D0542639

EXPERIENCE

By the same author

MARTIN AMIS
EXPERIENCE

JONATHAN CAPE
LONDON

Published by Jonathan Cape 2000

2 4 6 8 10 9 7 5 3 1

Copyright © Martin Amis 2000

Martin Amis has asserted his right under the Copyright, Designs and
Patents Act 1988 to be identified as the author of this work

First published in Great Britain in 2000 by
Jonathan Cape
Random House, 20 Vauxhall Bridge Road,
London SW1V 2SA

Random House Australia (Pty) Limited
20 Alfred Street, Milsons Point, Sydney,
New South Wales 2061, Australia

Random House New Zealand Limited
18 Poland Road, Glenfield,
Auckland 10, New Zealand

Random House (Pty) Limited
Endulini, 5A Jubilee Road, Parktown 2193, South Africa

The Random House Group Limited Reg. No. 954009

A CIP catalogue record for this book is available from the British Library

ISBN 0–224–05060–5
ISBN 0–224–06125–9 (Limited edition)

Papers used by The Random House Group Limited are natural,
recyclable products made from wood grown in sustainable forests; the
manufacturing processes conform to the environmental
regulations of the country of origin

Typeset in 11½ on 14½ Bembo by
SX Composing DTP, Rayleigh, Essex
Printed and bound in Great Britain by
Clays Ltd, St Ives PLC

to Isabel Fonseca

Contents

Acknowledgements

The author and publishers are grateful for permission to reproduce the following copyright material:

Kingsley Amis: *The Amis Collection* (Hutchinson, 1991), *Ending Up* (Jonathan Cape, 1974), *Girl 20* (Jonathan Cape, 1971), *I Want it Now* (Jonathan Cape, 1968), *Jake's Things* (Hutchinson, 1978), *Memoirs* (Century Hutchinson, 1991), *The Old Devils* (Hutchinson, 1986), *Stanley and the Women* (Hutchinson, 1984), 'What Became of Jane Austen?' from *The Amis Collection* (Hutchinson, 1991), reproduced by kind permission of The Random House Group Limited, *The Anti-Death League* (Victor Gollancz, 1966), *Lucky Jim* (Victor Gollancz, 1954), *One Fat Englishman* (Victor Gollancz, 1963), *Take a Girl Like You* (Victor Gollancz, 1960), *That Uncertain Feeling* (Victor Gollancz), reproduced by permission of The Orion Publishing Group, *The Biographer's Moustache* (1995), *The King's English* (1997), reproduced by permission of HarperCollins Publishers Ltd, 'A Bookshop Idyll' (1956), 'A Chromatic Passing-Note' (© 1967), 'A Dream of Fair Women' (1956), 'A.E.H.' (© 1967), 'The Huge Artifice' (© 1967), *I Like It Here* (© 1958), 'In Memoriam W.R.A.' (© 1967), 'Ode to Me' (© 1979), 'Real and Made-Up People' (© 1973), 'Something Does Not Work in My Car' (© 1962), 'Wasted' (© 1979), 'Ye Wearie Wayfarer' (© 2000), reprinted by kind permission of Jonathan Clowes Ltd., on behalf of the Literary Estate of Sir Kingsley Amis; Saul Bellow: 'A Silver Dish' from *Him With His Foot in His Mouth* (Secker & Warburg), *More Die of Heartbreak* (Secker & Warburg), by kind permission of The Random House Group Limited, *Ravelstein* (London, 2000), © 2000, reproduced by permission of Penguin Books Ltd; Jorge Luis Borges: 'The Circular Ruins' from *Labyrinths: Selected Stories and Other Writings*, edited by Donald A. Yates and James E. Irby, translated by James E. Irby, by kind permission of New Directions Publishing Corporation: C. Day Lewis: 'At Lemmons' from *The Complete Poems* (Sinclair-Stevenson, 1992), copyright © 1992 in this edition and the estate of C. Day Lewis; Don DeLillo:

Underworld (Picador, 1998), by kind permission of Macmillan Publishers Ltd; George Macdonald Fraser: *The Flashman Papers Volume III: Flash For Freedom,* by kind permission of HarperCollins Publishers Ltd; Christopher Hitchens: 'On Not Knowing the Half of It' from *Prepared for the Worst,* reprinted by kind permission of The Wylie Agency; Eric Jacobs: *Kingsley Amis: A Biography,* reproduced by permission of Hodder & Stoughton Limited; James Joyce: 'A Prayer' from *Poems Penyeach,* reproduced with the permission of the Estate of James Joyce – © the Estate of James Joyce; Franz Kafka: 'A Fasting-Artist' from *Stories 1904-1924,* translated by J.A. Underwood, reprinted by kind permission of Little, Brown and Company; Philip Larkin: 'Aubade', 'The Building', 'A Letter to a Friend About Girls', 'Livings', 'Money', 'The Old Fools', *The Selected Letters of Philip Larkin,* 'Self's the Man', 'This Be the Verse', 'The Trees', reprinted by kind permission of Faber & Faber; Vladimir Nabokov: *The Eye, The Nabokov-Wilson Letters 1940-1971,* edited by Simon Karlinsky, *Lolita, Pale Fire, Speak Memory, Strong Opinions,* published by Weidenfeld and Nicolson, reproduced by kind permission of The Orion Publishing Group Ltd; Siegfried Sassoon: 'Everyone Sang', copyright Siegfried Sassoon, by kind permission of George Sassoon.

While every effort has been made to obtain permission from owners of copyright material reproduced herein, the publishers would like to apologise for any omissions and will be pleased to incorporate missing acknowledgements in any future editions.

Part One

UNAWAKENED

Introductory: My Missing

– Dad.

This was my older son, Louis, then aged eleven.

– Yes?

My dad would have said, '. . . Yee*ess*?' – with a dip in it, to signal mild but invariable irritation. I once asked him why he did this and he said, 'Well I'm already here, aren't I?' For him, the Dad-Yes? interlude was a clear redundancy, because we were in the same room together and established as having some kind of conversation, however desultory (and unenlivening, from his point of view). I saw what he meant; but five minutes later I would find myself saying, 'Dad.' And then I would brace myself for an especially vehement affirmative. I was a teenager before I broke the habit. Children need a beat of time, to secure attention while the thought is framed.

This is from *I Like It Here* (1958), Kingsley's third and most close-to-life novel:*

> 'Dad.'
>
> 'Yes?'
>
> 'How big's the boat that's taking us to Portugal?'
>
> 'I don't know really. Pretty big, I should think.'
>
> 'As big as a killer whale?'
>
> 'What? Oh yes, easily.'
>
> 'As big as a blue whale?'
>
> 'Yes, of course, as big as any kind of whale.'

* In *The Amis Collection* (1990) KA wrote: 'I did once, out of laziness or sagging imagination, try to put real people on paper and produced what is by common consent my worst novel, *I Like It Here*.' I share the dedication page with my brother Philip and my sister Sally.

'Bigger?'

'Yes, much bigger.'

'How much bigger?'

'Never you mind how much bigger. Just bigger is all I can tell you.'

There is a break, and the discussion resumes:

. . . 'Dad.'

'Yes?'

'If two tigers jumped on a blue whale, could they kill it?'

'Ah, but that couldn't happen, you see. If the whale was in the sea the tigers would drown straight away, and if the whale was . . .'

'But supposing they did jump on the whale?'

. . . 'Oh, God. Well, I suppose the tigers'd kill the whale eventually, but it'd take a long time.'

'How long would it take one tiger?'

'Even longer. Now I'm not answering any more questions about whales or tigers.'

'Dad.'

'Oh, what is it now, David?'

'If two sea-serpents . . .'

How well I remember those vastly stimulating chats. My tigers weren't just ordinary tigers, either: they were sabre-toothed tigers. And the gladiatorial bouts I dreamed up were far more elaborate than *I Like It Here* allows. If two boa constrictors, four barracuda, three anacondas and a giant squid . . . I must have been five or six at the time.

In retrospect I can see that these questions would have played on my father's deepest fears. Kingsley, who refused to drive and refused to fly, who couldn't easily be alone in a bus, a train or a lift (or in a house, after dark), wasn't exactly keen on boats – or sea-serpents. Besides, he didn't want to go to Portugal, or anywhere else. The trip was forced on him by the terms and conditions of the Somerset Maugham Award – a 'deportation order' he called it in a letter to

[4]

Philip Larkin ('forced to go abroad, bloody *forced* mun'). He won the prize for his first novel, *Lucky Jim*, published in 1954. Twenty years later I would win it too.

The Rachel Papers appeared in mid-November, 1973. On the night of 27 December my cousin, Lucy Partington, who was staying with her mother in Gloucestershire, was driven into Cheltenham to visit an old friend, Helen Render. Lucy and Helen spent the evening talking about their future; they put together a letter of application to the Courtauld Institute in London, where Lucy hoped to continue studying medieval art. They parted at 10.15. It was a three-minute walk to the bus stop. She never posted the letter and she never boarded the bus. She was twenty-one. And it was another twenty-one years before the world found out what happened to her.

– Dad.

– Yes?

Louis and I were in the car – the locus of so many parental dealings, after a while, when the Chauffeuring Years begin to stretch out ahead of you like an autobahn.

– If nothing else was changed by you not being famous, would you still want to be famous?

A well-executed question, I thought. He knew that fame was a necessary by-product of acquiring a readership. But apart from that? What? Fame is a worthless commodity. It will occasionally earn you some special treatment, if that is what you're interested in getting. It will also earn you a far more noticeable amount of hostile curiosity. I don't mind that – but then I'm a special case. What tends to single me out for it also tends to inure me to it. In a word – Kingsley.

– I don't think so, I answered.

– Why?

– Because it messes with the head.

And he took this in, nodding.*

* * *

* I didn't notice, while writing this book (I only noticed while *reading* it, for revision), how often my free will has been compromised by fame (otherwise

It used to be said that everyone had a novel in them. And I used to believe it, and still do in a way. If you're a novelist you must believe it, because that's part of your job: much of the time you are writing the fiction that other people have in them.* Just now, though, in 1999, you would probably be obliged to doubt the basic proposition: what everyone has in them, these days, is not a novel but a memoir.

We live in the age of mass loquacity. We are all writing it or at any rate talking it: the memoir, the apologia, the c.v., the *cri de coeur*. Nothing, for now, can compete with experience – so unanswerably authentic, and so liberally and democratically dispensed. Experience is the only thing we share equally, and everyone senses this. We are surrounded by special cases, by special pleadings, in an atmosphere of universal celebrity.† I am a novelist, trained to use experience for other ends. Why should I tell the story of my life?

———

known as the media): stymied, finessed, crosspurposed. You're not meant to mind about this, because fame is meant to be so great. And I don't complain: I genuflect, and think of my friend Salman Rushdie . . . Actually there's a good reason, a structural reason, why novelists should excite corrosiveness in the press. When you review a film, or appraise a film-director, you do not make a ten-minute short about it or him (or her). When you write about a painter, you do not produce a sketch. When you write about a composer, you do not reach for your violin. And even when a poet is under consideration, the reviewer or profilist does not (unless deeply committed to presumption and tedium) produce a poem. But when you write about a novelist, an exponent of prose narrative, then you write a prose narrative. And was that the extent of your hopes for your prose – bookchat, interviews, gossip? Valued reader, it is not for me to say this is envy. It is for *you* to say that this is envy. And envy never comes to the ball dressed as Envy. It comes dressed as something else: Asceticism, High Standards, Common Sense. Anyway, as I said, I don't complain about all that – because fame is so great.
* V.S. Pritchett remains magnificently exemplary here; *The Complete Short Stories* (1990) is a series of dramatic poems about the thoughts of so-called ordinary people. I attempted something similar in *Money*: it is the novel that John Self, the narrator, had in him but would never write.
† It's not the case that in the future everyone will be famous for fifteen minutes. In the future everyone will be famous all the time – but only in their own minds. It is lookalike fame, karaoke fame. There's only one task it's equal to: it messes with the head.

[6]

I do it because my father is dead now, and I always knew I would have to commemorate him. He was a writer and I am a writer; it feels like a duty to describe our case – a literary curiosity which is also just another instance of a father and a son. This will involve me in the indulgence of certain bad habits. Namedropping is unavoidably one of them. But I've been indulging that habit, in a way, ever since I first said, 'Dad.'

I do it because I feel the same stirrings that everyone else feels. I want to set the record straight (so much of this is *already* public), and to speak, for once, without artifice. Though not without formality. The trouble with life (the novelist will feel) is its amorphousness, its ridiculous fluidity. Look at it: thinly plotted, largely themeless, sentimental and ineluctably trite. The dialogue is poor, or at least violently uneven. The twists are either predictable or sensationalist. And it's always the same beginning; and the same ending . . . My organisational principles, therefore, derive from an inner urgency, and from the novelist's addiction to seeing parallels and making connections. The method, plus the use of footnotes (to preserve the collateral thought), should give a clear view of the geography of a writer's mind. If the effect sometimes seems staccato, tangential, stop-go, etc, then I can only say that that's what it's like, on my side of the desk.

And I do it because it has been forced on me. I have seen what perhaps no writer should ever see: the place in the unconscious where my novels come from. I couldn't have stumbled on it unassisted. Nor did I. I read about it in the newspaper . . .

Someone is no longer here. The intercessionary figure, the father, the man who stands between the son and death, is no longer here; and it won't ever be the same. He is missing. But I know it is common; all that lives must die, passing through nature to eternity. My father lost his father, and my children will lose theirs, and their children (this is immensely onerous to contemplate) will lose theirs.

On the shelf by my desk I have a small double-sided picture-stand which contains two photographs. One is black-and-white and of passport size: it shows a teenage schoolgirl in a V-necked sweater, shirtsleeves and tie. Long brown hair parted at the centre, spectacles, the beginnings of a smile. Above her head she has written, in block capitals: undesirable alien. This is Lucy Partington . . . The second photograph is in colour: it shows a toddler in a dark flower dress, smocked at the chest, with short puffed sleeves and pink trim. She has fine blonde hair. Her smile is demure: pleased, but quietly pleased. This is Delilah Seale.

The photographs are kept together, and for almost twenty years their subjects lived together in the back of my mind. Because these are, or were, my missing.

Letter from School

Sussex Tutors,
55 Marine Parade,
Brighton, Sussex.
23rd Oct. [1967]

Dearest Dad and Jane,★

   Thanks awfully for your letter. So we all appear to be working like fucking fools. I seem to be flitting manically from brash self-confidence to whimpering depression; the English is all very fine, but the Latin I find difficult, tedious, and elaborately unrewarding. It would be so boring if it buggered up my Oxford Entrance paper. I spend about 2–3 hours per day on it, but I feel a painful lack of basic knowledge – not being one of those little sods who has been chanting 'amo, amas, amat', from the age of eighteen months. Anyway, the set book (Aeneid Bk.II) is pretty splendid, and if I slog through that with sufficient rigour I should be O.K. on that part of the 'O' level paper.

   Mr. Ardagh decided that the best plan for Ox. Ent. is to choose about 6 chaps and know them pretty thoroughly, rather than farting about with a bit of everyone. I have chosen: Shakespeare; Donne and Marvell, Coleridge and Keats; Jane Austen; [Wilfred] Owen; Greene; and possibly old Yeats as well. I do enjoy the English but I must say that I get periods of desperately wanting something else to

★ The novelist Elizabeth Jane Howard: my stepmother from 1965 to 1983. My half of this embarrassing correspondence is to be found at the Huntington Library.

occupy myself with. The prospect of teaching has lost its glow because it means that I will be dealing with the same *sort* of thing for the next 4 years without much of a break. I hope you don't think I'm off the idea of Eng. Lit., because I find myself suffused with an ardour for sheer quantity of consumption. In my last few days in London I read 'Middlemarch' (in 3 days), 'The Trial' (Kafka is a fucking fool – in 1 day) and 'The Heart of the Matter' (in 1 day), and even here I manage a couple of novels a week (plus lots of poetry). Its [*sic*] just that I'm a bit cheesed off with applying myself to the same ideas all the time – but I shouldn't think its [*sic*] anything that a paternal – or step-maternal – harangue won't correct. I'm sorry to be a bore, and it's probably merely a phase – might even be character-building, who knows.

I thought it very representative of your integrity, Jane, to warn me of the defficiencies [*sic*] of Nashville.* Much as I'd love to see you both, it does seem that I'll be doing too much fire-ironing and pie-fingering (I'm sure Jane could adapt that to one of her swirling mixed metaphors), to be able to get away for a full 2–3 weeks. I *might* have an interview at Oxford as late as the 20th of Dec. and various replies *could* start coming in as early as Jan 1st. This, coupled with the dire deterrent of U.S. T.V. being *lousy*, will, I fear, prevent me from coming over. It *is* a pity because I would dearly love to see you both.

I see young Bruce† pretty regularly, but not regularly enough, it seems, for him to contrive to secure adequate stocks of fish-cakes for my visits. However he seems in fine form . . . Predictably enough the very word is like a bell to toll me back to Latin Unseens, prose constructions, and like trivia.

Please write soon, I miss you both terribly,

All my love,

Mart x x x

* Kingsley was at this time a visiting professor at Vanderbilt University, in Nashville ('known, unironically I suppose to some, as the Athens of the South'), Tennessee.
† 'Bruce' was the nickname that, for some reason, my brother and I assigned to Jane's brother, Colin – a member of the household for many years.

P.S. Convey my cordial regards to Karen – there are no doleful regrets there because, as far as I can remember, she should be about 9′ 6″ tall by now.

P.P.S. On [*sic*] retrospect I consider 'Middlemarch' to be FUCKING good – Jane Austen + passion + dimension. Very fine. Love Mart.

Rank

The point about Karen and her being nine-foot-six was that I was then about five-foot-two (and had only another four inches to go). Everyone kept saying to me, 'You'll suddenly shoot up', and, after a while, I kept saying to everyone, 'What's all this about me suddenly shooting up? It *hasn't happened.*' I minded being short chiefly because it seemed that about half of womankind was thereby rendered unapproachable. When I was even younger and even shorter I had a girlfriend who was over six-foot-one. We had an unspoken agreement. We never stood upright at the same time. And we never went out. Apart from that it was like a normal relationship, with one other peculiarity: when we lay down on the bed we never quite got into, my feet seemed to be level with Alison's waist.

It would be nice to say that I 'make no apologies' for my early letters, which will punctuate the first part of this book. But I do: I make fervent apologies for them. And they get worse. It all gets worse. I really am very sorry. The toiling periphrases, the tally-ho facetiousness: this I can forgive. My dismissal of Kafka is ridiculous,★ and is only partly counterbalanced by the approximate justice of the PPS – and what *was* it with me and the word *fine*? But at least, here, I can recognise myself. Elsewhere this letter seems to have been written by a stranger: I mean its tone of pampered intolerance, its political stupidity; I am repelled by the thought-clichés and un-examined formulations, herd formulations. And there's also some-thing else. Which I suppose I'll get to.

★ I should have been directed to the stories, which are of course immortal. Kafka's dream-shaped novels are brilliant – but they are nightmares. *He* couldn't finish them either.

When I arrived at Sussex Tutors, late in 1967, I was just eighteen and coming out of a bottomless adolescent *cafard*. You remember how it was: it could take you an entire day to transport a single sock from one end of your bedroom to the other. And that day would be a good day. The torpor wasn't merely physical. I was eighteen and averaging one O-level every other year. The comforting thing was supposed to be that I had a knack for English. I took the A-level, rather precociously, at the age of fifteen or sixteen. And despite the fact that I fell down the stairs in plain view of three hundred young people, half of them girls, as I approached the examination room, I came out of there full of confidence. The difficulties associated with this A-level lark, I said to myself, had been much exaggerated. 'Martin!' my mother shouted up the stairs as I lay reeking in bed one morning in a house on the Fulham Road. My mother usually called me Mart. The full Martin was always a . . . 'You *failed*.' Not even an E. An *F*.

The trouble was that I didn't like working because I had no powers of concentration. *Concentration* was a fortress it never occurred to me to scale; and I remember gaping through hours of tuition without a thought in my head. I didn't like working. What I liked was bunking off school and hanging out with my friend Rob and betting in betting shops (not the horses: the dogs) and mincing up and down the King's Road in skintight velves and grimy silk scarves and haunting a coffee bar called the Picasso, and smoking hash (then £8 an ounce) and trying to pick up girls. One time I said,

– Let's go down King's.

Rob turned away. I should point out here that Rob was and is about my height.

– Come on. What's the matter? We'll pick up girls.

– Where? In the Picasso?

– In the Picasso.

– I can't cope with the Picasso. I can hardly cope with being in my room.

As usual we had smoked ourselves into a state of clinical paranoia.

– What's wrong with the Picasso? Okay, we won't go to the Picasso. We'll pick up girls somewhere else.

– Where?

– Uh, that other place. Beyond the Picasso.

– But we'll end up in the Picasso.

– We won't go to the Picasso.

– I always feel such a short-arse in the Picasso.

– Me too. That's why we won't try and pick up girls in the Picasso. Come on.

– Okay. But I don't want to end up short-arseing round the Picasso trying to pick up girls.

But that's what we would end up doing. Whole school terms went by like this: wondering whether to go to the Picasso. A while later, and very briefly, Rob and I hit the deb scene. It looked good at first but here we faced the giantesses of the gentry. The women were all elongated by centuries of huge meals, and so were all the men, and we felt, we admitted, as if we were walking around between everybody else's legs.

Sussex Tutors was the end of the road: my last-gasp saloon. Even I knew that. My secondary education was in tatters. In the course of it I had attended Bishopgore Grammar, in Swansea, Cambridgeshire High School for Boys in the capital of that county, the International School in Palma, Majorca, and Sir Walter St John's in South London – and then, after the grammars, the crammers, private establishments that allegedly specialised in rescuing the academic careers of public-school dropouts and others, the children of peripatetic, disorganised but always solvent parents. Sussex Tutors was a *boarding* crammer, intended for extreme cases. I needed four or five more O-levels (including Latin more or less from scratch) and three A-levels with good enough grades to enable me to sit the Oxford Entrance papers in December. I had a year.

And it had worked, so far. *I* had worked. The town was arranged like rows of seats around a stage – the sea; and Sussex Tutors, a ramshackle warren that seemed to be all attic, stood on an urban cliff above the pier and the pebbly beach where the breakers flopped and trawled. It was said that the building had once been a nursing home, and it was adjacent to a nursing home and surrounded by other nursing homes. Brighton itself was a nursing home; and on warm days the elderly would be helped or wheeled out on to the terraces and fenced rooftops, tier after tier of candyfloss hair and vague, freckled, upturned faces, enjoying the sun and the unvaryingly barbarous wind. I felt like a convalescent, too, after the obscure and wholly passive exertions of adolescence: the headaches, the dizziness, the aching bones. When I arrived in Brighton I was in love – first love. It came, then stayed, then went; having filled me, it then emptied me. I wanted to be in love again, and, of course, every last non-working man-hour was dedicated to the attempt to bring this about, wandering, staring, blushing, longing, waiting. But now at least I was in love with literature – particularly with poetry. I read poetry for days and days. Look out of the window: there are gulls in the sky and I feel sad. I read poetry and I wrote poetry. I was being edified. Was I thereby being improved?

The nineteen-year-old hero of my first novel was described in one review as 'both a gilded and a repulsive creature'. I accept this description, for my hero and for myself. I was an Osric. ('*Hamlet* . . . [*Aside to Horatio*] Dost know this water-fly?')★ What elicits my hoarsest moan of shame was the plumed and crested manner I vainly tried to cultivate. Private schooling had given me unwonted contact with the children of the rich and grand (one of my fellow pupils at Brighton was the Earl of Caithness, a gangling, gawping figure, and certainly no great ad for the aristocracy). It gave me ideas – which couldn't and didn't last long. Martin was the forename of half the England football team; and when I looked up Amis in a dictionary of surnames I was confronted by the following: 'Of the lower classes, *esp.* slaves.'

And after that brief conversation with Kingsley, I knew I had to call the whole thing off.

– Dad.

– Yes?

– Are we *nouveau riche*?

★ I was recently reminded that Kingsley played Osric in a college production at Swansea in 1953. Now I recall his Osric routine, very flirtatious, all eyelash and limp wrist. As Osric says of Laertes: 'an absolute gentleman, full of most excellent differences, of very soft society and great showing.' That was me, in 1967.

1966. We were in the kitchen of 108 Maida Vale, where Kingsley and Jane had set up together. I and my brother were recent additions to the household. We had stopped living with our mother and started living with our father. It was Jane's initiative. She could see we were both heading for the street . . . The kitchen was a prosperous one, goodlooking but also potently stocked, it seemed to me, and continually replenished by men in white topcoats. *Jane* was quite posh, after all, and I felt I had gone up in the world. Naturally I knew that nouveau riche was a bad thing to be, and I complacently awaited my father's assurance that we were a little bit better than that.

– Well, he said. *Very* nouveau. And *not at all* riche.

– Dad.

Thirty years later: the car again, Louis again.

– Yes?

– What class are we?

From the wheel I said ruggedly,

– We aren't. We don't buy that stuff.

– Then what *are* we?

– We're outside all that. We're the intelligentsia.

– Oh, he said, and added in deliberate falsetto: Am I an intellectual?

– Dad.

This was number-two son, Jacob, then aged nine.

– Yes?

– Why do you say Fri*dee* and Mon*dee* and Thurs*dee*?

– What do you say? Fri-*day* and Mon-*day*.

– It's bound to sound stupid if you say it in *that* voice. And do you say birth*dee*?

– Yes. Birthday. Birth-*day* is what your grandfather would call a spelling pronunciation. Or I suppose you say pro*noun*ciation.

– What's it mean?

– A spelling pronunciation is when you follow the spelling and go against the rhythm of the spoken language. Like saying *offten* instead of *offn*.

– Do you say yester*dee*? asked Louis.

– Yes.

– But you don't say *to*dee, do you.

– No. Of course not.

– And you don't say *dee*. What a lovely *dee* it is.

– Early the next *dee*, said Jacob.

– What *dee* would suit you?

– No of course I don't.

– Then why do you say Mon*dee* and Fri*dee* and Sun*dee*?

– Jesus. I trained myself to do it in my teens because I thought it sounded posh.

– Why d'you do that? asked Louis with sincere puzzlement.

– Because it used to be cool to be posh.

His head snapped round.

– *Did* it? . . . *Christ* . . .

Over in Tennessee interesting things were happening to my father, in 1967; but it was of course grimly typical of Osric that he failed to take notice of this. Flip ahead a page or two and see the first paragraph of the next Letter from School: a prose poem of stupefied incuriosity. And how listlessly I shrugged off the chance to visit Nashville during the holiday. I was working, true, and there might have been interviews to attend. And I didn't want to lose a whole fortnight's worth of wondering whether to go to the Picasso.

My father arrived in the South to find the usual streetscape: 'To evoke it you need not a description but a list, or the mere start of a list, and one that everybody knows.' He found too that 'liquor by the drink' was still state-banned. You brought your own bottle to the bar and ordered a *setup*: a glass with ice in it. Kingsley goes on: 'The same rules applied to restaurants, of which there seemed to be only two (in a town of nearly half a million), one providing bad, the other very bad food and service, but united in accepting no bookings.' Elsewhere, as an Englishman, he was treated like an aristocratic curiosity: '"We have *another* gentleman from Britain with us tonight," [said the chairman], displaying the modest pride of a provincial zoo official who reveals its possession of not one but *two* Arabian oryxes.' More saliently, he found himself involved in conversations such as the following (the woman is the wife of the Professor of Iberian Languages):

> 'Did you happen to see,' she said in her no more than averagely unbelievable tones, 'the movie Surr Laurence Oh-livyay made of Shakespeare's *Oh-thello*? . . . And what did you think of it? – I don't mean the movie so much, I mean *him*.'
> 'Well . . . I thought he was very good.'
> 'But they made him look like a black mayun!'
> 'Yes, they did, didn't they?'
> 'But he even toked like a black mayun!'
> 'Yes, perhaps a bit – '
> 'But he even *woked* like a black mayun! . . . But how could a real lady fall in love with a man like that?'*

More saliently still, Kingsley found himself in an English Department where a fellow professor, and a fellow novelist, could turn to him and say, '(verbatim), "I can't find it in my heart to give a Negro [pron. nigra] or a Jew an A."'

Gilded, repulsive (and never built to last), Osric would have dismantled himself after ten minutes in Nashville. So it used to be cool to be posh, did it? Yes, Louis, I quite agree: *Christ . . .*

---

* This reminds one of the fact that in certain cultures *Othello* is regarded as a tragedy in which *Iago* is the hero. These quotes are from KA's *Memoirs* (1991).

Letter from School

Sussex Tutors
55 Marine Parade,
Brighton.
4/11/67

Dearest Dad + Jane,

I received your letters simultaneously – and very fine they were too. Sorry to hear that you're not getting on too well with the colonials – are they *all* crappy? And you're working hard too. Still, you'll be back before you know it. Yes, that's when you'll be back.

That little goblin Mr Ardagh has pretty well definitely got me a job at Rottingdean. I'll be taking the little sods for games. How can this be? They're going to spend all their time beating me up and composing ingeniously wounding nick-names for me. Still, its [*sic*] a challenge etc.

B.H.Q. [Bastards' Headquarters] is now based at Brighton. We have had ten days of torrential rain punctuated with blizzards, hurricanes, whirlwinds, earth-quakes, and like upheavals. My only comfort is indulgence in gruelling, man-of-the-elements walks through the blinding rain. I have also been known to look out of my window and silently determine, with haggard stoicism, that I shall wear white flannel trousers and walk upon the beach.

I have a snippet of ego-nourishing news for each of you.

First, Jane's: I met a fine girl called Charlotte a couple of weeks ago and I went round to her flat in Hamilton Terrace to take her out. I was introduced solemnly to her mother who, after asking if she could offer me a drink, expressed a desire to know where I lived. I told her and she exclaimed ecstatically: 'Oh! You must live near Elizabeth Jane Howard!' I calmly told her just how near Jane Howard I lived. She was suitably impressed and went on to eulogise 'After Julius'. As it happens, I went on to make Charlotte mine; a complement to an enjoyable evening.* And a conquest in which Jane may well have played no inconsiderable part.

Next, my distinguished father. A friend of mine asked dutifully what book of yours I recommended. 'Lucky Jim' I told him. He promptly bought it and, one evening, I went into his room and he was retching into his sink, with tears streaming down his face, recovering from a laughing fit induced by a passage in the said novel.† Jolly good for you.

By the way, I hope and trust that you won't begrudge me the opportunity of getting some books on the bill – all respectable volumes, I may add. I know [sic] have a hallowed library of about 25 books (mostly paperbacks), which will do me proud when I go to university.

Another thing that veritable little hobgoblin Mr Ardagh has done is put a burning queer in the room next to mine. He rushes in without knocking every night between 12 and 1, with eyes aflame, hoping to catch me at some stage of undress. He wants to bugger me you see, but, somehow, it doesn't help knowing this. I've considered retaliation – putting bogies [nose-pickings] in his coffee, spitting on his toothbrush, stealing his shampoo, soiling his pyjamas etc., but I don't see how this would help. In the end I suppose I'll have to outline my reasons for being unable to see why he doesn't fuck off.

I saw poor old Peter Yates' new film 'Robbery' tonight. Its [sic]

---

* This is an empty boast as well as an outright lie. I thought Charlotte beautiful and intelligent (and posh, and short). I tried my hardest and got nowhere with her.
† *Which* passage, you fool? The 'said novel', indeed . . . But I mustn't heckle my past self too raucously. I have made no changes in this armpit-scorching archive, except to protect the innocent. And the really generous reader will concede that I was innocent too.

trendy – i.e. consciously bad – you know, 30 minute scenes in total darkness – that sort of thing.

Off I go to bed then, miss you both, write soon.

    All my love,

      Mart. X X X X X

By the way Jane, I did Lawrence's 'The Rainbore' for A level so I feel qualified to say why he's no good. I shall read the others before the interview and, I fancy, 'War and Peace', and – at that arch-hobgoblin's suggestion 'Daniel Deronda'. More lighting [*sic*] opinions –

Ezra Pound – Trendy little ponce.

Auden – Good, but I feel he *must* be an awful old crap.

Hopkins – Great fun to read, but doesn't stand up to any analysis.

Donne – Very Splendid.

Marvell –   "   "

Keats – All right when he's not saying 'I'm a poet. Got that?' 'La Belle Dame Sans Merci' – almost my favourite poem.

      more soon – M.

Women and Love – 1

We sat in high-bourgeois splendour, my father and I, in the house outside Barnet, having a pre-lunch drink and talking about his first published story, 'The Sacred Rhino of Uganda' (1932: he was ten). Now it was 1972, and he had just turned fifty, an occasion he marked with a poem: 'Ode to Me' ('Fifty today, old lad? / Well, that's not doing so bad . . . '). He was then at the height of his prosperity and productiveness; and his marriage to Jane was still cloudless – or so, at any rate, I believed. 'The Sacred Rhino of Uganda':

– It was awful in all the usual ways. And full of false quantities. Things like: 'Raging and cursing in the blazing heat . . .'

– What's wrong with that? I mean I can see it's old fashioned . . .

– You can't have three *ings* like that.

– Can't you?

– No. It would have to be: 'Raging and cursing in the . . . intolerable heat.'

You couldn't have three *ings* like that. And sometimes you couldn't even have two. The same went for *-ics*, *-ives*, *-lys* and *-tions*. And the same went for all prefixes too.

After lunch I went up to my room and spent a few hours with the novel I was about to submit for publication. Later, over a pre-dinner drink, I said,

– I've been going through my book. And guess what. It's doggerel.

– I'm sure it's not.

– It is. It's all 'the cook took a look at the book'. It's like a nursery rhyme. Hickory dickory dock, the mouse ran up the clock.

– You're exaggerating.

Yes, but I did revise the novel yet again: making war on the *-ings* and the -*ics*, the *pre*-s and the *pro*-s.

It was the only piece of literary counsel he ever gave me. And, of course, he had never expressed any desire that I should pursue the literary life, despite all the evidence that I had such a life in mind. I attributed this to sheer indolence on his part, but I now think he was obeying a parental instinct, and a good one. Five years later, when I was back-half editor of the *New Statesman*, a well-known writer visited me in my office with his son. The boy (seventeen?) wrote poems, it was explained, and the father wanted me to look at them; perhaps I might accept one or two for publication. I was ten years older than the poet. I sympathised with him. But I think I pointed out immediately that nobody writing in English had ever done anything of much merit before the age of about twenty (no, not even poor Thomas Chatterton, 'the marvellous boy', who was seventeen – and destitute, after early successes – when he poisoned himself with arsenic). The well-known writer gently persisted. And I thought, all right, it's conceivable: Rimbaud was the same age when he wrote 'Le Bateau Ivre'. I looked at the son's poems. And I sent them back to him with a letter saying that I thought they were promising, and (equally truthfully) that I would be happy to keep an eye on his stuff as it came along . . .

In the arts, when the parent invites the child to follow – this is a complicated offer, and there will always be a suspicion of egotism in it. Is the child's promise a tribute to the superabundance of the father's gift? And historically what long odds you face; there's Mrs Trollope as well as Anthony, and Dumas *père et fils*, and that's about it. What usually happens is that the child is productive for a while, and then the filial rivalrousness plays itself out. I think literary talent is strongly inherited. But literary stamina is not.

Quite soon afterwards I heard that the well-known writer and the poet son had fallen out. This was the beginning of a long rift. The last poem the son sent me was about the father: a lightly versified tirade.

I can't imagine what my adult life would have been like if any such breakdown had afflicted Kingsley and me. There is murk, there is poor visibility, in the motives of literary ambition – *nostalgie*, acidic isolation; and there is already quite enough going on between fathers and sons. I felt the squeeze of immediate hurt when Kingsley, who claimed to have liked my first novel, said he 'couldn't get on' with my second. But there it was: I knew him to be incapable of equivocation or euphemism on any literary question. And he had an apologetic, almost imploring look in his eyes when he spoke . . . (And he didn't like Nabokov either, or anybody else, except for Anthony Powell.) Otherwise we had fights and rows and many hot exchanges, but never anything that wasn't cleared up the following day. Only once, when I was turning thirty, did I find myself entertaining the prospect of a *froideur*. Kingsley – out of fondness for her predecessor – had spoken brusquely of the woman I had just fallen in love with. 'What did you think of her?' I asked on the phone the day after I presented her to him, expecting a paragraph of ceremonious praise – a sonnet, a psalm. 'I don't mind you bringing her to the house,' he said, 'if that's what you need to know.'* My roused feelings were roused further. For a few seconds a rift seemed attractively romantic, like a duel at dawn. I remember delectating it, this *froideur*. And then I dismissed it, convulsively, like an expectoration. Hoik. Phthook! Plus the thought: Don't ever consider that again. I was turning thirty and he was contemplating sixty. We were approaching the hinge of

* The family commitment to anecdote inclines me to reveal that the ex-girlfriend was Emma Soames. The present girlfriend was Mary Furness, later to be persecuted by the press as the outgoing Countess of Waldegrave. Kingsley loved Emma Soames, who had been at my side for two years, because she was loveable; but there was, I suspected, ancillary admiration having to do with the fact that she was Winston Churchill's granddaughter. His admiration was historical, not social. Only once did my father encounter Emma's parents. Jane drove him down to the Soameses' country place for lunch, where I was spending one of many weekends. While serving drinks Sir Christopher (as he then was), with that gentle, concerned, passionately solicitous frown he had (inherited by all three of his sons), asked Kingsley: 'Would you like to wash your hands before we go in?' And Kingsley said, 'No thanks. I washed them behind a bush on the way down.' Lunch was an unqualified success – a wall of sound from start to finish (present, too, were Emma's imperial-sized senior brothers, Nicholas and Jeremy). But, lor, how much stuff there was about class in those days. Whatever else she did, Margaret Thatcher helped weaken all that. Mrs Thatcher, with her Cecils, with her Normans, with her Keiths.

age, and would soon be needing each other in complicated ways . . .
My father never encouraged me to write, never invited me to go for
that longshot;* he praised me less often than he publicly dispraised
me; but it worked.

With my own children I intend to be more liberal in my praise.
Although I like the writer's life – day to day – much better than
Kingsley did, there will be no encouragement for my children. No
encouragement. None.

It is mid-November 1973, about fifteen months after the 'doggerel'
conversation, and that first novel is about to appear.† The event
passed in what now seems to be improbable tranquillity. No
interviews, no readings, no photo sessions. And no party – or no
publisher's party. It was a first novel, admittedly, but there wasn't any
outside activity when my second novel was published either, or my
third. That's the way it was in those days. A minority-interest field.
All quiet.

No official party, then, in 1973 – a quarter of a century ago,
almost to the hour, as I type these words. But I had a party anyway.‡
I was living in a small but fancy maisonette, with Rob and his
girlfriend Olivia. I couldn't afford it, and Rob, who had sunk the
whole of a small inheritance into the lease, couldn't afford it either.

* Unless you count the following exchange. At some point in our late teens
Kingsley asked my brother and me what we wanted to do in life. 'A painter,'
said my brother, who became one. 'A novelist,' I said. 'Good,' said Kingsley,
rubbing his hands together rapidly, even noisily, in that way he had. 'That
means the Amises are branching out into the other arts while keeping their
stranglehold on fiction.' He meant Jane, too.
† The single print run was so tiny that an individual copy of the novel is now
worth twice the original advance. For the record: my agent, Pat Kavanagh,
and my chief publisher, Tom Maschler, also handled my father, and I had
known both of them since youth. So, yes, the whole thing was tacitly
nepotic. Any London house would have published my first novel out of
vulgar curiosity.
‡ KA's calligraphy was more regular and upright than mine, but sometimes
our hands exactly correspond. That *anyway*, in my manuscript, could have
been his: an exact forgery.

The arrangement would collapse very soon: within a month or two I would find myself in a dust-furred bed-sit in Earls Court. But we had a great time that night. My brother Philip contributed a *magnum* of whisky. And my sister was there and my father was there. I remember him coming up the steps to the sitting-room with that glint of maximum anticipation (he looked forward to treats of any kind with youthful, childish intensity, the result, I suppose, of the eventlessness – and siblinglessness – of his childhood and youth). Kingsley's old friend, the Sovietologist and poet Robert Conquest, was there. And Christopher Hitchens was there, handsome, festive, gauntly left-wing. And Clive James was there, with his biker's build and beard and hairdo, not that long off the boat from Australia and 'madly excited' (like Charlie Citrine in the Bellow novel) to have reached the city of words.

What can I tell you? It was the Seventies: the joke decade. Clive wore denim hipsters and a poacher's jacket. Hitch would have had on his controversial patchwork jeans with the stain like a dull sovereign just to the right of the warped fly (I think he acquired them, or maybe disposed of them, by barter in Moscow). I, like Rob, was almost certainly sporting a dagger-collared flower shirt and green velvet flares – crushed velvet, too, so that their non-threadbare sections gave off a sickly sheen. Even Kingsley's trouser cuffs had an inch or two of extra play. It amazes me, now, that any of us managed to write a word of sense during the whole decade, considering that we were all evidently stupid enough to wear flares. That night Rob and Olivia gave me a blue T-shirt with the title of my novel embossed on it in purple capitals. I slipped into this for the rest of the evening. And there stood a copy of my book propped on the little TV.

It was a shocking rout, and ended some time between four and five. Those of us who met up for lunch the next day looked and felt like extras in the galactic-speakeasy scene in *Star Wars* (itself still a thing of the future: four years distant). Several new romances started on that night, the Hitch and my sister Sally, for example, repairing to the nearby Cadogan Hotel. At dawn Rob and Olivia went to bed together, upstairs, and I went to bed alone, downstairs. I was not in love. In fact I couldn't seem to get a girlfriend of any kind. I still dream about this relatively brief period of my life: dreams imbued with feelings of disconnectedness, unattachedness – and of course unattractiveness. Profound unattractiveness. When you're without a woman, it is astonishing how quickly you become loathsome to yourself. It is astonishing, too, how quickly this news gets around: every woman you meet seems to know all about it . . . Things would eventually look up – in a way that even then seemed completely spectacular. Early in the summer of 1974 I would be in the Cadogan Hotel myself, having an introductory and gently inquisitorial tea with the parents of the teenage Tina Brown. But I had my Earls Court time to get through first, days, weeks, months, without a woman.

– Get your hair cut, said Kingsley doggedly. Get your hair cut.

There was no one else in the room, but he wasn't telling me to get my hair cut. Over the years Kingsley must have told me to get my hair cut ten or twelve thousand times. But he wasn't telling me to get my hair cut. The year, now, was 1984. I was newly married to an American academic called Antonia Phillips, and there was a child on the way. I didn't need to get my hair cut.

– Get your hair cut . . . Get your hair cut.

This suggestion was being offered to the television set, more particularly to the actress Linda Hamilton every time she appeared on screen. We were watching a tape of *The Terminator* (again). An old science-fiction hand, Kingsley was a great fan of *The Terminator*, and seven years later he would make no secret of his admiration for *Terminator 2* ('a flawless masterpiece'), which I took him to at the Odeon, Marble Arch.

– Get your hair cut . . . Get your hair cut.

In *Terminator 2* (1991) Linda Hamilton wore her hair up or back. In *The Terminator*, on the other hand, she was decidedly full-maned, as people were then, in 1984.

– Get your hair cut . . . Get your hair cut.

– I hope you're going to stick with this, Dad, I said. I hope you won't weaken if anyone accuses you of being boring or repetitive.

– Get your hair cut . . . Get your hair cut.

[27]

– Because there are some who might point out that this film has already been made. Even if Linda Hamilton could hear you, and even if she thought it was a good idea, she couldn't go back and get her hair cut.

– Get your hair cut . . . Get your hair cut.

– But don't listen to them, Dad. You've set your stall out. Now it's up to you to see this thing through.

– Get your hair cut . . . Get your hair cut.

After a while, when the action started and it became clear that Linda Hamilton wouldn't have time or leisure to get her hair cut, Kingsley stopped telling her to get her hair cut.

Jane left Kingsley in December 1980. That was nearly four years ago, and there'd been nobody else. As I was getting ready to go I said,

– How are you really, Dad?

– Oh, all right . . . But you know it's only half a life without a woman.

– *Is* it?

I was surprised and in a way delighted to hear him say this. It sounded uncharacteristically forgiving, and I had thought him more chronically embittered. Embittered for the long haul. It wasn't so much his manner or the things he said. It was evident in his novels – specifically in the anti-romantic curve leading from *Jake's Thing* (1978) to *Stanley and the Women* (1984), which appeared to cancel any hope or even memory of comfort from that quarter. I wasn't making the elementary error of conflating the man and the work, but all writers know that the truth *is* in the fiction. That's where the spiritual thermometer gives its reading. And Kingsley's novels, around then, seemed to me in moral retreat, as if he were closing down a whole dimension – the one that contained women and love. So I asked him, surprised not by the formulation (which I knew to be true, and half a life isn't very much at all) but by the fact that the words were his:

– *Is* it?

– *Yes*, he said. And turned away.

Thereafter Kingsley lived the rest of his life without romantic love. But his fiction came back to it. Forgivingly in *The Old Devils* (1986), nostalgically in *You Can't Do Both* (1994), and assertively and even ringingly in *The Russian Girl* (1992). In *Jake's Thing* he had his hero announce:

> They [women] don't mean what they say, they don't use language for discourse but for extending their personality, they take all disagreement as opposition, yes they do, even the brightest of them, and that's the end of the search for truth which is what the whole thing's supposed to be about.

And in the barroom atmosphere of *Stanley*, we get the following evocation of feminine 'offences against common sense, good manners, fair play, truth, all those' (the speaker in the following is a medium-level film producer called Bert, and his drunken accent, at least, is being effectively satirised):

> You could fill her with what's that truth drug stuff, that's right, scopolamine, you could dose her up to the gills with fucking scopolamine and she'd still deny it . . . She's a . . . she's a *fucky nuck* case, that's what she is. Ought to be put away. For her own protection.

All this changed (and I know why). In *The Russian Girl*, which he wrote at the age of seventy, love is exalted not only above politics and – far more surprisingly – above poetry;* it is also exalted above truth.

The critique of womankind that seeps its way through *Jake* and *Stanley* is certainly not without interest or pertinence (both novels are sinisterly vigorous). Nor would it clinch matters to say: Listen, the female attitude to truth is exactly counterbalanced by the male habit (explored in tens of thousands of novels by women) of speaking and behaving *ex cathedra* ('with the full authority of office . . . implying infallibility': *COD*). My objection to these novels is simpler than that:

* Here we go back to 1973 and a piece called 'Rondo for my Funeral': '. . . I should state that, since starting to find it in my early teens, music has given me more pleasure, and more intense pleasure, than any other art . . . Further yet: only a world without love strikes me as instantly and decisively more terrible than one without music.'

[29]

I can feel Dad's thumb on the scales. T.S. Eliot suggested that literature was an 'impersonal' use of words. The great critic and utopian Northrop Frye improved on this, I think, when he said that literature was a *disinterested* use of words: you needed to have nothing riding on the outcome. And Kingsley was interested. He was keeping score with love and women, and with Jane.

He always knew better, and would know better again. An early poem called 'A Bookshop Idyll' has the KA figure casually browsing through a 'thin anthology' from the poetry shelf:

> Like all strangers, they divide by sex:
> > *Landscape near Parma*
> Interests a man, so does *The Double Vortex*,
> > So does *Rilke and Buddha*.
>
> 'I travel, you see', 'I think' and 'I can read'
> > These titles seem to say;
> But *I Remember You, Love is my Creed,*
> > *Poem for J.,*
>
> The ladies' choice, discountenance my patter . . .
>
> Should poets bicycle-pump the human heart
> > Or squash it flat?
> Man's love is of man's life a thing apart;
> > Girls aren't like that.
>
> We men have got love well weighed up; our stuff
> > Can get by without it.
> Women don't seem to think that's good enough;
> > They write about it,
>
> And the awful way their poems lay them open
> > Just doesn't strike them.
> Women are really much nicer than men:
> > No wonder we like them.

> Deciding this, we can forget those times
>   We sat up half the night
> Chockfull of love, crammed with bright thoughts,
>   names, rhymes,
>   And couldn't write.

This is a young man's poem, for all its wit and its luxurious technique. In the last stanza we sense regret, at the male deficiency; but we also feel that the author will soon be reconciled to it.* Men cannot write on the crest of emotion. Emotion must be tamely 'recollected' in the Wordsworthian tranquillity. On the other hand 'A Bookshop Idyll' suggests that the writing will in the end be all the better for that, stronger on precision and authority and other (male) virtues . . . What strikes and intrigues me now is the colloquialised quotation from Byron, where, in the second line of the couplet, 'Girls aren't like that' does duty for ''Tis women's whole existence'. Perhaps the poem intimates that the obverse is also true: Women's art is of women's life a thing apart; boys aren't like that. Art is, or tries to be, men's whole existence. And it might have seemed that way to a young poet at the top of his game. In his sixties, though, when he no longer had a woman's love, he acknowledged what this left him with: only half a life.

* When told of the death of a friend (I am again paraphrasing Northrop Frye) a man can burst into tears; but he can never burst into song. Women's fiction and poetry, it seems to me, has a bit more 'song' in it. Over this we can argue . . . Kingsley *loved* Elizabeth Barrett Browning; he had not much time for Jane Austen, rather more for George Eliot, and none at all for Virginia Woolf. Of Woolf he said he found her created world wholly contrived: when reading her he found that he kept interpolating hostile negatives, murmuring 'Oh no she didn't' or 'Oh no he hadn't' or 'Oh no it wasn't' after each and every authorial proposition. Despite his real admiration for Iris Murdoch, Elizabeth Taylor and Elizabeth Jane Howard, my father, I think, regarded women's writing as essentially occult – not a genre so much as a movement, like vorticism. Nabokov (no soulmate of Kingsley's) also confessed to being exclusively 'homosexual' in his literary tastes. He said, too, that a good translator must be (a) reasonably competent in the 'out of' language, (b) hugely skilled in the 'into' language, and (c) a man.

[31]

Dad's Telling Us the Lot

One summer afternoon, in Swansea, South Wales, some time in the mid-1950s, my mother told her two sons to attend their father in his study. Kingsley takes it up in the early pages of his *Memoirs*:

> Philip and Martin came in, their expressions quite blank,
> innocent in every way possible . . . They were, I suppose, seven
> and six years old. The short monologue I gave them slipped out
> of my head afterwards at the first opportunity, though I know I
> did get in a certain amount of what might be called hard
> anatomy and concrete nouns, although again I must have used
> the word 'thing' a good deal and talked about Dad planting a
> seed. Well, what would you? I have never loved and admired
> them more than for the calm and seriousness with which they
> heard me out. I knew they knew, they knew I knew they knew
> and so on to the end but never mind. They left in a silence that
> they courteously prolonged until they were out of all hearing
> . . . In no sphere is it truer that it is necessary to say what it is
> unnecessary to say.

There was a later and less anatomical induction. That night, I remember, I was engrossed, with maximum pleasure and concentration, in a pinball machine – so the locale changes to Spain, and my age is upped to twelve. Gripped though I was, I fell into line without hesitation when my brother approached and said simply: 'Quick, Mart. Dad's telling us the lot.' We sat before him at the restaurant table and mutely listened . . . In a sodden schoolyard, at the age of five, I had heard a friend explain the facts of life. And my reaction was, I should say, universal: my mother would never let my father – the bastard! – do *that* to her. But in Spain, in 1962, I came away with all the very best thoughts and feelings: my father and my mother loved each other, and I and my brother and my sister were somehow the creation of that . . . The family was returning, by car and boat, from a ten-day trip to Majorca, where we had stayed at the *posada*, or guesthouse, of Robert Graves. As we drove north from Barcelona something very fundamental started going wrong with the car: I spent my thirteenth birthday helping, quite happily, to push it up the Pyrenees. Six weeks later, Kingsley met Elizabeth Jane Howard.* And by the following summer his marriage was at an end. My father never had and never did stop loving my mother. Still, as the *Letters* clearly show, Jane Howard was a *coup de foudre*.

'It's an exceptionally smart man,' writes Saul Bellow in 'A Silver Dish' (one of the greatest short stories of all time), 'who isn't marked forever by the sexual theories he hears from his father . . .' During our mid-teens Kingsley continued to beguile my brother and me with apothegms of romantic promise. 'The most attractive part of a naked woman,' he said, 'is her face.' Which sounded very good. But what really put the cat among the pigeons was the following: 'The physical sensations of sex are hugely magnified by love.' So *that's* why you went after love: for the sex. No. Philip and I were as coarsely energetic as most boys our age; but we wouldn't be our father's sons if we had shown no impatience to experience the real thing. When I was sixteen I read *The Anti-Death League* (1966) in typescript. I was mesmerised by the two brief questions which the (previously unloved) heroine asks herself as she feels the first surge of attraction towards the hero: 'Is it now? Is it you?' And then, a little later, the two brief subvocalised answers: 'It is now. It is you.' I was always asking myself those two questions, and always hoping to hear those two answers.

So how was I otherwise, in November 1973?

My life looked good on paper – where, in fact, almost all of it was being lived.

That first novel had been such a long time coming that I was already halfway through its successor. I had a fulltime editorial job at

---

* At the Cheltenham Literary Festival. The panel discussion which Jane had organised and which Kingsley attended was on 'Sex and Literature': one of God's dud jokes.

the *Times Literary Supplement.*★ I was writing reviews and articles, for the *TLS* and elsewhere. In the November 23 issue of the *New Statesman* the Books section opened with my 1,500-word review of John Carey's study of Dickens, *The Violent Effigy*. A week previously, and a week prematurely, the Books section had closed with the novelist Peter Prince's 500-word review (last in a batch of three) of *The Rachel Papers*. I have the review before me now† and I only intermittently disagree with it.

A young first novelist is condemned to write about his own consciousness, but Mr Prince saw no irony, no stylisation – no difference at all between me and my narrator, with his 'cheesy little *bon mots*' and 'dingy little *aperçus*'. He is halfway there, though, on the Osric factor ('the Early Bloomer, the Sixth Form Sneerer, that combination of middle-class privilege and A-level meritocracy') and the herd-instinct sexism. This was the worst review that came my way. Everyone else showed leniency, and some showed

---

★ I got this job quickly but not immediately. For four months I worked in a small art gallery in Mayfair, showing the punters around the place, dusting frames in the basement, making the tea and coffee, hand-addressing the invitations to the private views, and reading about a book a day. Then I got taken on as a trainee copywriter at an ad agency, J. Walter Thompson, just up the road in Berkeley Square. The ad world used to be something of a refuge for literary types. But I feared for myself at J.W.T. It seemed to be entirely peopled by blocked dramatists, likeably shambling poets, and one-off novelists. The whole place felt like a club-world sunset home for literary talent. I resigned after a week (but only because I had somewhere else to go), serving two more before starting at the *TLS*, at that time located in an annex of the old *Times* building in Blackfriars – above a pools firm monitored by tublike turnkeys with whiskers of formidable wingspan.

† Not in some paranoiac's scrapbook (and there won't be much, hereafter, about reviews) but in a bound volume of the magazine. Six years' worth of bound volumes formed part of my leaving present, in 1979. If I may speak elegiacally: the old *Staggers* was for many years a very great thing (my contemporaries there, for instance, were James Fenton, Christopher Hitchens and Julian Barnes). Its front half, the political half, started to die with the conscience of the Labour Party. The back half had the cohesion available only to a minority-interest field, and lasted a little longer.

indulgence.* They seemed to think that it must have been extra difficult for me, coming out from behind my father, but it wasn't; his shadow served as a kind of protection. And I felt no particular sense of achievement, either. It's a strange surprise, becoming a writer, but nothing is more ordinary to you than what your dad does all day. The pains, and perhaps some of the pleasures, of authorship were therefore dulled to me. It was business as usual. I was working very hard, I was full of endeavour, but it seemed to be the least I could do.

And I still felt like a student. The *TLS* felt like a library, the sessions with the literary editors felt like tutorials, and my articles felt like weekly essays. My large, carpetless, dust-whorled room in the mansion flat in Earls Court made me feel like a student. My clothes, particularly my donkeyjacket-like jacket, made me feel like a student. My lone dinners, my interminable instant coffees, made me feel like a student. My headaches and faceaches (and my vestigially sebum-rich complexion)† made me feel like a student. The high principles, or essential indifference, of the girl I was futilely orbiting (kisses, nothing more) made me feel like a student. At the same time, although I was edging forward into it, the adult world of promotion and preferment still looked alien and menacing to me. There was still the suspicion, despite all the current evidence, that you would not only fail but actually go under. Perhaps everybody has this. Christopher Hitchens had it: we called it 'tramp dread'. Earls Court was certainly very fully furnished with tramps, drunks, beggars, babblers. And in the mansion flat itself there was an old doctor, close to retirement, who sometimes showed up for the night; I would see him slumped over a sherry bottle in the lino-draped kitchen, or staggering and flailing around in a beltless

---

* Auberon Waugh, son of Evelyn, was very generous. Nobody – literally nobody – was in a position to be more sympathetic. And *he* wrote his first novel when he was nineteen.

† The popularity of the Beatles haircut owed a lot to the fact that it covered the top third of your face. 'What's under that fringe of yours? A galaxy of acne, no doubt.' This was Kingsley's accurate surmise, some years earlier. The haircut was gone. The galaxy took much longer to fade.

[35]

bathrobe and unbelievable Y-fronts (shapelessly swilling, and mackerel-grey) . . .

I was twenty-four, and this is the condition: pretending to know everything, while knowing nothing; pretending to be sure, while being always uncertain. I felt like a student and I was not in love. But there was another world, one I felt I could control and order – which was fiction. And I have always been in love with that.

Over the Christmas of 1973, experience – in the form, as I now see it, of an acquaintance with infinite fear – entered my life and took up residence in my unconscious mind. This happenstance has shown me, through long retrospect, that even fiction is uncontrollable. You may think you control it. You may feel you control it. You don't.

But before we face experience, that miserable enemy, let us have some more innocence, just for a while.

Letter from School

55 Marine Parade,
Brighton, Sussex.
7/11/67.

Dearest Dad and Jane,

Another letter so soon, you see, because I want to ask some
rather delicate questions which I hope will not alarm you too
much. Strange as it may well seem, I've forgotten what plans we
made re my accomodation [sic] from Jan–Jun/July. I think we
agreed on a boarding house, did we not? Also, I vaguely remember
suggesting a flat, and Jane said I wouldn't like that and I agreed.
Well it has just struck me that I rather would like that: but it is
more than grandiose caprice. What would a boarding-house cost
per week? About £3-£4? Well a flat in Brighton (bedroom, sitting-
room, bathroom, and kitchen) would cost £6 to £7. I would gladly
pay the difference. You see I'm anxious to have a *bit* of
independence during my last days of independence, as it were. At
any rate I don't see why this period should introduce extra
restrictions. Independence does not entail riot, insurrection,
disregard of personal health, and general wanton behaviour. I just
want to be comfortable, to have a sense of establishing my own
discipline by doing certain things for myself, and to fuck girls (a
litotes I couldn't resist and not to be given unfair emphasis).*

★ Litotes ('ironical understatement')? No, this is just a clunking attempt at
bathos. More generally, I ask my male readers to remember what they were
like at eighteen. And I ask my female readers to remember the kind of boys
they were having to deal with then, and what *they* were like.

As for washing-up, cooking, laundry etc. I could probably continue to use the school facilities: I would have lunch at Rottingdean or wherever, and supper at Marine Parade.

I think this would really make all the difference as to whether I am to look forward to an enjoyable but disciplined 9 months or start settling down to reaping 'the rewards which courage brings'. I hasten to add that I'm quite confident that I will be saying this after 3 mths of running a flat by myself.

Somehow sitting in one room, of a weekend, marking papers is a sorry prospect. I have far more space here. Also, the idea of sharing a bathroom with 13 or 14 lorry-drivers is daunting. I know it's not relevant, but having shared a bathroom with you two, I couldn't imagine you joining in a baleful queue in a draughty corridor every morning . . .

You know that if you say I cannot have a flat then I won't make *too* much fuss, and you know that I'm not going to refuse to stay in Brighton if I don't get my own way. But haven't I earned the right to make something of my stay here in the way of having a nicer life as well as doing my stuff so far, so please don't dismiss the idea, and please don't assume that I won't be able to handle it. If it doesn't work then I could always leave the flat + get digs – there would be no lease-complications as with Phil's flat.

Anyway, sorry to have been so boring, but I think you'll see that it is a seriously conceived suggestion – 'not a present thought but by duty ruminated' – and I hope that you will consider it as such. On that heavy note,

    Lots of love

    Mart x x x x x x

P.S. Could you give me a cursory reply as soon as poss. Because I'd like to get the whole ugly business resolved quickly. – M.

On rereading this I feel I must emphasise that I am not contemplating orgies and parties as I write, but comfortable surroundings for stuff-doing. I wouldn't know how to go about falling into bad company or anything like that – and anyway that goblin Mr Ardagh can keep his beady eye on me.

Learning About Time

In the gap between school and university English men and women are traditionally expected to hike to the Philippines or care for the sick in Madagascar. I can account hardly at all for my '9 months' – except for the three weeks I spent sitting behind the till in my step-uncle's record shop in Rickmansworth. But some travel happened. This happened.

There were four of us in the Mini Moke, me, Rob, and Si and Fran (who were a couple). Attired in the usual chaos of flowered scarves and crushed velvet, unsolicited and unheralded (and reasonably stoned on hashish), we were about to disturb the peace of one of the world's greatest living poets, Robert Graves.

– Will he remember you? someone asked me.

– Not by sight.

But I said I thought he would, probably, after I'd lengthily explained. I certainly remembered him.

This is my father doing Lord David Cecil, the handsome, theatrical, effortlessly affected and above all aristocratic English don (who among other distinctions failed Kingsley's B. Litt. at Oxford):

'Laze . . . laze and gentlemen, when we say a man looks like a poet . . . dough mean . . . looks like Chauthah . . . dough mean . . . looks like Dvyden . . . dough mean . . . looks like *Theckthpyum* [or something else barely recognisable as 'Shakespeare'] . . . Mean looks like Shelley [pronounced 'Thellem' or thereabouts]. Matthew Arnold [then prestissimo] called Shelley beautiful ineffectual angel. Matthew Arnold had face [rallentando] like a *horth*. But my subject this morning is nòt the poet Shelley. Jane . . . Austen . . .'

[39]

Square brackets in the original (*Memoirs*). I am surprised to see 'Austen' there in straight roman: in Kingsley's spoken rendering the first syllable – *Auth* – was always viciously stressed.

When *I* say a man looks like a poet, I mean he looks like Robert Graves. Tall, angular, the lips sullen-sensual, the crushed but still diagrammatically aquiline nose, the rheumy eyes and their thousand-mile stare – and, with all this, a loose-limbed physicality, large, gestural: I remember him scaling the rocks that leaned up from the sandless shore – and bounding over them as he came back the other way and leapt flailing into the water. Here indeed was the warrior-poet. And yet I knew him to possess a forgiving soul. One night, back in 1962, he had had the Amis children over for dinner while my mother and father went out on their own. Graves's wife Beryl was there (surprisingly manly, straitlaced and countified, and always flanked by her two giant poodles), as well as members of his own progeny and entourage. Towards the end of the meal Graves proposed a party game: the oral composition of a poem, with everyone round the table contributing a line in turn. Philip and I sat there, slightly enfeebled by several hours of best behaviour. And when Graves said, 'Philip. Why don't you begin?', my feared, revered and much-adored brother instantly and typically reached for the most subversive – and above all the nearest – thing to hand. He said: 'There was an old farmer who sat on a rick . . .' My ears hummed: we're for it now, I thought. Because this 'poem', taught us that morning by our father, continued: 'Laughing and waving his big hairy fist / At the sailors who . . .' And so on.* Graves smiled and, glancing downwards, said lightly, 'You're not meant to know that poem.' I think it was Beryl who got us going on something about domestic animals. The only line I remember was one of Graves's: 'The cat was grey, and Siamese . . .' A perfectly understated iambic octosyllable – as I would come to realise, years later.

– What's he like? said Rob. How should we act?

By now we were passing through the village of Deya, saying

---

* This ditty, like others ('As I was going to St Paul's / A lady grabbed me by the elbow'), dealt in unmet expectations.

'Señor Graves?' and *'El poeta?'* to passersby, who confidently waved us on. At this time Graves had just finished his five-year term as Oxford Professor of Poetry. One of his historical novels, *I, Claudius*, had recently been televised, and his scholarly books – *The White Goddess*, *The Greek Myths* – were still very much current. He would now be seventy-three.

– Oh don't worry, I said. Just go on as if he's a god.

Graves seemed baffled but on the whole rather pleased to see us. He was perhaps fractionally diminished from the striding colossus of a few years earlier, but still very straight and head-in-air, the ancient coin of his face quite undulled. I introduced my friends and said,

– I'm sorry about this Robert, but you must get some very weird people coming to see you these days. Now you're so famous.

– Oh I do, I do. Some *extraordinary* people come to see me now. *Extraordinary* people.

The five of us looked out on the rocky acres – spurs and tors, terraces, arthritic olive trees. Then Rob said to Robert,

– Make that mountain open up.

– What?

– Turn it into a volcano.

– What?

– Go on. You can do it. Make that cloud go away.

– Oh, you're –

– Summon a tidal wave.

– You little –

– Make the moon come out.

– Ooh, you –

– Make the –

And Robert got hold of Rob and roughly tickled him.★

★ This seems to have been Graves's usual response to friendly mockery. In post-First World War Oxford somebody made a joke about his height: 'This encouraged me to a ragging pretence of physical violence; but I immediately stopped when I caught the look on his face. I had surprised his morbid horror of being touched' (*Good-bye to All That*, 1929). Not Rob, this time, but T.E. Lawrence. I shouldn't have worried about busting in on Robert Graves. He did the same thing to Thomas Hardy, and was just as generously received.

A couple of hours later the Mini Moke was edging its way down the drive. Graves kept running back to the house to bring us more fresh-baked bread, more labelled jars of pickles and homemade jam.

It was 1968, the time of devaluation and currency restrictions (and of much else): the upper limit on trips abroad was £50 per person. I had taken £50 out of the country. Rob had taken less than £50 out of the country because, the day before our departure, he had gone to a betting shop. After two or three years of near-daily patronage, I had stopped going to betting shops. I stopped when I suddenly noticed that betting shops were populated not by rich people getting richer but, rather, by poor people getting poorer. I shared this observation with Rob, who nonetheless persisted. Anyway, by the time he got to Majorca (where we stayed free at Si's father's house), he didn't have enough money to get back.

This soon became academic. As we drove north from Barcelona something very fundamental started going wrong with the car. I spent my nineteenth birthday as I had spent my thirteenth: pushing a car up the Pyrenees. It wasn't quite the same, because this car also had to be pushed *down* the Pyrenees. The thing wouldn't even coast. In a piece of 1962 called 'Something Does Not Work with My Car' Kingsley wrote:

> After ten miles we came to a slight upward slope. That was that. We were in a small town called Le Boulou, a name I shall never be able to see on a map (which is as close as I ever intend to get to the place again) without horror.

And that's where we were. Le Boulou.* I had loved all this the first time around: late nights, virile inadvertencies. But now, as I watched Rob approach the nearest house (hoping to call a garage on its telephone) and knock on the knocker and say, with pitiful insouciance,

---

* Kingsley did not thaw to Le Boulou when I told him, years later, that Nabokov wrote a novel in a hotel room there: *The Defence* (1930).

[42]

'*Bon après-midi!*' – well, even before the door was slammed in his face, I had a sense of the length of the road ahead.

Eventually the car was towed back to Perpignan. We responded to the crisis in the manner of middle-class adventurers the world over: we phoned home for more money. I reached my step-uncle Colin (Kingsley and Jane were on holiday themselves). 'Uh, we need some money sent.' 'Why? Can't you get a job?' 'Get a job? What job? A job doing what?' I waited in the post office while Rob tried his mother.

– What did she say?

– She said, 'Get a job.'

– Christ. What's all this about getting a *job*?

We did not get a job. I went on at Colin until he relented. It would take time for my father's accountant to arrange the transfer (a complicated and perhaps semi-legal procedure). Rob and I spent freely until our money ran out the next day, the last few francs going on Coca-Colas and a pinball machine, and then settled down to a week of patient trembling and starving and hanging around the post office. We slept in a state-run Y. During the day we would sometimes tremble and starve in the public gardens. Here we would mingle with enormous, and enormously evolved, hitch-hikers (Germans, Swedes), nordic titans of self-reliance who regularly girdled the earth on a dollar a year. They were grateful for our bulk-bought Spanish cigarettes.

– You come up from Barcelona? In Barcelona is it easy to find a job?

Rob and I looked at each other. One of us said,

– It depends.

– How about the docks? Can you get a job at the docks in Barcelona?

Rob and I looked at each other: our pallor, our want of inches, our soiled flower shirts. And, in voices that suddenly sounded mid-adolescent, we began:

– Well it's reasonably easy.

– It can be done.

– I mean, but you can't just *walk into* a job at the docks in Barcelona.

[43]

The money came through in the end, of course. After reclaiming the car we reckoned we had about fifteen francs for supplies. Rob went off and came back with some glacier mints, some coffee-cream biscuits and some orangeade – a combination which, even on paper, still makes me flinch. The neck of the orangeade bottle snapped off as I tried to open it (during a hysterical thunderstorm in Perpignan's northern suburbs), dramatically gashing my hand. More blood was to be seen the next morning when I managed to cough some up in a layby: out of my mouth came a translucent jellyfish with a dot of plasma in the middle of it. My only spell at the wheel lasted about fifteen minutes: a cigarette end, flicked from the rear seat towards the driver's window, went straight down the back of my hipster jeans, causing me to swerve into the path of an oncoming pantechnicon. That was my shot. Rob drove all night. We signed an IOU on the channel ferry and reached home on our last gill of gasoline.

I was very short of money when I was a baby. I slept in a drawer and had my baths in an outdoor sink. My nappies bore triangular singe marks where they had been dried on the fireguard. It was tough. My father's dinner would often consist of the contents of the doggybag that my mother brought back from the cinema café (the Tivoli) where she worked. (*Memoirs*: 'Swansea'.) Kingsley would sometimes write to Philip Larkin pleading for the loan of a fiver – or even a *quid*. It was really tough; but I don't remember any of it.

One day in 1978, in another car, Rob said to me as I dropped him off,

– Sorry, Mart, but could you spare a tenner?

I could, and usually I did. But this time I wouldn't.

– A fiver. Okay a quid.

– Okay. A quid.

That week in Perpignan was my only experience of privation, of hunger. It would happen differently for Rob, who was no mere trier-out of hard times, and proved to have a genius for adversity – not ordinary disasters either but extraordinary disasters. By his example well-born Rob schooled Osric in Fri-dee and Satur-dee, in *sofa* and *lavatory*, in *[with]drawing-room*, in *miffy*.* Still, there was nothing bourgeois about his trials and labours. You would not know, gentle reader,† with your attentive brow, your soft hands on the spine, his ordeals of park bench, of winter coalhole, or shelterlessness, and prison. As a child Rob attended the ancient prep school, Christ's Hospital. Then he went to the ancient secondary school, Westminster. Then he went to Wormwood Scrubs.‡ He's fine now, in 1999. Some people cannot play by the prevailing rules; other rules might have been okay, but not the prevailing. Thirty years ago his face was Nureyevian; then experience imbued it, for a while, with something medieval: self-inflicted wounds, unembitteredly borne. He's fine now, but Rob – but going under – lives very close to what I write.

From 'Agua, No' to 'Agua, Si'

On a tube train in Earls Court I saw a young man reading *The Rachel Papers*, about a week after its publication. He was enjoying the book, and in the best possible way: a reluctant smile, an unreluctant smile, a reluctant smile, and so on. I still regret that I didn't go up to him. But I told myself: listen, this will be happening all the time – get used to it. I need hardly add that it didn't happen again for about fifteen

---

* It was a bad thing to be *miffy*. Being *miffy* meant that you were the kind of person who, when pouring a cup of tea, habitually put the Milk In First. M: And that's common [working-class], is it? R: Yeah. M: Why? R: I'm not sure. It just is. M: . . . What happens when you put the milk in second and the tea's too strong and there's not enough room in the cup to make it milky? R: Then you get up and pour *some of it down the sink* and go back and try again.

† One of the meanings of 'gentle' is that risible word *posh* (port out, starboard home?). *Macbeth*, Duncan: 'This castle hath a pleasant seat; the air / Nimbly and sweetly recommends itself / Unto our gentle senses.' Our posh senses. Posh reader . . .

‡ An eight-month sentence for a domino effect of drink-driving offences. It could happen to anyone, more or less; but it happened to Rob.

years (someone in a headset, on an aeroplane, scowling at *The Moronic Inferno*). When my first novel won the Somerset Maugham Award I told myself the same sort of thing: get used to it. And that *never* happened again.★

The terms of the prize, much resented by Kingsley when he won it, as we have seen, required that the author spend some months abroad. My father had taken us all to Portugal. I went to my mum's in Spain. Spain: we're in Spain again. Spain is my other European country, not Italy, not France. Spain . . . At that time Mum (for that is what I call her and how I think of her: I have to concentrate for an instant to remember her name – Hilary) was hoping to turn a profit running a bar in Ronda, Malaga. She has always fancied herself as having entrepreneurial talent in the catering line. Years later, back in England, at six a.m. every morning she would get behind the wheel of one of those burger-and-furter vans you see lurking in the lay-bys. Her one major success, with which she was then still flushed, was a fish-and-chip shop she had co-run in Ann Arbor, Michigan – a place called Lucky Jim's. She was prospering in 1974, with a new husband (her third) and a new baby (her fourth). Her house, Casa de Mondragon, was the little sister of the adjacent *palacio* of the same name.

It was in one of the palace bedrooms that I worked, filling, to the disgust of the next occupant, two litre bottles with cigarette butts while taking my second novel from manuscript to typescript. For lunch I would walk across the bridge and into town, and spend an additional half hour feeling the warm breath of raptly attendant *niños*

★ The Norwegian translator of *The Information* was not long ago given ten bob and a sash for his work on that book, but that's the closest I've come to a prize since 1974. Kingsley won only two: the Maugham, and then the Booker, in his mid-sixties. I conclude that our novels are not good at creating a consensus, and conclude further that in some ways this is a virtue. The secret reason for the media's interest in the Booker Prize is as follows: it demystifies and declasses the writer. Writers become something you can bet on, and when lottery-night comes round you can watch them on TV being reduced to what Yiddish calls *schwitzers* – stealthily perspiring into their tuxes, their dimity. My father said the only sayable thing about literary prizes: they're obviously all right if you win them.

on my fingers as I played the pinball machine. Hemingway★ – in every bar in Andalucia there is a signed photograph of Hemingway getting or staying drunk with the owner – recommended Ronda, and in particular its casino/club/hotel in the main square, as the optimum setting for an elopement. There is nothing much going on at the casino any more: a billiard table with no pockets, a smattering of old men playing chess in the uncerebral Spanish style, smacking the pieces on to their squares with a snarl and a taunt. But Ronda remains prodigious – physically exciting to inhabit. It stands on a high plateau split by an abysmal gorge. Look over the drop and you see birds in flight a hundred feet below.

Spain is my mother's other country too, and she and her husband are back there now as I write, living in the primitive *casita* whose land they attempted to subsistence-farm in the late 1970s. The extent to

★ I saw a couple of bullfights in my teens and went on to read *Death in the Afternoon* plus a few more books on the subject, including Kenneth Tynan's *Bull Fever* (renamed 'Bull Shit' by Clive James). At first I was not immune to the powerful and immediate affect of the spectacle, but the excitement soon lapsed into something far stranger: a kind of brutalised vacancy. Once, in Barcelona, after an hour of messy kills, we saw a matador gored and tossed startlingly high in the air – and the whole family fiercely cheered. Hemingway argued that the bullfight was not a sport but a ritual, a tragedy, in fact, because the bull can never win. What, then, is the bull's tragic flaw? That he's a bull? (Besides, in both the traditional and the modern bullfight it is the horses that suffer most and longest.) In 1974 I went to another bullfight, there in Ronda (the 'cradle' of Spanish bullfighting), and witnessed the ritual in its decadent form, the goaded bulls underbred and cowering beneath their pre-blunted horns. I also glimpsed something of the other side of it: Hemingway's hero, Antonio Ordonez, now retired, was perhaps Ronda's premier personage, and I frequently saw him around town – though never in the Antonio Ordonez, one of my favourite bars despite all its Ernestiana. He was embarrassingly handsome and charismatic, and he glowed, as if under a spotlight and an omelette of makeup. On fiesta days he would take the reins of a coach and pair with his glamorous wife and his glamorous daughters (the town's top two vamps). Ordonez's inner glow came from reverence-assimilation. A man of proven courage – a bullkiller who went in *over* the horns, not around them – but, withal, one of the classical artists of the ring. He was treated like a war hero who also combined the attributes of a Pavarotti and a Pelé.

[47]

which my mother has made herself mistress of the language can best be conveyed anecdotally. On one occasion the victim of an irresolute sexual assault by a local youth, she screamed at him, *'Venga! Venga!'*★ Even so – to glance at Robert Graves – this was her country, beloved by her best; and I think I know why. We were strolling down the main shopping street, one afternoon in 1974, and we encountered Rafael, a famous local figure. You were never in danger of forgetting in those days (Franco would rule for another year) that Spain had a large population of cripples, clumpers, crutch-wielders, and all the rest; but still Rafael stood out. Wholly benign despite his furiously contorted face, he was a spectacular spastic with an unbelievable gait. He looked like Marcel Marceau putting absolutely everything he had into an imitation of a stage drunk. How could a stride so uneconomical (you wondered) ever really get him anywhere? As Rafael, a flailing blur, inched along, and as passersby greeted him with cries of *Eh, coño!*† and an embrace and a mock left hook, my mother turned to me and said,

 – I *love* living in Spain. I now regard him as *completely* normal.

It struck you, or it struck me, that Ronda was a place that had yet to experience dental selfconsciousness. Many a perfectly moulded visage would unreservedly open out to you – revealing a bag of mixed nuts or, more typically in Andalucia, a bag of mixed nuts and raisins. This suited me down to the ground, because I hadn't smiled unreservedly for at least five years. My mother and father had been tooth-sufferers all their lives and it was already clear that I was booked in for more of the same. 'Take him home,' our Welsh dentist told my mother (wiping his hands after a heavy session), when I was ten. 'He's a *wreck*.' And my teeth were now undergoing a deterioration that a later dentist would characterise as *dramatic*. In my late teens one of my top incisors had been elbowed in, right-angled, by my brother (during a rare bit of three-handed rough-housing with Kingsley), and a few years later one of my *lower* incisors had been snapped off at the gum when Rob flung a handful of poker chips in my face (after great

★ *Venga* means 'come on'. I think my mother was searching for *fuera*, which means 'go away'.

† This word means what you think it means. But here it has no greater force than 'man' or 'dude' or 'guy'.

provocation, and not at all forcefully). They just felt wrong. They didn't fit, didn't fit; when I clenched my teeth, they didn't fit. The mouth is uniquely vulnerable to obsession. If there's anything going on in there, then that's where you live: in your mouth. One of the characters in the novel I had nearly finished was a dental monomaniac (incapable, throughout, of considering any other topic), and this was very nearly my case. So I understood and participated in my mother's love of Spain. It was simple: the standards were lower, and less shame attached itself to the body.

My half-brother Jaime was two years old in 1974, and it is therefore almost certain that the following incident belongs to a later summer. I tell it now, though, because it seems to me a sharp satirical commentary on my romantic life as it was then developing . . . Like many children in Spain, Jaime was allowed to accompany his supper with a glass of red wine,* heavily qualified with water. On this particular night Jaime kept a strict eye on the dilution procedure. *'Agua, no,'* he kept saying, with raised forefinger, every time my mother moved to the tap. *'Agua, no.'* He probably got two or three glasses down him – and then, before anyone could prevent it, he seized and drained an unattended gin and tonic. What followed was a stark paradigm of drunkenness, astonishingly tele-scoped. Jaime laughed, danced, sang, bawled, brawled, and passed out, all within fifteen minutes. Then about half an hour later we heard a parched moan from his room. Jaime was already having his hangover. The voice was faintly saying, *'Agua! . . . Agua! . . .'*

– *Agua, si*, said Kingsley when I told him about it.

– Exactly. All the way from *agua, no* to *agua, si*. In an hour.

Such avidity, solipsism and indiscipline seemed to mark my own love life; and there was very often this feeling of time being speeded up – and gambled with. The love affair with Tina Brown† was a love

---

* I didn't find this at all shocking. In my house, back in South Wales, you could have a cigarette on Christmas Day at the age of five.

† As an undergraduate Tina was already famous (and this at a time when *no one* was famous): fringe playwright, journalist, looker, prodigy. To get to her room in college I would have to step over waiting TV crews, interviewers, profilists.

affair (the answers to the questions 'Is it now?' and 'Is it you?' were both clear positives), but it was over too soon, as if something much longer had been confusingly compressed into six or seven months . . . When my father made his Maugham trip he was thirty-three and fronting a family of five. My mother was my mother when she was twenty-one, and was Philip's when she was twenty. This was the pattern of their generation. The pattern of mine was to marry late, have children late.★ I didn't know it then, but there was an awful lot of bachelorhood to be swum through. And the beginnings of a pattern were also emerging in me. Ardour dwindled. Three months, six months, twelve months, with the affairs tending to elide. Tina, pointing to a lacuna in my emotional repertoire, would later say that I had never had my heart broken. And I can now recognise that I somewhere harboured an unconscious distrust of love (to this I will return). But at the time it just felt like a process, increasingly familiar and inexorable. Ardour, then diminishing ardour, and constantly starting again. All the way from *venga* to *fuera*. All the way from *agua, si* to *agua, no.*

One of the briefest of these affairs – one of the most condensed in time – caused me to pay another visit to my mother, not long after her reluctant return to England in 1977. I said I had a story I wanted to tell her. And a photograph I wanted to show her.

– Yes, dear.

Nearly three years ago, I said, I had an affair with a young woman called Lamorna. She had been and still was married to a rather older man, Patrick, whom I had known, slightly, for some time ('He went out with Gully, Mum,' I said, referring to the dedicatee of my first

★ I well remember the smile of sadistic satisfaction that came over John Updike's face as we talked about this during an interview held in the canteen of Massachusetts General Hospital. Updike had fathered four children when (as he has said) he was pretty much a child himself. He enjoyed hearing what it was like, humping infants around at thirty-five: spongey knees, mortified spines – all this baffling news about the body and time.

novel, and my mother smiled, now feeling more at home in all this).
Patrick and Lamorna, I continued, had not been getting on well, and
their marriage at that time was chaste.

– Yes, dear.

I said that Lamorna and I were still friends and that I had recently
had lunch with her . . . I did not go on to tell my mother that Lamorna
had impressed me with her general bearing and burnish – her beauty,
her sanity. Lamorna suffered from manic depression – a condition
once frivolously but memorably described by a psychologist as the
Arnold Schwarzenegger of mental illnesses. I had seen her, and would
again see her, in a state of tranquillised agitation, disorganised in
thought, and seemingly beset by small fears, small enemies. That day
at lunch it was I who was agitated (a current matter of the heart); and
I remember Lamorna suggesting that I order something non-
monolithic, like a stew or a fricassee, rather than face the edifice of a
steak or a chop. She knew about agitation. She knew all about
agitation . . . The restaurant was the old Bertorelli's in Queensway,
opposite the bookshop (both long gone, as unsorrowfully noted by the
narrator of *Money*), and Lamorna looked handsome and polished
among its dark wood and bright linen. I was, as usual, obsessively alert
to the health and prettiness of her dentition; as she bit into her tarama
on toast, pink plumelets appeared in the tiny vertices between her
teeth. I thought she had never seemed stronger or happier. I thought
she had found equilibrium. And I was wrong: diametrically wrong.

– She talked about her daughter. And then there was the
photograph, Mum. She gave me the photograph.

– Yes, dear.

It was ready in my pocket. It showed a two-year-old girl in a dark
flower dress, smocked at the chest, with short puffed sleeves and pink
trim. She had fine blonde hair. Her smile was demure: pleased, but
quietly pleased.

My mother snatched it from my hand.

– Lamorna says I'm her father. What do you think, Mum?

She held the photograph at various distances from her eyes. She
held it at arm's length, her free hand steadying her glasses. She
brought it closer. Without looking up she said,

– Definitely.

Lamorna was still some months away. As I sat at my desk in the *palacio* (the building had about it the air of immobility that precedes decay), I had a different consanguineous absence on my mind. On my mind? In my mind. Somewhere at the back of it.

. . . There were many reasons why my mother loved living in Spain, not least of them being that you could, in most pharmacies, buy speed over the counter. After a while the stuff she liked was declared prescription-only; so she had to put on ten layers of clothing and go to the hospital and pretend to be suffering from obesity (a routine business in winter, but not so easy during the African heat of July and August). She regarded the drug mainly as a labour-saving device. You could always tell when Mum had scored because the house suddenly became the scene of large-scale cleansings and reorderings. You would see her going from room to room, singing, with a sofa under one arm and a sideboard under the other. And just this one time, during the summer, I found her doing a major ablution, with her usual thoroughness but with none of her usual zest. I think I asked her if she'd run out. She reminded me that my aunt Miggy was expected for a short stay. And, of course, my mother would want the house to be looking at its best for her sister. We said no more.

My aunt's visit set me thinking, if that is quite the word I want, about the unassimilably dismal event of the previous December. Can you think about something you can't assimilate? I don't think you can. Or I don't think you do.

Typically in that era I would spend Christmas Eve buying all my Christmas presents and then drive around London in the white Mini (which started at least 50 per cent of the time), picking up my sister, my brother and perhaps my brother's girlfriend and then heading for the big house north of Barnet, the car full of presents, bottles, crisp bags, beercans and joint-ends, and feeling like a vampire racing against the sunset in his packed coffin to get to the castle before dawn. Christmas was a dark time in England, the lights going out everywhere from 24 December to what felt like late January, so that the whole world was as black as Aberdeen.

The house on Hadley Common was a citadel of riotous solvency – not just at Christmas but every weekend. There was a great sense of in-depth back-up, a cellar, a barrel of malt whisky, a walk-in larder: proof against snowstorm or shutdown. I think it was that Christmas morning that all four Amises, with breakfast trays on their laps, watched *Journey to the Centre of the Earth* – then the visit to the pub, then the day-long, the week-long lunch. And with Kingsley the hub of all humour and high spirits, like an engine of comedy . . . I felt so secure in that house – and, clearly, so insecure elsewhere – that I always experienced a caress of apprehension as I climbed into the car on Sunday night, any Sunday night, and headed back to the motorway and Monday, to the flat or the flatlet, the street, the job, the tramp dread, the outside world. An apprehension much magnified after this endless Christmas, a swathe of Sundays, Sundays squared and cubed. And, more than this, the outside world now had someone missing from it. On the night of 27 December 1973, my cousin Lucy Partington disappeared.

We had dined late, in the Spanish style, and I was in the kitchen with my mother and my aunt. They were over by the draining-board, preparing a hot drink, while I remained at the table, deep in an unpleasant, unconstructive and above all familiar dental reverie; a recent explosion in the top deck had made the righthand side of my nasal cleft tender to the touch – and so of course I kept touching it, feeling it, testing it . . . I woke up when I realised that the two sisters, for the first time in my presence, were talking about Lucy. Now, I have a deep background of love for my aunt: she and her four children – particularly the elder pair, Marian and David – were indispensable figures in my childhood and early youth, and Lucy herself was always pressingly vivid to me. So my heart was fully engaged. But where was my imagination?

After all, this was not the first time I had been close to an absence. When I was six my two-year-old sister fell from the garden table and landed head-first on the stone floor. For a day and a night her life was in danger.* Quite unready, quite unscheduled to face this or any other contiguous death, I felt enveloped by a sinister secret, a sinister privacy and quiet. I had this sense of exclusion, of approaching colourlessness and silence, a second time, in puberty, when after a long separation I began to suspect that I would never see my father again . . . But these two experiences had given me no understanding of the weight and depth of the present calamity. Understanding, or a glimpse of it, was still a great distance away, not in place but in time. It happened in the countryside beyond Ronda, a few miles from where we sat that evening, when my three-year-old son went into the garden to 'explore', accompanied by my mother-in-law's dog. Fifteen minutes later the dog returned, alone; and it was perhaps another hour before the child was found. What struck me, after a very short while, was the way the feeling of apparently maximal nausea and panic continued to escalate. But that was 1987, and this was 1974.

My aunt was leaning against the counter, with her hot drink, holding it close with joined hands. And she said in a steady and unemphatic voice that not a minute passed without her thinking of Lucy and wondering where she was . . . I cowered inwardly away from this – at the depth of my incomprehension of it. I ducked my head. I was turning twenty-five but how very young I was, how really terribly *young*. And how long it lasts, youth, that time of constant imposture, when you have to pretend to understand everything while understanding nothing at all. You understand nothing about *time*. I ducked my head and I thought: poor Miggy! What a terrible thing. She still thinks about Lucy every minute, and it's been . . . nine months.

Nine *months*?

* Sally recovered fully and quickly from her fractured skull. A year later she would have another confrontation with death. She was staying with her paternal grandparents in Berkhamsted. One morning, soon after my grandfather left for work, my grandmother had a stroke and fell down dead. On his return, ten or eleven hours later, he found Sally unharmed, but strangely dressed, and strangely daubed – with her grandmother's makeup. As it filtered down to my brother and me, the story was that Sally had 'opened the front door to him'. But that couldn't be right. Still, I wonder how my grandfather survived that homecoming.

Letter from School

Durham O.K. now.*   55 Marine Parade,
                                     Brighton, Sussex.
                                     30/11/67

Dearest Dad and Jane,

    I have more or less finished the exams, which, to me, were an immense disappointment. I had a complete break-down last week – a mild glandular fever: head-ache, fiendish sore throat, sweating, temperature 104! I lay in bed groaning and dribbling into my pillow for 3 days. Anyway I didn't feel quite with-it during the exams, and I felt that I was completely inequipped to do the paper, which in fact was quite within my capabilities. The goblin [Mr Ardagh] noticed this and, having read my papers, said that although not disastrous, they were well below my norm. Mrs Gibbs [the goblin's mother], who supervised my illness as it were, has procured a certificate which the goblin has despatched with my papers. I got a horrible feeling of inadequacy and had that awful feeling of exam hysteria of tearing up my first few attempted answers and ending up sobbing softly after 20 minutes. I'm sorry if I've buggered up my chances at Oxford – let's hope not anyway.

    Equally disturbing is the trend of affairs concerning Rottingdean. I went for an interview today. The chap said I wouldn't be teaching *any* English *or* History. Just Maths (NEW Maths too) to the 8 and 9 yr olds and, of course, cricket and rugger

* This refers to Durham University, where I was to be interviewed for a place.

[55]

every afternoon. It's pretty obvious that they just want some duffer; how's this supposed to benefit me. Apart from not being good for *me*, it's not going to be *good* for me, if you know what I mean. Part time means full-time but part-wage (5 gns); I'll be there from 9–7. I fail to recognise this as a formula for the stew of Eng. Lit, however much I might like that stew. What's our game? I can't convince myself that this is what you had in mind . . . I'll have no time to read because I'll be too busy having a nasty time. Where lies the profit? I've been dreading and fearing this thing for months, conceding in moments of euphoria that at least it'll be quite fun doing a Shakespeare play. I really can't tolerate the idea of making a fool of myself on the rugger pitch *every* day. Since I can't accept that this idea is calculated as a purge of recent sins and failures because there haven't been any, what do we think we're playing at. It's not even academic for Christ's sake. And I beg you not to come to the general conclusion that somehow, considering all, one way or the other, it might well end up doing me some kind of good. I'll need something more tangible than that. I didn't fail *ALL* my 'A' levels you know – I picked up one or two. I say, without any bitterness, ★ that you arranged all this without *once* consulting me – unless you count asking me whether I would be prepared to insinuate myself into the general state of affairs that you had delineated. In retrospect it seems incomprehensible to me: are you sure I haven't committed some heinous crime which I've forgotten and for which this is a grim protracted punishment? I repeat that I'm quite unembittered by this – I just don't know how you mean.

You're probably anxiously awaiting a suggestion that I should be furnished with a Park-Lane penthouse and a £500 allowance. No, dammit, I think that would be unreasonable. But why shouldn't I get a completely ordinary job, in which the rewards that courage brings would be closed to me, and stay on in Brighton, and have lots of lessons with the goblin? It would save you lots of

★ What is making me so very, very bitter here is the fact that I didn't fail any of my A levels, not this time. I got English (grade A), History (B) and Logic (D).

money (can't be wrong) and would allow me to get on with my reading at a far more spanking pace. Since the teaching bit has turned out to be spectacularly non-academic, why not try something unspectacularly academic. Let's please not think we have to go through with it because its [*sic*] gone this far.

Anyway the goblin agrees that Rotters is out + is ringing around but if there are no developments that we think make it worth-while, have I your permission to throw it?

Sorry if this seems querulous/petulant/spoilt etc. Love

Mart x x x

P.S. Dad. I didn't know you like your poetry to contain passion . . . . . . *much* passion.

P.P.S. (Could you reply *as soon as possible*).

Bus Stop: 1994

While rooting around among my papers I recently unearthed another letter, from my cousin David Partington – preserved by some miracle, because I do not keep letters and have kept none of my father's.

The letter is undated. But my cousin refers to the effect of parenthood on my new book, which he names. The boys were born in 1984 and 1986, and the new book was *Einstein's Monsters*: 1987. Julian Barnes has said that novelists don't write 'about' their themes and subjects but 'around' them, and this is very much my sense of it. The book consisted of five short stories *around* nuclear weapons and an introductory essay that was very definitely *about* them. Of course, the mid-to-late Eighties was one of the warmer phases of the Cold War: the time of the Reagan build-up, or spend-up; 'the evil empire'; Star Wars ('the force is with us'). Gorbachev had yet to show his hand, and it was hereabouts that Reagan accused the Russian language of having no word for *détente*.

This is from the polemical introduction, entitled 'Thinkability':

> When I told [my father] that I was writing about nuclear
> weapons, he said, with a lilt, 'Ah. I suppose you're . . . "against
> them", are you?' *Épater les bien-pensants* is his rule . . . I am
> reliably ruder to my father on the subject of nuclear weapons
> than on any other, ruder than I have been since my teenage
> years. I usually end by saying something like, 'Well, we'll just
> have to wait until you old *bastards* die off one by one.' He
> usually ends by saying something like, 'Think of it. Just by
> closing down the Arts Council we could significantly augment
> our arsenal. The grants to poets could service a nuclear
> submarine for a year. The money spent on a *single* performance

of *Rosenkavalier* might buy us an extra neutron warhead. If we closed down all the hospitals in London we could . . .' The satire is accurate in a way, for I am merely going on about nuclear weapons; I don't know what to do about them.

Having read the *Letters*, I now know that Kingsley was genuinely – and, it seems to me, hilariously – infuriated by my taking up this position. He wrote to Robert Conquest saying what 'a fucking fool' I was, coming to 'leftiness' so late (a fucking fool, in his lexicon, meant someone just about bright enough to know better). At the end of the week that saw the publication of *Einstein's Monsters* I took my three-year-old boy, as usual, to Sunday lunch at my father's house; and Louis, I remember, was aghast at our opening exchange:

– I READ YOUR THING ON NUCLEAR WEAPONS AND IT'S GOT *ABSOLUTELY BUGGER-ALL* TO SAY ABOUT WHAT WE'RE SUPPOSED TO DO ABOUT THEM.

– WELL IT'S NOT SURPRISING IS IT BECAUSE AFTER FORTY YEARS NO ONE ELSE KNOWS WHAT TO DO ABOUT THEM *EITHER*.

Come to think of it, he did look genuinely infuriated: as hostile as I ever saw him. My brother Philip does a flawless imitation of Kingsley in this state: the whole head vibrating, the eyes dangerously swollen, the tensed mouth in a violent false smile, and (most tellingly) the nails of the forefingers scrabbling, almost bloodily, at the cuticles of the thumbs . . . Your feelings about nuclear weapons depend among other things on your date of birth. I know exactly what happened to me. When I was a child my form-master regularly told me to get down on the floor and hope that my desk lid would protect me from the end of the world; I sensed violence and absurdity that lay beyond contemplation, and I expelled it from my conscious mind. Then fatherhood, at thirty-five.* Worked-up protective instincts

---

* This was Kingsley, at thirty-five (in a letter to Larkin): '. . . by christ, I have just heard an air-raid siren & feel so scared I could faint . . . Only testing the siren I expect, *to make sure it's in working order when they need it*. I prefer not to think about all that.' His sons were eight and nine at the time. What were they thinking, and feeling, about all that?

[59]

made me reexperience that shelved or resisted anxiety: that silent
anxiety. And the feelings were there to have and the stories were
there to write.

'Do you remember', my cousin wrote in that letter,

> how we used to talk when we were twelve* about what we
> would do if suddenly everybody except us disappeared, leaving
> the world otherwise intact? With you in Cambridge and me in
> Gretton we would make contact and meet up. We may even
> have agreed a plan.

Do I remember? Yes, David, I do remember – I remember
everything. Because all this is connected in my mind. And I
remember thinking about you, and your younger sister, and your
mother, when I wrote:

> I am sick of them – I am sick of nuclear weapons . . . They are
> there and I am here – they are inert, I am alive – yet still they
> make me want to throw up, they make me feel sick to my
> stomach; they make me feel as if a child of mine has been out
> too long, much too long, and already it is getting dark.

At certain times, for certain periods, David was able to persuade
himself that Lucy was still alive – alive, but elsewhere. Naturally all
the Partingtons attempted something of the kind. My mother, too,
attempted it. I attempted it. Lucy was serious, resolute, artistic,
musical and religious. Even when we were children the message I
always took away from Lucy was that she wasn't going to be
deflected, she wasn't going to be deterred. Only with difficulty could
you imagine her having the inclination to vanish; but it was the work
of a moment to imagine her having the will. So she was in a nunnery,
somewhere; she was a violinist in Melbourne, a pseudonymous poet
in Montreal. Of course, these reveries kept running up against an

---

* David was twelve and I had just turned thirteen when Kennedy blockaded
Cuba: 22 October 1962.

obstacle: the fact that Lucy was gentle, was kind, was sane. To which
the one available rejoinder would be: well, I must have been wrong
about that, and I suppose it can deeply surprise you, the people who
turn out to be prepared to disseminate hurt. Thus the argument
continued (very faintly after a while, and then almost inaudibly, given
my distance from the event) for twenty-one years.

It was David who drove Lucy into Cheltenham on 27 December
1973.

And now it was 1997.

– I could *so easily* have driven her back. I offered to.

But Lucy had decided to take the bus; and there was no point in
arguing with her about a thing like that.

– If I had insisted . . .

– You could go on for ever, I said, with this chain of *ifs* . . .

David was one of the great requited loves of my childhood. We
see each other seldom, now, in our ponderous adult guise, but the
connection remains more than cousinly. My brother★ is of course
irreplaceable, and so is my half-brother, Jaime. But for much of my
childhood I earnestly wanted David to be my brother, and he wanted
it too, and the affinity is still there. When I was writing the novel
London Fields I faced the minor task of thinking of a name for the
narrator's brother: it took me about a second to come up with
'David'. (The character was Jewish – and, I now notice, died
young.) . . .

This meeting with David Partington took place on 31 October
1997: Halloween. Lucy's fate had been public knowledge since
March 1994, no, more than public. Along with those of the other
victims, Lucy's fate was *national* knowledge: part of something that all
citizens felt themselves duty-bound to have in common. And from
that time David would need to nerve himself to open a newspaper.
Because it was all ready to begin again: waking in the middle of the
night and getting up to sit for hours weeping and swearing. This was

---

★ I had run into Philip the previous day. He was passing me in a
supermarket, and I was impressed by the sureness with which my peripheral
vision identified him, by his shape and volume, as if there was a template of
him in my mind which he alone could occupy.

his condition on the day after the disappearance. 'Lucy didn't come home last night.' There was nobody in her room and the made bed had not been slept in. There was certainty of disaster. And there was my poor cousin (I hate thinking about this), out in the courtyard, crying and raising his clenched fists and saying, 'If anyone has done anything to her . . .'

Weeping and swearing, cursing and sobbing: there ought to be a word for that. In November, 1918, the news of the Armistice inspired Siegfried Sassoon to claim: 'And I was filled with such delight / As prisoned birds must find in freedom . . .' Robert Graves felt differently: 'The news sent me out walking along the dyke above the marshes of Rhuddlan (an ancient battlefield, the Flodden of Wales), cursing and sobbing and thinking of the dead.' Cursing and sobbing and thinking of the dead: there ought to be a word for that. 'Grieving' won't quite serve. This is something anterior. It is, I think, not a struggle to accept but a struggle to believe.

– As you drove into town. Do you remember what you talked about?

– I was trying to justify my current girlfriend, who was – you know, sexy, but thick. Lucy was being very accommodating. Not at all critical. But I still felt I had to justify myself.

– Six years after she disappeared – remember? When we talked about it. You were saying that you wanted to avenge her. With your own hands. Do you still?

– No. But now or at any other stage I would give up my life so that Lucy could have hers. Because my life is . . . And hers . . .

– I understand. But don't be hard on yourself. I think you're a paragon.

– Me?

Later there was a silence as we followed a line of thought: the same line of thought. On the night of 27 December 1973, Lucy Partington was abducted by one of the most prolific murderers in British history, Frederick West. We knew what had happened to her after death. She was decapitated and dismembered, and her remains were crammed into a shaft between leaking sewage pipes, along with a knife, a rope, a section of masking-tape, and two hairgrips. But the terrible imponderable was what had happened to her when she was still alive. Records showed that just after midnight on the morning of 3 January 1974 West appeared at the casualty department of Gloucester Royal Hospital with a serious laceration to the right hand. 'It seems only too possible that she was kept alive for several days,' writes one commentator. And yet the evidence remains entirely circumstantial. 'It is possible', writes another, 'that [West's] wound occurred as a result of the dismemberment of a corpse, but it is just as possible that it did not, which is the inference I should prefer the family to make.' I said,

    – I've read all the books, and there's no . . .

David veered back from this, just an inch or two, as if shocked that I had survived exposure to something that for him was so much more thoroughly steeped in revulsion. The books: I was assiduous in hiding them in a cupboard when, a couple of months later, my cousin came to spend the night. Well, the books are what they are, but they had given me something I needed David to hear.

    – I've read all the books, and there's no hard evidence that it wasn't all over there and then at the bus stop.

And I added, hoping to give comfort (but why would this give comfort?), 'Lucy was just very unlucky, David. Your sister was just incredibly unlucky.'

It was Sunday, 10 July 1994, and one of the most beautiful days of this or any other year. A faultless morning, a blue-planet afternoon. I had no idea that a crucially significant – a transfiguring – experience lay before me. I was living, or enduring, or just lasting, from moment to moment, and from hour to hour . . . Like many people who have not yet turned forty, I used to give the Mid-Life Crisis little credit and no respect: it was the preserve of various dunces and weaklings who, for one reason or the other, were incapable of walking in a straight line. When my crisis was over (and they do end: a crisis can't go on being a crisis), I saw that it was intrinsic and structural. It had to do with things that were already wrong and were not being faced. The Mid-Life Crisis compels corniness and indignity upon you, but that's part of the torment. More materially it puts you on a beachhead of pain that your cliché has created. But later you see that there was a realignment taking place, something irresistible and universal, to do with your changing views about death (and you ought to have a crisis about that. It is critical to have a crisis about that). People say that a growing child can successively 'understand' the death of a pet, the death of a grandparent, and then even the death of a contemporary. Only in adolescence do we hear the first rumours of our own extinction, these rumours remaining vague until the irrefutable confirmation of the mid life, when it becomes a full-time job looking the other way. Youth has finally evaporated, and with it all belief in your own impregnability. The knowledge marks you: it makes your hair whiten and wither, it smears the grime into the orbits of your eyes . . . That Sunday – 10 July 1994 – I was as glued to the present as Captain MacWhirr in Conrad's 'Typhoon', watching the shoes he has flung off 'scurrying from end to end of the cabin, gambolling playfully over each other like puppies', as the dark storm begins to show its might.★ I expected no saving illumination. But it came.

I had two other reasons to feel unreceptive that day. First, I had, of all things, a toothache: a joke toothache, something you'd see in a tabloid cartoon set in a dentist's waiting room (I might as well have tied a pillowslip round my head); the bulge on the side of my jaw threatened closure of my right eye. Second, I was having the only regular bad time I ever have with this matter of writing fiction: severe anxiety, rising sometimes to purulent levels, while finishing a long novel . . . The toothache had begun on Friday, in Oxford, with a night of sleepless pain at the house of Ian McEwan (another mid-life-crisis artist, like all my best friends – though his was forced upon him), followed by a horrified self-inspection in the bathroom. Over the next day and a half the abscess stopped hurting and concentrated on swelling. It was spectacular, even by prevailing standards (and the whole business with the teeth was at that stage near-terminal, and the

★ It goes on: 'He threw himself into the attitude of a lunging fencer, to reach after his oilskin coat; and afterwards he staggered all over the confined space while he jerked himself into it.' That lunge. Conrad was the kind of writer who kept his eyes open when most of us would prefer to keep them shut.

next move richly dreaded). Pressing an icetray to my cheek before the mirror, I saw that I had acquired an attribute casually granted to one of my more brutish minor characters: penny-farthing nostrils. The right side of my face was telling the left side of my face what it would look like when it was very fat. No one remarked on it, that weekend. Close family because they understood; others through tact and decorum and gentle myopia, and because reunions are like that, and you take a forgiving view of a half-remembered face distorted by stroke or palsy or some other mudslide caused by time.

In logistical terms the weekend had so far been pretty typical for one in my generic condition. Up to Oxford with the boys on Friday, down to London with the boys on Saturday, up to Oxford with the boys on Sunday (to transfer them to my estranged wife, who lived in London but was staying in Oxford) – and then onward. As we continued north-west, the three adults in the car, I and my mother and my brother, could now talk (and smoke, and cough) and prepare ourselves for the afternoon. Like well over a hundred other souls we were converging on the Religious Society of Friends Meeting House, in Cheltenham, Gloucestershire, to attend a memorial gathering for Lucy Katherine Partington, 1952–1973. The funeral itself had been postponed because Lucy's remains were still being held as evidence by the police. We drove on. My mother relied, for her ashtray, on the empty and sealable tin of throat pastilles she carried round with her. She warned her sons that she would not be sitting with them or near them or in their line of sight. This was accepted and understood (for reasons that had better be disclosed elsewhere). All three of us smoking, coughing, thinking, we drove on . . . David would later tell me that the moment he heard about the exhumations in Gloucester he knew that Lucy would be among the dead. In early March I had been abroad and knew nothing until I opened a newspaper in the taxi from Heathrow. There was the photograph I had last seen on a missing-persons poster twenty years ago.

In a justly celebrated essay* Lucy's elder sister Marian quoted from the diary she kept at the time of the excavations:

* 'Salvaging the sacred', published in the *Guardian*, 18 May 1996.

[65]

Saturday, March 5 10.15 phone call from the police saying they
would like to come over to talk to us [Marian and her mother].
They have some 'news' for us. That half-hour of waiting for
them to arrive was full of a terrible restlessness and anxiety . . .
palpitations and nausea. The numbness and muteness of shock
began to invade . . . Numerous messages on the answering
machine on our return. The Pain Vultures sounding as if it's
unquestionable we should call them back (TV and tabloids). We
don't. . . . I hardly slept that night. I felt a paralysing feeling of
weight, fear and a pain in my heart. This is enormous. Shock
brings you into the present like giving birth. All your energy goes
into focusing on survival. Some people die of it.

For a while my mind kept conducting involuntary thought-
experiments, or feeling-experiments: I would imagine each of my
sons finding themselves, as their distant cousin had, in such a violent
force field, and I would imagine the moment when they sensed the
magnitude of the undifferentiated hatred that was ranged against
them. The first time I did this I teetered backwards on my feet, and
there was a palpable rush or whoosh, as if I had approached the
entrance of a wind tunnel. And this tunnel a mere vent or flap,
leading to the room occupied by Lucy's parents and siblings. Again at
several removes from them I experienced an apprehension of defeat,
of obliterating defeat. The hope that things might have turned out
differently could now be seen as the pitifully fragile thing it was, while
the braced body began its labour to live with the other outcome.

We were very early. An hour passed before we joined my aunt
and my cousins, and all the others, at the meeting-place.

Lucy Katherine Partington, 1952–1973.
    This was Marigold Palmer-Jones, daughter of Marian:
    'Twenty years ago my mum's sister, Lucy, went to visit a friend
in Cheltenham. She left the house to catch the bus home and was
never seen again. I can remember clearly how my mum told me this.
I must have been about four and we were looking at some

photographs of her and her family. There was one photograph of four children sitting on a pony. I didn't recognise one of them so I asked her who it was. She said it was her sister but she had disappeared when she was twenty-one. At the time I think I was too young to grasp the idea of her sister just "disappearing". But I remember feeling really confused when I looked at my mum because she was crying and I couldn't understand why . . .'

This was Susan Bliss, a childhood friend:

'. . . Guinea pigs featured largely in our lives in those early years. They had this strange habit of multiplying! We spent hours in various hutches and huts in friendship with our guinea pigs . . . We had been nursing a sick guinea pig for some time. I think that it was actually Beryl's guinea pig but as we all shared so much it didn't seem relevant. Eventually the sick guinea pig died and we were three little girls in a hen house saying goodbye to the poor little chap. Lucy and Beryl kissed him goodbye and passed him to me. I was scared to kiss him as he was dead. Lucy was very angry with me. She told me fiercely that just because something dies it didn't mean that you should stop loving it and that everyone deserved to be kissed before going to heaven. Humbly I kissed the guinea pig and today offer the same tribute to my beloved friend.'

This was Mary Smith, a teacher at Pate's Junior School:

'. . . She wasn't smug; however much she loved books, however brilliantly she did her homework. She was never a pious little goodie-goodie sitting in the corner. She would argue with anybody, but it was always because she wanted to know the truth . . . We had, some of you may remember, an annual ritual at Pate's – called Race week. The school would assemble, neat and tidy and silent, to wave to the Queen Mother as she went by. Well, I remember in the fifth year Lucy rebelled against this. She may have heard the story that the Queen Mother once said to the Town clerk, "What is the name of the school for the deaf and dumb girls who come to wave to me?" Well, Lucy was not very pro-monarchy; she sat in the form room and discussed her anti-monarchy views and the state of the country and the state of the world and what sort of poetry she should study next, and so the time passed . . .'

[67]

This was Elizabeth Christie, a childhood friend:

'. . . The very last time I met Lucy was in the summer of 1973 at Gretton and she spoke very enthusiastically about her Mediaeval English course and wrote out from memory ["slightly mistakenly"] a particular poem . . . And I kept it and over the years it became for me a sort of epitaph for Lucy. It's a mediaeval poem about the Virgin Mary:

I Sing of a Maiden

I SING of a maiden
    That is Makeless:*
King of all kinges
    To her son, she ches.†

He came all so stille
    There his mother was
As dew in Aprille
    That falleth on the grass.

He came all so stille
    To his mother's bower
As dew in Aprille
    That falleth on the flower.

He came all so stille
    There his mother lay
As dew in Aprille
    That falleth on the spray.

Mother and maiden
    Was never none but she
Well may such a lady
    Goddes mother be.'

* (1) matchless, peerless; (2) mateless, husbandless.
† chose.

This was Marion Smith, a childhood friend:

'. . . When we did the school play *The Crucible*, I don't know if any of you remember that – Lucy was Abigail and I was Mary Warren – and we had to scream. So we had to spend hours rehearsing screaming in a field. Lucy was just wonderful at it and the rest of us just stood around to boggle at it. Next term in the sixth form we did *Middlemarch* and Lucy was the enthusiast and the scholar . . . I was going to read something from *Middlemarch* and have been going back through it. Poor Dorothea wasn't up to Lucy you know. Dorothea had this long life at the end and she was very nice and people thought she was wonderful and she didn't really affect anyone very much. Even in the short life that Lucy had – I think as everyone has said here today – she affected an awful lot of people and goodness knows what she would have done – You know, Dorothea stand back – Lucy had it all.'

This was Elizabeth Webster, a teacher at the Arts Centre:

'. . . She came to see me when she was at Exeter, just before the last year, and I said to her, "now that you are grown up what are you going to do?" and she said, "I don't mind what I do as long as I do it absolutely to the hilt." – and then I said, "yes that's fine but where are you going?" and she thought awfully hard, then she said, "Towards the light . . . Towards the light."'

And this was Marian Partington:

'. . . Four months after Lucy died I had a dream. And in the dream she came back and I said, "Where have you been?" and she said, "I've been sitting in a water meadow near Grantham," and she said, "If you sit very still you can hear the sun move." And in the dream I was filled with a great sense of peace . . .'

Very soon it was clear to me that something extraordinary was happening. As I wept I glanced at my weeping brother and thought: how badly we need this. How very badly my body needs this, as it needs food and sleep and air. Thoughts and feelings that had been trapped for twenty years were now being released. They were very ready. I have known literary catharsis and dramatic catharsis, and I

[69]

have mourned and I have been comforted; but I had never experienced misery and inspiration so purely combined. My body consisted only of my heart – that was my sense of it. Formulaically, perhaps, but without mysticism, I can assert that I felt bathed in her presence (and felt unrecognisably the better for it). This is where we really go when we die: into the hearts of those who remember us. And all our hearts were bursting with her.

The Onion, Memory

– Are you going back to Oxford now? asked my mother as I dropped her off at the house.

– No, Mum, I'm not going to Oxford. What a wonderful afternoon.

– Yes. It was. Give my love to Isabel.

On the day I told her and my father that I was leaving home, my mother shed silent tears, unemphatically, unwillingly. That made three out of three. (Or three out of four: Jaime was twenty then, and is still single.) But then she wiped her cheeks with the back of her hand and accepted me in my new reality.

I didn't go back to Oxford. I went back to my flat in West London – the work studio that now served as home. The place was comfortable enough under normal circumstances, but it had had the boys in it on Saturday night: their camp beds thus commanded most of the sitting-room floorspace, and the entire apartment was strewn with comics, empty crisp packets, video-game cartridges, yoghurt cartons, and various effigies of various ghouls and goblins and boglins, of buffed-up superheroes, of predators, terminators, robocops . . .

With an ice-bag pressed against my cheek I sat among all the detritus, my heart still raw and swollen as I communed with my murdered cousin.

More than a hundred had been there that day. Their differing degrees of pain went back twenty years and would continue for another twenty, forty, sixty. And that hundred each knew another hundred who sympathised, who worried and winced. And my cousin was not the only victim but one of eleven, or perhaps thirteen, or perhaps more . . . The murderer, in a sense, presides over this little universe, with all its points and circles, but of course there is no place for him within it. He caused it, but he is not of it.

So I hadn't intended to say very much about Frederick West. Earlier on I conceived of a short chapter that would describe an average domestic day at 25 Cromwell Street, ending – after a scarcely credible inventory of troglodytic squalor, including theft, violence, incest, rape, sexual torture, whoredom, pimpdom, peeping-tomdom (daughter: 'my bedroom was like a sieve'), pornography, child prostitution and paedophilia – ending, as I say, with West's oft-repeated goodnight to his large and various brood: 'When you go to sleep, my life begins' . . . My family cannot understand the extra-ordinary collision that allowed him to touch our lives, and I have no wish to prolong the contact. But he is here now, in my head; I want him exorcised. And Frederick West is uncontrollable: he is uncon-trollable. For now he will get from me a one-sentence verdict and I will get from him a single detail. Here is the sentence. West was a sordid inadequate who was trained by his childhood to addict himself to the moment when impotence became prepotence.

And here is the detail. West had Quilpian eating habits. He would take the hind end off a loaf of bread and top it with a brick of cheese. He would stroll around the house eating an onion like you'd eat an apple.

An *onion*? When she first met him, at the bus stop (a different bus stop), Rose thought Fred's teeth were 'all green and manky'. A determined enemy of the washbasin and the bathtub, West, we can be sure, was no friend of the waterpick or the dental floss. Still, he could chew his way unconcernedly through an onion. His teeth were strong enough.

But what about his *eyes*?

Learning of this detail, my mind went back to an evening in the late 1970s when I was lounging around with my brother Philip, and I drew his attention to a new book of poems I was reading: the first collection of my mentor and protégé and friend (and ex-tutor), Craig

Raine, *The Onion, Memory*. We talked about the title: how the onion, like memory, is arranged in folds with a common nub. And I said,

– What else have they got in common?

– They make you cry, said my brother.

In May 1994, Marian Partington had travelled to Cardiff with two close friends. She went to bless her sister's bones:

> I lifted her skull with great care and tenderness. I marvelled at the sense of recognition in its curves and proportion. I wrapped it, like I have wrapped my babies, in Lucy's 'soft brown blanket', her snuggler. I pressed her to my heart.

And when, late in 1995, Frederick West's interrogation tapes were played, and his version of events appeared, unchallenged, in the press, Marian campaigned, and won a public rebuttal. This is a rebuttal, I think, that I must confirm, solidify and perpetuate. Because otherwise these things are lost, lost in the daily smudge of newsprint; and I never again want to hear anyone ask me how Lucy Partington got 'drawn into' the orbit of the Wests.

West said he killed my cousin because she wanted him to go and meet her parents.* He and Lucy were having an affair ('purely sex, end of story'), and Lucy, now pregnant, had 'come the loving racket' and 'said I wanna come and live with you and all this crap, and I just grabbed her by the throat'. '[H]er wanted me to see her parents, her wanted me to do bloody everything.'

That is what it said, in the press, unchallenged. I rebut it. This book rebuts it.

At the end of that day – 10 July 1994 – I went over to Isabel's. We talked about my cousin and about Isabel's brother, Bruno, himself a family prodigy of charm and innocence, who had died a month and a half earlier at the age of thirty-six. I chewed experimentally on my dinner, using about 8 per cent of my mouth, which was all that was

* Roger Partington, Lucy's father, was at this time living on Teesside.

available. At one point Isabel said: You've got to go to a dentist. At least go and *see* a dentist . . . I hadn't been to a dentist for five years. I had been writing the novel for five years. I said: If I get into the dentist's chair I'll never get out. I'll finish the novel. Then I'll get into the chair.

Letter from School

55 Marine Parade,
Brighton
Sussex

Dear Jane, and Dad:

Thanks for the very cheering + very fair letter. I've spoken to the goblin who agrees as long as Mrs Gibbs agrees. However, Rottingdean will probably only require me on a part-time basis because the chap they thought was leaving might have decided to stay instead. Mrs Gibbs and that grand-high-arch-hobgoblin are emphatic that Rotting. is so easily the best prep-school in S. England that I should accept this. This means that I wouldn't get a living wage (only £6 or £7 per week) but, on the other hand, I might well be teaching the scholarship boys who, I am assured, are as bright as buttons. What do you think? I'm rather pleased because I don't want to spend much time teaching 7 yr olds how to divide decimals etc. But the question is whether this should effect [*sic*] my bid for a flat. I shall leave this entirely up to you, and if you think it O.K., then adjust away at will.

I have just learnt that Durham are pestering me for an interview, which was to have been on Monday (21st). But Col★ was so tardy in forwarding it that I will not be able to go. It arrived today (Sat) and I would have to have gone tomorrow – but owing to Bruce's negligence it may not now be. It's bloody boring because I expressly told him to be very careful because offers must be

★ My then step-uncle, Colin Howard; a.k.a. Bruce and Monkey.

answered within a week or else they are withdrawn. It's not all that serious because they might accept my apology and postpone the interview – but they could easily not. (Let us not forget that there are 37 people entered for every Eng. Lit. place). I shall have to write him a biting letter – otherwise I'm sure to find an unconditional offer from Bristol in a tattered, 3 week old envelope, which Col thought was 'not worth forwarding'. Anyway, not a real disaster.

Anyway let me know the verdict,

Lots of Love, Mart X X X X X

The Hands of Mike Szabatura

It is now a bright Monday morning in the autumn of 1994. I am
sitting in a coffee shop on Madison Avenue. The novel is finished
(though there is still some tweaking to be done); and I am here for
the chair. I said that it was five years since I went to a dentist. This is
no longer the case. In the new reality, it is five days since I went to a
dentist. And now I'm back again. In twenty minutes something very
terrible is going to happen to me.

Courage was needed for the first visit: I could, in theory, still walk
away. For the second visit all that was asked of me was stoicism.
Because I no longer had a choice.

When I was a child, and the whole thing was beginning, I used to
look forward to being older. By virtue of being older I would be brave
– unavoidably, automatically. Courage would just come upon me: I
wouldn't be able to get out of the way. Look at the adults, I said. Adults
didn't refuse to get out of bed in the morning because they had a dental
appointment later in the day; they didn't spend their lunch hours
snivelling in the toilet; they didn't come home and tell their mothers
that, yes, they had been to the dentist when in fact they hadn't – when
in fact they had wandered the streets, helpless, tranced by a mysterious
failure of will, failure of courage. Courage would be conferred by age.
The two words seemed to me to be connected: age would give me
coeur. Age would give me heart. Anyway it didn't happen. When I was
forty I just stopped going. And now I was forty-five.

The first visit to Mike Szabatura took place at eight in the
morning on the previous Wednesday. My name was called and I went
on through. The handshake of Mike Szabatura: masonically medical.
Dentists' hands: their warmth, their strength, their godly cleanliness.
Two beautiful young women, luminously brown-skinned in pink

worksuits, swayed around us. I needed no second invitation to lie down. The words formed easily. For many years I had been writing them in my head.

– I'm in for a bad time. But then so are you. You've got to look inside my mouth. My lower teeth are merely very poor. But my upper teeth . . . I have a bridge that runs from ear to ear. All that's keeping it in, as far as I can tell, is habit. The whole trouble is hereditary, together with inadequate care early on. My mother had okay teeth and bad gums. My father had okay gums and bad teeth. I've got bad teeth and bad gums.

– Let's take a look.

– Steel yourself, I said, and opened wide.

Half an hour later Millie helped me out of the lead vest I had donned for a fusillade of X-rays. I always think of my cousin Lucy when I am being X-rayed, when I am being restrained; and I always think of her whenever I find myself in church . . . I waited in the waiting-room. It was not yet nine in the morning and other tooth-sufferers were gathering. For what? Local tremors and disturbances, probably, and not tectonic shift. Millie beckoned. I was shown – most ominously, it seemed to me – into another room, a darker and quieter room, a room that might as well have been called the Bad News Room, where Mike Szabatura stood bent over an X-ray chart. Mike is a large solid man with a fleshy, mobile, almost cartoonishly expressive face. As he talks he wags his head and tubes his lips and pops his eyes. It is a face that has been trained over many years to dramatise positives and negatives – trained to say, On the one hand, *this*, on the other hand, *that*. But my case would not test his repertoire. Today there was no other hand.

– The uppers are shot. The lowers are no good either. And look.

We stared at the moonscape of the X-ray. There was 'pathology' in the lower jaw: a ridge of darkness just above the chin. This, I learned, could be one of three things: a cancerous growth; a growth with a long name that would keep coming back; a growth, but something manageable and unexotic. Anyway it would have to come out. For months, months, I had felt something new and strange down there: pressure, activity, occupancy . . .

[77]

– The uppers are shot. At any meal you could be sitting there with your teeth *in your hand*. They go Monday. You don't have a choice.

We spent the intervening weekend at Isabel's family spread in Long Island, with her brother, the painter Caio Fonseca. There used to be another brother, and another painter: Bruno. But Bruno died, here, in June. His mother Elizabeth said to me: 'I still don't think of him as dead. I think: He's back in Barcelona. I never see him anyway,' she added with a shrug. 'He's in Barcelona!' Bruno was the dreamboat who always danced with the wallflower; and now his ashes flowed with the ocean. The last time I saw him he was, like Eliot's Christ, an infinitely gentle, infinitely suffering thing. In the dark groundfloor room, surrounded by the dully glowing machinery of home care, I sat and read to him. He liked the sound of my voice and would sometimes put in requests for a session; but every paragraph that left my lips seemed to be a sinisterly poetic commentary on his condition. From Borges's 'The Circular Ruins':*

No one saw him disembark in the unanimous night, no one saw the bamboo canoe sinking into the sacred mud, but within a few days no one was unaware that the silent man came from the South and that his home was one of the infinite villages upstream . . . The purpose which guided him was not impossible, though it was supernatural. He wanted to dream a man: he wanted to dream him with minute integrity and insert him into reality . . . For a moment, he thought of taking refuge in the river, but then he knew that death was coming to crown his old age and absolve him of his labors. He walked into the shreds of flame. But they did not bite into his flesh, they caressed him and engulfed him without heat or combustion. With relief, with humiliation, with terror, he understood that he too was a mere appearance, dreamt by another.

* Translated by James E. Irby.

From Kafka's 'A Fasting-Artist'* (*Die Hungerkünstler*):

Those were his last words, but his shattered gaze retained the
firm if no longer proud conviction that he was fasting yet.

'All right, deal with this mess!' the foreman said, and they
buried the fasting-artist together with the straw. Into the cage
they now put a young panther. It was a palpable relief even to
the most stolid to see this savage animal thrashing about in the
cage that had been bleakly lifeless for so long. He lacked
nothing. The food he liked was brought to him by his keepers
without a second thought; even freedom he did not appear to
miss; that noble body, endowed almost to bursting-point with
all it required, seemed to carry its very freedom around with it –
somewhere in the teeth, apparently; and sheer delight at being
alive made such a torch of the beast's breath that the spectators
had difficulty in holding their ground against it.

Perhaps it was Bruno's example that shored up my sense of
proportion, but all that weekend I was, as the saying has it, a model
of calm. That cliché is actually very telling and descriptive (like many
other clichés: 'beside yourself', for instance); I felt modelled,
moulded – and selfconscious and semi-paralysed; and yet I was calm.
Calmly I walked on the beach. Calmly I played tennis. Calmly I
watched the Canadian geese as they gathered for migration. Calmly I
smoked and drank and took tranquillisers. Calmly I cleaned my teeth.
The lowers only, of course, because the uppers would be in a dustbin
before ten o'clock on Monday morning. Cleaning my teeth used to
be a big part of my life. Fifteen years on a hygiene regime meant that
I had used up something like eight thousand hours cleaning my teeth:
the picks, of wood and water, the interproximal, the floss, the electric
brush. I switched on the TV for something to watch while I cleaned
my teeth and what do I get? An ad for dental implants. Look at them
go: crunching into carrots and apples, attacking corn cobs in a way
that put you in mind of electric typewriters, getting through the

* Translated by J.A. Underwood.

drumsticks and throwing them over their shoulders like Henry VIII – and kissing. Forcefully kissing. 'Doing all the things they used to do. Dial 88-TOOTH' . . . The ad gave the impression that these people had suddenly been readmitted to a party – an orgiastic banquet of immortality and joy. Seeing the pain of their exclusion now turned into such happiness, I found I had tears in my eyes. Then I realised that these people were just actors who had had perfectly good teeth all along.

This was the physical climax of my life. Or better say that it was the third-act climax. Next would come the fourth act (conventionally a quiet act). And then the fifth act. Two weeks ago I had straightened up from the last pages of *The Information* and gone into the bathroom and looked at a face containing three or four toothaches and TV-shaped with swellings and said out loud, 'You're not prepared for this. The master plan didn't work. You're not prepared.' But I was prepared. Or at least I was ready. The master plan had always been as follows. Persist until you can persist no longer. Persist until it cannot be borne. Persist until *anything* could be borne more easily. It was a bad plan. A good plan would have been to keep on going to the dentist. It was a bad plan, but it had worked. My respect for the unconscious continues to grow. My unconscious mind might not have thought much of the plan either, but it worked round that and made its preparations. Really, the conscious mind can afford to give itself a rest. The big jobs are done by the unconscious. The unconscious does it all.

I was calm, I claim, but the Canadian geese were not calm. They had turned the whole back field into the departures section of an American airport – though any Americans, any humans, seeing a concourse as busy as this, would have turned on their heels and got back into the cab, adjusting their schedules with resignation and relief. The Canadian geese were thrilled, exalted, ecstatically communicative. For them, no check-in and seat-allocation. They waited in throbbing wedges and trembling phalanxes, their energy growing in an eagerness free from all impatience; they would choose when to go, needing no clearance from the tower. Their time was coming. And so was mine. I too was going to another place . . . Then, yes, now:

they were away, not as one body but in peeling teams and relays, volleys, salvos, forming every shape a blade could make, swordpoint, arrowhead, smooth or jagged. At each vertex the alpha bird, powerfully yet subtly responsive, ducked and shouldered its way through the thermals – off to Boca Raton, to Terceira, to Santa Cruz, to Barcelona.

Were the birds auspicious (*auspice*: 'the observation of bird-flight in divination')? Tomorrow would mean the end of my mouth as I knew it, so there was some comfort to be had from the following line of thought. My mouth has done wrong, and deserves chastisement. My mouth has bad habits – it drinks and it smokes and it swears. Like the hands of Humbert Humbert, my mouth has hurt too much too many people. It has lied and falsely promised. It has kissed insincerely, incautiously, intemperately . . . At the party where I first exchanged whispers with Lamorna Seale the attraction was so immediate that we disappeared into some unattended shadows; and when I emerged into the light my girlfriend★ burst into tears. 'What's the matter with you?' I asked, with defiant innocence – and with that mouth of mine, which was smothered in lipstick. (This was one of the few occasions when I rivalled my father, whose sexual recklessness, as we shall see, often approached the psychotic.) . . . My mouth talks too much. Only a week earlier my mouth had soured a *New Yorker* dinner at the Caprice in London by indulging in this 'exchange' with Salman Rushdie:

– So you *like* Beckett's prose, do you? You *like* Beckett's prose.

Having established earlier that he did like Beckett's prose, Salman neglected to answer.

– Okay. Quote me some. Oh I see. You can't.

No answer: only the extreme hooded-eye treatment. Richard Avedon would need a studio's worth of lights and reflectors to rig up this expression on an unsuspecting Salman. At the moment, though, a passing waiter with an Instamatic could have easily bettered it. Nobody spoke. Not even Christopher Hitchens. And I really do hate

★ The dedicatee of my *second* novel, Julie Kavanagh. I'm sorry, Julie; and I still owe you that letter.

Beckett's prose: every sentence is an assault on my ear. So I said,

– Well I'll do it for you. All you need is maximum ugliness and a lot of negatives. 'Nor it the nothing never is.' 'Neither nowhere the nothing is not.' 'Non-nothing the never –'

Feeling my father in me now (as well as the couple of hundred glasses of wine consumed at the party we had all come on from), I settled down for a concerted goad and wheedle. By this stage Salman looked like a falcon staring through a venetian blind.

– 'No neither nor never none not no –'

– Do you want to come outside?

End of evening.* My mouth wasn't any good at knowing when to stop. And tomorrow the matter would be taken out of its hands. It didn't have a choice.

That last weekend every meal was an awful adventure. Each time the uppers met the lowers they experienced a kind of electrical repulsion that made my head jolt. And sometimes, as I chewed, the whole top rank would shiver and shift, and give a resilient twang.

---

* We didn't go outside. The next afternoon (Salman and I had briskly made up over the phone that morning) I was to be found at Paddington Sports Club, working out on the quiz machine with my friends Steve and Chris. On the screen the following question appeared: Who wrote 'The Old Devils'? The multiple-choice answers were: A: Kingsley Amis; B: William Golding; C: Salman Rushdie. Pressing the A, I pointed to the C and said, 'I had a row with him last night. He offered me out.' Steve said, '*Did* he? Well I hope you took him outside and gave him a fucking good hiding.' Now now, I began, resuming the usual debate, though in more colloquial terms than I had recently used while arguing the point with George Steiner (who was inexplicably obtuse on this question). 'What is it? "Taxpayers' money"?' (E.M. Forster said that 'women and children' was the 'phrase that exempts the [English] male from sanity'. Now it's 'taxpayers' money'.) 'That's money *well spent*. Or you'd like to see your country rolling over for a load of towelheads in . . .' I noticed Chris: his silence, his immobility. He was tensely hunkered forward, giving me his shocked stare. Self-made tycoon, onetime national judo champ, ex-bouncer: a great cube of muscular mass. Over the years I have worked on Chris and the Rushdie question, telling him to abandon his stock response and live up to his own IQ. I think I have nearly succeeded. But what he said then was: 'Offered you out? I wish he'd fucking offered *me* out.'

Like when you're driving round a corner and engage the indicator at the exact point where it is calibrated to self-correct, and the stick resists, and bristles with its own will.

I missed my boys.

The Tunnel

Monday morning on Madison Avenue. Before me on the coffee-shop table: my notebook, and a pensive cappuccino. I was saying goodbye to my upper jaw, but my upper jaw wouldn't have thanked me for any kind of farewell treat. A salami sub, perhaps. Or a steak sandwich. One for the road. Another thing I was declining to do with my teeth was to grit them. I was all through with gritting them, and it hurt too much anyway. The next hour was nothing: I was going to sail through it. How? Because I could look into my soul and see the courage, the strength, the simple heroism of a man who has taken a tremendous amount of Valium.★ Oh, let other pens dwell on the symptoms of fear. And yet . . . and yet there was no hiding from the deeper moment of it. Really, I was saying goodbye to myself. I would be different hereafter. How different, I didn't know. But different: a changed proposition.

I looked at my watch. One more sip of coffee, and a final cigarette in the street while I cautiously sucked on a spearmint Lifesaver. I gathered my things. As I headed for the door a svelte young man emerged from my peripheral vision and tremulously asked,

– Are you Martin Amis?

Yes, I answered. And I thought that this would not feel strictly true for very much longer.

– Love your writing. Keep it up!

– Thank you very much.

If he has this book open before him, that gentle reader in the

---

★ Advice. Take a near-fatal dose on rising, of course. But take a near-fatal dose *the night before*, in addition. Then numbness descends on numbness. Then you are two distances away from your reality.

coffee shop will now know how close I was to collapsing into his arms. But he did his bit: he did his bit to help me to the other side. In the significant elevator, my launch pad (press the button marked Barcelona), I said to myself: Yes, there is that: the writing. I am not an opera singer or a trombonist or an actor. My writing doesn't need my mouth. And that part of me, which is the best of me – that won't change. Eating will change, and so will smiling, talking and kissing (*kissing*), but writing won't change . . . Here we are: the fifteenth floor . . . *Carry me along, taddy, like you done through the toy fair.*

Goodbye, I subvocalised as I climbed quickly into the moulded *chaise longue.*

Millie stands by with her secondary implements. The smocked shoulders of Mike Szabatura bend into their work. First the sour tweakings and piercings of the jabs, one after the other (twelve, fifteen?), until my eyes seem to be brimming with them. Next Mike Szabatura produces the deep plastic horseshoe and starts lining it with the potent adhesive. A civilised pause as we wait for things to solidify, things to liquefy.

Goodbye. Goodbye. This is goodbye. You hated me. I hated you. I loved you. Be gone. Stay! Goodbye. I love you, I hate you, I love you, I hate you. Goodbye.

The hands of Mike Szabatura, with the horseshoe now wedged against my palate, bear down, and tug. In the rhythmical creaking something gives and something catches. My right forefinger flickers up to indicate the right canine: unwilling to abjure its talent for pain, this tooth will fight to the very end. Another trio of injections. And Millie is close, with her rinser, her vacuum-cleaner, her masked face. A further San Andreas of wrenching and tearing – of ecstatic sundering.

– Wait. Your teeth are still there.

I cannot control my tongue which dances up to meet the dangling bridge. Something light drops on to it – a piece of severed root – and slithers off sideways. The aromatic hands of Mike Szabatura are now exerting decisive force. And it is gone – the gory remnant whisked from my sight like some terrible misadventure from the Delivery Room.

[84]

Clearly and firmly I said,
— I find I can talk.

Now (finally) the writer proposes to invite the reader into the bathroom. I have just received a backclap from the hand of Mike Szabatura, and I am still drowning in the sorrowful solicitude of Millie's soft brown gaze, but I am also gliding and staggering through the office and past the reception desk and down a passage, where a mirror awaits me. I lock the door behind me and stand there in the dark. What would it be? 'Nutcrackerish', like Dorothy Wordsworth? Or the squidgy compression of an Albert Steptoe? Or just a lot more age, all at once? I torch the light.

The bathroom mirror, over recent years, had familiarised me with spectacles of convexity. It could happen without warning — without pain. On my way out to dinner I would step into the bathroom to brush my hair and be met by a face like a chaotic potato. I knew about the convex. But here was the concave. Nothing too dramatic: the face does not altogether collapse. I looked gormlessly lantern-jawed, as if I had an underbite (an underbite under what?). I recited the alphabet: all okay except *f*. And I looked all right as I talked, so heavy and pendulous was my upper lip — from decades of not smiling. But now I opened my mouth to its full extent. The realisation, the recognition, was instantaneous.

I claim that a writer is three things: literary being, innocent, everyman. Well this thought was *all* everyman. Not every man will have to see what I saw; but every man will think this if he does . . . Four or five years ago I overheard my mother saying to an old friend, 'Oh I've lost all mine.' And adding, very straight: 'I know what I'm going to look like when I'm dead.'

This was not yet my case. Hopelessly compromised and contingent, my lower teeth were still there. But in the new space above them, impossible to misidentify, was a darkness, a void, a tunnel that led all the way to my extinction.

Letter from Home

108, Maida Vale,
W.9.
Maida Vale 7474,
12.2.68.

Dearest Dad and Jane,

Thanks for your letter, Jane: I must say that Acapulco sounds eminently nasty – did you hire a crack squad of experts to map out a visit abroad which would embrace as many horrible places as possible? What I can't understand, you see, is why you didn't come straight back when the term ended. Did you for one minute fancy that Mexico was going to be *nice*? I'm afraid that hearing about Nashville in all it's [*sic*] horror has indoctrinated me with a virulent xenophobia of which even the exacting Monkey would be proud.

It's good about the Latin,★ is it not? Another thing that cheeky little goblin got right – he told me three weeks before the exams to do nothing else but Latin, so, the syllabus having been completed within this period of time, I passed. A pleasing extra is that the awful little Hun called Schicht, with whom I took the Latin exam, who got up after three quarters of an hour saying 'Interesting . . . interesting', *failed*. The Hobbiegobbie himself has fixed me up with lessons once a week in Brighton. I go to an old shag called Mr Bethell who, I should say, is experiencing puberty for the second,

---

★ Osric surprisingly and narrowly passed the necessary O level. But Latin would be needed again if he got into Oxford, so Osric thought he had better defend it.

or possibly the third time. This old dullard can speak seventeen languages fluently, including Latin, Ancient Greek, Welsh, Anglo-Saxon, Romney [sic], and the language of the tinkers. He says things like 'There are 140 first conjugation deponent verbs': I say 'Well I never' and he says 'They are Venor, Conor' and so on and on and on. He is also a high-priest of B.O. well versed in its most secret arts, and master of the most esoteric precepts of his craft. He still enjoys frequent use of his limbs although they taper off, after the second joint, to gangrenous supporating threads. But we do get through a large amount of work each week.

Working for Col is great fun – one of my more demanding duties is winning money off him at backgammon. We play an average of about 10 games every day and are fairly evenly matched so there are no vast sums of money changing hands. However there was a game, wrought with much splendour, which was an eight shilling game in which I scored a *backgammon*. Col was so depressed that, after putting a lightbulb down the wastemaster,★ he went to bed (6 p.m.). But 108 life is largely tragedy-free at the moment apart from the fact that Sarg† is being [given] a dull time by a girl he seems to be rather keen on.

On to the literary syndrome (yawn). I've decided that translations *really* must be a good idea after reading 'Exile's Letter' by Ezra Pound, who, I admit, isn't often awfully edifying. The poem itself is so very fine that it doesn't matter what Rhaiku meant, although, on the other hand, I don't purport to know anything about the original poem itself. Of course there are a myriad modes of appreciating Art.

★ My editor at Cape, Dan Franklin, has queried this point. 'Is "putting a lightbulb down the wastemaster" slang for having a stiff drink?' Which made me think of that bit in KA's *The Green Man* (1969), where a character who really is about to visit the Bishop makes another character wonder if *visiting the bishop* is 'a family euphemism for excretion'. Dan took the lightbulb stuff 'literally'. But then so did Colin. Putting a lightbulb down the wastemaster was his most dependable pick-me-up.
† Sargy Mann, the painter, who lived with the Amis/Howards for many years.

Well, see you in five weeks then. Alright? Right. Goodnight.
(Alan Freeman's Catch Phrase). *

Lots of love then, and write soon,

Mart.

By the way, I am reading 'The Outsider' by Albert Camus
(pronounced: Albong Camwow).

---

* Freeman was the wall-eyed DJ on *Thank Your Lucky Stars*.

Failures of Tolerance

Jacob, aged six, said reflectively,

   – I've never seen Kingsley move.

   – What do you mean?

   – I don't think I've ever once seen Kingsley move.

   – Move?

   – Move.

   – Bullshit. Every time we have lunch there he moves. He goes to the toilet at least once.

   – That's true, Jacob allowed.

   – And what about the time you knighted him? He moved then, didn't he?

   – . . . That's true.

Kingsley had said nothing about his knighthood and was no doubt planning to announce it at dinner: he was expected at seven. But the news had come through on the radio, and we were ready for him . . . It was 1990. My life, around then, now seems surreally uncomplicated. I had married late. I was forty, and living with my wife and two sons (six and four) in a tall narrow house off Ladbroke Grove. The long novel *London Fields* lay behind me; the short novel *Time's Arrow* lay ahead of me. My father came to dinner one night every week.

The bell rang on the stroke of seven – for Kingsley was a man of Naipaulian punctuality. I let the door swing open to reveal the boys, promiscuously accoutred in various plastic breastplates, gauntlets and Viking moose antlers, and slowly raising their grey plastic swords. In silence Kingsley went down on one knee (no trivial undertaking), there on the doormat, and the boys, also silent, and unblinking, dubbed him in turn with a touch of the blade on either shoulder.

[89]

A minute later Kingsley was being led downstairs by Antonia for his first drink: chilled gin and cocktail onions. Jacob followed, still with some show of pomp (a raised spear, perhaps), but Louis lingered, impatiently throwing off the thighpieces, the shinguards. This stuff had come out of a very old trunk. Even the boys had had to dig back deep for it.

– Why is he a Sir?

– Why?

– Because they don't *need* . . . *knoights* any more. There's nothing for them to *do*.

I was delighted for my father (he would have his visit to the Palace, and his tender, dream-fuelling moment with Corky),* but I must admit that I agreed with my son.

At the time I automatically assumed that Kingsley was fiercely gratified by his KBE, but I can remember little evidence of that now. When writers crave honours, they usually crave them very thoroughly: one hears of novelists who can name the cats and dogs of every bureaucrat in Stockholm. He never talked about the knighthood (and we never talked about prizes, or advances or sales). And once, when I brought up the example of Ferdinand Mount,† who had effectively dispensed with his title as an encumbrance and a thing of the past, Kingsley just shrugged and nodded. It wasn't too little but it *was* too late.‡ I hope he got some pleasure out of it in his

---

* Kingsley's dreams about the Queen were themselves pretty reverential and almost entirely chaste. K: I had another dream about Corky last night. M: What happens in these Corky dreams of yours? (We tended to call her Corky, once a widely used sobriquet, I thought, but I can't find it in Brewer or Jonathon Green.) K: Oh nothing much. I kiss her a bit and say something like 'Come on, let's go off somewhere.' And she just says things like 'Kingsley, I can't' or 'No, Kingsley, we mustn't' . . . That was as far as it went with Corky. Kingsley always got much further with Margaret Thatcher.

† Novelist, baronet, and editor of the *TLS*.

‡ It is curious how seldom and how tardily novelists receive this honour; and they usually get it not for their novels but for something else. Services to PEN (V.S. Pritchett), for instance, or to the London Zoo (Angus Wilson). I suppose Kingsley got it partly for being audibly and visibly right-wing, or conservative/monarchist. It is equally curious how soon and often

last five years. Becoming a Sir must have satisfied any vestigial aspirations formed by his upbringing (lower-middle-class, lapsed Baptist, work ethic), and surely must have silenced for ever the sound of his father's voice, which never quite stopped saying, 'This writing game is all very fine and large, but one day, you know, you'll have to pull yourself together and get a proper . . .' The newly elevated Kingsley probably walked that much taller at his club. And at last he could hold his head up at home, in the *ménage* he maintained with my step-father (Lord Kilmarnock) and my mother (Lady Kilmarnock).★ It was only because of a technicality that the teenage Jaime remained untitled: he was born out of wedlock and so had to struggle on without his honorary 'Honourable'.

Edward Upward said that he felt the aging process at work in him when he experienced 'little failures of tolerance'. Well, Kingsley was never much of a tolerance-cultivator; and his failures were big failures. As his sixties settled on him, as heavy as a bathyscope, and as his seventies loomed, my father underwent a fluctuating series of inner ravages. His articulation was sometimes amorphous; he tilted

---

playwrights get it. Whenever I run into my contemporary Sir David Hare, he amuses me so much that I can't think why he isn't more amused by being called Sir David Hare – a ridiculous appellation, like Sir Johnny Rotten or Lord Vicious. Why would such a fiery excoriator of the establishment suddenly want to be a Knight of the British Empire? But maybe the dramatists are getting it for something else too: services to the tourist industry, perhaps, or to the union that looks out for drivers of minibuses and charabancs. I apologise for my tone (and I don't want a knighthood), but I will now take the chance to repeat my contention that the drama is handily inferior to the novel and the poem. Dramatists who have lasted more than a century include Shakespeare and – who else? One is soon reaching for a sepulchral Norwegian. Compare that to English poetry and its great waves of immortality. I agree that it is very funny that Shakespeare was a playwright. I scream with laughter about it all the time. This is one of God's very best jokes.

★ My mother has never cut a very ladylike figure, and she said she felt fraudulent, like a thieving baglady, whenever she used her chequebook at the supermarket. But she surprised me, and made me laugh, when I once complacently asked her: 'That wasn't a big attraction for you, was it, Mum? Alastair being a lord and all that.' She frowned deeply and said, 'Ooh *yes*.'

himself, with that inconvenienced grimace of his, like a smile of pain, and pointed his good ear towards you; he had lost all trust and ease in his body (he would book a cab for a journey of a hundred yards: his legs hurt). Kingsley never mentioned these cerebral ruptures and blockages, these little *coups de vieux*, and you weren't supposed to mention (or notice) them either. When they happened they had the tendency of making him turn away from the world. To him, at sixty-eight, in certain moods, revealed creation looked worthless: and, therefore (because he trusted his instinct and thought himself never wrong), it *was* worthless, and could be wholly repudiated. In a completely central way Kingsley always declined to make allowances, for himself or for anybody else.

There was another consideration. This is from *The Old Devils* (1986):

William set the car in motion. 'Seat-belt, Dad.'

'Sorry.'

'I can see you'd like to get out of it if you could. You know you're enormously fat, do you? Fatter than ever? No-joke fat? Well of course you do. You could hardly not. The booze I suppose mostly, is it? I'm not saying I blame you, mind.'

'That and the eats . . . I'm sitting on my arse with the telly finished and I start stuffing myself. Cakes mostly. Profiteroles. Brandy-snaps. Anything with cream or jam or chocolate.'

My father didn't expect us not to notice that his weight had practically doubled over the past few years. When I was twenty-five Clive James said hauntingly to me: 'It's not that you *get* fat. One day your whole body just *turns into* fat.' But that wasn't how it happened with Kingsley. With him, getting fat was more like a project, grimly inaugurated on the day Jane left him in the winter of 1980. This would become the era of the late-night carbofests, the two-hour supersnacks with which Kingsley would start the process of soothing and numbing himself into sleep. His gustatory style now strikes me as manifestly bizarre, like something that ought to be done in solitude; but my reaction, then, was unreflectively filial – you just accepted the new reality. As if in the interests of successful hibernation he would load up his cheeks with confectionery at about twice the rate that he ingested it. 'Jesus, Dad,' I once said, 'what's going on in there? Your face is the size of a basketball.' It took him about ten minutes of disciplined mastication before he could reply. 'Seems to calm me down,' he said, and started loading up again. He ate for comfort; the tranquillising effects of starch and glucose helped to allay fear. But I now see that his nocturnal gorging was a complex symptom, regressive, self-isolating. It cancelled him out sexually. It seemed to say that it was over: the quest for love, and the belief in its primacy.

Soon after *Stanley and the Women* was published, in 1984, he said to me,

– I've finally worked out why I don't like Americans.

I waited.

– Because everyone there is either a Jew or a hick.

– . . . What's it like being mildly anti-Semitic?

– It's all right.

– No. What's it *feel* like being mildly anti-Semitic? Describe it.

Stanley, or rather Stanley, had been accused of anti-Semitism (and, with more reason, of misogyny) on the basis of first-person asides like the following: 'I went out and picked up a taxi on its way back from dropping somebody at one of the Jewboys' houses in the Bishop's Avenue.' But anti-Semitism, in *Stan*, is structural: the narrator's inherited and unexamined prejudice is contrasted with the violent babblings and scribblings ('EVIL LIVE VILE LEVI') of his son Steve, who has succumbed to the miserably trite belief-system of schizophrenia. And it *is* a system, a wretched little rhomboid: Jews, spies, aliens, electricity . . .

– What's it feel like? Well. Very mild, as you say. If I'm watching the end of some new arts programme I might notice the Jewish names in the credits and think, Ah, there's another one. Or: Oh I see. There's another one.

– And that's all?

– More or less. You just notice them. You wouldn't want anyone to *do* anything about it. You'd be horrified by that.

[93]

– Fascinating. Did you see John Updike's review of *Jake's Thing* in the *New Yorker*?

– No.

– He said that all your objections to women could be summed up by Professor Higgins's line in *My Fair Lady*: 'Oh, why can't a woman be like us?'

– Yeah, said Kingsley with slow emphasis. *That's* right.

A Sunday lunchtime, eight years later, in 1992, and Kingsley was expected: expected without great enthusiasm, I have to admit . . . More than once, in general chat, he and I had reached a modest conclusion about social and familial behaviour. There is a moral duty to be cheerful. There is a solemn duty to be cheerful. And, just recently, this was a duty that Kingsley had been failing to discharge. His low spirits took aggressive form: having cast me as a dutiful plaything of multicultural correctness, he would then attempt to scandalise me with the ruggedness of his heresies. I found this routine easier to deal with at the end of the day – numbed by alcohol and exhaustion. The fact that Kingsley was coming for lunch and not dinner was itself a minor victory for the old school. We had wearily squabbled about it: 'I hate lunches,' I said. 'Nonsense.' 'I hate all lunches. I hate drinking in the middle of the day.' 'How can anyone *hate* lunches?' 'You sound as if you don't believe me.' 'I *love* lunches.' 'I don't believe you.' 'You're mad.' 'I love dinner. I hate lunch.' 'Well, at my age, lunch *is* dinner.' Yes, and at my age lunch is still lunch, and three hours of you, mate, without a few stiff ones and the comforting prospect of that minicab at 9.45 . . . .

The doorbell rang. I was downstairs in the kitchen – but the boys would let him in. Putting my book aside I assembled the doings for Kingsley's cocktail and made sure that his chilled tankard was in the icebox next to his giant can of vandal-strength lager: Carlsberg Special Brew. Then I heard the cautious creak at the top of the stairs.

– Hi, Dad, I said, and we embraced.

– . . . What's that you're reading? Some *Jew*?

I turned my back on him and kept it turned. The book referred to was *If This Is a Man*, by Primo Levi . . . Not many months earlier my novel about the Holocaust, *Time's Arrow*, had appeared, and *I* had been accused of anti-Semitism.★ What I didn't want was another syllable of loose talk on this subject. So as I fixed my father's drink, the gin, the white onions, I kept my head down and said something like:

Actually I was going to tell you about it. A really clinching thing about sex difference. When the Fascist Militia rounded him up he was taken to a huge detention camp, in Italy, in the north, I think. Then the Jews were singled out and told that they would be deported to Auschwitz the next day. The men all spent that last night drinking and fucking and fighting. The women all spent it washing their children and their children's clothes and preparing meals. And, he writes, something like – when the sun came up, like an ally of our enemy, the barbed wire around the camp was full of children's washing hung out in the wind to dry.

At last I turned with the drink in my hand. And my first thought was to reach for a kitchen towel. How had he had *time* to cry so much? His motionless face was a mask of unattended tears. He said steadily,

– That's one thing I feel more and more as I get older. Let's *not* round up the women and the children. Let's *not* go over the hill and fuck up the people in the next town along. Let's not do any of that ever again.

✳ ✳ ✳

Despite his failures of tolerance, Kingsley liked coming to the house

★ It began with a review (saying I had looked to Auschwitz for 'profit') in the *Spectator*, which then printed my letter of rebuttal. The reviewer was James Buchan, a fellow novelist, and a humourless worthy. And by calling him humourless I mean to impugn his seriousness, categorically: such a man must rig up his probity *ex nihilo*. (Incidentally: I don't know if Mr Buchan is a parent, but I often wonder how the humourless raise their children. How does it *get done* without humour?) Anyway this was enough to entrain a minor controversy in the British press, where a tradition of 'neutrality' sees to it that opposed views are given equal play. When the novel was published in America I expected more animus: mistakenly. There was none; nor would there be any in Germany, or Israel. In England, though, the slur of anti-Semitism is evidently not that serious, and can be reached for along with anything else that lies to hand. Soothingly sprinkled with octogenarian exclamation marks, Buchan's replies to my personal letters sought in effect to reassure me about this.

off Ladbroke Grove: 'One of the few places', he said, 'where I can be sure of good.' Then, in the spring of 1993, after ten years there, I moved out of that house – a development (an upheaval, a terrible failure) that Kingsley could hardly have welcomed as he turned seventy-two. But he cleaved unquestioningly to the new reality, as did my mother. All our marriages kept falling apart; and here was another second-generation collapse . . . I still took the boys to lunch at Kingsley's place on Sundays – at the *ménage* in Primrose Hill; for our midweek meetings, though, we relied on a restaurant, an Italian place called Biagi's near Marble Arch, where, on and off and in various configurations, we had been coming for thirty years.

It was here, in 1966, surrounded by flasks and fishing-nets, by six-foot peppergrinders and bottles of Chianti in their wickerwork cradles (the place is more streamlined now), that I closed out one of the strangest nights of my youth – awed, and sumptuously relieved, to find myself in a restaurant rather than in a jailhouse: in Biagi's, not Brixton. It was seven o'clock in the evening when I crept home 'from school'. In fact I had spent the day in unstinting truancy, accompanied by Rob: first, the betting-shop (where, with our accumulators and reverse forecasts, we had actually *won* something); next the pub (where we had tried, and as usual failed, to drink alcohol: even a half of shandy would give us immobilising back-aches); and then a hugely promising afternoon listening to records with two worldly girls who had their own flat and, moreover, their own dope. When I came through that front door I was already wholly unmanned by hashish.* My intention was to go down to the

---

* Hashish has never done anything for my courage (and I question the suggested etymology of 'assassin': oblique plural of *hassas* – hashish-eater). This drug had recently denied me the control of my sphincter: that prince of all the muscles. I was walking down Gloucester Road, blearily singing a Beatles song, when the pavement turned viscid beneath my feet. The workman whose wet cement I had just disfigured (there was, I now saw, a sign saying WET CEMENT) reared into my face. 'You long-aired little *cunt*,' he said, and swung his pickaxe above his head. I raised my stoned arms in propitiation or self-defence. But the *mano-a-mano* situation had already been clarified by a single hot jet in my black flares. My black flares, with the special sewn-on creases. I was eventually allowed to stumble off in them.

kitchen for a supersnack of starch and glucose. But then a deep-voiced summons drew me into the sitting-room, where my father, my step-mother and my step-uncle were unmistakably arrayed against my freedom . . . Kingsley did have the power to make me frightened of him, though it was a card he played only when roused by a co-parent (anger was effortful: it was too much like work). Here he was doing his stuff, frowning and glowering; but I sensed Howard knowhow in this triumvirate of adult unanimity. I was busted, in short. Not for drugged truancy: just for drugs. Busted, and grounded. Much more stunningly, my brother Philip (only 375 days my senior),* as a result of this night's work, had already *left home.* Drugs had been found in one of his clothes drawers. It was no great feat of detection, finding Phil's drugs, because they were kept in a box with PHIL'S DRUGS written on it in eyecatching multicoloured capitals. And my brother, always more rebellious than me, more headlong than me, would *not* be grounded. 'We know you're on drugs,' Kingsley intoned. 'Phil claimed you weren't,' said Jane, 'and tried to defend you. But he's not very good at that kind of thing. And it came out.' Then we had a talk about the legal position and the possibility of 'calling the police' . . . When he went to see President Nixon and offered himself as a figurehead in the war on drugs, Elvis Presley was not at his best: already a heroin-addict, the King, at this presidential audience on drugs, was on drugs. I too was far from clear-headed, as I blabbed, feigned contrition, and gaped with paranoia. But then the evening descended, or rose, into inconsequentiality and magical realism. I was taken out to dinner at Biagi's, where Kingsley (drunkenly, I now realise) tried to persuade me that the international traffic in marijuana and hashish was 'a Communist plot' designed 'to weaken men in the field' – more specifically, the American forces fighting in Vietnam. All these

---

* For quite a long period as a child I used to torment Kingsley with the following exchange about Philip and me. 'Dad.' '. . . *Yes?*' 'Are we twins?' '. . . *No.*' I saw this drive for enhanced consanguinity repeated in my half-brother Jaime. He always refused to call the Spanish boys he grew up with (they were no relation) his 'cousins'. They were his brothers: *mis hermanos,* he would insist.

views, in broad daylight and full consciousness, he would later defend and elaborate. At the time I just kept my head down, over the prawn cocktail, the steak and chips. When I went to bed that night I rolled back the covers and found a note from my brother which said something like: They know *I* do but they don't know (*you* know). I had been deceived: this was experience. But the far larger fact was that the identical bedroom next to mine was now empty: this was existential.

I thought of Philip with disquiet, with wonder, with envy. He wouldn't be on the street. He would be at Rob's, in the arms of Rob's glamorous and neurotic elder sister, Jane, and calmly smoking one of the foot-long, three-pronged joints that Rob then specialised in rolling. But I was full of anxiety. Phil had done something that I wouldn't do for another five years. And he never came back. He came back in a different way, as an adult, but he never came back as a child of the house. He was gone.

Kingsley was forty-four then, in 1966.

But I was forty-four now, in 1993, and I had left the house – a different house.

And he was seventy-one. The Vietnam War had ended twenty years ago. If the traffic in hashish was once a plot to promote Communism, then that plot failed, and so did Communism. And for a long time now, too, Philip and I had routinely smoked joints in front of our father. He lurked back from it slightly, with a superstitious air about him, but the disapproval he expressed was also routine. Once I came into the room and Philip said, by way of greeting (a common form between us), 'Got any dope, Mart?' I told him that I certainly had. 'Yes,' said Kingsley, 'I could tell there was something *wrong* with you when you came in here.' We laughed. It went no further. Geopolitically, on the other hand, he seemed sincerely antic. What *was* it with him? He could still bring himself close to tears when rehearsing the 'tragedy' of the American collapse in IndoChina; he owed his humblest gratitude to nuclear weapons for getting us so safely through the Cold War; true, the velvet revolutions

of 1989 had left him a bit short of obvious villains and hate-figures –
until, incredibly, he settled on Nelson Mandela. Having read the
Letters I am tempted to conclude that most of the time he was just
winding me up, because his correspondence is largely free of
obviously provocative folly. Still, we continued to argue about all
this, and viciously. But not now: not in 1993. What compelled us,
every week, for months, for years, was something that lay much
closer to home.

'Stopping being married to someone,' he had written, ten years
earlier,★ 'is an incredibly violent thing to happen to you, not easy to
take in completely, ever.' He knew I was now absorbing the truth
and the force of this. And he knew also that the process could not be
softened or hastened. All you could do was survive it. That surviving
was a possibility he showed me, by example. But he did more. He
roused himself and did more. 'Talk as much as you want about it or
as little as you want': these words sounded like civilisation to me, in
my barbarous state, so dishevelled in body and mind. Talk as much or
as little . . . I talked much. Only to him could I confess how terrible
I felt, how physically terrible, bemused, subnormalised, stupefied
from within, and always about to flinch or tremble from the effort of
making my face look honest, kind, sane. Only to him could I talk
about what I was doing to my children. Because he had done it to
me.

And he responded, and he closed that circle: his last fatherly
duty.

His 'allography' (writing about others), entitled *Memoirs*,† was
two years behind him. The book ends with a poem ('Instead of an
Epilogue'), and here are its first and last stanzas:

★ In *Stanley* (1984). I was mildly surprised to see, when checking the date,
that the novel is dedicated to my mother: *To Hilly*. *Money* (dedicated to my
wife) came out the same year. 'I bought your book today,' said Hylan
Booker (Louis's godfather, and a black American). 'I bought your daddy's
book too.' Kingsley loved this, adding: 'That sentence will only get said
once in the history of the world.'
† Dedicated to Hilly and also to Philip, Martin, Sally, Jaime and Ali.

To H.

I

In 1932 when I was ten
In my grandmother's garden in Camberwell
I saw a Camberwell Beauty butterfly
Sitting on a clump of Michaelmas daisies.
I recognised it because I'd seen a picture
Showing its brownish wings with creamy edges
In a boy's paper or on a cigarette card
Earlier that week. And I remember thinking,
What else would you expect? Everyone knows
Camberwell Beauties come from Camberwell;
That's why they're called that. Yes, I was ten.

III

In '46 when I was twenty-four
I met someone harmless, someone defenceless,
But till then whole, unadapted within;
Awkward, gentle, healthy, straight-backed,
Who spoke to say something, laughed when amused;
If things went wrong, feared she might be at fault,
Whose eyes I could have met for ever then,
Oh yes, and who was also beautiful.
Well, that was much as women were meant to be,
I thought, and set about looking further.
How can we tell, with nothing to compare?

Fancy Woman

On the last page of his memoir about V.S. Naipaul,* *Sir Vidia's Shadow*, Paul Theroux – rather tendentiously, some may feel – depicts

* My own dealings with the great man have been remote but pleasingly symmetrical. I outline them on page 356.

the senior writer as 'scuttling' away from him down a London street. Well, I know a scuttle when I see one, and my father definitely scuttled down that gravel drive on the day he left the house in Madingley Road, Cambridge, in the summer of 1963. He was carrying a suitcase. A taxi waited . . . I am a good three or four inches shorter than my father, but our bodies are similarly disproportionate, with a low centre of gravity: 'almost the same height standing up as sitting down,' as Kingsley put it in *That Uncertain Feeling* (1955), adding that this kind of physique is not untypically Welsh.* Such legs are *made* for scuttling. He was en route from one reality to another; that taxi was part of a tunnel to a different world. I didn't know, then, as I watched him through the window, that I would inherit his body type (minus the self-inflicted corpulence, so far); nor, of course, that I was destined to do some scuttling of my own.

Not long ago (early December, 1998) I ran into another theatrical knight, Sir Richard Eyre, at a good party given by yet another theatrical knight, Sir Tom Stoppard, in honour of the Czech philosopher-king, Vaclav Havel.† Sir Richard and I left in a group of four with our wives. We recalled that he had been a student of

---

* Despite tenacious inaccuracies in the press, and despite my sister Sally's birthplace (Swansea) and middle name (Myfanwy), and despite the ridicule of my sons ('A Welshman through and through, born in the heart of Wales to wholly Welsh parents who can trace their Welsh lineage back to . . .'), and despite the legs, I can lay no claim to a single drop of Welsh blood. Kingsley was sensitive on the legs issue. This is Jenny and Patrick at the cricket match in *Take a Girl Like You* (1960): 'Oh, I am wild at missing you wearing your pads.' '. . . What? Why did you want to see me in my pads?' 'It'd be a new view of the little legs, in the little pads. Have you got special short ones made? Or do you get a lend from one of the juniors?' Patrick does not take this well ('Why, you cheeky little bitch'), and humourlessly defends his legs for more than half a page.

† Looking slightly lopsided from long confinement, broken health and waning power, Havel was, I thought, an impressively sympathetic figure. And I liked his controversial new wife: Helga. Much younger, blonde, round-faced, round-haired, she looked as though she used to spin the clock on one of the early TV gameshows. She also attended to her husband with what Saul Bellow has called 'a TV brightness' in her manner. You wanted the very best for them, but you could see how all this might be looking in the Czech Republic, as Havel's presence edged towards the margin.

Kingsley's at Cambridge. The house on Madingley Road differed from every other don's house in the city: students could be found in it, regularly. They stayed the night. They drove the car. They read or dozed in the garden. They made some of my meals. I enjoyed their presence. Three of them were real friends to me, and one of them, Bill Rukeyser,* was an exceptional friend to me. They were all men, these friends; Kingsley's students were all men. There were young women around too: I can remember generous and aromatic female entities but I can't individualise any of them: clear proof of my unawakened state. When we saw something of each other again, fifteen years later in America, Bill Rukeyser gave me to understand that 9, Madingley Road was the locus of considerable sexual activity, 1961–63, but I witnessed, or noticed, little of that. Certainly the atmosphere was lawlessly, and in some way innocently, convivial. It was no big thing (for example) to watch my mother and our family friend Theo Richmond,† both of them exhausted by laughter, riding through one of the sitting-rooms on Debbie, our pet donkey, who, every morning, would stick her head through the kitchen window and neigh along with Radio Caroline.

As we approached our cars I said to Richard,

– We must have come across each other back then.

– Oh yes. You were so unhappy.

– . . . Was I?

– You were *so* unhappy.

Was I? I was unlucky thirteen, overweight and undersized: I had reached that clogged point in youth, where childhood (in my case happy, even idyllic) was obviously running out, and yet no alternative mode of existence seemed available or even possible. This is the time of the bathroom and the mirror, of eyes transfixed and then averted in the school showers, the time of odious comparisons, dire predictions. The little voice is still caught inside the body, which mutinously burgeons . . . 'You're too fat for that suit, Mart,' said a

---

* Now the well-known broadcaster and financial analyst, and sometime editor of the magazine *Money*.

† The author of that formidable monument of Jewish remembrance, *Konin* (1994).

student, with shattering justice, in the summer of 1963. Until that
year I had got by without sartorial ambition, without sartorial self-
awareness, content, even proud, to make do with my brother's cast-
offs. But now Osricisation was well entrained. In the hall of the house
in Madingley Road I had just slipped off my shorty mackintosh to
show the household my new made-to-measure from Burton's. The
design specifications were my own, and thus the suit was a genuine
dog's dinner, the trousers as tight as tights, the jacket a blunt denial of
the human shape, with two gold buttons, no lapels, and no collar
except for a hank of black velvet at the back of the neck (soon to
become a trough of sparkling dandruff). Another thing about the
jacket was that it only went down as far as my waist: a crucial demerit.
For at that time I had a complex about something very simple.
Returning from his boarding-school for the Easter holidays, my
brother (who was tall and slim, who was through, who had made it
to the other side) composed the following entry in his diary:

> Mum told me she found Mart crying in the night about the size
> of his bum. I do feel sorry for him, but a) it *is* enormous, and b)
> it's not going to go away.

I was particularly impressed by clause b).★

So, yes, averagely unhappy for my age, perhaps. But essentially
secure. My parents' marriage, I believed, loomed like a translucent
horizon – a belief memorably reaffirmed by my father the summer
before, in Deya, Majorca, where (late at night, admittedly) he had said
to my brother and me: Never doubt that I love your mother. Never
doubt that we will always be together . . . And I didn't doubt it.

✳   ✳   ✳

★ But it *did* go away. I felt the moment of its passing: six years later. A big
teen crowd had gathered at my mother's house in Ronda. And as we walked
into town that evening the rank of girls trailed behind the rank of boys on
the wide street above the gorge. When we reached the bar in the main
square a female voice (whose? whose?) said in my ear: 'We were comparing
all of you on the way in, and we voted. You won best bum.' With a final
shriek my complex evaporated into the Spanish night.

Maybe Richard Eyre remembers me from my last weeks in Madingley Road: some time after the following exchange around its kitchen table:

– You know your father's got this fancy woman★ up in London, don't you?

– No. I didn't know.

My informant was Eva Garcia (pronounced *Gah*cia). And Eva Garcia *was* Welsh, classic Celt-Iberian, as was her husband, Joe, a kind, cubiform, semiliterate, longsuffering grafter who was actually *taller* sitting down than standing up. Eva was terrible and great; she was one of the divinities of my childhood, and so it was quite right, I suppose, that she should be the one to end it, at a stroke, with that sinister sentence . . . Eva the great: some days, in Swansea, I would return from school to find her belting out a song as she made my tea, and elegantly swivelling on the slab of her orthopaedic boot (early polio) with a shake of her hair and real delight in her hispanic eyes. Eva the terrible: on other days you would find her leaning palely against the kitchen wall with a hand to her cheek and a red bandanna knotted tight around her brow, and your childish spirits would brace themselves for an evening of silence and even tranced immobility, such a martyr was Eva to her migraines. At such times, as the day dimmed, she would talk in a gradually strengthening voice about the various disasters that had befallen her peers. Nothing brought Eva round more quickly than the contemplation of the sufferings of others.

It was Eva I was thinking of, thirty-odd years later,† when I suggested that the word *Schadenfreude* was not German but Welsh. Once, down on the Mumbles road along the coast, the family encountered a traffic jam caused by a serious accident. In the car there was a murmur of anxiety that Sally – then two or three – might see something frightening. Finally we approached the crossroads, and there on the verge was a twitching, blood-bespattered figure half

★ 'Mistress' (with overtones, here, of vulgarity, superficiality, etc); cf: fancy man.

† In the novel *Night Train*. The Welsh character was called Rhiannon, in deference to the heroine of *The Old Devils*.

covered by an old overcoat. We seemed to be safely past when Eva propped Sally up on the back seat and said, 'Look at him, Sall. *Writhing in agony* he is.'★

– No. I didn't know.

Eva had come down from Swansea alone, for a visit, and to put herself about at this painful time. Now I met her gaze across the kitchen table. It was clear to me even then that she couldn't possibly have been given the authority to tell me this. I knew, too, that for Eva the dissemination of bad news was no short-straw occasion but a privilege to be vied for. Was she, in her zeal, overstating the case? I said,

– Has he really?

She addressed me with the narrowed stare and flat smile of reckoning I remembered from my childhood in the valleys. She said gauntly,

– Ooh aye.

The next morning, or perhaps the morning after that, my mother and I made our usual run to Cambridgeshire High School for Boys. As we approached the final crossroads she told me matter-of-factly that she and my father were going to separate (there was no mention of the fancy woman). My mother kept her eyes on the road ahead; she was driving, after all, and smoking one of her menthol cigarettes: a Consulate. Mum has stayed with it, but she was never a serious smoker, in my view: she takes a drag and then puffs out quickly, as if to get it gone. Even at thirteen I reckoned I was twice the smoker that Mum ever was . . . Still, she needed her Consulate, this morning. I did see that. She asked me if I understood, and I think I said I did. I climbed out of the car and paused before the gates in the sunshine.

★ 'Eva, can I have a glass of milk with my lunch?' She was wedged into her chair by the Rayburn (a squat black Aga) and I saw her legs swing up for purchase and then relax again. She had been going to say yes but now she said no. 'Gnaw,' she said firmly. 'Oh. Why not?' 'Because I knew a man who had a glass of milk with his lunch . . . and he *died*.' I was sure this was nonsense, and perfunctory nonsense too: she was just generally succumbing to a rare attack of laziness. All the same, until I was an adult I avoided glasses of milk at lunchtime, in case I died; and once I was an adult the question of having a glass of milk with my lunch simply stopped coming up.

My mother's plan, she later told me, was to deliver the news at a moment when I couldn't brood on it. And the plan was a good one as far as it went. There stood the school and all its chalk-opera, duties, games, trials, friends, fears. It only took a few seconds to leave the weightlessness, the zero-gravity of childhood and feel the true mass of the world. Thinking something like, 'Yes, the easy bit's over. I've done the easy bit,' I moved into the yard with my satchel and cap.

It was November when I next saw my father: a winter midnight, in London. His astonished form, pyjama-clad, moved back from the doorway.

– You know I'm not alone . . .

In the background, wearing a white bathrobe, was the fancy woman with her waist-long hair.

– *You* don't even know what *sophisticated* means!

My mother turned on me sharply. I should repeat that she was twenty-one when I was born. I have never been much younger than her and she has never been much older than me. Another school run: Swansea, in the late Fifties.

– Ooh I *do* know what *sophisticated* means!

– No you don't. Not what it *really* means.

– Yes I do.

– Go on then. What does it mean?

I now see my mother's profiled face, lightly frowning in concentration as she listed some of the more attractive attributes that went hand in hand with being sophisticated – all of them worth the aspiration of a bashful country-girl from Berkshire. I said,

– That's not what it *really* means.

– All right then. What does it *really* mean?

– *Corrupt.*

My mother was innocent. Then experience came, and she experienced it. And then she got her innocence back again. I have always wondered how she did that.

Letter from Home

108 Maida vale,
W.9.*

Dearest Dad and Jane,

My last letter appears to have rendered you speechless,so I am going to try,rather nervously,to resolve the controversial matter of my immediate future.I hope I can now dispense with the stirring rhetoric and unrelenting dialectic to which you must by now have grown accustomed.That Goblin rang up various schools all of which were busy requiring masters conversant with the new mathematics.That worthy then suggested that I get a job at a bookshop,and he is going to look around during the holidays.He says I'll probably learn more that way,and I'm inclined to agree-he also says that he and I could do some Anglo-Saxon next year.How does that strike you?
I went for my interview at Durham and it all went quite well.The chap who interviewed me at the Eng. Dept. turned out to be an ex-pupil of Dad's (SWAN) and claims to have met me several times.I didn't get his name but he was an odd looking little chap with lots

* I was now going back and forth from Brighton to London (on an obsolescent train called the Brighton Belle). Already I seem to have formed the bad habit of not dating letters. And I have also started typing. Over the years I have become incredibly good at typing (novelists, particularly those who write long novels, should get prizes, not for writing, but for typing), and seldom make more than three mistakes per line; but I wasn't any good at it in December, 1967. Here I preserve the eccentricities. This young man has ceased, on the whole, to repel me. He is no longer quite Osric: that flirtatious valetudinarian. But he and I are becoming wordier.

of dark wavy hair.I've also procured an interview at Exeter★ in
January.Which is the better university? I thought Durham was a
beautiful town I must say,and the college looked very comfortable
from all points of view.†But let's hope I am accepted at either
Oxford or Bristol.

There are only 4 days to go until the Oxford interviews and,since I
haven't received a telegram, it seems that I've passed the first
hurdle.There are now about three serious candidates for every
place. I am rather dreading the interview:shall I be refreshingly
different,stolidly middle-brow,engagingly naïve,candidly matter-of-
fact,contemptuously sophisticated,incorruptibly sincere,sonorously
pedantic,curiously fickle,youthfully wide-eyed? Should I bow my
head in solemn appreciation of the hallowed atmosphere of
learning? Should I play the profound truth-seeker,the seedy anti-
hero,the crusty society-observer,the all-discerning beauty-
appreciator.? No,I suppose I shall end up. . .just. . .being. . . . .
myself.

Your letter (Jane) came in the middle of this one,so I will just say a
few words about it.You must see that what was fixed up for me is
the sort of thing that is usually acompanied [sic] by some form of
coercion.I thought the sole aim of the operation was to do me
good.I accepted this-with certain qualifications-but when I saw just
how much good this was going to turn out to be,I began to
question the worth of the project.I fully see now that it wasn't
intended in quite that way.I'm sure that the Goblin(devil that he is)
will come up with something more interesting,and I hope that our
trans-atlantic battles-of-wits may go no farther.

I now have unusually short hair.Although my seering [sic] jaw-line
is more meaningfully described,I think.I look like a particularly
nasty and petulant Baboon.

(Changing to pen + ink after 11 hours at the typewriter).

★ In 1973 Lucy Partington was in her last year at Exeter University, reading
English.
† The poverty and defeatism of this sentence reinforces my suspicion that I
would have settled for Durham around now. Around now Bristol seemed
unlikely and Oxford grandiose.

On to the arts. I think Dad is being very silly about Donne, who is surely not as 'cold' as your Marvell, who is too immaculate to supply the passion you seem to expect. Marvell, I think, does all his feeling *before* he does his writing, while Donne, I always feel, is gritting his teeth as he writes. Read 'S. Lucies Day' + 'The Apparition', and then 'The Definition of Love' or even 'To His Coy Mistress', and I think you'll see some of what I mean.

First Impressions:

Conrad: Great romantic-power bore.

James: Eloquent + rather funny + polished.

I read 'War + Peace', and thought it was bloody good – Forster's 'great chords' strumming away like mad.

By the way, what would you have me do about your presents – I'll send them on before very long and you'll be getting them in due course.

Lots of Love, Mart XXXXX

Him Who Is, Him Who Was!

Weak-toothed Osric talked about John Donne 'gritting his teeth' as he wrote 'S. Lucies Day'. This is an erroneous view of Donne, and an erroneous view of how poetry gets written. Fourteen years later I would grandly scold John Carey (q.v.) for promoting it in his book *John Donne: Life, Mind and Art*. The conjunction of the names caused me to look again at 'S. Lucies Day', or 'A Nocturnall upon St. *Lucies* day, Being the shortest day'. Although, as a critic, Professor Carey knows that lyric poems are 'works of the imagination', the biographical helmet is a heavy one: 'Wordsworth, after all, needed no actual death to mourn his Lucy. But if Donne's Lucy poem is about a real dead woman, then his wife is the only candidate worth considering.' He describes 'S. Lucies Day', which rhymes and scans, as 'suicidal'. Suicides write notes, not elegies. The last lines are unforgettable, but the sentiment they express is a commonplace of the elegiac form:

> Since shee enjoyes her long nights festivall,
> Let mee prepare towards her, and let mee call
> This hour her Vigill, and her Eve, since this
> Both the yeares, and the dayes deep midnight is.*

---

* On perhaps the year's longest day in, I think, 1975, at a party given by Claire Tomalin, when midnight neared Harold Pinter was asked to read 'S. Lucies Day', and he expertly obliged. In the silence that followed the perfectly modulated climax, Claire's secretary, Sally, burped and said, 'Nice one, Cyril.' A football catchphrase, used here with deflationary intent. (I was impressed by the tolerance of Pinter's laughter.) *Sally*, in fact, was suicidal. She killed herself the following year. Then there was another suicide, that of Claire's daughter Susannah, aged twenty-two, in 1980.

The *Encyclopedia Britannica* is skimpy and the *OED* silent on the identity of St Lucy, or St Lucia. *Brewer's Dictionary of Names* has the following: 'The Caribbean island was named by Christopher Columbus for the day on which he discovered it, Tuesday 13 December 1502, the feast of *St Lucy*, Sicilian virgin martyr.' December 23 is now established as the shortest day – the year's midnight. Lucy Partington disappeared on December 27. There was an energy crisis that winter, and no street illumination that night. The year was 1973 but the darkness was seventeenth-century.

Gritting my teeth was something I couldn't do, in November 1994. A mystical notion: the sound of one jaw gritting.

I knew that all Sikhs bore the same surname, but I was getting what comfort I could from the idea that a great fraternity of Singhs was tenderly driving me around New York during this difficult time. My daydream didn't deserve to last very long: Inderjid Singh drove me in from the airport; and promptly had a crash.★ And again it was Charon Singh, eerily, who drove me to my first appointment with Todd J. Berman, DMD, Diplomate of the American Board of Oral and Maxillofacial Surgery. Todd it was who faced the professional challenge of my lower jaw: a series of extractions, the removal of the tumour, the rebuilding of the chin with cow bone pre-tested for AIDS, and the bedding down of the implants.

But it fell, appropriately, to Charjit Singh to take me on an eleven-dollar ride uptown for the eleven-hundred-dollar catscan. My friend Chris, the one who wished that Salman Rushdie had offered *him* out, recently had a catscan, or tried to have one. 'I found out something about myself,' he told me. 'I've got claustrophobia. I didn't know they put your *whole head* in there. I went *berserk*.'

★ Just a sideswipe and, for Inderjid, no big deal. My host in New York, Richard Cornuelle (who is now my stepfather-in-law), was once very briefly hospitalised after a cab crash. He said to the hard-pressed doctor that he supposed it was a myth – all this about New York cabs crashing the whole time. The doctor said: 'A myth? Listen. When there's a cab strike this place is *deserted*.'

They do put your whole head in there. With an emery board between my jaws, a blue showercap on my head, with straps over my brow and chin, I was sucked backwards into a kind of cyclotron where I remained for ten minutes. The confinement, or interment, made me think helplessly about Lucy Partington. Shaw was wrong. Suffering *is* relative.

. . . In my late twenties I started having panic attacks on the underground. And for a while I thought I would inherit my father's lavish array of phobias: aerophobia (he flew once, as a child: a five-shilling 'flip' at the seaside. That did it), acrophobia (when he took his children to the top floor of the Empire State, in 1959, it was only our presence, he said, that stopped him from screaming), and nyctophobia, or fear of the night.* Nyctophobia overlapped with partial monophobia. There were many things he couldn't do alone. When he paid his visits to Swansea, my sister escorted him there and went back to fetch him. Once, stranded in Newcastle, he took a taxi to London. Most crucially, though, he couldn't be alone in a house after dark. He just couldn't do it . . . My panic attacks were cured by a single sentence of advice, delivered in a pub, by one of Kingsley's close friends, the psychiatrist Jim Durham. He said, 'Just remember that the worst thing that can happen to you is that you might make a fool of yourself.' It worked then, and it worked in the cyclotron. My spirit settled down for ten minutes of quiet durance.

When I emerged, the piped music was sympathetically featuring 'Candle in the Wind'. Waiting to pay, I sat around with two elderly ladies. One of them was engrossed in a magazine called *Modern Maturity*, with the usual couple of great-shape oldsters on its cover. The ladies were drinking from Barium Dispenser Cups, nonchalantly and congenially, as if enjoying their morning coffee. The piped music switched from Tchaikovsky's First to 'Let It Be' . . . I paid and went outside. The Singh brothers, rather hurtfully considering my recent

---

* There are some ridiculous words, and some ridiculous phobias, in the relevant sub-section of the *Thesaurus*. Kingsley did not suffer from triskaidophobia, or fear of the number thirteen. Nor did he suffer from autophobia: he wasn't at all frightened of referring to himself.

ordeal, were all elsewhere, and I resorted to Jorge Palomino to get me back downtown.

Immediately after my rendezvous with the hands of Mike Szabatura, Isabel very cannily took me to lunch in the Lower East Side. While I paused to spit blood into the gutter she said,

– Remember, this is freak city. Look around. Nobody's going to notice *you*.

I looked around. It was true. It was great. Babblers, brown-bag artists, panhandlers, all with astounding distributions of biomass, saturated fatsoes, human pool cues; and wheelchair riders and walking-frame wielders, trashcan prospectors, addicts, hookers, crazed Vets. This corner was a drug corner and today's salesmen were standing there, leaning at an angle without visible means of support,★ like a diagonal stroke: /. And rubbish everywhere, ankle-deep and everywhere. On the auriferous arcades of midtown I would constitute an embarrassment to the social scene. But down here on Second Avenue I walked with my head high, unregarded and unremarked. There even seemed to be room for significant deterioration.

Excellent company, then, here on the street. Excellent company across the lunch table, too, as Isabel, like a flight controller in an airport movie, talked me through my chicken soup. And I had excellent company elsewhere: in the mind.

★ The Tower of Pisa effect is the 'junkie lean', as distinctive as the pimp roll. I had to wait three years to have this explained to me.

Touts serve as living billboards – walking, talking advertisements for the chemicals coursing through their bodies. A tout who staggers to his post and simply stands there – vacant-eyed, at a thirty-degree junkie lean, telling passersby that the Spider Bags are a bomb – is earning his keep.

From *The Corner* (Broadway Books, 1997), by David Simon and Edward Burns. This is a truly redoubtable piece of work, as is David Simon's earlier book, *Homicide* (1991), an epic of egregious futility and hilarity, recounted in impeccable prose.

Question: How many of these three noted stylists – James Joyce, Vladimir Nabokov, and Martin Amis – suffered catastrophic tooth-loss in their early-to-middle forties? Answer: All three.

'My teeth are very bad,' muses Stephen, in the first chapter of *Ulysses*, and goes on to ask the great and useless question: 'Why?'

> Why, I wonder. Feel. That one is going too. Shells. Ought I to go to a dentist, I wonder, with that money? That one. This. Toothless Kinch, the superman. Why is that, I wonder, or does it mean something perhaps?

Why? Heredity? Celtic tapwater? A noxious introversion? Even in his early twenties Joyce would squirm with pain while eating warm soup. In 1907 he wrote to his brother Stanislaus from Marseille: 'My mouth is full of decayed teeth and my soul of decayed ambitions.' Joyce was born in 1882. His teeth lasted until 1923. He spent two weeks recovering from the extractions in a sanatorium, but according to Richard Ellmann's (near-transcendent) biography, *James Joyce* (1959), the loss 'did not greatly bother him'. As he told his son Giorgio, with wonderful simplicity, 'They were no good anyway.'

Joyce suffered a greater haunting: the Miltonic (and perhaps Homeric) wraith of blindness. By 1922 he had finished *Ulysses*; and his teeth, after all, weren't going to help him write *Finnegans Wake*. 'I always have the impression that it is evening,' he told his friend Philippe Soupault in the same year. The dental operations were slipped in during a three-stage optical sphincterectomy (preparations for the latter included the application of 'five leeches to drain the blood from the eye'). Emerging from these violences to his face, his head, his mind, Joyce wrote his first poem for over half a decade: 'A Prayer'. 'The speaker's attitude', glosses Ellmann (biography is always heavy work), 'confuses desire and pain, [pain] because his mind associates his subjection to his beloved with other subjections – to eye trouble and to death.' And to toothlessness. 'A Prayer' (from *Pomes Penyeach*) is generally assumed to be 'addressed' to Nora Joyce. But in my universe it is addressed to Mike Szabatura. The second of the three stanzas runs (beautifully and, to me, unbearably):

I dare not withstand the cold touch that I dread.
Draw from me still
My slow life! Bend deeper on me, threatening head,
Proud by my downfall, remembering, pitying
Him who is, him who was!

I first read this poem in 1992 or 1993. I see that I have written in the margin here – 'the inevitability of submission'. And I wasn't thinking about a woman.

On 23 November 1943, Vladimir Nabokov (b. 1899) began a letter to Edmund Wilson without preamble:

Dear Bunny,

some of them had little red cherries – abscesses – and the man in white was pleased when they came out whole, together with the crimson ivory. My tongue feels like somebody coming home and finding his furniture gone. The plate will only be ready next week – and I am orally a cripple . . .

When my face is reflected by some spherical surface, I have often noticed a curious resemblance with the Angel (you know – the wrestler); but now an ordinary mirror produces this effect.★

The experience waited a while, as experience usually does, before distilling itself into fiction. In *Pnin*, published in 1957, the 'heroic' Timofey eventually trudges off to his rendezvous with the man in white. Afterwards:

★ From *The Nabokov-Wilson Letters 1940–1971* (1979), edited by Simon Karlinsky. This book is an enthralling duologue of heavyweights. Bunny's early generosity to Volodya is impressive and endearing, and Volodya can sometimes be brashly satirical at Bunny's expense. Of the supposedly lascivious women characters in Wilson's novel *Memoirs of Hecate County* (successfully prosecuted for obscenity in 1946) Nabokov wrote, 'I should have as soon tried to open a sardine can with my penis.' Both humanly and intellectually, though, Volodya prevails. He is right, and Bunny is wrong, about almost everything that matters: prosody, politics (the USSR), and the alleged genius ('I admit that he has no sense of humour,' writes Wilson, as if dismissing a merely captious stricture) of André Malraux.

A warm flow of pain was gradually replacing the ice and wood of the anaesthetic in his thawing, still half-dead, abominably martyred mouth . . . His tongue, a fat sleek seal, used to flop and slide so happily among the familiar rocks, checking the contours of a battered but still secure kingdom, plunging from cave to cove, climbing this jag, nuzzling that notch, finding a shred of sweet seaweed in the same old cleft; but now not a landmark remained and all there existed was a great dark wound, a terra incognita of gums which dread and disgust forbade one to investigate.

This desolation soon bleeds into another, when Pnin's fiercely anticipated reunion with his ex-wife (the terrible Liza) comes to nothing – to *nothing*. His gentle American landlady, Joan, finds him in the kitchen:

> Pnin's unnecessarily robust shoulders continued to shake . . .
> 'Doesn't she want to come back?' asked Joan softly.
> Pnin, his head on his arm, started to beat the table with his loosely clenched fist.
> 'I haf nofing,' wailed Pnin between loud, damp sniffs. 'I haf nofing left, nofing, nofing!'

What else did Nabokov and Joyce have in common, apart from the poor teeth and the great prose? Exile, and decades of near pauperism.★ A compulsive tendency to overtip. An uxoriousness that their wives deservedly inspired: the omnicompetent and artistic Véra

---

★ In 1922 Joyce received a letter from his father, John, asking for a pound to help him through Christmas. James, who was in Rome, got the pound off Stanislaus, who was in Trieste, and sent it to John, who was in Dublin. It has been said that there are only two types of Irish male: the hard man, and the desperate chancer. In life, Joyce was a desperate chancer. But in his work he was a hard man. Tell a dream, and lose a reader, said Henry James. And we all know that the pun is the lowest form of wit. Joyce spent seventeen years punning on dreams. The result, *Finnegans Wake*, reads like a 600-page crossword clue. But it took a hard man to write it.

Slonim (she translated *Pale Fire* into Russian), the sublimely unliterary Nora Barnacle ('He's on another book again,' she said, referring with some exasperation to *Finnegans Wake*). More than that, they both lived their lives 'beautifully' – not in any Jamesian sense (where, besides, ferocious solvency would have been a prerequisite), but in the droll fortitude of their perseverance. They got the work done, with style. You could say that Joyce overdid his elder-brotherish frigidity towards Stanislaus, and preferred Ibsen's dramas to Shakespeare's;★ and you could say that Nabokov was sometimes guilty of a certain Parnassian triumphalism: but the lives they led were unfaltering. When I reflect that D.H. Lawrence, perhaps the most foul-tempered writer of all time (beater of women and animals, racist, anti-Semite, etc., etc.),† was also, perhaps, the most extravagantly slapdash exponent of language, I feel the lure of some immense generalisation about probity and prose. But the fit reader, the ideal reader, regards a writer's life as just an interesting extra. On good days, when you have the sense that you are a mere instrument of the work you were sent here to do, this is what a writer's life actually feels like: an interesting extra. And there is no value correlation between the life and the work. Some writers will be relieved to hear this said.

'My English is patball to Joyce's champion game,' said Nabokov – with, I should guess, very considerable but by no means complete sincerity. I might say the same about Nabokov. Still, I claim peership with these masters in only one area. Not in the art and not in the life. Just in the teeth. In the teeth.‡

★ I agree with my father's entry on 'Shakespeare' in *The King's English* (1997): 'to say or imply that the man of this name is not our greatest writer marks a second-rate person at best.' And I agree with Nabokov: 'The verbal poetical texture of Shakespeare is the greatest the world has known' (*Strong Opinions*, 1978).

† Yet I shed a tear at the end of Brenda Maddox's *A Married Man*. She quotes Sam Johnson: 'It is so *very* difficult for a sick man not be a scoundrel.' Lawrence's teeth were once likened to black pumpkin seeds. But they lasted him his short stay on the planet: forty-four years.

‡ John Updike made a transparent attempt to crash the tooth club with the doubly questionable chapter in his memoir, *Self-Consciousness* (1989), called 'On Not Being a Dove'. In this essay Updike tries (and fails) to link his

The War Against Shame

My first word was *bus*. Apart from infantile renderings of 'Mummy' and 'Daddy' and 'Philip', *bus* was the first word I ever uttered. And throughout my childhood in Swansea I had a helpless passion for the great blood-red doubledeckers, and I would ride them, with no destination in mind, for hour after hour and day after day. Once, when I was seven or eight, I overheard a conversation between the bus-conductor – a much grander personage, then, with the metal ticket-dispenser strapped to his chest like a silver accordion – and one of his female passengers. She gave the name of her stop and said,

– I've been bad. Terrible I've been.

– Oh aye? It's the hospital then is it?

– Aye. Toothache.

– Have them all out and be done with it is what I say.

– Saves all the bother.

– Common sense.

Using the overhead strap, he leaned his face into hers, as if hesitating before a kiss, and out flashed the full vista of his flawless Chiclets.

– Ooh. Lovely. There's posh.

---

opposition to the Vietnam peace movement, or rather his opposition to the sort of bullying he got from the sort of people who were part of the Vietnam peace movement, with his own 'war effort' in the dentist's chair. Vladimir, James and I, however, have blackballed Updike. His teeth are far too good. Look at him: still grinning his head off at sixty-nine. It's not everyone, you know, who can jostle shoulders with Joyce, who can hobnob with Nabokov. In his criticism, by the way, Updike writes about Nabokov perceptively and responsively but without real excitement. And yet he paid Joyce the vast compliment of trying to write like him for many years – trying to modernise and Americanise *Ulysses*. See *Couples* (1968). It didn't work out, but much else did work out, for Updike. I also concede that he bows to no man in his struggle (also explored in *Self-Conciousness*) with psoriasis. His fellow-sufferer, Nicholson Baker, in his great book *U and I* (1990), gave the bays to the Updike character who starts every day by hoovering out his bedclothes. Would it be altogether heartless to suggest that Updike should form an alternative club of his own, starting with Nick Baker and enlisting, as I'm sure he can, many a distinguished forerunner?

Osric in funds: this photograph, which was taken in a spare office at the *TLS*, appeared on the back flap of *The Rachel Papers* (1973).

Top left: Philip and Martin in the outdoor sink, when we were poor.
Left: I am perhaps putting my father on record about combat between killer whales and sabre-toothed tigers, while my mother and Sally look on. (*Hulton Getty*)
Top: Outside our first house: 24 The Grove, Uplands, Swansea. (*Hulton Getty*)
Above: Outside the cottage in West Wratting, just before our period in Cambridge (1961-64). My leanness didn't last (see following).

Portugal, in 1955. Philip (see bottom right) was much taller than me: people thought that two
or three years divided us (rather than 375 days). In the course of this three-month exile (volubly
resented but actually enjoyed by KA) Philip once rescued Sally when she was engulfed by a herd
of goats. I see it now: him carrying her along above the bobbing horns.

My mother and father in Martha's Vineyard, 1959.

I am on the far left, tubbily slumped against the car. It is 1962 and I am turning thirteen.
From the right: Robert Graves, KA, Tomás Graves, Hilly.

Eva.

Crewcuts and whitewalls: Princeton, 1959.
We never used the American names we had prepared for
ourselves. Mine was Marty. Adapting one of his middle names,
Philip had come up with Nick, Junior.

Phil down the Fulham Road, checking his Vespa, c. 1966, while a rozzer (or 'tithead') patrols the pavement.

Sally finishing a salad in Spain: 1973

Rob (top) and I spent much time (and money) pouting into photo booths. 1967.

Barnet, early 1970s.
Kingsley is pretending to be a French intellectual and is saying something like, 'If existence precedes essence . . .'

These interlocutors were about twenty years old.

Here was the trailing edge of a culture that actually *liked* dentures, regarding them as a more practical and more personable simulacrum of the real thing. It remained a preference of the working and lower-middle classes only, of course; Evelyn Waugh has a sneer at it, noting, with a thrill of disgust, the 'grinning dentures' of a travelling salesman in *Brideshead Revisited* (1945).* Today, most bourgeois readers would take the foregoing duologue as an illustration of proletarian credulity. But the preference was also an aesthetic preference, and an embrace of the new, just as nylon was preferred to cotton, plastic to wood.

Teeth were clearly, or apparently, connected to rank – which was bad news for the lower classes, and bad news for Osric. Thirty years ago, feeling the trouble coming on and already knowing that it would never go away, I sensed an additional question mark over my claims to high birth. And anyway the dental demographics were changing. Those shocking gobfuls of the poor were becoming a memory. Observational evidence soon established that *everyone* had better teeth than me: football hooligans, junkies, tramps. Nor, back then, could I adduce the counter-example of the noble Nabokov, in whose veins raced the grape blood of emperors . . .†

---

* We know from the *Letters* that Waugh's teeth didn't quite go the distance. He was manful about it, and felt quite undeclassed.

† A footnote for Nabokovians. Recently (23/4/99), at the centenary celebration organised by PEN, where twelve hundred people filled a theatre on Forty-Third Street, I said that Nabokov was my novelist of the century. At a different event – one for Bellovians – I could have said that Bellow was my novelist of the century, without equivocation. I have always maintained that these two are my twin peaks. Nabokov, ridiculously, once dismissed Bellow as 'a miserable mediocrity', an evaluation based (I am confident) on slender acquaintance with his stuff; perhaps too he associated Bellow with the sort of Big Idea novels that Edmund Wilson would sometimes press on him. Besides, Nabokov clearly derived sensual pleasure from being dismissive: it is the patrician in him. At the PEN event his biographer, Brian Boyd, told me that on one occasion VN 'marked up' an anthology of short stories by various hands, giving an A-plus to Joyce (for 'The Dead') but giving Lawrence, and other writers of hemispherical reputation, a Z-minus. For his part Saul Bellow has his doubts about Nabokov. I know he passionately admires *Lolita* and *Pnin*, but there is something in Nabokov that doesn't sit well with him: that

The other key dental connection, of course, is with sexual potency.
Freud has much to say on the subject – how, for instance, dreams of
tooth loss are manifestations of sexual doubt and fear. Interestingly,
Nabokov, who had a somewhat over-cultivated contempt for 'the
Viennese quack' (and his world of 'bitter little embryos, spying, from
their natural nooks, on the love life of their parents'), acknowledged
and vivified this association not only in *Pnin* and elsewhere but also in
one of the very greatest paragraphs in *Lolita* (1955). These sentences –
beautiful, dreadful, flinching and groaning with pain and grief – show
us the moral soul of the entire enterprise. 'She did haunt my sleep',
writes Humbert Humbert of Lolita, when she has gone,

> but she appeared there in strange and ludicrous disguises as
> Valeria or Charlotte,* or a cross between them. That

---

suspicion of aristocratic triumphalism, detectable in the Russian novels *Mary*
(1926), *Glory* (1932) and *The Gift* (1937), and in that Russian novel written in
English, *Ada* (1969). I agree, or rather I sympathise. The characters seem head-
in-air: they don't walk, they 'stride'; they don't chew, they 'munch'; they feel
entitled. But I would also argue that it has nothing to do with snobbery (of
which Nabokov was always a witty enemy). Looking again at *Speak, Memory*,
I noticed that he habitually writes about his father, and no one else, in this
supercharged vein ('he had burst into my room, grabbed my [butterfly] net,
shot down the veranda steps'). Vladimir Dmitrievich Nabokov (1870–1922),
whose country house held fifty servants, was a hugely capable lawyer,
journalist and politician ('a liberal of noble family, the son of a former tsarist
minister, Nabokov – almost symbolic in his self-satisfied correctness and dry
egotism': this icy description is Trotsky's). He served in the Provisional
Government of 1917, and might have gone on (or so his son always felt) to
'lead' Russia in some sort of Kerenskyite administration. Exiled to Berlin, he
was assassinated by a 'sinister ruffian' of Tsarist affiliation ('whom, during
World War Two, Hitler made administrator of émigré Russian affairs'). So
perhaps the Nabokovian triumphalism can more properly be seen as nostalgia
for the paternal qualities of robustness, decisive vigour, innate confidence:
aristocratic (and anachronistic) virtues, but still virtues. I cautiously suggest that
this slight disequilibrium in his work was brought about by thwarted filial love.
* Humbert's previous wives, Valeria, 'the brainless *baban*' from his Paris
period, and Charlotte, 'she of the noble nipple and massive thigh', the
onetime Mrs Haze, Lolita's mother. Now please go back, if you would, and
start the passage again.

complex ghost would come to me, shedding shift after shift, in an atmosphere of great melancholy and disgust, and would recline in dull invitation on some narrow board or hard settee, with flesh ajar like the rubber valve of a soccer ball's bladder. I would find myself, dentures fractured or hopelessly mislaid, in horrible *chambres garnies* where I would be entertained at tedious vivisection parties that generally ended with Charlotte or Valeria weeping in my bleeding arms and being tenderly kissed by my brotherly lips in a dream disorder of auctioneered Viennese bric-a-brac, pity, impotence and the brown wigs of tragic old women who had just been gassed.*

I sometimes believed that sex and teeth would be coterminous.

* Once, in 1990 or thereabouts, I challengingly read this passage out loud to my father. Thirty years earlier he had written a long, hostile and, in my view, wilfully philistine review of *Lolita* just before it was published here in 1959 (and it was published here very warily: the matter was discussed in Cabinet). The book, he announced, was 'thoroughly bad in both senses: bad as a work of art, that is, and morally bad − though certainly not obscene or pornographic'. Having fulfilled the necessary condition of wholly identifying Humbert with Nabokov, Kingsley was free to land some rough punches: '. . . the many totally incidental cruelties . . . bring the author into consideration as well, and I really don't care which of them is being wonderfully mature and devastating when Lolita's mother . . . is run over and killed [there follows a long quotation, ending:] "a dead woman, the top of her head a porridge of bone, brains, bronze hair and blood." That's the boy, Humbert/Nabokov: alliterative to the last.' Kingsley's oblique stroke, here, is the slash of a vandal. And that 'I really don't care' (where the reviewer throws off the critical shackles to pull one back for common decency) should be taken literally as a boast of indifference to literary truth . . . When I read the quoted paragraph out loud to him he said, 'That's just flimflam, diversionary stuff to make you think he cares. That's just style.' Whereas I would argue that style *is* morality: morality detailed, configured, intensified. It's not in the mere narrative arrangement of good and bad that morality makes itself felt. It can be there in every sentence. To Kingsley, though, sustained euphony automatically became euphuism: always. His review of *Lolita* is collected in *What Became of Jane Austen?* (1970).

Love would end. In some of my more tremulous fantasies I thought that I would slip out of the country and head off to a land – Albania? Uzbekistan? South Wales? – where nobody else had any teeth either. Or, less adventurously, I would locate and sign up with the right kind of amatory crisis-centre, where we would all sit around in a fug of peppermints and fixatives, with various mouthfuls of pottery clacking like castanets, until, perhaps, I would repair to the bar with Dorothy Wordsworth, her with her Corsodyl cocktail, me with my tumbler – so much more frank and manly – of Plax on the rocks . . .

As for the transitional period, the week of oral nudity, of Kinchdom: it seemed to defy contemplation. But I reckoned I would be comfortable enough in my coalhole or in the cupboard beneath the stairs among the fuseboxes and the geranium bulbs, with somebody rolling the odd thermos of soup under the door. When the day came I would unfurl myself from the foetal position and emerge, as pale as a Sex Pistol, for the first fitting.

When I was much younger and stupider I came up with another strategy for dealing with it: suicide. It was always a fantasy, a way of deferring fear, and could never have been an option while either of my parents was still alive. But it seemed to help. The only style of exit I ever envisaged was a nihilistic debauch of Valium and alcohol – with decorous trimmings, though, like the note on the door telling the hotel staff to alert the authorities. All the same, none of this prevented a sluggish, passive, low-level death wish from slowly establishing itself in me. I became, by my standards, very un-frightened on aeroplanes, ethereally calm in the most bestial turbulence.

Suicide disappeared even as a fantasy in November 1984, on the day my first son was born. I had a toothache on the day my first son was born. I had a toothache on the day my second son was born. I had a toothache on the day I communed so vitally with the spirit of Lucy Partington . . . Now I had these children and I had these toothaches and I no longer had suicide – suicide as a pleasant distraction; these births had killed off suicide. I'm glad. I'm glad I shook the habit. I was soon to find out a little more about suicide:

that, for instance, it is sinful (and an insult to suicides) to think about suicide when you know it isn't in you.

So there was nothing to do but live it. I didn't have a choice.

Encouragingly (I thought), I only had to Kinch it for three days before I could go and try on the temporary. In the morning I rose believing that a considerable treat lay ahead of me. But the first omen was not a good one. After five minutes on northbound Sixth Avenue I found out where I stood with the Singh brothers. Oh, they had made their feelings very clear . . . I bounced uptown contemplating the seamed neck of Nelson Rojas, with Isabel at my side. She was there to give support but she also had an appointment with Mike Szabatura: there was evidently room for improvement somewhere among her crystal battlements. I once put it to a dentist that women have better teeth than men, and he did not demur. Better teeth, like better hair. Imagine a planet of filamentary equality: women with the blue lagoons of male-pattern baldness (what other pattern is there?), women with thatch-jobs, with comb-overs . . . Horrified at first – 'it was like a poor fossil skull being fitted with the grinning jaws of a perfect stranger' – Timofey Pnin learnt to love his 'new amphitheatre of translucid plastics': 'It was a revelation, it was a sunrise, it was a firm mouthful of efficient, alabastrine, humane America.' Soon, then, like Pnin, and like the teenage bus-conductor back in Swansea, I would be telling everybody to have all their teeth out 'first thing tomorrow. "You will be a reformed man like I," cried Pnin.'

'The mouth,' gentle Millie told me as I took the chair, 'is remarkably adaptable.' Mine was about to suffer an intrusion; over time, my enemy would come to feel like my enemy's enemy: my enemy would feel like my friend. The gadget was borne into the room, and shyly awaited its introduction. Here it came, my ticket to good looks and fine dining, to the head thrown back in vivid laughter, to nuzzling and honeying, to goopy kisses.

But wait. This wasn't the grinning jaw of a perfect stranger. Nothing could have been more hideously familiar. This was me, myself: this was my old bridge, my bridge of sighs with its weight of gold, ear-to-ear under the great pink saddle of the palate. In it went. I lay there flattened, utterly decked, by the sheer mass of the prosthesis. And when I tried to express my general dismay I heard the voice of a perfect stranger who seemed to be standing somewhere well behind me. Millie's face was aswim with sympathy. She said,

– It's like getting used to new shoes.

Yes, I would have said if I could. A new shoe: in your mouth. No, a football boot: in your mouth. A boot forged from an element quite new to our periodic table: an element called nausium. Millie produced a handmirror. I made the acquaintance of the nutty professor. And I missed my boys and felt them missing me, and knew that the hardest part, perhaps, would be to face them with this face.

People walk out of doctors' offices with a quietly satisfied spring in their step or, alternatively, in a meek and burdened shuffle. It was in the latter style that I introduced myself to Madison Avenue. Isabel offered me a sip of orange juice: the flavour took several seconds to get to the back of my throat, and was followed by a cataract of saliva. Smoking a cigarette was no piece of cake either. Smoking a cigarette was no picnic. But imagine a piece of cake. Imagine a *picnic* . . . Gulping, gagging, trying to smoke and trying to swear, I leant heavily on Isabel's arm.

We walked three blocks and entered Brentano's. It was my notion to buy some books that would transport me from the quotidian, the merely sublunary, the bluntly dental. I approached a tall redhaired youth and said,

– The astronomy section, please.

– Excuse me?

– The astronomy section.

– The what?

– Astronomy.

– Excuse me?

– Astronomy.

– What?

At last he seemed to understand. He led, I followed. And found myself in Astrology . . . For hundreds of years rational men and women have been expecting astronomy to subsume and then entirely displace astrology. But it hasn't happened.★ Here it all was, shelf upon shelf upon shelf. I didn't need it. I didn't need its charts and graphs and cusps and casts to tell me that it wasn't my day.

Not my day. But it was my night.

Poor Pnin had nothing. He had nothing left, nothing, nothing. Such was not my case.

That night you came bellydancing out of the bathroom wearing (a) your silk bathrobe and (b) my teeth. Both were then removed.

This was the war against shame.

The next morning I woke early and lay there quietly laughing and weeping into the pillow. I felt fragile, guileless, and exquisitely consoled. The quality of the happiness made me think of a poem – early Yeats – that I had once copied out for my sister to memorise, thirty years ago. Had I the . . . the dark cloths of night and light and the half-light . . . I have spread my . . . Tread softly because you . . .

'Because you don't fall in love like that,' my mother told me. 'It's a terrible thing, what's happening to you. A *terrible* thing. But it's all right if you're loved. Because you don't fall in love with someone's teeth, do you.'

No. It wasn't over. And now, perhaps, more life could be created.

★ Proviso: in astrology everything is 100 per cent false except everything about Scorpios, which is 100 per cent true.

Letter from Home

108 Maida Vale
London, W.9.

Dearest Dad and Jane,

It's pretty fine about the Exhibition, isn't it?* There's still some adrenalin coursing through my veins. It's £40 by the way. (Is that £40 per year or for the 3 yrs?). Anyway it's not so much the money but the distinction and fame which will undoubtedly accrue and the awe that my new intellectual rank will inevitably excite. Mr Ardagh told me that [John] Carey at St. John's was embarrassed by the state of my languages but [Jonathan] Wordsworth at Exeter, who doesn't care about that, and, I suspect, is rather proud of the fact that he doesn't care about that, has advised me that I have been elected to an open Exhibition.

Hope you had a good time in Mexico. Meanwhile, back in Maida Vale, everything is much the same as ever. Colin flits from long work-outs on his bed to dangerously prolonged sun-ray lamp sessions, and then buckles down to his meditation. Consequently he is dreamy, swarthy, and serene. The only reason I can venture to

---

* I had been expecting to say here that this was my least favourite sentence from the Osric archive; but I thought I had written 'rather fine', not 'pretty fine', and 'pretty fine' is not as bad as 'rather fine'. An exhibition (£40 per year) places you between the scholar (£60 per year) and the commoner (nothing). The admissions dons use the 'awards' as an intercollegiate trumping system to get the students they want. I was made a scholar in my last year and got the telltale longer gown. I was probably very pleased about that. This letter reverts to manuscript.

explain his intermittent correspondence is that he has been very busy not ordering enough Weetabix. Sarg gets some hours in on the same employment. Apart from this grave negligence they are looking after me splendidly.

Catsaca, while not putting robins to the sword, staggers and dribbles, allowing us all full knowledge of her naked flesh; Princely Hugo spins away the hours in his habitual placid wonderment. Malfi has the run of the house at all times. If there are rows then Catsaca is hustled into Niger's study – however she has not favoured any of the furniture with her urine.*

I spent Xmas with Mum. At Maida Vale the festive season was never really acknowledged. There was a sullen exchange of presents on Xmas-eve-eve and then everyone buggered off. But spirits are always high and your return is the only desired complement to the general contentment. We are thinking of coming to S/Hampton in a Lincoln Executive, which is about 40 yards long – that should do it nicely. I shall enjoy watching Col clearing the hall of his hi-fi stuff which has been growing steadily until it now constitutes an amorphous expanse of wires, cases and tubes. I am looking forward more than I can say to your return,

> Lots of Love
> Mart XXX

P.S. Sorry if this seems a bit of a 'stream of consciousness' letter but I'm still excited.
P.P.S. How does Virginia Woolf mean?

---

* These three were the house cats, all of them great beauties and exotics (though Catsaca was moulting with age). Niger, or The Niger (pronounced like the river), a fictive figure whom Kingsley would sometimes impersonate, was an uncontrollably successful black gangster who had a fleet of 'pink Cadillacs *doubleparked*' outside his house.

The City and the Village

At the memorial service for Lucy Partington one of the speakers, Sara Boas, charmingly introduced herself as follows: 'I'm Sara and my mother is Lucy's father . . . I mean Lucy's father's sister. Good start, isn't it?'* Sara, in other words, is Lucy's cousin on the father's side. I am Lucy's cousin on the mother's side. We are, in that odd-looking phrase, german cousins (*COD*: 'in the fullest sense of relationship'). Lucy and I shared two grandparents, Leonard and Margery Bardwell, who were themselves cousins – german cousins. When I was about ten I asked Lucy's sister Marian to be my bride; and she accepted. Had that secret engagement come to fruition, then David (at last) would have been my brother, in a way, and Lucy would have been my sister. Not my german sister but my sister-in-law.

I once said to David, experimentally rather than jeeringly,

– You're a country bumpkin and I'm a city slicker.

– No, he said. You're a city bumpkin and I'm a country slicker.

And the ten-year-old David, I felt, had truth as well as wit on his side. But it remained the case: the Amises were of the town, the city, and the Partingtons were of the country, the village. They were more innocent than we were. And I partook of the Partingtonian innocence whenever I went to stay with them – in Gretton ('Nr. Winchcombe', I used to scrawl on my letters): quite close to the spa of Cheltenham, in Gloucestershire. It has been said that Italian cousins are closer than Irish twins. David and I were definitely Italian

---

* It was a good start, and it was a good finish, too: '. . . I have heard a number of people describe Lucy as sensible and I remember when I was about ten and I talked with Lucy about how sensible she was and she said to me, "Well the thing is that I like to be opposite of what people around me are doing."'

[128]

cousins, for many years. The intimacy came to an end, as did so much else, when Eva Garcia ('You know your father's got this fancy woman up in London . . . Ooh aye') hoisted me out of my childhood, in Cambridge in 1963. It was the summer before, I think, that David paid his last visit to the house on Madingley Road.

During his stay he was deputed to inform me that a much-loved dog (Nancy, a gentle Alsatian) had been put down.★ He knocked and entered my – our – room and said, 'Mart, I'm sorry to have to tell you . . .' And he didn't linger; he gave me a sternly encouraging nod and left me to my grief. Nancy had recently produced a large litter – eight or nine strong. I spent the next hours with the orphaned pups in the dark outbuilding, giving and seeking consolation as they crawled over me, unaware that things had changed. So even in the city there were dogs and cats and the donkey. There was plenty of innocence. But I was not as innocent as the Partingtons.

Towards the end of the famous drunken-lecture scene in *Lucky Jim*, the hero starts denouncing the ethos he has been assigned to praise: the folk culture of 'Merrie England'. These are Jim's last words before he blacks out at the podium: 'It's only the home-made pottery crowd, the organic husbandry crowd, the recorder-playing crowd, the Esperanto . . .' Such, more or less, was the ethos of Kingsley's in-laws, the Bardwells: the grandparents I shared with Marian, David,

---

★ Weeks earlier Nancy had been hit by a car. Her right foreleg was broken, and the dragging paw became inflamed and then infected . . . Once, in South Africa, on a visit to a game reserve, my sons and I inspected a crocodile that had undergone the Mike Szabatura experience in jungle conditions: its entire upper mandible (about a third of its head) had been wrenched off in some unspeakable croc rumble. It lay there steaming and gurgling and reeking and, above all (being a reptile), waiting, waiting, waiting (waiting, in this case, for a bucket of food to be upended on to its tongue). I didn't feel that the animal was aware of any significant reduction in its quality of life – any absence of a certain je ne sais quoi . . . It was different with Nancy, unfortunately. She was brave, and skipped along as best she could, but I kept thinking I saw sorrow, bewilderment and even disgrace in her frown and her hot brown eyes. I had become even closer to her after the accident. She was laid up on a mattress in the TV room, and every evening I had to persuade Nancy that it was all right for her to pee where she was. It took a long time; again the eyes, and great anxiety.

Lucy and Mark. Margery Bardwell, like Mrs Welch in the novel, had money: the remains of a Victorian merchant fortune (she gave half of it to cancer research. Her parents went to China as missionaries). Leonard Bardwell, an ex-civil-servant, was a benign eccentric with a passion for popular art. And they were innocent, they were both innocent. My grandfather, I'm pretty sure, did not speak Esperanto, but he had gone to the trouble of mastering three languages of limited utility: Swedish, Welsh and Romansh (heard only in the Swiss canton of Grisons); and I certainly grew up believing that he knew Romany *and* the tongue of the tinkers. He was also an amateur musician and a morris dancer – they're the people who caper about in formation dressed in ribbons and bells.★ I loved him, and was always amazed by the amount of energy he devoted to entertaining me. He moved with a swiftness and agitation rare for a man of any age; and I would notice, as he showed me some stunt with a drawing on a folded piece of paper, that he was even more excited than I was. Daddy B.,† dressed in his trademark blue suit of janitorial serge, had wafty white hair, few teeth, and a skittishly highpitched voice. In a letter to Philip Larkin, Kingsley described him as resembling 'a music-loving lavatory attendant' – and I'm sorry, Mum, but the writer in me knows a bullseye when he sees one. In fact Daddy B. emerges as a great comic figure in the *Letters*, where he survives the hostility levelled at him with cheerful self-sufficiency.‡ Kingsley cultivated an ornate resentment

★ Sordidly trolling up and down the King's Road, with Rob, one Saturday in the late Sixties, I came across a troupe of morris dancers performing in a garden square. 'My granddad used to do this stuff,' I was saying, when a costumed figure pressed a pamphlet into my hand. I opened it: and there was a photograph of the now-deceased Daddy B., in full rig, delightedly leading the Abingdon 'side'.
† The senior Bardwells were referred to by my parents as Daddy B. and Mummy B., the senior Amises as Daddy A. and Mummy A.
‡ For instance, who is the winner in this anecdote (addressed, again, to Larkin)?

The best time was when I was lying in a partially filled bath with him in the room underneath accompanying on the piano, his foot regularly tapping, folk tunes he was playing on the gramophone, there being a

towards his father-in-law, but the truth is that he was irritated by Daddy B.'s innocence. My father, as we shall see, was generally irritated by innocence. And the Bardwells were so innocent. I could tell they were innocent when I was *six*.

My last memory of Mummy B. is now coloured by some retrospective shame – though the occasion seemed no more than an embarrassing absurdity at the time. At the time (1970) I was a drawling, velvet-suited, snakeskin-booted undergraduate: Osric on a roll (but actually getting slowly less stupid). Already widowed, Mummy B. had unwisely agreed to take me out to lunch in Oxford, at the Randolph Hotel (where, in the postwar years, Kingsley used to be wined and dined by generous friends like Bruce Montgomery* and Kenneth Tynan). It was clear from the moment Mummy B. walked in that she was overwhelmed – was utterly engulfed – by the scale of the place. She had been there at least once before. On 21 January 1948, a family tea was held at the Randolph to mark my parents' wedding. Mummy B. had to be inveigled into joining the celebration by Mummy A. – as did Daddy B., and as did Daddy A. Well, my mother was nineteen, and pregnant with Philip; but it was Rosa Amis who had to persuade the other three to stop behaving like

difference in pitch between the two sources of sound of approximately one-3rd of a full tone. As one vapid, uniformly predictable tune ended and another began I found that the hot tap was now dispensing cold water, and getting out of the bath, began drying myself.

I sympathise, but my vote goes to the regularly tapping foot. Kingsley's portrait has its kinder moments. At one point he allows that there is 'no harm' in the old boy. And we mustn't forget the sweetness and decency shown by his fictional counterpart, Professor Welch in *Lucky Jim* ('Poor old Daddy B.,' wrote Larkin, on finishing it), over the matter of the scorched and savaged bedding. Letter to Larkin again (and I like the defeated tone): 'I can see now what makes fathers fling their children out of the house with a few bob at the age of 11; mine ran up to him [Daddy B.] with cries of delighted welcome.'
* My godfather and a fantastically bountiful one – especially when compared to my brother's godfather and namesake: the lenten Larkin. Bruce was a minor composer who also wrote and anthologised crime fiction under the name of Edmund Crispin.

automata of their time . . . It wasn't that the Randolph had grown since Mummy B. was last there. Mummy B. had shrunk. She seemed no taller than the tabletops, and she sensed it, too. With an expression of painful shyness and unworthiness (with flashes of undisguised fright) she accompanied her sauntering grandson into the dining-room. For the first ten minutes she ignored what I said to her and kept muttering the same sentence. The sentence was: 'We should have gone to Debenham's.' Mummy B. was feeling too old to be doing this – too old, too small, and too deaf. I raised my voice and had to go on raising it, as her panic attenuated into exhaustion. After a while I was about three-quarters of the way to my maximum volume. Silences fell and heads turned all over the room, throughout our lunch, as I continued to scream various questions and answers about the health and whereabouts of my parents, siblings and cousins. I should have done better. I should have taken her to Debenham's. Mummy B. died the following year.

The Bardwells endowed their children with legacies on or around their twenty-first birthdays. My mother got enough to buy us our first house, a terraced three-floor near Cwmdonkin Park (and near the Cwmdonkin Drive that Dylan Thomas was supposedly the Rimbaud of), Swansea, for £2,400. This is either a preternaturally early memory or an often-visualised family anecdote, but I see and hear Kingsley and Hilly running around 24 The Grove, Uplands, Swansea, yelling and hooting and growling as they celebrated their new space and freedom.

Even I inherited money from the Bardwells, on or around my twenty-first birthday, as did my siblings and all my cousins: £1,000. My mother and, I believe, my aunt, and perhaps my uncles (whom I never really knew), also inherited innocence.

And the Partington children came into some of that. And the Amis children came into some of that – but maybe not so much. We had Kingsley in us too.* And they were of the village, and we were of the city.

* I don't want to be mistaken here. My father had the innocence you need to be a novelist, and the greater innocence you need to be a poet. But he answered strongly to experience too; it roiled in him, and in us.

✻ ✻ ✻

Innocence and nakedness, like Adam and Eve, used to go hand in hand. 'With naked honour clad / In naked majesty, seemed lords of all,' writes Milton in Book IV of *Paradise Lost*.★ In Book IX the serpent leads Eve to the tree of 'knowledge forbidden'. She eats, and urges Adam to do the same ('On my experience, Adam, freely taste'):

> each the other viewing
> Soon found their eyes how opened, and their minds
> How darkened; innocence, that as a veil
> Had shadowed them from knowing ill, was gone,
> Just confidence, and native righteousness
> And honour from about them, naked left
> To guilty shame . . .

And inducing Adam's terrible lament:

> cover me ye pines,
> Ye cedars, with innumerable boughs
> Hide me . . .

Nuditas virtualis: virtuous, prelapsarian nakedness. Astoundingly, we still glimpse something of this in ourselves, every year. On holiday, whether in Nailsea or in some brochurish 'paradise', we go through the motions of feeling less ashamed of our bodies. On the first morning, as your quivering, death-grey foot broaches the sand, you think only of your shocking etiolation – the stripped creature, so pale, so parched. Then, after a while, the body becomes the focus of a cautious complacency. How one primes it with oils and unguents, how one braces it with the alerting asperities of sand and salt and solar fire . . . The nudity is of course only partial (as, God knows, is the

---

★ Kingsley and I agreed, by the way, that the last forty-odd lines of *Paradise Lost* were incomparably the greatest thing in non-dramatic poetry in English.

virtuousness), but the connection* is still available to us in the little Eden of the seaside.

Early in our friendship David astonished me by playing naked on the beach in Swansea. It wasn't his nakedness – it was his indifference to it. He just knelt there, building a sandcastle, digging, shaping, patting, with serious eyes. I realised that I had long lost that kind of freedom, summers ago. A thing had appeared in me that was still absent in him. He was of the village, I was of the city. Was that it? . . . One startling summer day in the village of Gretton, Gloucestershire, Marian performed a sensational streak: out of the house and once round the garden. The four boys there – me, David, my brother Philip, and another, much vaguer cousin or second cousin – stood and giggled. She called for the hose to be turned on her. I remember her bobbing, shrieking figure. I remember the relationship between the curve of her back and the arcs of the water. Once, very late at night, in Swansea, on the top floor of the second house we had there, 59 Glanmore Road, Marian and I took our pyjamas off and got into bed together. It was innocent, innocent.† Afterwards (that word should be wearing two epaulettes of inverted commas) we lay in the dark and for a long time busily whispered. I asked,

– Will you marry me?

---

* A couple of years ago, after being thoroughly nosed by a salt-and-pepper Alsatian (Nancy! How could you do this to me?), I was stripsearched for drugs at Venice Airport. 'The dogs are never wrong,' said the spivvy plainclothesman, dressed in full entrapment gear with earring and neck bracelet. I was guided into a back room. The first thing I saw was a man flexing and wriggling his fingers into a raised rubber glove, and I thought – No, you ain't going to do that, are you? I wanted to say: You've got the right guy but you've got the wrong trip. (And there would never be a right trip, not after this.) Isabel was there. I started taking my clothes off. When I got down to my boxer shorts I was told to lower them. This I did, and was then contemptuously dismissed. It felt like the crime of indecent exposure in reverse. More than this, though, my nakedness had proved my innocence. A tenuous connection had been made.
† Technically it was also my first fiasco. A structural fiasco: we were asking each other to double in age. No reproaches were voiced. And I didn't have to lie there with a hand spread limply across my forehead, going on about my homework and the pressures facing the contemporary eight-year-old.

– . . . Yes.

Yes. And I thought something like, well, it's a bit early – but it's sometimes good to get these things out of the way.

I have said that my childhood was idyllic (and the times I spent with the Partingtons were arcadian. The lion lay down with the lamb, and the rose grew without thorn). But I couldn't have spent time thinking about the fate of Lucy Partington without remembering that where there was grass there would also, necessarily, be serpents.*

Innocence attracts its two main opposites: experience and guilt. *Nuditas virtualis* attracts its theological counterpart, *nuditas criminalis*. The paedophile, for example, wants more from children than their physical beauty; the paedophile is so interested in violation that only children will do. I was young, and the world was younger, almost unimaginably younger. And yet there always are these enemies, who see innocence and need to do something to it.

It Im Again, Dai

I was idling away at the kind of thing that eight-year-old boys find very fascinating. A plump pebble was wedged between the bars of a drain in the gutter, and I with a sandalled foot was trying to kick it through, to stomp it down, to hear that satisfying plop as it joined the waterways of the city's innards.

– Oi! You by there! What ewe doing with that drain?

– Nothing! I'm just . . . I'm just . . .

He was about fifteen, swarthy, curly-haired, his good looks undermined by his fraudulently bright green eyes. It was dark, it was wet – but in Swansea, in winter, an inky drizzle was the very air you breathed. 'When the lights come on at four / At the end of another

* Frederick West was always very much of the village, then, later, very much of the city, too. Unsurprisingly, his early, yokellish brutalities were visited on animals.

year,' wrote Larkin, well north of us in Hull; but he needed his assonance and his monosyllable, and couldn't say 'half past two'. Still, memory informs me that the time was illicitly late. I shouldn't have been tarrying with this pebble, this drain, this green-eyed boy.

We stood on the busy and well-lit foothill of Glanmore Road. Now we started off together, up into the steepening gloom. In a practised but roundabout way the youth asked me if, following his leniency with the pebble and the drain, I might consider doing him a favour. 'What?' I asked. He said he would give me a chocolate toffee, a Rollo – 'or possibly two' – if I would oblige him. 'What is it?' 'Oh, it won't take a minute. Just show me . . . ewe willie.'

I came to a halt and received the pressure of tears on my chest. Strange: we know that children cry from fear, but this felt more like *grief*. I crossed the road. He watched me as I climbed the hill. I said nothing to my mother when I got home.

A couple of weeks later I reencountered the boy with green eyes. I was a block from home, on a side street I crossed every schoolday (it had a good dirt lane, a shortcut, up the other end of it). Again it was dark, late, wet.

– Oi. What ewe doing down here on my road?

He had a companion with him, a stocky little boy, considerably and reassuringly younger and shorter than me. This terrible toddler, I would soon learn, was called David and answered to the usual Welsh diminutive.

– What ewe doing down here on my road?

– Your road?

– It him, Dai.

With explosive alacrity, like a fast bowler at the moment of release, Dai hurled his closed fist into my forehead. I didn't know that boys that size could hit that hard. But I did know two things. One, that the attack was revenge for the favour earlier denied. Two, that little Dai, at least to begin with, had enjoyed Rollos by the tubeful. But Christ knows what they turned into, this pair. And Christ knows what *their* children turned into.

– Who said ewe could walk past my house?

– I didn't know it wasn't allowed.

– . . . It im again, Dai.

And so on for about ten minutes, the same question, and the same command. When I got home I told my mother how I had come by my swollen face. I gave her the bare facts, and not the subtext. Immediately she leashed up the three big dogs: Nancy, certainly, and Flossie? and Bessie? With anxious adoration I watched her go down the hill, like Charlton Heston or Steve Reeves wielding the reins of the chariot. The dogs, no less indignant than their mistress, were almost upright on their leads.

She returned half an hour later, still furious and still unavenged.

I was returning from the playing-field to my class. Cambridgeshire High School for Boys, during the Cuba Crisis, which places us in the week of 22–28 October, 1962, and puts me two months into my teenhood.

The Cuba Crisis, I am sure, had a far heavier effect on me than the relatively minor violation I am about to describe – which might itself have been crisis-borne. I remember it★ as one long dankly gleaming twilight: darkness at noon, a solar eclipse, an Icelandic winter morning. The planet's children suffered this crisis – the most severe in human history – dumbly, with abject dumbness. I could talk about it afterwards (with David, for instance) but I said not a word to my friends at the time; and I don't recall hearing any reassurance (or any effective reassurance) from my mother or my father. When the TV showed the kill targets, the concentric circles, the fallout forecasts, I bolted from the room. At school we had had our nuclear drills, where, I repeat, we were invited to believe that our desk-lids would save us from the end of the world. What were we supposed to do with such a notion? And what did it do to us?† The children of the

---

★ We all remember it. To paraphrase Christopher Hitchens's pertinent inversion: Like everybody else, I remember exactly where I was standing and who I was with at the moment that President Kennedy nearly killed me . . . Except it wasn't just a moment, it wasn't just a week. It began with the first Russian test, on 29 August, 1949, and it lasted for forty years.

† In Don DeLillo's novel *Underworld* (1997), which is an 800-page meditation on this query, the schoolchildren are issued with *dogtags*:

nuclear age, I think, were weakened in their capacity to love. Hard to love, when you're bracing yourself for impact. Hard to love, when the loved one, and the lover, might at any instant become blood and flames, along with everybody else.

I was returning from the playing-field when I was jumped on by a group of older boys and dragged into a classroom. Some major inadvertency (perhaps this was connected to the crisis, too) had brought it about that an entire school outbuilding was left uninvigilated all afternoon – long enough, at any rate, for eighteen or twenty of the younger children to get the treatment that was waiting for me. The maximal resistance I gave was the result of primitive panic and remained unsubdued by blows and threats as I was spread out on the absent master's desk and roughly stripped. On the blackboard someone had chalked up a kind of manifest; I thought for a moment that it was a school timetable, but in fact it was just a scorecard, giving each victim's name, his age, his form, and the state of his sexual development, if any. For the record, my entry concluded: TINY. NO HAIRS AT ALL . . . Well, I could live with that. *That* wasn't the end of the world, I thought, as I ran away clutching my belt in one hand and a shoe in the other. If fear is simply the intense desire for something to be over, then I had indeed been horribly frightened, that day. Frightened by their hysteria, their self-goading mob energy, all splutter and grinning spittle. Was there nihilism in it? Who cared? We were all dead anyway. But the essence, the gravamen, was the forcible restraint and what that does to the spirit.

I was lying in bed on a bright summer evening. We are not in the city and we are not in the village. We are in the suburbs of Princeton,

---

The tags were designed to help rescue workers identify children who were lost, missing, injured, maimed, mutilated, unconscious or dead following the onset of atomic war . . . [The children] were expecting a drill, the duck-and-cover drill, which they'd rehearsed before the tags arrived. Now that they had the tags, their names inscribed on wispy tin, the drill was not a remote exercise but was all about them, and so was atomic war.

New Jersey: Edgerstoune Road, a stretch of detached single-storey houses backed by woods and hillocks . . . My parents were giving one of their parties, and I could hear it, like a baritone schoolyard, several walls away. Sometimes at these events my brother and I served as paid waiters: $3 each, on one famous occasion. But it was apparently too late for me to be up, though the room felt full of day and I seemed a great distance from sleep. It was 1959 and I was nearly ten – and fully Americanised, for now: accent, crewcut, racing bike with whitewall tyres and electric horn . . .

The door opened and a dapper middle-aged man smiled and confidently entered, followed by a woman in a grey silk blouse beneath a black jacket, dark-haired, handsome, even distinguished, with artistic bones. At the sight of me her face 'lit up': it is the what-have-we-here? expression of the adult who lacks all talent with children (under more normal circumstances they approach on tiptoe and address you in an idiocy-imputing singsong). Throughout she remained by the open door, one hand holding a cocktail glass, the other flat on her breastbone. The man came towards the bed and sat down on the foot of it. After some general inquiries he introduced the notion that he was a doctor and that it would be a good thing if he examined me. Grateful for the diversion, I slipped readily out of my pyjamas.

Now, looking back, I wonder how many children came before and after me, and I wonder how far it went. In my case it went as far as what is usually called 'fondling', though the word is blasphemously inapt, suggesting that the man touched me 'lovingly' (he was not a lover. He was a raptor). And what kind of *mission* was this anyway, to come to the house of a friend or a colleague, to find a solitary boy-child, and, risking everything, to conspire against his trust?

This third violation has taken on a new resonance in my mind, following the exhumation of Lucy Partington, because it involved grown adults and a *folie à deux*.* Significantly, perhaps, my memory of the man is vacant – a shape, a tone, an outline. But my memory of

* Frederick West, like Rosemary West, was a paedophile. He raped and sexually tortured his own children, and murdered two of them. 'Your first child should be your dad's,' he used to tell his girls – a line that seems to have

the woman is intact and entire. How she leant against the open door, maintaining her tall-eyed, all's-well smile as she turned, every few seconds, to glance down the corridor. I must have noticed those glances at the time, their frequency, their dissimulated stealthiness. All this had to melt down through me.

It didn't feel like an unpleasant experience at the time but it clearly *was* an unpleasant experience. Why didn't I mention it to my mother the next morning, or any morning, chattily, innocently, over breakfast or on the way to school? As with the other incidents, I kept quiet, and was obliged to make my own sense of it. These are insults. These are thefts. They take something from you that you never quite get back.

Paedophilia means 'love of children'. And paedophiles will say that that is all they are doing: loving children. Like suicide, paedophilia is an evasive subject, and little understood. But some statistical emphases point you in a certain direction. When violating girl

---

a kind of caveman rectitude about it (you could imagine it being parlayed into some sententious village-idiot couplet, beginning, Unless first child by father be / . . .). 'I made you,' West would say in answer to his daughters' protests. 'So, I can touch you.' In *Out of the Shadows*, the gauntly painful memoir she wrote (with Virginia Hill), Anne Marie, West's eldest, reveals that her father succeeded in making her pregnant when she was fifteen. The ectopic foetus was surgically removed; Anne Marie was told that the operation was 'something to do with her periods'. Years later, after complications with her two subsequent pregnancies and a full hysterectomy at the age of twenty-three, she saw her medical records and then confronted her father. 'You don't do things like that to children. I was just a child. I loved you. You abused that and me,' she told him, among other things. Before saying that he wasn't going to listen to 'this fucking rubbish' and stalking out of the house, West, absolutely floundering, came up with: 'If you're going to bring up all that stuff – well, you're no bloody daughter of mine.' In 1994 Anne Marie left flowers on the gate of 25 Cromwell Street and a note to her murdered sibling: 'To my sister Heather, I've searched and sought, I've wept and prayed we'd meet again some sunny day. Missing you so very much. Will always love and remember you. All my fondest love, Big Sis, Anna-Marie.' As I was finishing this book Marian Partington told me that Anne Marie (the name changed), with whom she is in touch, was lucky to survive a recent attempt at suicide. She has all Marian's sympathy, and all mine.

children, for instance, the paedophile shows a marked preference for sodomy. And those under paedophiliac assault are very likely to be additionally hurt, too (never mind, for now, about the 'untold damage' of an intrusion into the sensorium of a child); and, secondly, with these supererogatory beatings, the younger the child the greater the danger. The *younger* the child . . . That tells me something. And so does this. When I have handled my babies I have had the wayward thought, the thought suggested by their beauty and their innocence. It feels like a sexual thought but in essence it is a violent thought. To act it out in any way would be like dashing the naked body to the bathroom floor. Paedophiles hate children. They hate children because they hate innocence, and children *are* innocence. Look at them. They come here naked – but not quite. To the fit pair of eyes they come here thoroughly armoured: with native honour clad.

Syzygy

Here is a geographical epiphany. At the most westerly point of the Welsh peninsula, on the tip of its lower talon, lies St David's, widely but quietly famed, in the 1950s, as the smallest city on earth. It was a village that had a cathedral in it. It was a city that was also a village.

One summer I went there on a camping holiday with my aunt Miggy and her four children: Marian, David, Lucy, Mark. That time lives in my memory as a stretch of unpunctuated delectation, as if the sea salt in my throat was continuously succumbing to the taste of icecream. As we got ready for bed in the great tepee I felt I was shedding my towny complexity and mire, and that I was entering a calmer universe than the one I would (eventually) return to. Aunt Miggy was my mother and yet not my mother. David was my brother and yet not my brother. This was my family and yet not my family. Night was only a cone of canvas away, but I was fully protected. In *Speak, Memory*, writing about his uncle, Nabokov is economically elegant on the child's sense of secondary, or additional, security:

'Everything is as it should be, nothing will ever change, nobody will ever die.'

Some freak perihelion or syzygy caused the sun to hang unnaturally low in the late afternoons. A tennis ball would cast a shadow two yards long. As David and I, anticipating an evening snack, went to visit some new friends on the site, our hosts – two men sitting with their back to us around a fire – would start calling out greetings when we were forty feet away. We were growing boys. We were immensely proud of our shadows.

When the time came these new friends agreed to drive me back to Swansea. 'We'll be getting to your place about *lunchtime*, Martin,' one said. 'We'll be getting to your house around the time that people have *lunch*,' said the other. The great Eva Garcia was alerted.

Throughout the journey I sat hunched forwards on the back seat, praying that Eva would be at her best and not staring tragically out from under her red bandanna. We arrived, at 24 The Grove (the house had somehow been passed on to the Garcias). And Eva's welcome was warm to the point of flirtation. My heart swelled as she laughingly and lavishly served up her speciality and staple: fried eggs, chips, toast and tea. Eva's eggs: the pale sun of the yolk, the succulence of the glair.

It was not Eva's fault, of course, but it was her peculiarly Welsh privilege, in Cambridge, in 1963, to tell me that all this was over. The first act was over. Only when I came to write the present book did I realise how much I lost and how far I fell in the course of that brief sentence: 'You know your father . . .?' Childhood, the grandparents, the Partingtons, the village, the animals, the garden, innocence, even Eva herself: all wiped out.

And my father, too, was gone or going.

To the end of his life Kingsley maintained the following: 'the idea was' that he would have his holiday with Jane, and then return to the family (and then go on seeing her as often as he could). Still, he knew he had crossed a line with my mother. He did come back to the house on Madingley Road. I imagine he must have been very frightened to find it empty, vacated by animals, children, wife. He didn't like empty houses anyway. There was nothing there, not even a note.

We had absconded to Soller, Majorca, to a villa the family had already rented for an experimental year abroad. I can't describe it because I can't remember it – golden walls, an orange grove, much sun, great gloom. In his useful if curiously repetitive biography,* Eric Jacobs writes:

> It may be that their marriage unravelled more by miscalculation than by plan, certainly with no deliberate intention that it should on Amis's side. Perhaps, he thought, Hilly had gone off to Majorca as a way of calling his bluff, in the hope that he would rush off after her full of contrition and eager to renounce Jane. If so she was mistaken.

No. My mother had crossed a line too. The idea of Kingsley 'rushing off' to Spain is fantastic. If Mum had taken us off to Miggy's (as Miggy, once, had come to her), then my father might have fought his way to Gretton. But Soller? To accomplish this he would have needed: someone to make all the bookings, someone to get him to Southampton, someone to share his cabin on the boat, and someone to lead him from Palma to Soller and right up to our front door. The only possible candidate for the task was Elizabeth Jane Howard. Anyway, it didn't happen. The marriage was still very far from loveless, but my mother had made a decision. She tells me, now, that she fantasised about Kingsley 'rushing off' to Spain, but never expected it. My mother understood the force of that old precept (or tautology) about character being destiny. Of course, it is idle to quarrel with the *fait accompli* of the past, idle of me to 'wish' that my father had stayed with my mother. Divorces are like revolutions: accomplished fact. But I am struck by the symmetry of it: the same phobias, the same neurotic timidities that kept them apart in 1963 would reunite them, in 1981.

After a few weeks in Soller my brother and I fell into a wordless

---

* *Kingsley Amis: A Biography* (1995). See, in due course, Appendix.

routine. After breakfast we went through the orange grove to the iron gates and sat on the wall and waited. We were waiting for the post-man. We were waiting for something from my father – something that his occasional notes and postcards weren't bringing us: they seemed paltry, tangential, wholly incommensurate. What took us out there every morning? What did we need to know? It got paler and paler, this waiting. We said little. The oranges were orange and the leaves were green. The postman's motorbike was red. The letters were white or brown and the postcards colourful. But I couldn't see these colours. The oppression did not appear to originate from my own heart: the world was doing it, subtracting clarity from things. We were almost comatose by the time my mother put us on the plane.

I can see Kingsley now, in his striped pyjamas, rearing back from us in histrionic consternation. London, midnight, the harsh doorbell. The plane was late, the warning telegram had not arrived. It wasn't just that he was surprised to see us. He was horrified to see us. We had busted him *in flagrante delicto*: in blazing crime . . . Our mother had been terse (though never critical) in her descriptions of his living arrangements. And Eva's unconfirmed figment of the 'fancy woman' (all bangles, cleavage, and electric red hair) had faded in my mind. Kingsley, we had come to understand, was living in a 'bachelor flat'. When I thought of my father, during the later weeks of that four-month separation, I pictured him in the unlikely role of a functioning, indeed rather houseproud single man: Kingsley heating up a philo-sophical TV-dinner; Kingsley frowning as he chafed that stubborn stain on the saucepan; Kingsley ironing a shirt . . . These were his opening words to Philip and me, nicely phrased, I thought (even then): 'You know I'm not alone.'

Devastated, and scandalised, the brothers shrugged coolly, and entered.

In her white towel bathrobe, with her waist-long fair hair, tall, serious, worldly, Jane loomed beyond him – already busying herself, cooking eggs and bacon, finding sheets, blankets, for the beds in the spare room. It would have been an impossible heresy for me to admit that any woman was more beautiful than my mother. But I could tell at once that Jane, while also being beautiful, was certainly more *experienced.*★ And experience accounts for the well-attested attraction, to the Young Man, of the Older Woman. It isn't just a matter of sexual experience. The older woman brings with her the glamour and mystery of life lived – people met, places seen, experiences experienced. Jane had been around, and at a high level – higher than my father's. I acknowledged the appeal of that with simple resignation and I did not feel disloyal to my mother.

That week passed in a spree of expert treats – gimmicky restaurants, the just-released *55 Days at Peking*† in Leicester Square, the Harrod's fruitjuice bar, a new LP each (mine was *Meet the Searchers*, featuring 'Love Potion Number Nine') – counterbalanced by long, fumbling and (for us) inevitably lachrymose discussions between father and sons. Outwardly calm, unusually quiet-voiced, Kingsley set about the task of explaining how marriages unravel. He took everything we threw at him, even when Philip said (incredibly, to me – but then again the words were tearfully blurted), 'You're a *cunt.*' These talks served a vital purpose, though it wasn't one of elucidation. All I can remember, from Kingsley's end of it, is a derisory ramble about china tea – how Dad liked it, and Mum never remembered to buy it, and now here he was, contentedly awash in Earl Grey . . . Towards the end of our visit the journalist George Gale‡ came to dinner. Pretty soon he was putting on his coat again and heading off to Fleet Street. The telephone had rung. This was a call from the real world. '*No!*' my father shouted into the mouthpiece. Jane wept. That was where I was and who I was with when I learned that Lee Harvey Oswald had killed President Kennedy.

As soon as we got back to Spain we entered the swirl of school – in Palma. This establishment, run by a theatrically pedantic

★ Jane was in fact a few years older than my mother – close to my father's age (forty-one at the time). Philip and I had just turned fifteen and fourteen respectively.
† After a while, Kingsley got off his seat and lay down on the floor every time Ava Gardner appeared on screen. Ava Gardner was the co-star, opposite Charlton Heston; and *55 Days at Peking*, according to my Halliwell, runs for 154 minutes. In all, Kingsley must have spent a good half an hour stretched out on our shoes.
‡ A.k.a., satirically, George G. Ale.

Yorkshireman, was casual and cosmopolitan and above all coeducational, featuring the daughters of businessmen and diplomats: wonderful, terrifying, and inconceivably distant young women. Fascistic and Catholic, Spain nonetheless showed considerable laxity towards the young, and Philip and I were starting to enjoy new freedoms. My mother appeased us with dirt-track motorbikes which we crashed about eight times a day. We could order a beer at the cafés in the town square after school; and once, with a friend, we had a brandy each *before* school (where we would be known, thereafter, as Los Tres Coñacs). Spanish cinemas acknowledged no rating system, and we paid several visits to a perfunctorily dubbed *Psycho*.* There was a girl of sixteen who often commuted with us on the Soller-Palma train. Saying it was an experiment, she once kissed me on the mouth with parted lips. I thought: This is heavenly, but shouldn't it be happening to Philip?†

The locomotive we rode on had a rating system, and one strictly enforced. Its first-class carriage was a mobile drawing-room, a thickly carpeted boudoir, with sofas, paintings, and swaying chandelier. Second class was a bourgeois barber shop of leather and mirror and antimacassar. But when I travelled alone I always chose the bare wood of third, for a reason that still makes me feel slightly serpentine. In those packed, silent, orderly carriages there was a better chance of seeing something you never saw in the Protestant north: nursing

* This was another film that had a notable effect on my father. I was especially pumped-up for it, after this conversation with my mother in Cambridge a year earlier:
 – Mum. Why is Dad following you about and making you go to the bathroom with him?
 – Because we saw a very frightening film last night.
 – What was it about?
 – . . . It's about a man who thinks he's his mother.
 Her answer satisfied me. I thought: Yes. That would do it.
† Needless to say, it *was* happening to Philip, very thoroughly, with somebody else. An Older Woman, too. I couldn't believe his luck when he told me about it. I was only a year behind him, true, but years lasted a very long time in those days, and were not the mere afternoons, the mere evanescences, they have since become.

mothers. And although the back of the baby's head looked nice enough, I have to confess that the bit I liked came before and after. Nobody else watched; nobody else noticed. In a country where tourists in bikinis were arrested at gunpoint, there was still this virtuous nudity, invisible to all except a furtive young foreigner whose thoughts were no longer pure.

My brother and I were undergoing the integral ordeal of turning into men, but we had ceased to be deeply unhappy. In a late interview, talking about this time, Kingsley said that he partly owed his survival to the forgiveness of his children. Yet forgiveness, in the sense of full reacceptance, was never in doubt. Philip and I now knew that our father, while no longer with us, while no longer married to our mother, was still our father.

In the late spring we went back to England. From then on it was all city, all London, and all experience.

When I go back to the core of my childhood Lucy Partington seems always to be in the peripheral vision of my memories. I keep thinking that if I could only shift my head an inch and change its angle then I would see her fully. Just as Marian, a year my senior, was magnified in my mind, so Lucy, two and a half years younger, was additionally reduced (and little Mark was no more than a pair of legs in shorts, running off to where he needed to go). Only David did I see four-square . . . Some people, alas, live and die without trace. They come and they go and they leave no trace. This, at least, was not Lucy's destiny.

She is off to one side, always off to one side, with a book, with a scheme or a project or an enterprise. Or with an animal. There were animals everywhere – it was like *Big Red Barn* with additional humans. And there was always a great succession of ponies and horses, gymkhanas, rosettes. I remember Marian practising jumps in the field beyond the garden. I remember Lucy in riding gear, her spectacled face eagerly smiling under a cloth-covered helmet. Every afternoon, to rusticated chants of 'The *cays* are coming', the cows did come, like a slow-motion Pamplona, dozens of them, with that rolling, shouldering trudge, down Duglinch Lane, which they basted with their steaming breath and their steaming dung. The cows never glanced at the small herd of children that watched them so intently every day. Like other Bardwells – like my mother, for example – Lucy Partington understood the innocence and mystery of animals, and she wrote about them with a clairvoyant eye, even as a child. In my clearest image of her she is crossing the small courtyard between the stable and the house, looking downwards and smiling secretively, privately, as if sharing a joke with the mouse I knew she had in her pocket.

I was, on the whole, an equable little boy, easily the 'easiest' of the younger Amises. I loved my sister Sally, and often considered myself to be her appointed guardian;* I was capable of shedding tears of sympathy when she was distressed. But the Amises were, in configuration, a rough and ready boy-boy-girl (as opposed to the platonic perfection of the Partingtons' girl-boy-girl-boy). Philip, therefore, exerted his will on Martin, and Martin, therefore, exerted his will on Sally. I did some terrible things to her,† often in concert with Philip. So as a ten-year-old, say, I might have looked at Lucy (seven and a half) as someone I could mock or manipulate. But such an impulse was quite absent in David, and instantly vanished in me. It was a straightforward matter: you simply wouldn't dare. You wouldn't dare tangle with Lucy, and not just because you feared her

---

* Sally was born on 17 January 1954, at 24 The Grove. I was allowed on the scene soon afterwards, and I have an utterly radiant – and utterly false – memory of my hour-old sister, her features angelically formed, her blonde tresses curling down over her shoulders. In fact, of course, she was just like the other Amis babies: a howling pizza. Larkin celebrated her arrival with 'Born Yesterday', a poem that Sally, over the course of her life, often rewrote, its opening line, 'Tightly-folded bud . . .', becoming, at one point, the no-nonsense 'Fat pod . . .', and so on.

† This was the worst. From my bed I once flung a small pair of scissors at Sally, or in her direction, as she slept. The point struck her forehead – and yet she slept on. Only when I was wiping away the few drops of blood did she stir. 'What are you doing?' she asked. 'I'm just wiping your brow.' Then she said, unforgettably, 'Hanks,' and, with a sigh, resumed her rightful slumber.

rectitude and her wit. Her presence was somehow infinitely self-sufficient and self-determining. She was autonomous because she was *powerful*. And the idea of encroaching on her universe still makes me quail. When I think of Lucy being bound or restrained my nerves and membranes feel her moral force and its demand for release. This, together with the fact that her assailant was without physical courage, is my best reason for allowing a passionate hope – that it was all over quickly – to grow into something very like a belief.

Then there are the photographs. Lucy's poetry and prose were collected on her twenty-second birthday, 4 March 1974, just over three months after her disappearance. On the last page of the pamphlet – the *Poetry and Prose* – we see the author (aged eight) and her grandmother (Mummy B.) sitting on deckchairs in February sunshine. Lucy is in wellington boots and tartan trousers. She has an exercise book open on her lap. Almost fully camouflaged, the mouse Snowy nestles in a crook of her white rollneck sweater. Death has come to all three creatures pictured here. My cousin and my grandmother are both wearing spectacles, and they are smiling the same smile. I know that smile.

Then there is the photograph I keep in my study (the glasses again, the school tie: 'undesirable alien'), back to back with the other photograph: the two-year-old girl in the sandals and the flower dress, my daughter, Delilah.

Then there is the photograph you will find in all the books, the smiling face among the other smiling faces of the other murdered girls. I know that Bardwell smile from a photograph of my mother when *she* was twenty-one, sitting with Kingsley (and Mandy, the dog) outside Marriner's Cottage, near Oxford – and expecting me.

Letter from Home

108 Maida Vale
London, W.9.
9/1/68.

Dearest Dad and Jane

Thank you both for your respective letters. It's nice to know
you expected it of me: while I knew that failure to secure a place at
Oxford would not be complemented by my being thrown naked
into the streets, I did, however, enjoy the calm reassurance that
neither of you would ever speak to me again. *VERY seriously*
though, thank you, O Jane, for quite literally getting me into
Oxford. Had you not favoured my education with your interest and
sagacity, I would now be a 3–O-levelled wretch with little to
commend me. I have a huge debt to you which I shall work off by
being an ever-dutiful step-son.

By the way, the idea of commuting to Brighton thrice-weekly
sounds fine to me, but that limber elf, the celebrated hobbiegobbie, takes a more cautious line. I see his point, or rather mine,
but I think staying in Brighton for 6 months of solid . . . [The
present letter is incomplete, so this is definitely the time and the
place to clarify the structural function of these letters, what with the
author's sudden and florid reOsricization (the symptom, now, not
of torpor but of pride). Down in Brighton there had previously
been an auxiliary English master (it was usually the Goblin who
gave us our Shakespeare, Coleridge, Lawrence), and he had fingered
me, I felt, for an anti-talent – a powerfully facile anti-talent, but an
anti-talent. What was his name? A disappointed, passionate,

longsuffering being, with an air of intelligent melancholy; if they
had made a film about this man, then only Denholm Elliott could
have played him. In an essay on Wilfred Owen I wrote something
like: 'To extricate himself from the Georgians, Owen needed the
Great War; as a poet he was animated by the shocks and
amazements of great suffering.' Denholm Elliott had underlined the
last seven words and suggested: 'Why not just say "it"?' With Osric
here, what we are seeing is the first pass, the first lunge at language.
Always a painful sight – but ignore it. Structurally, that's what these
letters are for: to allow the reader, hard-pressed by the world as it is,
to enjoy a few moments of vacuity, of luxurious inanition, before
coming to the matter ahead.] . . . erchiefs for Xmas. Deeply moved,
I reciprocated the gift with a featherweight gilt-edged mirror which
is doubtless the pride of that good housewife's home.

Life here at 108 with Monk and Sarg is all very well but I can't
help feeling that it would be enhanced by your presence. What's
your game? Only 2 months though.

I saw "Darling" the other day and Rob said that he fancied that
Jane must have looked like Julie Christie 10 years back. Anyway, *he*
meant it as a compliment.

See you in March,
All my love,
Mart XXXXXX

P.S. Dad: thought your poems were fucking good. Especially
'A.E.H.', which I know by heart. Extremely moving, and I think
that the Nemo one★ is very funny.

★ 'L'invitation au Voyage', from *A Look round the Estate* (1967).

The Problem of Reentry

In November 1994 I lost my face. It was something I was very attached to, and we went back a long way. And it seemed to me that I was changed, transformed utterly.

The reality wasn't as bad as I thought it looked. My face did not much resemble that of Albert Steptoe, the senior – the resoundingly senior – ragman in the early proletarian TV soap, *Steptoe & Son*, whose characteristic expression was a kind of embittered, split-level munch. Nor had my mouth become crimplike with countless vertical nicks. I also had the choice of two impostors to impersonate. When I wore the Clamp I looked like a minor extravagance from the island of Doctor Moreau: half man, half rabbit, and all geek – the male lead in *Revenge of the Nerds*. When I didn't wear the Clamp I looked . . . My face seemed to me, not vacant (far from it), but strangely vacated. And when and if I opened my mouth before a mirror there was that void, that tunnel to oblivion. In addition, my eyes, I thought, showed the knowledge of that tunnel, and of what it meant.

With the return to London I now had to negotiate the problem of reentry. To meet everyone anew, to meet their half-averted gazes anew. There it was, and I didn't have a choice. I had to see my sons and they had to see me: I knew what lay ahead. Experience told me this.

During the summer term of my second year at Oxford I received a visit from my mother – at the time an elusive and nomadic figure. She was recently back from a two-year stint in America, with her second husband,* and would soon be off to Spain, where she would

---

* Professor D.R. Shackleton Bailey, a.k.a. Shack – though the former appellation is the more descriptive. Shack is still a world-class authority on Cicero. He was, moreover, I always thought, the diametrical opposite of my

meet her third.* Mum was, as she put it, 'flush', having made an entrepreneurial killing in Ann Arbor, Michigan, with the fish–and–chip shop called Lucky Jim's. She had brought my sister Sally with her and a celebratory bottle of Asti Spumante . . . My mother has always had eccentric taste in drinks, unable, for instance, to get through a glass of dry sherry without adding a couple of sugars to it; and her two favourites are Green Chartreuse and a really piercingly dulcet liqueur, violet in hue, called Parfait Amour . . .

It was a lively afternoon, and my mother was volubly proud of her Oxonian Osric. But I felt like an actor in a saddening dream. Because my mother had changed. There had been talk a while back of some sort of terminal showdown with the man she always referred to (no doubt to cheer herself up) as 'Peter Sellers's dentist'. And it had happened. My mother had been Kinched, then Pninned. It wasn't the effect of the change that harrowed me (her prettiness was probably undiminished) but the fact of it. I went cold at the sight of this parody mother. And I felt my heart make a tactical withdrawal from her. Because you'd better not commit too much love to someone who has suddenly become changeable. Mothers, fathers, aren't supposed to change, any more than they are supposed to leave, or die. They must not do that.

✳ ✳ ✳

---

father: a laconic, unsmiling, dumpty-shaped tightwad. I used to say to myself: Mum's had enough of charm. Still, Shack had an interesting head. For twenty years, before he took up the professorship at Michigan, he was the Cambridge University lecturer in Tibetan. And I was once around the place when he experimented, as they say, with LSD. To me he seemed to be on the verge of total freakout for several hours, but he later pronounced himself pleased with the exercise.
* Ali, Alastair Boyd, a.k.a. Lord Kilmarnock: the second great love of my mother's life. I learn from the Eric Jacobs biography of my father that Alastair's title is of the sort I used to have sex dreams about when I was fifteen. No money or anything – but it goes back seven centuries. An earlier, treasonous Lord Kilmarnock was executed at Tower Hill for his part in the Jacobite Rebellion of 1745. 'But for this blot on the family escutcheon,' writes the biographer, 'Alastair Boyd would now be the fourteenth Earl of Kilmarnock.'

[153]

In New York I struggled to be obedient to the words of the gentle Millie; I tried to let my mouth adapt itself to the grotesquely prodigious intruder. I don't want to bore the faithful and patient reader with an encyclopedic account of my sufferings, but I would be shirking my task if I failed to suggest that dental reconstruction goes on for far longer than anyone can possibly imagine.

I was in a new world but I wanted to be back in the old one, with its pitifully ineffectual dental floss, its icepacks and waterpicks – and all the toothache and all the denial. Denial, I believe, has been much maligned; there were paragraphs in praise of that state in the novel I was still tinkering with, *The Information*. I have got a lot of time and respect for denial, and I feel the same way about toothache. Later in the year I would run into my old friend John Gross★ while escorting my sons to Tower Records in the mall that takes up half of Queensway, near where I lived for most of my twenties, surrounded by fireprone hotels, in Kensington Gardens Square. This was the first time I had seen John since his successful double-bypass surgery, and, as the boys shopped or prospected or merely pollinated the shelves, he described the heart attack that introduced the crisis. 'The pain

---

★ John Gross was one of my two significant early editors, along with Terence Kilmartin of the *Observer*. He instilled a rule in me, one I still follow in fictional prose as well as journalism and book reviews. Never start consecutive paragraphs with the same word – unless (I add to myself) you begin at least three paragraphs this way and the reader can tell that you're doing it on purpose. John is right. It looks uglily inattentive, clunking against the eye as well as the ear. I have to say at once that this rule has been ignored by many great writers. Conrad and, of course, Lawrence were insensitive to it. Forster seemed only intermittently aware of it. Nabokov observed it, on the whole and increasingly: there are no para-opening 'reps', as New York magazine editors call them, in *Speak, Memory* or *Pnin*; and when, on pages 107–9 of *Pale Fire*, we get three *He*s followed by three *The*s we know that something (large-scale modulation) is up. Joyce did not observe it in *Dubliners* and the *Portrait*, but places himself beyond inadvertency in the obsessive pages of *Ulysses* and *Finnegans Wake*. The tirelessly fastidious Henry James sometimes faltered, though his paragraphs are of sufficient obesity to muffle both ear and eye (you sometimes have quite a few pages in your left hand when you turn back to check). Early Bellow does not observe it. Later Bellow observes it. The same goes for KA.

wasn't too bad,' he said. 'Bearable. I've had worse toothaches.' And it seemed natural that John should place the toothache at the zenith of civilian, non-mortal pain.

Agreed. I know all about the expert musicianship of toothaches, their brass, woodwind and percussion and, most predominantly, their strings, their strings (Bach's 'Concerto for Cello' struck me, when I recently heard it performed, as a faultless *transcription* of a toothache – the persistence, the irresistible persuasiveness). Toothaches can play it staccato, glissando, accelerando, prestissimo and above all fortissimo. They can do rock, blues and soul, they can do doowop and bebop, they can do heavy metal, rap, punk and funk. And beneath all this anarchical stridor there was a lone, soft, insistent voice, always audible to my abject imagination: the tragic keening of the castrato.

Yes, but at least the toothaches were me, and the Clamp is not me, even though it is trying to live in the middle of my head. It's strange. I'm okay if I'm just sitting there, reading, writing. But talking, walking . . . all public interactions immediately exhaust me.

Today I accompanied you and your mother Betty on a shopping mission to Union Square (to buy, among other things, football shirts for the boys) and I felt the full force of gravity – I felt it wanting me down there at the centre of the earth. How can these extra few ounces, carried in the mouth, assume the weight of a full army pack (after a twelve-hour march)? The oppression can only be spiritual; it must be of the spirit.*

Everyone is being incredibly nice to me. Your sister's smile is soft. The food your mother cooks is soft. It's a *good* thing that I've always regarded eating as something of a chore, good training, because now every meal is a punishment, every mouthful cruel and unusual. It's a *good* thing that I've never had a discerning palate (often kissing my bunched fingertips over a bottle of corked wine), because now I don't have a palate at all: my mouth needs ten seconds to distinguish between sugar and salt.

But that isn't it.

---

* It is physical, too. I have since read that nausea is itself exhausting. The body's struggle with it is exhausting.

The Clamp gives me the impression that something is holding my mouth in *its* mouth. But that isn't it. And never mind all the gagging and retching, as compulsive as a fit of the hiccups, nor the sudden Niagaras of drool. For several years I didn't go to the dentist's. Now the Clamp makes me feel that I am at the dentist's all day long. And all evening, too. And then it sits there in the glass, confronting me with its snarl or sneer.

Soon I must go to London and show the boys my face.

Dunker Castle

I first made front-page news when my age was in single figures. The banner headline of South Wales's premier evening paper (it was the *Evening Post*, I think) ran as follows: THE SAGA OF THE AMIS BOYS.

It turns out that I am a much more anxious parent than my mother ever was. I once spent half an afternoon – Spain, a picnic, I was a childless twenty-eight – standing with my arms outspread under one tree or another in case Jaime, then four or five, fell out of it. My mother looked up from her sandwich, and flicked a hand backwards through the air.

– I let him do *everything*. I let *you* do everything.

She did. She let us do everything. We spent all-day and all-night car journeys on the roof rack of the Morris 1000, the three of us, in all weathers, slithering in and out while my mother frowned into the windscreen . . . I don't think we did this when our father was in the car, and he was perhaps in general rather more cautious. As for the decisions leading up to the saga of the Amis boys, well, he wouldn't need or want to be consulted about a matter to do with the open air. He was in his study. He was always in his study.

The Amis boys, and primarily Philip, put it to their mother that they should canoe alone from Swansea Bay to Pembroke Bay, a distance of several miles west along the (notoriously and, in that direction, increasingly unpredictable) Welsh coast. And my mother said yes. In secret I had always thought this an ambitious plan. I was not exactly emboldened when I saw the height of the sea at our starting point (Swansea Bay was usually much more docile than the others we would pass), and saw also the extreme difficulty we were having in getting the boat past the surf. Repeatedly and brutally the waves rebuffed us until, already half drowned, we were in our slots and paddling, Philip up front, towards the bay's western limb. All went well for several minutes. Then our paddles fell silent as we assimilated an oceanic effect that remains unique in my experience. A violently confused kiloton of water was driving *laterally* along the bay towards us . . . I have seen seas disgracefully tousled and disorganised, in the epilogue of hurricanes, sick-green and crapulent after their atrocious splurge, and meaninglessly milling, flapping, cringeing. The cross-tide we now faced, while formidably muscular, had the same deracinated air as it sidled loutishly towards us. We could have turned back (this was my firm preference); but I knew that Philip would not turn back. On the whole the younger brother has an easier time of it, watching his elder not turning back – going on, into unlit territory, and not turning back. Philip was, as always, positioned ahead of me. But this time I was in the same boat. Staring straight ahead he shouted,

– Goodbye, Mart.

And we paddled at battle speed, at attack speed, at ramming speed into the advancing foam. 'Saga' suggests something endless and arduous (and uncomplainingly Nordic); but those few seconds, as we slapped and bounced our way through, were really the extent of our adventure. That was in any case quite enough for me. Reaping much fraternal disgust, I asked to be dropped off at the next beach along. I called home from the snackbar at Caswell Bay; then I stood on the steps leading up the cliff and watched Philip as he tried, again and again and again, to manhandle the tall canoe over the taller breakers; and each time, with his boat all over him, he came thrashing back into the shallows. His body was untiring; I couldn't see his face but I knew it would have an implacable look on it by now.

At Pembroke Bay my mother and I spent the afternoon vainly scanning the mountainous seascape. And at this point the alarm was raised . . . But let's face it. The *Evening Post*'s front-pager, adumbrating an ordeal of maritime endurance that would have stunned a Patrick O'Brian, was a near-total sell. Because my brother never did get the canoe past the breakers. And all the time the coastguards were unscrambling and the helicopters were clattering down the coast, Philip was drinking Tizer and trying the phone in the snackbar on Caswell Bay.

I felt more embarrassed than flattered by the headline. My position was especially fraudulent, Philip having at least *tried* to go on getting killed.

So the press got everything wrong. But this was the first and last time that it cast me (wrongly) as a hero.

When my parents' marriage broke up, in the Sixties, the newspapers covered it. And when my marriage broke up, thirty years later, the newspapers covered it (with noticeable differences in the journalistic approach). When my father had his teeth fixed, in the Sixties, the newspapers didn't cover it (his teeth weren't in the papers but his new smile was: he had never smiled like that before). And when I had my teeth fixed, thirty years later, the newspapers covered it. My teeth made headlines. But let me tell you something about experience. It outstrips all accounts of it – all ulterior versions. A man having a fullscale epileptic fit on the street corner does not mind about the tittering of nearby children. He is involved in his own triage.

In 1993, over dinner, my father said,

– Say as little as you want or as much as you want.

And I told him about my recent visit to Cape Cod to see my children, and their mother – to whom I had become a stranger, from whom I was *estranged*. The boys sensed that there was a possibility of reconciliation. On the first morning Jacob pushed my coffee cup an inch nearer my right hand and said, 'Enjoying your stay so far?' . . . Five days later, as I prepared to leave, the pond outside the house was obediently reflecting the mass of doom stacked up in the sky. My sons were constructing a miniature zoo on a patch of grass; Louis showed me the little stunt where you dropped a coin down a complicated tunnel and were then issued with your ticket of admission. But I wasn't staying, and they knew it. They knew I was leaving. They knew the thing had failed – the whole thing had failed. I said goodbye and climbed into the rented car.

– I just can't stop thinking about it. I just can't get it out of my mind.

– There's nothing you can do with things like that. You can only hope to coexist with them. They never go away. They're always with you. They're just – *there* . . .

Yes, always available for delectation, and always undiminished in their power. On the nightflight back to London I performed what seemed to me to be the extraordinary feat of shedding tears throughout the full six hours, even during the shallow sleep I kept snapping out of. I wondered about the physiology of weeping: questions of storage and supply. In my delirium I was vexed by the parenthetical thought that there was an indicator flashing in the cockpit, something like the watering-can symbol on the dashboard of a car, telling me that I had at last used up all my spray.

Now another nightflight over the Atlantic, to see the boys. And I was Kinch, I was Pnin, I was the parody father. I was even more estranged.

A brief preamble.

The Swansea-Cardiff train slowed, and came to a contentedly sighing halt. Vaguely the passengers in our car turned to the window, and all conversation likewise halted – but on the instant, like a radio suddenly unplugged. We stared at each other and looked out again. If this was a hallucination, then the hallucination was shared. What we saw out there was a simple arrowed sign directing sightseers to a place called Dunker Castle . . . At the time I was eleven years old, and excitedly bound, with two schoolmates, for Cardiff Arms Park, there to watch an under-21 rugby international. I was probably meant to be too young to know that 'dunker', in South Wales and perhaps elsewhere, was slang for 'condom' . . . There was a young man sitting opposite me: collar and tie, curt haircut. I will never forget the serious, sorrowful frown that slowly invaded his face, and the recoil of hurt disbelief with which he said (as if registering a crucial solecism in the order of things), 'Dunker *Castle* . . .?' My friends and I were feigning innocence: we were trying not to burst out crying with laughter. But the young man spoke for all of us, and eloquently. Dunker *Castle*?

On the day of my return to London, in November 1994, I had two teeth-related chores to get through, which in a way felt about average, because my most recent stretch of time in New York, when the Clamp was making me feel I was at the dentist's all the time, I was also, in actuality, at the dentist's all the time, being fitted and finetuned by Mike Szabatura, for the denuded upper jaw, and being scoured and scraped by Todd Berman for the dreadful sink of the lower.* I am, at this point, as I step off the plane, dry-eyed, but stunned and deafened by it all, and wraithlike, and drastically gaunt. Still, I had had some good news in a setting where so much bad news has come my way: at the dentist's. The tumour in my chin (this will be excised next month) is almost certainly non-cancerous, and is very likely unexotic. And the costly catscan has revealed, in my maxillo-facial surgeon's words, that I have 'a *great* lower jaw', adequate, with the aid of a frontal bone graft, to receive the titanium implants.

Remarkably, my two dental trials, on Day One of Reentry, did not involve my being at the dentist's. One trial was comic, the other tragic in coloration, and both were rites of passage. But there it was and I didn't have a choice.

Put simply, the first trial featured an exchange of money for goods: the maiden acquisition of a dentrifice with which only my very oldest readers, I think, will be tolerably familiar. It is trade-marked Steradent and comes in tubes. The tablets, in contact with warm water, give off a festive fizz; and it is in the resulting solution

* During the gluey cast-taking procedure, at Mike's, I was obliged to sit for a few minutes with what felt like a coating of tasteless bubblegum in my mouth. Whereas Joyce and Nabokov tell me, down at the tooth club, that *they* had to spend half an hour, twisting and retching, under a throatful of puréed rotten eggs – the favoured flavour of such concoctions in their dental era.

that the Clamp, overnight, will sneeringly wallow . . . As I geared up for the job – indeed, as I circled a couple of plausible outlets – I realised that this business sharply reminded me of another business: buying condoms for the first time, thirty years ago. It was the type of connexion you initially make, not with the mind, but with the body: the same feeling, the same chemical disposition. And it made me give a groan of defeated laughter. Because the earlier initiation was one of potent arrival, prefiguring insuperable treats, whereas the second – well, the second was all travesty, and pointed in the other direction with its mottled and rigid thumb. Otherwise, though, the similarities were hard to shirk.

(1) You will try to make sure that the chemist who serves you is a man and not a woman and certainly not a young woman. (2) You will hang around for a long time staring at hairsprays and deodorants until the chemist's is empty, but in both cases, as you commit yourself to the till, a coachload of silent eighteen-year-old girls will come through the door. (3) You will of course buy something else too, as a (ridiculous) diversionary tactic. Products altogether unrelated to the contraband you seek. No Vaseline or Philisan (which, Kingsley used to say, fiftified the over-forties). Innocent things like shampoo or vitamin C (but not E). (4) You will endeavour to give the impression that these articles are not for your own use: you are the mere errandboy of a shadowy satyromaniac or nonagenarian. You may even brandish a list, and mutter, or consider muttering, something about the indolence of your older brother or the forgetfulness (and immobility) of your poor old gran. (5) Whatever happens, you will leave the shop with your face burning.

Also, of course, you will go to a chemist's you have never visited before, in the present case a dank little joint which I enter to the tinkle of a bell. True, the cashier is a woman, a milky-haired old dear, but otherwise the place is perfect for me. Outside on the pavement, like a poem of poverty, stands a senior citizen in warped gymshoes and *flared trousers*; and inside it just gets better and better, unreconstructed, practically pre-war, all coughdrops and corncutters and flesh-toned gauze, and the air thick with the smell of decaying penicillin. No sunglasses or beachbags to attract the young and healthy. Only the desperate necessities of lumpen self-maintenance – plus a Prescriptions counter for those customers who, in that fearful phrase, find themselves 'under the doctor'. To the side, entirely dominating the dental-care section, stands a shrine of Steradent, which is represented in three flavours.

The shop stayed empty as I picked out a few manly items – razor blades, an elbow support – and moved to the till, pocketing my list. In a few seconds this would be over. Now I faced the old lady. And noticed that something strange was happening to her eyes: delighted dilation.

– You're Martin Amis! Oh. Oh. My nephew. My nephew thinks you're just . . . Jim! Jim!

Jim was the jovial old soul in the stall behind Prescriptions. I wrote out and autographed an encouraging note for the nephew (an aspiring writer – and, again, good luck to you) on the back of an order form. Then I came out on to the street with my face in flames. But the old pair had been sweetness itself, and I was laughing, too, at fate's casual brilliance. *That* never happened in the old days of the condom. I wondered how, say, child star Macaulay Culkin managed, in these ever more condom-conscious times. Perhaps he got his dad to buy them for him. As Kingsley once did for my brother and me, and with a broad hand.

That night I plopped a tab of Steradent into the glass, and, too elderly itself, perhaps, it didn't work. But the next one did, causing the Clamp, still within me at the end of a long day, to give a brief and enfeebled leer.

Both my parents kept an unvaryingly impeccable distance from the love lives of their children. My mother did so instinctively, but with my father I felt it was also a result of considered policy. At the house in Maida Vale a girlfriend of mine, searching for the bathroom, stumbled in on Kingsley and Jane, waking them in the early hours. The next morning I gingerly picked up the note that was waiting for me outside my door. Written in my father's hand, it said: 'Your friend is very welcome to stay for breakfast. Just be discreet with Mrs

Lewsey.'* In fact my girlfriend had been anxious about spending the night, and I was uncertain too, and she hadn't stayed. So I wasn't just being excused: I was being sympathetically notified of a new freedom. This was clarifying.

– What's so funny?

– I've just come to the bit about masturbation.

The year is now 1995, and I am lying, for a brief moment, on a patch of grass in a London park, looking again at Kingsley's *Memoirs*, while my sons, perched on rollerblades, totter past, and now pause.

– And?

– When Kingsley was your age his father told him that it 'thinned the blood and the victim eventually fell into helpless insanity'.

– Did he?

– Yes. And by the way, it doesn't.

– Good.

That was the only sex tip ('which he topped up every so often') Kingsley ever got from William Robert Amis. And before 'you start grinning, reader, if that is what you feel like doing,' KA goes on, '. . . a chum told me how at his school each class as it approached puberty was taken on a little tour of the supposed masturbation-mania ward of the local mental hospital', where real schizophrenics and manic-depressives were passed off as average veterans of self-abuse. My father claims, in his memoir, that he was 'sensible enough' not to believe such warnings, and I think he really did survive the prevailing conspiracy of hypocritical deception and menace, a phenomenon that today we can only interpret as hatred of youth. Or maybe the whole thing was an awful game played by disappointed mediocrities, my grandfather somehow persuading himself that if he had 'left himself alone' in his youth he might have aspired to more than a senior clerkship in the City, and of course he would be wanting better for his boy . . . It seems fair to say that the relationship between father and son never recovered from the former's aggressive mystification on sexual matters. It wasn't that Kingsley needed hard information on

* Domestic treasure and culinary anti-talent. Even the cups of instant coffee she sometimes kindly brought round were not just undrinkable but also (the household agreed) unrecognisable.

[163]

the birds and the bees. 'Sex instruction in the home', as he says, '. . . is not instruction but a formal permit'; and 'it must be given'.

Kingsley would go on to tell the following birds-and-bees joke to his sons, and I would duly pass it on to mine . . . The farmer's wife says to the farmer: 'The time has come for you to tell our George about the birds and the bees.' The farmer drags his feet: 'Ah come on, love. I mean, it's a bit embarrassing for a bloke . . .' But finally he accedes. The hot afternoon, father and son alone in the glade, the twisting coils of birdsong, the murmur of innumerable bees. 'George. The time has come for your dad to tell you about the birds and the bees.' 'Yes, Dad.' 'You know what you and me did to them girls in the ditch last Friday night?' 'Yes, Dad.' 'Well the birds and the bees do it too' . . . My opinion of this joke, as a joke, fluctuates, I find. But I won't forget my younger boy's response to it: a full three seconds of stunned assimilation before his first voluptuous shriek.

In 1943, by which point Kingsley was a 21-year-old Oxford undergraduate and a lieutenant in the army, William discovered that his son was having an affair with a married woman.* It is depressing work, trying to imagine the 'explosion' this caused in the Amises' straitened suburban cottage. And six years later came William's prideful boycott of the wedding of my parents. On that occasion Mummy A., Rosa (in my memory she is just a dark presence, richly embroidered, aromatic, calorific), managed to talk him round. But she herself was hardly a free spirit – scowling over the garden wall, for instance, when a neighbour used the word 'honeymoon' in front of her child, who was then fourteen. In general William and Rosa couldn't have 'restricted my choice of friends', Kingsley writes, 'or my chances of seeing them, more unflaggingly if there had been a long family history of male prostitution or juvenile dipsomania'. My father loved his mother without much complication, as things turned out; but I never saw him altogether easy in the company of my grandfather.

Whom I remember as a sallowly handsome man, and

---

* And this was no casual dalliance. It was KA's exaltedly melancholy first love. See 'Letter to Elisabeth', which opens his Collected Poems.

conventionally dapper – though the sallowness may be just a back-formation from my memory of his last hours, when he glowed dull orange with jaundice. He spent a good part of his widowhood (1957–63) as a member of our household – to Kingsley's vast inconvenience, I now realise – and a considerable fraction of that time keenly and inventively and rather sternly playing with my brother and me. I admit without reservation that he was one of the grand passions of my childhood – so much so that he once reduced me to a tantrum of misery when he found himself maintaining that it was 'natural' to have 'more feeling as a grandfather' for the first-born son. As far as I was concerned it wasn't a question of what was *natural*. This was a question of love: of insufficiently requited love. He tried to soften it but he wouldn't unsay it; he wouldn't bend to the severity of my distress . . . After the year in America he grew restive and moved back to London. And on his frequent and still yearned-for visits he would puzzlingly bring along a garish and garrulous ladyfriend.

Then it ended. I mean love ended: my love. I didn't feel it leave, but I remember the instant when I knew it to be gone. All that day, in Cambridge, my mother had been putting it about that a secret treat awaited me: a treat of the first echelon. Late in the afternoon we drove to a mystery destination (in fact Peterhouse, my father's college), and there, at the gates, stood the suddenly and hopelessly and utterly inadequate figure of Daddy A. I missed only half a beat before I leapt out of the car and embraced him. But in that single pulse of time I experienced a physical thud of disappointment and surprise. Daddy A. *used* to be a treat of the first echelon. He just wasn't any longer. I was thirteen, unlucky thirteen; and grandparents, at thirteen, are (alas) among the childish things you have to put aside . . . A year later he died of cancer, a couple of months before Kingsley left★ and Cambridge turned into a morgue of dead or departing animals. Philip and I were taken to the nearby nursing home for what was clearly a final visit. I am glad, now, that I was out of love. The awful rictus of

---

★ I wouldn't want to venture any connection between the two events. But the death of the father (and maybe particularly the death of that father) does embolden you, among other things.

his attempted smile, the eyes bright against the kippering jaundice, like a backlit pumpkin on Halloween. In private my brother and I were nervously callous about the experience – about Gramps. Or about death. Perhaps, too, my young heart still hurt from that day when I felt my love was scorned.

And when I felt, moreover, the fantastic obduracy of the man. He tried to soften it but he wouldn't unsay it. He wouldn't bend. He wouldn't tell a salutary white lie to calm a sobbing, squealing, supplicating child.

'You're like Kingsley,' I said to my son (the elder) as I drove him somewhere or other in the car. I continued,

– You're one of those people who can never admit they're wrong.

– Yes and *you're* one of those people too.*

Yes and Kingsley was one of those people and William was one of those people. 'As I came to sense the image in which my father was trying to mould my character and future,' says the memoir, 'I began to resist him, and we quarrelled violently at least every week or two for years.' And I can see it, I can hear it, like a bad marriage, Gramps, who wielded so little power in the external world, attempting by mere iteration to impose his will, and Kingsley, cleverer by many magnitudes, coming to learn that he could dominate the dance. In the end my grandfather simply persecuted my father with boredom (and what other novelist, since Dickens, is so mesmerised and then energised by 'the burning sincerity of all boredom'?). I think love was there on Kingsley's part but it was forced underground. Eventually it surfaced in a poem, a modest elegy straightforwardly called 'In Memoriam W.R.A.' and subtitled 'ob. April 18th, 1963'. When I read it and became more fully aware of it, I felt that something misaligned, something corrugated had been straightened out between my grandfather and me, too. But I don't think I caught the self-criticism, amounting to a delicate self-disgust, in the poem's last lines (having to do with emotional indolence, with resentment and obstinacy, and

---

* A couple of days later I said, 'I let you win *that* argument. The one in the car.' And he admitted it: tactically only, the argument in the car might have been a good one to lose.

with the Amis paralysis). The long argument was finally won – by mortality. The poet finds such an outcome banal, and the slightly perfunctory air he assumes is an acknowledgment of that. 'In Memoriam W.R.A.' ends with the 'I' of the poem imagining

> The on-and-on of your talk,
> My gradually formal response
> That I could never defend
> But never would soften enough,
>   Leading to silence,
>   And separate ways.
>
> Forgive me if I have
> To see it as it happened:
> Even your pride and your love
> Have taken this time to become
> Clear, to arouse my love.
> I'm sorry you had to die
>   To make me sorry
>   You're not here now.

Over dinner at Biagi's in the summer of 1965 Kingsley established that both his sons were sexually launched. He did this cheerfully and encouragingly and almost gloatingly. A day or two later he took us out to lunch in Soho and it was one of those times when he was comically extravagant while also being continuously subversive. 'Dad's great,' my brother and I said to each other, as we always did and still do. But I remember saying (or merely thinking), He's just thrilled we're not queer.* I was wrong, I think. A promiscuous man,

---

* Which is a bit early for me to be ascribing reactionary prejudices to my father. Osric tended to parrot Kingsley in those days, disgracefully (though very loyally) toeing the line, for example, on the Vietnam War. It didn't last. And I was no longer a hawk by the time he started recommending the involvement of British troops – men unincapacitated by hashish, if any could be found. We argued about Vietnam for the next thirty years.

and a promiscuous man in the days when it took a lot of energy to be a promiscuous man, Kingsley was excited by his contiguousness to yet more promiscuity. And he was feeling the justified warmth of the man who does not do what his father did, and, instead, becomes for his sons the exact opposite of boredom.

After lunch he led us to an ambiguous little outlet in a side street north of Piccadilly. Some will consider it appropriate that he bought for us there, among the Brylcreem jars and the jockstraps and the hernia supports, a *gross* of condoms: 144. But you have to think about the boys. Like the celebrants in the famous Larkin poem, we had never known success so huge or wholly farcical.* Of course the gift was largely symbolic: it represented the all-clear. But it also represented a saving of £14 12s., and spared us a total of 48 visits to the chemist's.

Kingsley used to tell the following anecdote about sibling rivalry – how he found me, when I was four or five, lying on the stairs in an ecstasy of grief, how he worriedly knelt at my side and, after several minutes, managed to quell my hiccuppy gaspings, my heaving chest. Then he said, 'Easy now . . . What is it?' When at last I could find and shape the words, I said, 'Philip had a biscuit' . . . In another version I reply, 'Philip had one more biscuit than me.' And that was the variant I kept thinking of in the summer of 1965. I couldn't lie down and weep on the stairs: I was turning sixteen. In any event, soon after the day with Dad – surreally soon, it seemed to me – I was back outside the chemist's, palely waiting for my moment, with my three shillings and my three pence.

It belatedly occurs to me that the signpost saying DUNKER CASTLE was not intended to direct you to a castle. It was intended to direct you to a chemist's. That's what chemists are to the young purchaser, scaling this particular rampart: dunker castles. To shore up this theory we need to establish the existence of a sister castle, or rather a sister signpost (with the arrow pointing the other way), directing you to Castle Steradent.

✻   ✻   ✻

* 'The Whitsun Weddings'. *The Whitsun Weddings* was published the previous year, in 1964.

Dental trial two, on Reentry Day One, sounds straightforward enough. I went to see the boys.

Even light things get heavy over time, and heavy things get heavier, and the Clamp was heavy in my jaw, after a heavy day.

There they were and I blustered on, but there seemed to be nowhere good to put my head, no bearable angle, no sustainable elevation.

The boys didn't look at me so much as watch me, their parody father. *That* father has gone; this father has come. Their faces appeared to be flickering. 'Dad. Something's happened to your face.' And I said, Yes, I know. But it is temporary. The change is only temporary.

As is the retraction of your love, I wanted to tell them – which was palpable and could not be evaded. But I couldn't say that. I could only try to imitate myself for a while, to imitate myself, then wish them goodbye and hurry down the steps scratching my hair with both hands.

The Fact of Wounds

Here is KA's 'A.E.H.', the poem I memorised at eighteen and still have by heart. It is a reverent pastiche of A.E. Housman, and it duplicates one of his characteristic effects. Normally better suited to light verse or doggerel, the trochaic meter – tum-ti, as opposed to the iamb's more stately ti-tum – is cast against type, in the service of solemnity.* The first line of the poem is also the personal mnemonic I seem to need for where the sun rises and where it sets.

* It has been suggested, by KA among others, that the preeminent war poet, Wilfred Owen, wrote with peculiar agony and tenderness about fighting men at least in part because of his homosexuality (however inert), and the same could be said of Housman. This seems entirely likely. (As a thought-experiment I tried to rescreen the opening minutes of *Saving Private Ryan* with a female cast, and found I couldn't get very far with it.) Owen also insisted on seeing the adversary, not as a nation or an ideology, but as a convocation of pressed individuals. 'Mental Cases': 'Snatching after us who smote them, brother, / Pawing us who dealt them war and madness'. Or

EXPERIENCE

A.E.H.

Flame the westward sky adorning
Leaves no like on holt or hill;
Sounds of battle joined at morning
Wane and wander and are still.

Past the standards rent and muddied,
Past the careless heaps of slain,
Stalks a redcoat who, unbloodied,
Weeps with fury, not from pain.

Wounded lads, when to renew them
Death and surgeons cross the shade,
Still their cries, hug darkness to them;
All at last in sleep are laid.

All save one who nightlong curses
Wounds imagined more than seen,
Who in level tones rehearses
What the fact of wounds must mean.

And what the fact of wounds must mean, of course, is that God is
absent, or immoral, or impotent.

Lucy Partington converted to Roman Catholicism three months
before her death, and in my view this raises questions of theodicy. It is
naïve of me, no doubt, but very often I find myself reflexively
wondering how the Vatican has the gall to go on standing after the
events following the Christmas of 1973. The kind of convolution
attempted in the closing lines of Graham Greene's *Brighton Rock* ('You
cannot understand, my child, nor can I, nor can anyone, the appalling

---

'Strange Meeting', with the most beautiful of Owen's half-rhymes: '"I am
the enemy you killed, my friend . . . / I knew you in this dark: for so you
frowned / Yesterday through me as you jabbed and killed. / I parried; but
my hands were loath and cold. / Let us sleep now . . ."' Kingsley always
shuddered at that: 'my hands were loath and cold'.

strangeness of the mercy of God') has always been eloquent but inadequate, because it asks us, here, to regard Lucy Partington's murderer as in some sense a divine instrument,★ and this is clearly an impossible notion. On the other hand, there was the feeling, expressed by more than one voice at the memorial service in Cheltenham, that her recent conversion fortified my cousin, so that (as Jane Kamar movingly put it), 'when she went she went with the full power of faith behind her'. And we must try passionately to believe that, just as we try passionately to believe that it was over very quickly: very quickly.

Another speaker at the service, Christina Kiernan, essayed a more ambitious consolation (broadly Buddhist/Hindu in tendency). She explored the intuition that Lucy's 'was a culmination of many lives': 'some people get the chance to . . . clear a lot of debris of lifetimes away, leaving them free to forge ahead next time, or in another layer of life'. We can respond to the poetic boldness of this inkling; and we could adduce an increasingly respectable philosophical theory (many worlds, many minds; or the relative-state interpretation of quantum mechanics), according to which there is a constant proliferation of universes – and, therefore, of other Earths where, perhaps, on the night of 27 December 1973, Lucy Partington safely (no: casually) returned to her mother's house in Gretton. 'I think we should see her life as a life completed,' said Christina Kiernan, 'not as a life disrupted and cut off too soon.' But here I could not follow. There we were, the congregants, so many of us Lucy's contemporaries; and we were all grown up, far advanced along our histories and worldlines. And where were Lucy's years?

This, again, is Elizabeth Webster:

> . . . I said to her, 'now that you are grown up what are you going to do?' and she said, 'I don't mind what I do so long as I do it absolutely to the hilt' – and then I said, 'yes that's fine but

★ Frederick West, childkiller, seeder of nightmares. I use the word murderer in the singular here, controversially yet advisedly. Rosemary West deserves to be in prison for ever, but a belief that she was justly convicted of murder cannot survive a reading of Brian Masters's book, *She Must Have Known* (1996).

where are you going?' and she thought awfully hard, then she said, 'Towards the light . . . Towards the light.'

Everything about her, even her name, pointed towards the light. Given this, I cannot find order or meaning in a darkness so deep and durable.

The death of Lucy Partington represents a fantastic collision (*collide*: 'from *col-* "together" + *laedere* "to strike"'). It is what happens when darkness meets light, when experience meets innocence, when the false meets the true, when utter godlessness meets purity of spirit, when this –

Hi May it your Dad Writeing to you. or lette me have your telephone number . . . or Write to me as soon as you can, please may I have to sort out watt Mr Ogden did to me, my new solicitors are Brilliant I Read What you sead about me in News of the that was loylty you read what Scott canavan sead he had –

– meets this:

> things are as big as you make them –
> I can fill a whole body,
> a whole day of life
> with worry
> about a few words
> on one scrap of paper;
> yet, the same evening,
> looking up,
> can frame my fingers
> to fit the sky
> in my cupped hands.

Letter from College

Exeter Coll.,
Oxford.
Wednesday, 13. Oct. [1968]

Dearest Dad and Jane,

It was really incredibly good seeing you both – I've been feeling really elated ever since. Especially because on that very afternoon I had my tutorial in which Wordsworth didn't say more than half a dozen words to that coy little turd I was telling you about, who, after 40 minutes of bulging his eyes and pouting his lips, tried things like curling up in a little ball, humming nursery rhymes, and gasping at the sunset over the chapel. None of these things had the desired effect – i.e. spending an hour talking about his emotions when he read 'The Exequy".★

The scout† washed the stairs yesterday and the whole staircase smells as if someone has run up and down it pissing on everything having just eaten 8 or 9 lbs of asparagus.‡ It's all very boring just

---

★ By Thomas King (lopsided inverted commas in my m.s.), and not to be confused with Peter Porter's equally great poem, 'An Exequy'. I am horrified to see that the above is an extremely ungenerous pen portrait of someone I became very fond of – someone who, in addition, is now one of my dozen favourite living poets: Christopher Reid. I'm awfully sorry, Chris, but you *were* a rather whimsical figure in those days; and I myself (as I bet you were well aware) was a terrible little guy.

† I.e., a college servant. At Cambridge, until very recently, they called them 'gyps'.

‡ I think this is the only strophe from the Osric archive that found its way into a novel: *The Rachel Papers*.

now because Marzipan (my room-mate [real name: Marzys]) is getting emotional about his work and I feel as though I should be on tiptoes the whole time. *BUT* he had a sort of attack yesterday – stabs in the liver – on account of some chocolate he had eaten. He can't touch spice or drink. Needless to say, I've littered the room with opened packets of ginger biscuits, figs, quince, turkish delight, and other delicacies. He'll be out for a year if it comes back. Take the silly grin off his face.

Thanks again for a fucking good lunch, Love to all, not least Miss Plush,★

Mart XXX

★ Jane's ruby Cavalier spaniel, usually known as Rosie. Plush was the 'surname' on her official pedigree. So there you had it: Plush was a posh *dog*. Rosie wasn't that long out of puppyhood in 1968. She became very right-wing in her middle age, and there is a vivid portrait of her (the Furry Barrel) in KA's *Girl, 20* (1971), where she belongs to the left-wing composer and political maverick, Sir Roy Vandervane.

Permanent Soul

I first met Saul Bellow in the fourth week of October, 1983, when I went to Chicago to write a piece about him for the London *Observer*. As the piece warmed up I said, *inter alia*:

> This business of writing about writers is more ambivalent than the end-product normally admits. As a fan and a reader, you want your hero to be genuinely inspirational. As a journalist, you hope for lunacy, spite, deplorable indiscretions, a full-scale nervous breakdown in mid-interview. And, as a human, you yearn for the birth of a flattering friendship. All very shaming, I thought as I crossed the dun Chicago River, my eyes streaming in the mineral wind.

A young writer, in Belfast, asked me how I could bear to squander 'mineral wind' in a piece of journalism. I don't think I confessed to the truth: it was Saul Bellow's anyway. Now I know how pushy it looks, to quote yourself, but I did relevantly continue:

The present phase of Western literature is inescapably one of 'higher autobiography', intensely self-inspecting. The phase began with the spittle of Confessionalism [in American poetry: Lowell et al.] but has steadied and persisted. No more stories: the author is increasingly committed to the private being. With all sorts of awkwardnesses and rough edges and extraordinary expansions, supremely equipped, erudite, and humorous, Bellow has made his experience resonate more memorably than any living writer.

His experience being primarily, not a matter of divorces and literary-political feuds, but the experience of the immigrant and, more generally, of the permanent soul in its modern setting.

Higher autobiography: I still do believe that in the development of the twentieth-century novel some such fluctuation occurred. And I was well placed to observe it . . . You can always tell when fiction is undergoing evolutionary change: very prolific – though not necessarily very literary – fiction reviewers start complaining about it.* A lot of people complained about the higher autobiography. *I* complained about it. As a reviewer, I hounded Philip Roth through his Zuckerman years. Roth was an extremist, naturally, and also a post-modernist. Writing about writers, writing about writing: his compulsive self-circlings, I felt, were stifling his energy and his comedy. Something was missing: other people.† We may note here too that Bellow was perhaps a modernist but never a post-modernist. His storytelling, as storytelling, is all earnest and no play. His only *ism* is realism. Meditative Realism, or Inner Realism, perhaps.

'What can you reveal about me', Bellow once asked a prospective biographer, 'that I haven't already revealed about myself?' One of the assumptions behind HA, I think, went as follows: in a world becoming more and more this and more and more that, but above all becoming more and more *mediated*, the direct line to your own

---

* The current complaint, which I have already seen a number of times, goes something like: Can we *please* have a moratorium on novels about science! There will be, of course, no moratorium on novels 'about' science. That is where the novel is now heading, to fill a vacuum created, perhaps, by the failure of the sister discipline, philosophy of science, and by the indifference or contempt in which scientists hold it. Scientists don't care what the novel says either. But novelists will almost certainly find themselves moving in here, as the uncontrolled and sharply escalating power of technology goes on annexing more and more of the human space.

† In the paranoid headline in *Portnoy's Complaint* (1969), remember, it was an ASST HUMAN OPP'Y COMMISH, and not a WRITER, who was FOUND HEADLESS IN GO-GO GIRL'S APT. Bellow's heroes are sometimes writers, but they write discursively, not imaginatively. They are thinkers, teachers, *readers*. The fact that Charlie Citrine is some kind of playwright does not seriously affect this point.

experience was the only thing you could trust. So the focus moved inward, with that slow zoom a writer feels when he switches from the third person to the first.★ In 1983 I was finishing a novel, *Money*, which was narrated in the first person by a character called John Self. It would be a ferocious slander of Martin Amis (who was, incidentally, a minor character in this book) if I called *Money* autobiographical. It certainly wasn't the *higher* autobiography. But I see now that the story turned on my own preoccupations: it is about tiring of being single; it is about the fear that childlessness will condemn you to childishness.†

I knew that HA was truly if temporarily unavoidable when I watched my father following down that road, against his inclination, against his past practice, and against his stated principles. He didn't want to go there, but he went. And for me it was like watching him walk around naked. Saul Bellow, much to the furtherance of his spiritual insulation, writes about the self from the perspective of the soul, the permanent soul. Such a perspective was available to my father's poetry but not to his fiction, which is firmly social, quotidian and end-stopped; his world, in a judgment of John Updike's that I cannot get out of my head, is 'stiflingly human'. *Jake's Thing* ends with the hero's shockingly eloquent repudiation of womankind. *Stanley*, the later, post-Jane novel, *begins* with something far more radical: the author's cancellation of his own artistic androgyny. What followed was a book of such programmatic gynophobia that for quite a while it was unable to find any American publisher.‡ That was unprecedented. And so was this: before turning his hand to *Stanley*,

★ My novel of 1981, *Other People*, was written from a woman's point of view in the third person (as was a sizable fraction of *London Fields*). *Night Train* (1997) was written from a woman's point of view in the first person. Immediately, from the opening word ('I'), I felt something closing above my head. I knew I was much deeper in.

† It seems to me almost crassly appropriate that I got married on publication day. My first son, Louis, was published four months later.

‡ There was a muted fuss about this at the time, with cries, or murmurs, of 'censorship'. I of course supported Kingsley, but without any political enthusiasm. I didn't like his new attitude to 'females'. I should add here that I think both novels, especially *Jake's Thing*, have some great pages in them.

Kingsley had abandoned a novel in mid-stream. He abandoned it, he patiently explained to me, because he feared the HA imputation: the central character was homosexual.*

Filial anxiety, I now perceive, was metastasising within me when I went to Chicago in 1983. I wasn't prospecting for a new father, but I was seriously worried about the incumbent. His *life* was now steady enough, in its external dispositions. It was the state of the talent that bothered me. I always knew, pretty much, what my father was up to at the typewriter. His year with the aborted 'Difficulties', he implied, had been like a trek up the Cloaca Maxima; and he had given me a fair picture of where he was heading with *Stanley*. He had always been a contrarian, an unpopularity-courter, in his public dealings. Now he was trying to drag his art into the forum. If his soul was unhappy (and it was), then it couldn't be *his* fault. The world did it. Women did it. This was the new theocracy. There would be no more separation between church and state.

I feared he might be finished. The poetry seemed to be on the point of evaporation, and the novels were beginning to sound like a long argument all ready to continue into the night.† It seemed to me that his strategy was to shed sentiment as he moved closer to death.

---

* He worried particularly – and in my view preposterously – about 'what they would say' at his club. I couldn't believe it. That was supposed to be the *point* of Kingsley Amis: he didn't care what people thought about him. 'Let me get this straight,' I said, gathering my argument. 'You're giving up a year's work because a few old wrecks at the Garrick, who probably think you're also a Northerner [*Lucky Jim*] and a Taff [*That Uncertain Feeling*], may suspect, wrongly, and semi-literately, and against the evidence of all the other books, that you're queer.' '. . . Yeah THAT'S right,' he answered. Only the title, *Difficulties with Girls*, survived, serving for a later book (the sequel to *Take a Girl Like You*). I have since read the original fragment. It isn't without interest or insight, but it has a stalled feel. Maybe the Bateman-cartoon fantasy was KA's cover story for artistic unease. In any case he would return to the homosexual theme.

† *Russian Hide-and-Seek* fails, in part, because it is a bugbear novel: a fantasy that is also a 'warning'. This particular tub-thump went back a long way. Note how the affability of the fiftieth-birthday poem, 'Ode to Me', is unhinged by the Russian bugbear ('The going a good bit rougher/Within the Soviet sphere – /Which means when the bastards are here', and so on).

The indispensable value, romantic love, would therefore have to be exposed as an illusion. "'That slimy tune" I said, and got a laugh,/In the middle of old Franck's D minor thing.' These are the opening lines of 'A Chromatic Passing-Note' (written in the early 1960s). That tune, the poem goes on, had not always seemed so unctuous. In the poet's youth it had sounded like a 'paradigm':

> Yes, I know better now, or different.
> Not image: buffer only, syrup, crutch.
> 'Slimy' was a snarl of disappointment.

And that is what I was preparing to listen to, from here on in. The long snarl.

Saul Bellow was sixty-eight in 1983. Three marriages, three sons, and now a fourth marriage. This marriage too would end. But that's life. We all have *lives*. It was the writing that excited me. Milan Kundera has said that we go on being children, all our born days, because again and again a new set of rules is set before us, demanding decryption. At various stages you think you've got reality halfway straight; then suddenly that knowledge, so laboriously acquired, is of absolutely no use to you. In Bellow the sense of a child's vision is supreme and defining. But it is the *same* child, not a series of improvised or expedient selves.★ And in the novels, as they unfold, we see a man (we see a consciousness)

★ 'To grasp this mystery, the world, was the occult challenge. You came into a fully developed and articulated reality from nowhere, from non-being or primal oblivion. You had never seen life before. In the interval of light between the darkness in which you awaited first birth and then the darkness of death that would receive you, you must make what you could of reality, which was in a state of highly advanced development. I had waited for millennia to see this.' From the forthcoming *Ravelstein*. (Today – 10/6/99 – is the author's eighty-fourth birthday. He is due a call.) Compare Larkin, in 'The Old Fools': 'It's only oblivion, true:/We had it before, but then it was going to end,/And was all the time merging with a unique endeavour/To bring to bloom the million-petalled flower/Of being here.' But the poem continues, contra – or rather *pace* – the Bellovian view: 'Next time you can't pretend/There'll be anything else.'

heading towards death with his eyes open and his head high . . . When I was a child I would sometimes hear my father in the night – his horrified gasps, steadily climbing in pitch and power. My mother would lead him to my room. The light came on. My parents approached and sat. I was asked to talk about my day, school, the games I had played. He listened feebly but lovingly, admiringly, his mouth open and tremulous, as if contemplating a smile. In the morning I talked to my mother and she was very straight. 'It calms him down because he knows he can't be frightened in front of you.' Frightened of what? 'He dreams he is leaving his body.' It made me feel important – up late, holding the floor, curing a grown man: my father. It bonded us. But I always knew how it went with him and death, how personally he took it, how viscerally he feared and hated it.

Transcending the Purely Dental

Someone – Horacio Martinez, most probably – has sent me an article from the Bulletin of the History of Dentistry called 'James Joyce's Ulysses and Dentistry', by Horacio Martinez. Its subheads are, in order, Joyce Appreciated Dental Health, Joyce Abhorred Dental Disease, Joyce Advocated Prevention, Joyce Valued Dental Treatment and Joyce Observed Dental Habits. But I already feel that I am wronging Horacio Martinez, D.D.S. True, he says things like 'it is high time to extend Joyce's readership among members of the dental profession' and 'there is much in the book that transcends the purely dental', but he is not the thunderous literalist that I am in danger of making him seem. He has clearly derived much of the right kind of pleasure from Ulysses, and his quotes, despite an undeviating quality that I suppose would be hard to avoid, are a reliable delight: 'splendid set of teeth he had made me hungry to look at them'; 'He took a reel of dental floss from his waistcoat pocket and, breaking off a piece, twanged it smartly between two and two of his resonant unwashed teeth'; 'His breath, birdsweet, good teeth he's proud of, fluted with plaintive woe'.* Bloom at the chemist's: 'Smell almost cures you like the dentist's doorbell.' To which Sr Martinez appends the remark: 'Joyce may have been one of the many whose fear overpowers pain and rational conviction.' I don't think so. But all in all I applaud the responsiveness of this particular toothmeister. And I challenge Mike Szabatura, and my maxillofacial surgeon Todd Berman, to write as feelingly about the century's key novel.

It is 1994 (but not for much longer) and we have reached that stage in the flight where the excitement of travel (or transfer), if any, has quite evaporated, along with all our internal fluids. The drink and the meal and the movie (all of them much appreciated) have come and gone, and so has the five-minute nap; now we are sourly completing our US customs and immigration forms, and excuse me, please, I must scrabble in the overhead locker for my documents, enabling me to give passport number, flight details and visa-issuance date. In my carry-on bag, I see, is that recent letter from Janis Bellow, posted from the Caribbean, and cheerfully telling me among other things that Saul turns out to have a surprisingly 'delicate gorge' and is being driven crazy by the smell of the neighbours' cooking. We now know that this was an olfactory hallucination: the first symptom of a physiological catastrophe whose outcome is still unclear . . . The passengers are entering the seventh hour: before us lies the great task of rehydration. In Coach, where I ride, we are fully interpenetrated with each other's breath, kiss-of-lifing each other's yawns, giving each other blowdowns of each other's burps and sighs and sneezes. I am coming to New York for a string of dates with Mike and Todd, particularly Todd, who will perform the operation on my lower jaw.

* This footnote is for Joyceans and dentists only. 'Curiously,' writes Sr Martinez, 'when Joyce refers to some not exactly likeable characters, he again points out their teeth, but as if they belonged to animals – animals that have each one of the three masticatory mechanisms of the omnivorous human being, i.e., rodents, the herbivorous, and the carnivorous . . . In three successive occasions we read: "With rats-teeth bared he muttered . . .", ". . . smiling in all her herbivorous buckteeth . . .", and "cynically, his weasel teeth bared yellow . . .".' The page references (New American Library edition) are 249, 433 and 476.

My upper jaw is in my flight bag. In fact I sported the Clamp to the airport and as far as a departure-lounge toilet, but only in case the flight bag got turned over by Security. My mouth was just a good place to hide it: even a stripsearch would have come up empty. The truth is that, unClamped, I look and feel (and eat) much better; it is only the haunting softness of Millie's instruction (about oral 'training') that persuades me to wear the Clamp at all. 'Your teeth look okay again now, Dad,' said Louis, and full love returned; but I was thinking *What* teeth? It appears that I give nothing away. My upper lip is solidly pendulous, altogether atrophied by twenty-five years of not smiling . . . There is a slushy crush outside the British Airways terminal. Everyone is enlarged, fattened, baggy with impedimenta, with winter coats, padded, air-bubbled, taking up a lot of space, all Kingsleysized, and bumping into one another.

When did Horacio Martinez send me 'James Joyce's *Ulysses* and Dentistry'? I can't remember. But the innocent reader will be wondering *why* he sent it. Now, Horacio hails from Argentina, from Buenos Aires. As I type out this fair copy the year is 1999, and I have already publicly celebrated, with Ian McEwan, the centenary of Jorge Luis Borges (just as, next week, I will go to New York to celebrate the centenary of Vladimir Nabokov). 'Horacio *Martinez*' . . . Am I, perhaps, being drawn into a Borgesian maze, a singularity or circularity? Is Martinez, in fact, the *nom de plume* of one of Borges's collaborators or literary scions – for instance, his witty workmate Adolfo Bioy-Casares? The answer is no. Horacio Martinez is on the level. And I am on the mailing list of every dentist in the West.

I arrive at my future mother-in-law's house in Greenwich Village and I call you at home. Then I call Saul Bellow's number in Boston and speak to *his* mother-in-law (and junior), Sonia. The news is cautiously hopeful. He is still in intensive care but the medication has been decreased. He is *struggling* . . . Good. As Saul's youngest son Daniel said, after his septuagenarian father had gone over the handlebars of his bike on a dirt road in Vermont: You're a tough old guy. And that is what he is good at, struggling, fighting, working, working, working.

All the Lovely Times and Jokes

Kingsley said, one summer evening, in about 1975:
  − I'm going to get a gun.
  − . . . What for, Dad? one or other of his sons responded.
And he said it deliberately, like a poem, heavily end-stopped:
  − To fuck up
    Anyone who comes here
    Trying to take my stuff.
He was in the three-acre garden of the house on Hadley Common. Perhaps he was actually walking round its perimeter, in the late afternoon. This was a routine of his, a physical regime, for a short time, and only when the weather was good. It could well have been his first regular exercise since World War II.
  − You're going to get a gun . . .
  − I'm going to get a gun . . . to kill or otherwise *fuck up* . . . anyone who comes here . . . trying to take my stuff.
You would skirt the three descending lawns, which were gently staggered in size and elevation (the first and broadest had at its far end a massively self-sufficient Lebanon Cedar); then you turned left down a narrow and brambly path and came to a five-barred gate looking on to a five-acre field, also part of the property but never used by us − leased out free to two mildly and unflirtatiously lewd local girls and their two horses. Country girls, with rural accents. But this was neither the village nor the city. This was the suburbs, Barnet, a dormitory town on the tip of the Northern Line; and there it lay, beyond the horses, beyond the field, looking well-meaning and decent and sensible (or, as Kingsley put it in *Girl, 20*, 'looking rather serious over the distant treetops, as if someone in particular had once been beheaded outside its church or unique glassware formerly made there'). Suburbia in the Seventies, it seemed, was assuming a strained expression, and beginning to lose its unselfconsciousness about the garden gnomes, the pebbledash semis with names like Hizanherz and Dunroamin, and the all-Aryan golf club . . . Having admired the townlet, we would turn up the broad avenue, walk through the officially 'listed' barn ('full of empty cardboard boxes and pieces of wood shaped for some now

superseded purpose': ibid.) and head on past the conservatory into the paved courtyard – outbuildings, the gravel drive, the housekeeper's cottage, and Lemmons itself, mainstream Georgian, with its two staircases and its twenty-odd rooms. The most plutocratic item on the whole estate was the lawnmower: it had double headlamps and a pushbutton cigarette-lighter. So, in those days of conspicuous strikes and squats and students, Kingsley felt that he had much to defend – house, wife, and a vein of form that had given him *I Want It Now*, *The Green Man*, *Girl, 20*, *The Riverside Villas Murder* and *Ending Up*, plus a respectable clutch of poems, between 1969 and 1974.

How much did it mean to him, the high-bourgeois splendour? Quite late on in their marriage Jane wrote a magazine piece saying that her husband had less interest in money or his surroundings – 'or, indeed, in acquisitions of any kind' – than anyone she had ever met. I agree; but it turned out to be more complicated than that. Readers, and reviewers, of KA's *Memoirs* could be forgiven for questioning such a verdict on his character. That book hauls various acquaintances out of obscurity to denounce them for unshared restaurant bills and even for unbought rounds in the pub.★ 'It can't just be the money, can it?' asked Ian Hamilton in the *London Review of Books*. No, it wasn't the money; or, rather, it certainly wasn't *just* the money. But it was something he minded about more and more. Later, much later (it was at one of our last suppers at Biagi's in, probably, 1994), I lost patience and attacked him about it. For a couple of weeks he had been anticipating a lunch with one of his best and oldest friends who, Kingsley claimed, derived pleasure from never paying. That same night, as he came slouching into the restaurant, he had, I thought, a ragged and feral air about him. It had been building up in me and the argument was already there in my mind. I said,

★ For example (and I would have been sorry to lose this): 'When the drinks came, [the novelist Andrew] Sinclair [who already owed him one] plunged his hand confidently into his top inner breast pocket. As in a dream I watched that confidence vanish in an instant, to be as quickly replaced by puzzlement, disbelief, consternation. Soon he was doing an imitation of a free-falling parachutist frenziedly trying to locate his unpulled ripcord. Finally his movements slowed, ceased, and shame possessed him. "I must have left my wallet in my other jacket," he said.'

– Look at you – you're a fucking wreck. Who paid for lunch?

– *I* did.

– And you let it poison your whole day. Your whole week. Instead of having a nice time with your old pal. It's not *worth* it, Dad. You're the loser twice over. When I go out with Rob, I pay for everything. He says, 'Just pretend I'm a chick.' And I do pay for everything and I give him twenty quid for his taxi home. And I don't mind.

– Yes but Rob *couldn't* pay for anything even if he wanted to.

– So? It's like with the Hitch when he used to say, 'Whose turn is it to pay for me?' Some friends *do* get pleasure from dodging a bill. What you should do is indulge them. Anything's better than the suffering you go in for. Look at you. Christ. In its own way your attitude to money is as sick as your friend's.

Head quivering, voice quivering, the forefingernail of either hand seeking the cuticle of the thumb, he said, with genuine contempt,

– . . . *That's exactly what I* EXPECTED *you to say.*

Because, by his lights, I was young, modern, ignorant, corrupt; because I didn't revere or even recognise the values that he had been shaped by (values that were now recrudescing, in old age). Kingsley was a child of the low-church work ethic.* Dodging your share made you an idler or a niggard. More than this, though, it was secular sacrilege. And it rendered you *unmanly*.

That night we made peace, symbolically, over the bill. (We always made peace.) Kingsley tried to pay, although it wasn't his turn. My credit card firmly but gently prevailed.

It now seems to me that my father was lucky to survive that lunch of his. In the climactic scene of *The Old Devils*, the hero, Alun Weaver, is socialising with others at the house of a friend, Garth

---

* 'I cannot claim to be more honest and responsible and thrifty and industrious than most people, but I'm pretty sure that I would be less distinguished in these fields if I had been brought up quite outside the shadow of the chapel' (*Memoirs*). I have just remembered the following incident. When I was about sixteen I was seriously undercharged for a packet of cigarettes in a newsagent's. Hearing me crowing about this, my father took me back to the shop and looked on as I returned the money. I humoured him in what I took to be a ludicrous piety. Now I marvel, not at the piety, but at the energy.

[185]

Pumphrey. The first drinks are handed out, and then the host produces a pocket calculator. Alun speaks up sarcastically:

'Mind you don't forget to add on the cost of the first round.'

At this Garth moved the calculator aside, though not far. 'I regard that as distinctly uncalled for, Alun,' he said in a sorrowful tone. 'If not downright gratuitous. Those first drinks were not a *round* in any sense of the word. They were my freely offered hospitality. Good God, man, do you take me for some kind of Scrooge?'

Instantly Alun choked on his first large sip of whisky and water. Coughing with marked violence he shakily clunked his glass back on the sideboard, strolled a pace or two and went down sprawling with most of his top half across one of the sofas and his legs spread out on the thin carpet. This seemed even for him an unusually thorough imitation of a man collapsing with rage or revulsion . . .

Alun was breathing loudly and deeply through his mouth in the guttural equivalent of a snore. His eyes were wide open and to all appearance focusing, though not on Charlie or Peter, nor on Garth when he too bent over him. In a low voice but quite succinctly he said a couple of meaningless words and his mouth moved. Then his eyelids drooped and he stopped doing anything at all.

For many years I thought that Kingsley dishonoured Jane – and himself – when he turned revisionist about the strength of his feelings for her. He tried to rewrite the past, to unperson, to unlove; and you can't do that, or so I believed. His early letters to Jane, which I have now seen, are, in at least two senses, enviably eloquent on the power of the initial attraction.★ It was the sort of thunderbolt that fills the world with sudden colour. The evocations of the physiology of love in *The Anti-*

★ In one passage Kingsley describes how he silenced a room at a party in Cambridge in 1963. Everyone present was asked to list the things which, in the course of their lives, had least disappointed them. People talked of children, of work, of travel. When Kingsley's turn came he said, 'Love.'

Death League (1966) and *I Want It Now* (1969) caused at least one reader to murmur, with generalised humility and respect, 'God. Dad really has it bad.'* And for a long time the household had the confidence and humorous liberality that gathers itself around a dynamic marriage. In Maida Vale we all used to have breakfast together in the master bedroom (where, in addition, you could smoke). Sometimes I or my brother looked in too early. Philip used to do a very good imitation of our father being surprised in the act of making love: the lips were of course crenellated in concentration, but the voice was perfectly calm – 'Just hang on a while, would you, old boy?'

I once wrote, and still believe, that love has two opposites. One is hate. One is death. The notion may well have been planted in me by *The Anti-Death League*, which aggressively confronts the fact that love re-alerts you to death, and all suffering, and all mortal injustice. This is an uneven book (too much plot, too much dialogue, too much protocol); but it is something of a coup, I think, to have a whole novel turn on a *poem*. The poem is anonymously and subversively sent to an army clergyman, Major Ayscue, who is stationed at a secret base committed to the deployment of biological weapons. Its title is 'To a Baby Born Without Limbs', and its narrator is God:

> This is just to show you whose boss around here.
> It'll keep you on your toes, so to speak,
> Make you put your best foot forward, so to speak,
> And give you something to turn your hand to, so to speak.
> You can face up to it like a man,
> Or snivvle and blubber like a baby.
> That's up to you. Nothing to do with Me.
> If you take it in the right spirit,

* Catharine steps out into the street: 'She looked so beautiful in her white dress and white hair-band that Churchill had an instant of sincere puzzlement at the way the passers-by went on passing by, the farmer climbing into his estate wagon over the road failed to reverse the direction of his climb and come pounding across to cast himself at her feet, the man laying slates on the roof of the barber's shop managed to stay aloft. Churchill put his arms round Catharine and kissed her' (*The Anti-Death League*).

You can have a bloody marvelous life,
With the great rewards courage brings,
And the beauty of accepting your LOT.
And think how much good it'll do your Mum and Dad,
And your Grans and Gramps and the rest of the shower,
To be stopped being complacent.
Make sure they baptise you, though,
In case some murdering bastard
Decides to put you away quick,
Which would send you straight to LIMB–O, ha ha ha.
But just a word in your ear, if you've got one.
Mind you DO take this in the right spirit,
And keep a civil tongue in your head about Me.
Because if you DON'T,
I've got plenty of other stuff up My sleeve,
Such as Luekemia and polio,
(Which incidentally your welcome to any time,
Whatever spirit you take this in.)
I've given you one love-pat, right?
You don't want another.
So watch it, Jack.

The deliberate illiteracies ('whose', 'snivvle', that little sprain of mis-punctuation shortly after 'Luekemia') are explained away in the novel as a smokescreen (part of the author's attempt to disguise his identity). But I think they are also intrinsic to the style of the dramatic monologue, and make this one of Kingsley's best poems. Here we have the voice of omnipotent evil, but also the voice of atrocity, with its brutish facetiousness, its clunking puns. Here we have the 'murdering bastard' who can't even spell, who can't even parse, who can't even *write*★ . . . Perhaps the most revealing thing my father ever

★ In *The Anti-Death League* the chaplain, Major Ayscue, turns out to be no ordinary man of God. He reveals himself as a kind of tortured Manichee, declaring, for instance, that 'to believe at all deeply in the Christian God, in any sort of benevolent deity, is a disgrace to human decency and intelligence'. All the same, his spiritual hunger is palpable. Towards the end Ayscue

said was in response to Yevgeny Yevtushenko's question (King's College Chapel, Cambridge, 1962), 'You atheist?' He answered: 'Well yes, but it's more that I hate him.'* Kingsley could never share Saul Bellow's aspiration, that of establishing 'sober, decent terms with death' (death being 'the dark backing a mirror needs if we are to see anything'). It wasn't only that he feared death; he hated it, because it was the opposite and the enemy of love.

Death came to the family, not long after we moved into the house on Hadley Common. Jane's mother Kit, who had been with us for some years, suffered a heart attack in the ground-floor bedroom to which she was by then largely confined. That night, as if for a dare (we wanted the experience, new to us), I and my girlfriend, Tamasin, stole in to look at the body. Now I had never been especially fond of old Kit. And neither, to be sure, had Kingsley. He used to do a lot of writhing and groaning and swearing to sustain himself for his daily visits to her bedside (this was called 'doing Kit'), but make the visits he did. I thought her a snob and a grouch, and felt that she had been a harsh mother, particularly to my sweet-natured step-uncle, Colin. Kit reminded me of the governess Mademoiselle O. (a more extreme case) in *Speak, Memory*, of whom Nabokov writes, in valediction:

> She had spent her whole life in feeling miserable; this misery was her native element; its fluctuations, its varying depths, alone gave her the impression of moving and living. What bothers me is that a sense of misery, and nothing else, is not enough to make a permanent soul. My enormous and morose Mademoiselle is all right on earth but impossible in eternity.

---

offers a prayer, or a plea for leniency, on behalf of a sick friend (Catharine). 'Whenever he had prayed before it had been like talking into an empty room, into a telephone with nobody at the other end.' This time, though, he feels that there is somebody there on the line, 'not saying anything, nowhere near that, but listening. It frightened him rather.' On the last page Ayscue's beloved Alsatian bitch slips her lead outside the church and, 'too interested in something across the street', fails to notice an approaching lorry. The dog is called Nancy. She *is* Nancy, and she is luminously rendered.
* 'Yevgeny Yevtushenko', *Memoirs*.

Kit had, I suppose, been all right on earth. And her permanent soul, if it existed, was now certainly absent. She looked utterly emptied . . . Death is the complex symbol, and ours was a complex reaction to it. Tamasin and I laughed, we giggled, we reached out to each other with trembling hands. Even then I felt a judgment hanging over us. And it came: soon afterwards Tamasin's father, Cecil Day Lewis, then Poet Laureate, would die in this room, would die in this bed.

This room knew all about death and was well-equipped for it (I remember the elaborate and alarming handholds in the adjoining bathroom). Outside was the courtyard and the garden, but this room knew all about death. Day Lewis and his wife, Jill Balcon, went to the house as to a hospice: no other possible outcome. In April 1972 Kingsley wrote to Larkin:* 'Poor old Cecil D L is very ill, dying, in fact, and he will stay with us here until he dies. He's very weak but totally compos and cheerful (Christ) . . . Nobody can tell, of course, but somewhere between a week and a month seems probable.' It was a month. 'I do want to die well,' says a character in Iris Murdoch's *Nuns and Soldiers*: 'But how is it done?' *Contra* Dylan Thomas, it is done by going gently. Cecil went gently. As an admirer (and at one point an imitator) of his earlier, more romantic poems ('Short, short is the time') and, more recently, of his drolly colloquial verse translation of the *Aeneid* – and as a known lover of his daughter – I skirted round the dying Day Lewis. But his equanimity, his stillness, drew me in closer. It was an extraordinary demonstration. He was showing you how you could keep your self-possession, right to the end; you still had your permanent soul. Tamasin came. Daniel came. And the dying got done. These are the last lines of his last poem, 'At Lemmons':

> a bloom of
> Magnolia uttering its requiems,
> A climate of acceptance. Very well.
> I accept my weakness with my friends'
> Good natures sweetening every day my sick room.

* Who wrote, rightly but wrongly, in his last great poem, 'Aubade' ('Postmen like doctors go from house to house'): 'Courage is no good:/It means not scaring others. Being brave/Lets no one off the grave./Death is no different whined at than withstood.'

Earlier in the poem Day Lewis writes of 'the calm a loved house breeds'. That his was a good death is a tribute to him and to Jill, Tamasin and Daniel.* And the fact that we could absorb and assimilate it so frictionlessly tells me, more clearly than anything else, that the house was strong in love.

So my father, during those years, had much to defend. He was indifferent to his surroundings, indifferent to acquisition, but the big spread, as I say, was perhaps his clinching reply to *his* father, in the argument that is never over. For Kingsley, and for all the other writers I have known, prosperity attests to the health of the talent, the strength of the readership, and nothing more. It has not been sought; it can be done without.† To the best of my recollection (Kingsley would have considered that phrase a wooden Americanism, but it has been one of my principles in writing this book, and in such ways does the argument go on), only once did he attempt to be lordly or over-weening: and the result was custard-pie. It is hard work describing real-life slapstick (either it makes you laugh or it doesn't), but I will try to preserve the self-finessing quality of the moment . . . At a noisy lunch in the kitchen, with perhaps a dozen people present, Kingsley was experiencing an unusual difficulty: that of making himself heard.

* Daniel is of course the great actor, and the great *poetic* actor (see, above all, *The Last of the Mohicans*). I often think – though not as often as I'm sure Daniel does – of the pleasure Cecil would have taken in his ascendancy. At fifteen (to my twenty-two) he reminded me of my cousin David. But Dan's ferocious handsomeness was at this time obscured by acne. He liked sweets and sticky buns, and Tamasin, I remember, would indulgently traffic them to him.

† And I already felt the same way. I was growing up and becoming less stupid. Osric, like Kit, like Cecil, was past and gone. In 1974 I quit my job at the *TLS* and went to work on the back half of the *New Statesman*, the organ of the Left whose most famous editor, incidentally, was called Kingsley Martin. Two of my contemporaries there, Christopher Hitchens and James Fenton, were proselytising Trotskyists. They spent their Saturday mornings selling the *Socialist Worker* on Kilburn High Street. I moved to the libertarian left of centre. So my father and I entered our Kingsley Martin, or Kingsley-Martin, period, reliably disagreeing on every issue along (approximately) party lines. This would never change. And I am still having that argument, here in 1999.

I watched him as, again and again, he questingly raised his head and, after a few seconds, theatrically let it drop. He persisted for perhaps a minute and a half. Then he reduced the company to instant silence by slamming his unopened beer can on to the table. It made the cutlery jump. Coolly, grimly, proudly, he surveyed his chastened listeners, and, before at last giving utterance, reached to free the tab of his Heineken. The torrential upsquirt caught him full in the face. And the room re-erupted, with laughter. I thought, This could go either way. But he saw the funny side of it. There was no other side of it to see. He had gone against his nature. For once in his life he had behaved humourlessly; and humour had promptly corrected him . . . Answering a recent query, Lady Violet Powell* said that it was a pleasure to remember these years and 'all the lovely times and jokes'. Yes, exactly, Violet: all the lovely times and jokes. And Kingsley at the centre of everything, like an engine.

– So how's it go again, Dad? You're going to . . .?

– . . . I'm going to get a big gun.

– Oh it's a *big* gun now.

– I'm going to get a big gun . . . to kill, maim or otherwise *fuck up* . . . anyone who comes here . . . trying to take my stuff.

Of course he never did get that gun. And the big house disappeared anyway, and so did love.

---

* Wife of the novelist Anthony Powell. The letter was to Zachary Leader, editor of KA's *Letters*.

Letter from College

Exeter College,
Oxford.
[Easter? 1970]

Dearest Dad and Jane,

Fucking thanks for the lunch Dad (from Ros too).★
Did you see that I won £2 in the New Statesman
competition?† The best experience of my life.

I'm getting quite delirious about my prelims.‡ We won't finish
the course until about a week before the exams (i.e. next week) by
which time I'll have to be conversant with 2 books of Virgil, lots of
Old English texts, lots of Old English grammar, and all of Milton
whom we've only had six months on as opposed to the two terms
everyone else in Oxford has had on him. It's like Brighton all over
again but with no little goblin coming round to tell me what to do.

My only friend [Rob] came up last weekend. His arrival at Ros'
flat was heralded by increasingly panicky half-hourly telephone calls,
but he got here all right. The rise he'd been angling for for so long
turned out to be a cool 5 shillings a week, so he's leaving

★ My girlfriend, Rosalind Hewer.
† An honourable mention for an original idea, lamely executed. At this time
I was going under the name of M.L. Amis. Who started the double-initial
thing? D.H. Lawrence? L.H. Myers (Lawrence's exact contemporary, and
more or less the only other twentieth-century novelist okayed by F.R.
Leavis)? It's more austere: that's the point. It gives less away. M.L. Amis: my
first, but not my second, book review appeared with this by-line.
‡ Preliminary Examinations, sat at the end of the second term.

Biographic to start at the bottom somewhere else. All very depressing.*

How's your novel going Jane? I know what you mean about distractions. I actually find myself wondering whether I've got *time* to make myself coffee in the morning. I'll be *fucking* glad when term's over (15th, if you didn't know).

My love to Col and Sarg but *not* to Rosy who can look forward to 6 weeks of being well-bullied for not recognising me – I'll also do my best to see that she gets raped by a mongrel. See you in 3 weeks,

> Lots of love
> Mart.

P.S. Here are some expenses: Coffee etc – 15 0. Dry Cleaning – 1 15 0. Stationery – 8 0. Lunch (weekends up to end of term) – 2 0 0. Tip for scout – 1 10†: 5 8 0. The money you declined to send me earlier this term – +3 18. The money I owe Dad from when I came down for the day – – 1 0 0. *8 6 0*

---

* Biographic was and perhaps still is a small film company in Greek Street, Soho. Why I should claim to be depressed by Rob's struggles is unclear. Gore Vidal wasn't wrong when he said that it is not enough to succeed: others must fail (especially our friends). This sounds like a vice of sophistication, but I think there's something primitive in it. It has to do with fear of desertion. A couple of years later, Rob's career as an assistant director would seem to me, for a while, to be horrifyingly meteoric. I thought he would project himself out of my orbit. Then he fell – too fast, too far (things started getting out of hand on *The Stud*, an early sex-and-shopping movie starring Joan Collins). Last night (12/5/99) I had dinner with him and experienced a twinge of atavistic disquiet when he told me that his experiments with professional picture-framing were coming along reasonably well . . . I paid the bill. I gave him carfare. I had not moved out of his orbit. But I might have done.
† These are pounds, shillings and pence. Miserably predictably, Osric has tipped his staircase servant twenty-one shillings – or one 'guinea'.

Existence Still Is the Job

1995 did not stand on ceremony. It announced itself, on the first of January, with the prison suicide of Frederick West. (And in death, as it were, he drifts up from the footnotes and into the text.) . . . The act had been long premeditated. He volunteered for the shirt-mending detail at Winson Green, Birmingham. This gave him access to cotton tapes, which he eked out with the hems of his own bedding. He waited for the reduced invigilation of the public holiday. In the morning he played pool, used the exercise yard, and collected his lunch of soup and chops. There was a chair in his cell but it was the laundry basket that he kicked away from under him. A clattering chair might have brought the guards running. The laundry basket would have fallen with an unemphatic crackle.

There has been much speculation about the 'motive' for West's suicide. Was he unable to face his forthcoming trial? Did he despair when Rosemary spurned him after his arrest? One writer has suggested that West's *felo de se* might have been his final 'lust murder', the apotheosis of his addiction to death. But surely the circumstances and details point to a timorous departure. Two of West's children, Stephen and Mae, offer something much simpler and more credible. Mae: 'I always knew he would kill himself in jail. He was terrified, and forever watching his back in case someone had a go at him.' Stephen: 'Dad told me that if he didn't do it, someone in there was going to . . . He was in tears, crying his eyes out . . . [His suicide] was very selfish.'* It is necessary for me to

---

* These quotes are from Stephen and Mae West's book, *Inside 25 Cromwell Street*. Stephen elaborates: 'He was determined to keep out of trouble and

believe it, but I think these comments shore up the view that West was unusually susceptible to fear. He crept towards his death. He cringed out of existence.

When I heard about the suicide I felt shock and some reflexive pity (because suicide sends you a message from ultimate human collapse), but I felt no surprise: nil. Suicide and Frederick West were wholly congruent. Why did he kill himself? It would be much harder to come up with a 'motive' for his going on living. And I also thought something like: to Hell with him and his stark beseeching face. Excise it from the planet.

On the other hand, truth had taken a beating. That was immediately clear, and I could sense the deficit. All his life he had been a colossus of mendacity, the enemy and the opposite of truth.* And he would slander my cousin – from his grave. Suicide constituted his final evasion. Frederick West's brother, John, took his share of the truth with him when he, too, killed himself, in

---

he called everybody Sir. Even the other prisoners when he saw them. I was with him one day when another bloke came by. He was in there for murdering his whole family and Dad said: "Hello, Sir."' I am reminded of KA's poem in *The Anti-Death League* when Mae says of her father's suicide: 'I believe God has split us up and is trying to kill us all. If it's a nightmare then please God let me wake up now.'

* He lied as unstoppably as he stole. Stephen: 'He stole anything he could get his hands on. He was an incredible thieving machine.' Mae: 'At least 99 per cent of the contents of the house were stolen, including the lino on the floor.' It is impressive – it is astonishing – to hear such force of life in these two voices, and in the voice of Anne Marie, the most senior in years, in suffering and in isolation. Well, they had each other: one assumes that they created some kind of alternative world within Cromwell Street. The other children are or were: Charmaine (murdered, along with her mother, Rena, West's first wife), Heather (murdered), and then 'the young kids', Girl A, Girl B, Boy C, Girl D and Girl E, four of whom were halfcastes fathered by Rose's 'clients'. Girl A, Girl B, Boy C, Girl D and Girl E were taken into state care in August 1992, after the Wests were charged with abuse and neglect – eighteen months before the exhumations began . . . Frederick West's lying was chaotic and serendipitous. He would say, for example, that he owned a string of hotels, and had toured the world with the pop star Lulu.

November 1996.* He used the same means as Frederick. He even used the same knot on the noose – taught to the brothers, perhaps, when they were growing up in the Herefordshire village of Much Marcle, by their parents, Walter and Daisy, who also taught them physical and sexual brutality, as they were taught by their parents, in their turn.

I have before me a recent newspaper clipping which begins: 'The mother of [a missing girl, aged twenty-two] said last night: "I cannot close my eyes for fear of what I might see."' Her words have a fundamental eloquence. It strikes you as counterintuitive at first, when you come across it in the literature: the fact that the families of those who have been murdered usually *do* want to know how the victims died. But the reason is transparent. They want to retard or narrow down the swarm of horrors that will present itself for contemplation. Afterwards, at least, when you close your eyes, you know what you are going to see. This is *Pnin* (and Nabokov, we should remember, lost his brother Sergei in the Holocaust: his crime was homosexuality):

And since the exact form of her death had not been recorded, Mira kept dying a great number of deaths in one's mind, and undergoing a great number of resurrections, only to die again and again, led away by a trained nurse, inoculated with filth, tetanus bacilli, broken glass, gassed in a sham shower-bath with prussic acid, burned alive in a pit on a gasoline-soaked pile of beechwood.

On 1 January 1995, I could already feel my questions, my eyes,

* John West died while a jury was deliberating evidence against him on numerous sex offences committed at Cromwell Street. Anne Marie West alleged that, over a period of years, she had been forced to submit to him more than 300 times. Rosemary was sleeping with John too – and with her own father, Bill Letts, who had always been a domestic psychopath. And of course Frederick was regularly raping Anne Marie. It began when she was eight (Rosemary participating in the initiatory torture), and continued until her ectopic pregnancy at fifteen.

my guns, turning on Rosemary. Her committal and week-long
hearing would begin on February 6.

To say that the headline suicide 'brought it all back' is inaccurate and
inadequate, because such things never go away: with such things, as
Kingsley said, you can only hope to coexist; they're just *there* . . . But
it did entrain a new cycle of miserable and directionless meditation –
a quieter version of David's swearing and weeping: cursing and
sobbing and thinking of the dead. It would seem that I was anyway
in poor shape, as the year turned. It would most definitely seem that
I was in poor shape. Notebook: 'If weepy is poor shape, then I'm in
poor shape.' I am easily moved to tears and (for instance) rarely
survive a visit to the cinema without shedding them, racked, as I am,
by the most perfunctory, meretricious or even callously sentimental
attempt at poignancy (something about the exterior of the human
face, so vast and palpable, with the eyes and the lips: it is all writ too
large for me, too immediate for me). But that lachrymose, that
crybaby Christmas was a formative convulsion, new to my
experience. And then came 1995.

In ascending order of seriousness, I was structurally weakened
by various severances (some of them professional as well as personal
and all of them public), by the excruciating sunderings in the
dentist's chair (with their extended lessons, their conferences, on
anno Domini), and by the partings and separations from my wife and
two children over the summer and the autumn. The theme is clear:
partings, sunderings, severances, with the great depth-charge of my
cousin Lucy, with her beautiful but now sorrowful surname.
Additionally, alongside all this, my friend, mentor and hero Saul
Bellow was on a breathing machine in an intensive-care unit with
both his lungs whited out. The source of the massive attack on his
nervous system was still unclear. In the Caribbean, olfactory
hallucinations had given way to the symptoms of dengue fever. His
wife Janis almost had to skyjack him from St Martin to Puerto Rico
and thence to Boston. In hospital he suffered heart failure and
developed double pneumonia. One night he climbed out of bed

and had a fall. His back was so inflamed, the doctor said, that it looked like a forest fire seen from the air. And Saul was almost eighty years old.

Finally there was Bruno: Bruno Fonseca, 1958-1994. Finally there was that moment in New York, when all the lines of grief converged . . . At the end of the dinner – was it, perhaps, on Christmas Eve? – your mother passed round the table a series of drawings she had had bound together: drawings of your brother Bruno as he lay dying. Drawings of Bruno sleeping, staring, waiting, they looked like self-portraits by the ghost of Goya; and there on the last page, most shockingly, was a photograph of Bruno at the age of twelve – his smooth bare chest and arms, his innocently wondering slouch and pout. The slim volume was passed to your father, Bruno's father. All that year Gonzalo had been conspicuous for his composure. As one desolation followed another, I never saw him flinch or weep. He took it; a sculptor himself, he just deepened into the ground like one of his old stones on the hillside. Now I watched him while he leafed evenly through the pages. Gonzalo was faintly smiling in what I took to be acknowledgment of the quality of his ex-wife's technique (a technique maintained against intense emotion). Then, exhaling, he turned to the photograph. Suddenly, sharply, involuntarily, he sucked the air back in through his underteeth. It was the sound you make as a wintry sea slaps your chest, or like the sea itself when a wave starts regathering over sand and shingle. He recovered at once. That was all . . . Later, I would find that thinking about this moment went very heavily with me. It made a disastrous connection. Because it encompassed my own sons (in their limbs and lineaments so like the boy in the photograph), and the matter of thwarted parental love, and all the discontinuities and disappearances of 1994.

Nothing Cures That

Fate, disguised as Michael Ignatieff,* brought Bellow and me back together in London in 1985, where the three of us made a late-night, discussion-type TV programme. Saul and I shared a cab or two. There was a dinner, where we were joined by my first wife, Antonia Phillips. Saul seemed to be travelling alone. I now know that his marriage to the dedicatee of *Him with His Foot in His Mouth* (1984), his fourth wife, was over or ending. But I felt little curiosity about his personal life. I want to say that my feeling for him has always been based on – and formed and constantly refreshed by – literary admiration. That admiration is seldom more passionate than when, in his pages, he 'reads' a human face, a human presence. These readings are no mere impressions; they are visionary and biblical. So at that time I found his gaze testing. I felt tested by it. He could look at my face and tell exactly how much trouble was waiting for me.†

Early in 1987 I was asked to contribute a paper to a Saul Bellow Conference in Haifa, organised by the distinguished Israeli novelist A.B. ('Bully') Yehoshua.‡ My assignment was the forthcoming novel *More Die of Heartbreak*. With my wife I flew to Israel, arriving at the Haifa hotel very late at night, long after the kitchens had closed. I think we got an apple and a tomato out of them. Very early the next

---

* Gratifyingly, the gentle Michael shares a surname with the recurring villain in George Macdonald Fraser's Flashman books, Count Ignatieff, one of the most tirelessly vicious characters in popular fiction. (We shall return to Flashman later, unexpectedly, and in mortifying circumstances.)

† Oh, and I should say that I sent a copy of *Money* to him, too, as well as to Larkin, and his response had deeply thrilled me. But I was still vulnerable to that brown-eyed gaze. The TV programme we had made together was called 'Saul Bellow and the Moronic Inferno'. It occurred to me that Saul was Saul and I was Moronic. Or better say that he had a panoptic view of the modern confusion, and that I was within it, looking out.

‡ Bully's nickname was tremendously well-established, though I never saw the logic of it. In a formal after-dinner speech Shimon Peres would refer to Bully as 'Bully' without feeling the need for any elaboration. Peres was at that time leader of the Labour opposition. As Bellow himself observed in *To Jerusalem and Back* (1976), Peres is so impossibly youthful in appearance that you imagine he subsists entirely on organ meats.

morning there came a brutal squawk from the telephone: I was told that 'the Conference minibooce', even now, was revving in the forecourt. Unfed and half-dressed I journeyed to a university building that resembled a multi-storey bomb shelter and listened to a series of American academics lecturing on things like 'The Caged Cash-Register: Tensions Between Existentialism and Materialism in *Dangling Man*'. Saul was present. He was heard to say that if he had to listen to much more of this he would die, not of heartbreak, but of inanition.* Thereafter, Saul Bellow was not often to be found at the Saul Bellow Conference Centre. (Nor was I regularly seen there.) He was in stalwart attendance, though, on the last day, when I gave my paper alongside the novelists Alan Lelchuck and Amos Oz.

After exulting in the brilliance of the weather, and in the brilliance of the novel, I continued:

Here are further grounds for extreme complacence on my part: Bellow has been reading Philip Larkin. Now the narrator of *More Die of Heartbreak* grew up in Paris at the feet of heavy thinkers like Boris Souvarine and Alexandre Kojève who talked geopolitics and Hegel and Man at the End of History and wrote books called things like *Existenz* (note the powerful *z* on the end, rather than the more modest *ce*). I grew up in Swansea, Wales, and Philip Larkin was a good deal around. He didn't talk about post-historical man. He talked about the psychodrama of early baldness. Bellow quotes Larkin as follows: 'In everyone there sleeps a sense of life according to love.' Larkin 'also says that people dream "of all they might have done had they been loved. Nothing cures that".' And nothing – i.e., death – did

---

* At the time I thought he was merely embarrassed (and, of course, bored). But his pain was not only personal. 'The universities', as he remarked in an essay of 1975 ('A Matter of the Soul', collected in *It All Adds Up*), 'have failed painfully.' They quench literature of all its agitation and excitement, producing the BA who 'can tell you, or thinks he can, what Ahab's harpoon symbolises or what Christian symbols there are in *Light in August*'. Melville and Faulkner would have been tormented by such observations, just as Bellow was tormented that morning in Haifa.

cure that. Love was not a possibility for Larkin. Because to him death overarched love and rendered it derisory. He died in 1985: by Bellow's age, incidentally, he had been dead for years. For him, death crowded love out. With Bellow, it seems to be the other way around. More die of heartbreak, says the title. Well, Larkin never had any heartbreak, not in that sense. Perhaps one of many, many things the new novel has to say is that you *need* heartbreak, to keep you human . . . The right kind of heartbreak, mind you. Anyway, whether you need it or not, you are certainly going to get it.

I find this surprising, now, to see life behaving with such thematic obedience. Today (13/7/99) I came across the following in Allan Bloom's *The Closing of the American Mind* (1987): 'Very few men are capable of coming to terms with their own extinction . . . It is the hardest task of all to face the lack of cosmic support for what we care about. Socrates, therefore, defines the task of philosophy as "learning how to die".' Which made me think of Bellow's remark: 'Death is the dark backing a mirror needs if we are to see anything.' And that, in turn, brought me back to Larkin and his line, 'the costly aversion of the eyes from death'. Costly! Yes, it would be costly: prohibitive, steep, ruinous, dearly bought. And yet there he was, on 21 November 1985, heading off to hospital, packing his pyjamas and his shaving things, and summoning the ease, the humour and the generosity for one more letter: to my father. And Larkin's last words, addressed to the nurse who was holding his hand, were 'I am going to the inevitable'. His last words, spoken to the last woman in the last room.

The Conference ended and we all headed south – to Jerusalem, where (by my reckoning) Saul and I made friends.

– Is Saul Bellow in some sense your literary father?

This was a regular (and not unwelcome) query, in interviews, when the affiliation became known, and I usually replied,

– But I've already got a literary father.

And that was true, then, in 1987.

Lurid

As 1994 ended my life became lurid. *Lurid*, according to the condensed epic poem of the Fowlers' article in the *COD*, means:

> **1.** ghastly, wan, glaring, unnatural, stormy, terrible, in colour or combination of colours or lights (of complexion, landscape, sky, lightning, thunder-clouds, smoky flame, glance, etc.); **cast a ~ light on,** explain or reveal (facts or character) in tragic or terrible way. **2.** sensational, horrifying, *(lurid details)*; showy, gaudy, *(paperbacks with lurid covers)*. **3.** (Bot. etc.) of dingy yellowish brown.

In *The King's English: A Guide to Modern Usage*★ my father has this to say under the heading 'Single-handedly':

> Some illiteracies are presented in the name of literacy, or at least of regularity and common sense . . . Those who like to make words longer and more polysyllabic have not noticed or do not care that *singlehanded* is already an adverb . . . The lately fashionable *overly*, one of the ugliest intruders of this part of the century, is similarly an unnecessary extension of what was already a thriving and unquestioned adverb.
>
> There are plenty of other adverbs vulnerable to creative illiteracy through not ending in *-ly*. *Regardless* is in the forefront, having three syllables already and perhaps standing in need of rehabilitation by being blown up into *irregardless* by a different kind of illiteracy. But no word of this sort – an adverb not already ending in *-ly* – can be considered safe. When can we expect to see *quitely*? *Altogetherly*? What *nextly*?

★ When this book appeared, in 1997, it was widely assumed that the title was a nod to Henry and Frank Fowler's *The King's English* (1906). And so it was. But 'the King', along with Kingers, was a diminutive, one seldom used in Kingsley's presence although he knew about it and vaguely approved of it. Rob, for example, invariably referred to Kingsley as the King, as in 'How's the King?' or 'I saw the King on TV the other night'. So the title is apt: the book is about *his* English – the King's English – as well as everybody else's.

Here's what nextly. Yesterday (30/4/99) I heard Nato spokesman Jamie Shay use the phrase 'know fully well'. My first thought was to call my father but of course there was no father to call. Kingsley goes on (and here he gives a surrealistic glimpse of my lurid activities at this time):

> An award-winning actress was recently witnessed . . . thanking all those who had contributed to her triumph, 'lastly but not leastly' some easily overlooked minor figure. And a New York dentist says 'open widely' on his best behaviour, but 'open big' when in a hurry.

The dentist was Todd J. Berman and the actress was Jessica Lange. Reduced to near-total Kinchhood by Todd in New York, I flew to Los Angeles and luridly mingled with Jessica, and with Sharon Stone and Sophia Loren, with Tom Hanks, with Quentin Tarantino, with John Travolta. John and I would share two intimate dinners at his rented home in Beverly Hills, north of Sunset, and then a farewell lunch in his trailer on the set of *Get Shorty*.

Notebook: '15 Dec. Tenderly driven there by Subhindra Singh (oh, *now* they're sorry), I arrive at 307 E 49 under a near-fatal dose of Valium. Dick★ gets a better drug from *his* dentist: "It makes you feel you don't give a shit *what* they do to you." And Valium, I find, isn't quite that good. "Open widely."

'1) Explanation. 2) A dozen? injections. 3) Extractions (rt) extractions left accompanied by a dystopia of scrape and grind – and stitching, with the yarn like bloodied dental floss. 4) The scan on the backlit screen: the bridge connecting the lower canines, with one surviving incisor – a pathetic little buoy in a sea of disease. Then the removal of the "large cyst". "Do you want to see it?" I make a noise that means yes. It reminds me of a biology class in Swansea: a length of worm, dissected and opened out. 5) The endless deftness of the knitting. X-ray × 2.

★ The social critic Richard Cornuelle, Elizabeth Fonseca's second husband.

'Sit for an hour, waiting for bleeding to be staunched, in the "recovery" alcove. Scrips for penicillin and Valium. Also for Toradol and Percadan (Don DeLillo says that the names of pharmaceuticals sound like the gods of science fiction). "You'll have to be a grouch for a while," says Todd. No stretching the mouth. No smiling. I have my usual hundred bucks' worth of painkillers.

'That week: sleep (one day). Use the icepack. No sign of the expected discoloration. The whole jaw rigid and tender. In repose, not so much a pain as a presence, a wedge: the bone graft – cowbone, prescreened for AIDS. The Bug. Bruno.*

'And what about *my* bone, the smell and spume of my burning bone, with irrigator, vacuum cleaner, and two pairs of hands in my mouth, all at the same time, and the drill, and of course the other drill, capable of making your vision shudder.

'I advise dental patients to keep their eyes open during the procedure. It frees you, just a little bit, from internalisation. The dental patient must have something to stare at – the panels of the blinds, the framed certificates (Diplomate of the American Board of Oral and Maxillofacial Surgery. I once heard Todd say, in a dismissive boast, 'I haven't done any *dentistry* for years.' Well this sure feels like dentistry to me), the assistant's green smock, the surgeon with his tongue folded upward and outward over his upper lip, his straining eyes, his condomlike gloves which, during the third hour, are marked with fresh as well as dried and crusted blood, his hooked forefinger.

'21 Dec. SB still in hospital but out of intensive care.

'22 Dec. Stroll into Todd's for a leisurely checkup. But no. The stitches have come undone. "Open big."

'Another bloodbath and the most painful yet, despite the eight or nine jabs. Down on the lower jaw, where the cowbone lives, great scouring and scoring. How the instruments squawk and rasp.

'Once again staggering around 2nd Ave with a fat lip and a wad of bloodied Kleenex, like an old brawler who just never learns.'

*   *   *

---

* Bruno Fonseca contracted the virus at a brothel in Barcelona, where he was seeking to entertain an uncle visiting from Uruguay.

The only package holiday that the longsuffering travel agent, Martin, could put together ('What's the latest?' he kept wearily asking, as our plans chopped and changed) was five nights in Puerto Rico: San Juan, where, two weeks earlier, Janis Bellow had wheeled her dying husband across the tarmac . . . In preparation I bought a glow-in-the-dark linen suit from a chainstore called something like Sir Guy; once established at the Condado Plaza Hotel/Casino, I added a pair of black sateen flipflops which clacked incensingly at every footfall. It is a relief, sometimes, to embrace indignity. I embraced it. I would never wear the Clamp again. My lower jaw, I felt, was now too crippled to bear all that sneering mass.

Onset: Bellow's first symptom, I repeat, was a horror – a hatred – of food, not just the taste but the smell of it, the sight of it. In the early stages the loss of appetite 'seemed to merge with the malaise I had brought here from the North – a kind of uneasiness or dislocation, something like the metaphysical miseries'. At first, for his dinner, he could manage a bowl of cornflakes, and could still tell himself that such moderation was salutary, because 'like everyone else in the USA I am grossly overfed'. One night he could manage only a spoonful of the chicken soup that Janis had managed to procure and prepare for him. Making a joke of his failure, he recalled the immigrant mothers of his childhood who cried out, 'My Joey can't eat an ice cream – he turns away his head – he's got to be dying . . .' But Saul *was* dying . . . In London, when children go to hospital with stomach complaints, the doctor will test for appendicitis with the following question: 'Would you like a Big Mac?' If the answer is no then they've got it. They put that question to my son Jacob as he lay in Casualty, squirming with gastroenteritis. The pain came in waves, every minute; as they approached he shouted out, 'Help me Daddy! Help me Daddy!' And I couldn't help him . . . Saul, on the other hand, had no real notion that he was ailing. The sickness had now gone on to attack the 'sheath' of the nerves.

Among the Condado Plaza's restaurant concessions was Tony Roma's, billed as 'A *Place* for Ribs'. Clearly, Tony Roma's was no place for me. Kinch would eat a sandwich with a knife and fork in his room; or, wearing an eyecatching swimsuit, he would sit sucking on a french fry under a palm tree with a hi-fi speaker bolted to its trunk. I was surrounded, here, not by the bums and mendicants and diagonal dope-fiends of the Lower East Side. Far less consolingly, I was being swept along in a pageant of American health, wealth and micro-managed facial pulchritude. Saul was no good at eating and I was no good at eating. It seemed a lonely affliction, especially at the Condado, where eating was the principal group activity. They ate while they were eating but also while they were strolling, shopping, volleyballing, swimming, diving. Reduced by now to my lowest-ever adult weight, I might have found the verve to exult in my slenderness, among all this bronzed rotundity. 'Grossly overfed'? The hotel guests could not be mistaken for representatives of that strange capitalist innovation, the corpulent poor, who wear their obesity like a low-caste colour – and who, in sufficient numbers (after a daytrip, say, to a Native-American casino in Connecticut), can make the liner-sized ferry from New London to Orient Point wallow awful low in Long Island Sound . . . This was a different kind of casino crowd, middle-income, middle-weight, and disporting itself in a tropical setting. If the Caribbean, in Bellow's phrase, has been developed into 'one huge U.S. recreational slum', there was also much creaturely immobility, much sated torpor, on which to rest one's zestless gaze. I found myself increasingly attracted to one brontosauran family (mother, father, daughter, son). During the afternoons their four bellies would respire in unison as they slept, companionably and rightfully, as if after some demanding but success-ful collective effort. This collective effort, I suppose, was symbolised by lunch. Later, they liked to go and *stand* in the sea, neck-deep, perhaps to experience lightness, their biomass duly diminished by the weight of the water it displaced. I was thin and hollow and no good at eating; but I helped myself to the cafeterial sachets of salt (laid out with the ketchup and relish at the poolside commissaries), which hit the spot for my hourly mouthwash.

What was I reading? I want to convey a mood, and what you are reading is a constituent of how you feel. In biographies they should always tell us that, routinely, in the margin: what they were reading. What was I reading, in San Juan? As usual I failed to make a note of this valuable *aide-memoire* – but of course I remember what I was reading. I was reading you and I was reading me. In our room I lightly subedited *Bury Me Standing: The Gypsies and their Journey* and ponderously embossed the American proofs of *The Information*. A decade of work was disappearing from our desks. And for many a moment I felt wonderfully happy and proud* . . . The tumour in my underjaw now languished on a petri dish in New York. It was gone from me; I would soon know whether to expect it to return, and with what degree of virulence. 'Life-tenure', as Bellow puts it, had lost some of its substance. I trod softly through the after-tremors of my *coup de vieux*. A gnarled and arthritic thumb was bearing down on the Fast Forward. The body complained about this, but the body, suddenly a little less stupid, took what it could from the experience. All the same I was lurid with it, ghastly, numb-brown, like the reflection of my face, perched on the puddly linen suit – the reflection of my face, slithering over the gunmetal of the slot machines as I moved through the cold casino.

It would be years before I understood where Saul Bellow had ended up when he journeyed to the rented apartment on the tiny island of St Martin. He made a side-trip, a fantastic voyage to the limits of mortality and the ends of the earth. Quite right, absolutely right, to stop eating. Eating, it transpired, was what had taken him to intensive care. And what was he reading? That was also crucial. He was reading about the Iron Guard atrocities in wartime Bucharest – the slaughterhouse and the meathooks, the cleavings, the flayings. And he was reading about the marvellously 'appetising fragrance' of human flesh as it roasts on the headhunters' campfires in New Guinea, among torrents and cataracts of blinding flora.

* * *

* I recall that I was also rereading Dennis Overbye's *Lonely Hearts of the Cosmos* (HarperPerennial, 1992). Despite its so-so title, this is in my view the best popular book on modern cosmology: on the kind of human intelligence involved in it, and on the kind of questions the universe puts to that intelligence. Mr Overbye's pages offered another perspective on daily life at the Condado Plaza, with its talking lifts ('Going *up*'), its ferocious refrigeration, its great sprawl of negative entropy.

Notebook: 'Tailor-like fitting for the upper set, at the hands of Mike Szabatura. A blue spot is daubed on the tip of my nose, to help calibrate symmetry. Nazi-doctor measuring. That's how Nazi doctors spent much of their time: measure measure measure.

'Can't believe the US proofs of *The Info*. A termitary of imported commas, each one like a papercut to my soul.★

'Jan 3, 95. Big day. Todd. Stitches removed. No infection. Cleanout painless. Jaw feels freer, looser. *More* penicillin – 3rd dose in a month. The treatment, like the patient, is getting old.

'But good news, good news. The lab report on the pathology: the cyst is unexotic. I'm not dying. I will live. This is good news.

'On Seventh Avenue I got hold of a copy of *The Sun*. The prison suicide at Winson Green. The terrible pleading face. He looks like some wretch being led yet again to the stocks, and hoping, this time, for reasonably rotten fruit and vegetables. No bricks or spanners or roofslates.

'I am praised by my dentists: for holding still. Many patients, they tell me, are "moving targets". My unflinching rigidity makes the best results possible . . . Here's another thing they sometimes say: "Sorry for torturing you like that." My dear Mike, my dear Todd: if you had been *trying* to inflict pain, like the Nazi dentist, Szell, in *Marathon Man*, instead of trying not to . . . Besides, I am assuming that torturers never apologise. But do they ever explain?

'*Big* day. I can tell immediately by the breathiness of Janis's message on the Bellow answering machine that Saul is *much* better. He is getting ready to come home.'

※　　※　　※

★ '*And the function of the editor? Has one ever had literary advice to offer?*
'By "editor" I suppose you mean proofreader. Among these I have known limpid creatures of limitless tact and tenderness who would discuss with me a semicolon as if it were a point of honor – which, indeed, a point of art often is. But I have also come across a few pompous avuncular brutes who would attempt to "make suggestions" which I countered with a thunderous "stet!"' Vladimir Nabokov, *Strong Opinions* (1974). 'Pompous avuncular brutes' is exquisite: it commands satirical truth, skewering a whole generation of Anglophone publishers (now vanished – though the occasional throwback remains).

I too came home, and settled into the lurid and lugubrious New Year.* My notebook records that during this period I was busted in my study by my older son. 'Are you *crying?*' Louis asked. 'Yes,' I said. 'But don't worry. Things are so much better now.' Were they? My cousin was dead, and your brother was dead. But I wasn't dying and neither was Saul. 'The Forest Ranger', I informed my boys, 'is out of hospital.' They nodded solemnly . . . Years earlier, with their mother, on a trip to Vermont: the Nobel Laureate was to link up with us at a market in a small town near his house. He arrived in a jeep and dropped down from it wearing some kind of municipal combat jacket with (I think) the words FIRE SERVICE stitched into its shoulders. I told the boys he was a forest ranger. And they couldn't be blamed for believing me. That's what he looked like, towards the end of a summer of writing, walking, cycling and chopping wood. And now such exchanges as

– Who are you going to see?
– The Forest Ranger.

or

– Who said that?
– The Forest Ranger.

or

– What are you reading?
– The Forest Ranger.

have become commonplace . . . I talked to Saul on 9 January (Notebook: 'completely himself. Janis's voice so *moved'*) and a week later I would see him, in Boston, on my way to Los Angeles and my rendezvous with John Travolta.

In *Ravelstein*† (2000) – and doesn't *that* look weird – the narrator,

---

* Lurid, because my case continued to be widely discussed by the Fourth Estate. The gravamen, the crux of it was that I had demanded a big advance for *The Information* so that I could fritter a lot of it away on cosmetic dentistry. Plus all the usual other stuff.
† I have seen *Ravelstein* in three versions. Some of the quotes in this section have been cut from the final draft. In his foreword to the compact fictions that make up *Something to Remember Me By* (1991), Bellow writes: '[W]e respond with approval when Chekhov tells us, "Odd, I have now a mania

hospitalised and on the threshold of death, seems to be entertaining himself with hallucinations, delusions – 'fictions which did not have to be invented'. Bellow writes:

> A male hospital attendant on a stepladder was hanging Christmas tinsel, mistletoe and evergreen clippings on the wall fixtures. This attendant didn't much care for me. He was the one who had called me a troublemaker. But that didn't stop me from taking note of him. Taking note is part of my job-description. Existence is – or was – the job.

I second that. Existence still is the job.

---

for shortness. Whatever I read – my own or other people's works – it all seems to me not short enough." I find myself emphatically agreeing with this.' There followed, in 1997, the powerful but minimalist novella, *The Actual*. So Bellow's return, with *Ravelstein*, to an earlier, freer, more voice-driven exuberance is an astonishment to me. I have to keep reminding myself that the author was born, not in 1950, but in 1915.

Letter from College

Exeter College,
Oxford.
[Spring? 1970]

Dearest Dad and Jane,

I enclose my Battels – I haven't really looked at them but I
rather fancy that the coupon money (£6) is cancelled out by my
dinner credits (£6 – 6). In any case, I require a check by Friday
otherwise they'll fine me. It's so boring because I've never felt quite
so ill in all my life. I wake up every morning feeling terrible in a
completely different way from the morning before. Last Thursday:
my neck & top part of my back were alive with those fibrous
nodules that one gets between one's muscles (I can't see why I
should get those since I haven't drunk any Shandy* recently);
Wednesday featured a feverish chill; Friday – a bulging headache,
and on Saturday I had what felt like a coronary. Yawn, but I always
have this before exams. My morning sortie to get the papers now
invariably includes a call at the Chemist's.

I'm working so hard now that my work can't fail to come into
focus before next Monday. Anglo Saxon grammar has proved to be
the principal hang-up although I try & liven it up with awful jingles
to remember the sound-changes – but mostly it's just staring
gloomily at endless lists of verbs, swearing softly every few minutes.

I met an incredible reactionary yesterday who supports the

---

* Even a glass of lager and lemonade was too much for the flirtatious
valetudinarian. More testimony to his extreme lightness of head.

Arabs vs. Israel, Russia vs. Czechland, and *Nigeria* vs. Biafra. Rather like Peter Simple★ – I've stopped taking the Bellygraph since that 'Lost Bouquet' piece (how much better it was in 1830). I'll close now because I'm having an early night – I'll be very relieved to see you all in a couple of weeks.

      Ros. sends love.

         Love Mart X X X

P.S. Thanks for your letters. Love to all, not excluding Miss Plush.

★ Pseudonym of a right-wing humorist in the *Daily Telegraph*.

Women and Love – 2

1970: it all started going wrong in 1970. From a letter to Robert Conquest, written in 1991:

> I continue to lead a charmed life and never set eyes on the bag. Almost unbelievable that it's now *8 years last Nov* that I last did ... It amazes me now that for several months after she went I was v cut up about it, wanted her back, contemplated a *poem* on the subj if you don't fucking well mind. Now I wish it had happened in – well I suppose about 1970 would be right. Well it's all experience, though it's a pity there had to be so much of it.

This is an example of Kingsley in revisionist mode (and a relatively mild example, too: he is much more energetically ungallant elsewhere). I think I now understand the need for that revision, though I wonder if my father ever did; and it still pains me to see it. 1970? Surely not. But how would I know? In several senses, marriages are secrets, shared only by the principals. In the spring of 1976, at any rate, the writing was on the wall. There was the wall of the big house, and the writers were writing the writing on it, in italic capitals. It seemed that everything had changed in the space of a week. Now, the most incurious visitor, sticking his head round the front door for ten seconds, could have told you that the marriage of Kingsley Amis and Elizabeth Jane Howard was ineluctably doomed.

For reasons that may appear more obvious than they really are, I have lost all appetite for apportioning blame in matters of the affections – in failed unions, sunderings, divorces. The symbiosis, the dyad, it fails, and that's that ... It is very difficult, it is perhaps impossible, for someone who loves his mother to love the woman whom your father left her for.

Because the Other Woman has made you cautious about love: she herself has created caution in you about love. However this may be, I got very close to loving Jane. 'I'm your wicked stepmother,' said Jane, after the wedding. And she *was* my wicked stepmother – but only in the sense meant by my son, Louis, when he tells me (for instance) that he is 'wicked at Latin'. Jane was my *wicked* stepmother: she was generous, affectionate and resourceful; she salvaged my schooling and I owe her an unknowable debt for that. One flaw: sometimes, early on, she would tell me things designed to make me think less of my mother, and I would wave her away, saying, Jane, this just backfires and makes me think less of *you*. And she worked on this little vice, and overcame it. When I see her now I resent our vanished relatedness, cancelled by law but not by feeling. I also admire her as an artist, as I did then.* Penetrating sanity: they both had that, in their work. And I kept thinking, as I watched the household start to collapse, that if they could just stand back from this, if they could *write* it instead, then, surely, they would see . . . But writers write far more penetratingly than they live. Their novels show them at their very best, making a huge effort: stretched until they twang.

* As far as I am concerned she is, with Iris Murdoch, the most interesting woman writer of her generation. An instinctivist, but an elegant one (like Muriel Spark), she has a freakish and poetic eye, and penetrating sanity . . . Now I remember an incident from the later days at the house on Hadley Common: Kingsley regretfully yet rather dourly correcting a short story of Jane's (this would have been for the collection *Mr Wrong*, 1975, and one of her best books). He was correcting it in typescript, for grammar, and there were several marks on each page. When I later settled down to read it I thought that my father might have been captious, or carried away, or borne along by some parallel momentum (the two of them were already hoarding grievances against each other). But no. All the regularisations seemed conscientious and non-pedantic. There was only one that bothered me. The sentence, describing a suburban street, went approximately: 'The windows all had their curtains drawn, like houses asleep.' And Kingsley had crossed out *like* and inserted *as of*. I thought: You're right, but you've killed the poeticism, and crippled the rhythm. Jane, an autodidact (exercised about my education, perhaps, because hers had been threadbare and homebound), accepted the corrections with some meekness – and, as I remember, incorporated them all. Kingsley's expression said: What could I do? I didn't disapprove of what he had done, but I felt for her. And for him. He didn't have one marriage riding on this marriage. He had two.

[215]

What happened? Addressing this question, Eric Jacobs, KA's official biographer, muses: 'Both plain and mysterious forces are at work in such shifts. The decline of Amis's marriage to Jane was a bit like this: plain and mysterious, their relationship disintegrating even as it continued, like an art form moving slowly and imperceptibly towards exhaustion.'* Well, yes. The causes were both proximate and not so proximate, as always, both commonplace and inimitable. But the actual *precipitant*, I can disclose, was *The Mask of Fu Manchu* . . . Kingsley told me how it went. The whole day, he said, had been unusually enriched by the prospect of the Karloff classic (late screening). Dusk settled; midnight struck; and the film, when it came, was incredibly boring.† He sat up, alone, for another hour, in what he described as 'a trance of depression'. Something, he reasoned, must be missing from his life. And he decided that what was missing was London. He wanted to leave the big house . . . So the marriage might have been extended for at least an additional twenty-four hours, if *The Mask* had been any good. As it turned out, the marriage would last another five years. But it was over, effectively, the minute those credits rolled.

Men, I have noticed, can indeed be indifferent to their

---

* Earlier on I called Jacobs's book 'mysteriously repetitive'. The quote above is from p. 313. On p. 314 we get: 'One cause of change may be simple exhaustion, like an art form running out of steam.' And on page 315 we get: 'Exhaustion, like that of a literary genre running out of steam, played its part.' The proofreader must have been mysteriously repetitive too. See Appendix.

† Kingsley might have had this disappointment in mind when he wrote p. 31 of *Jake's Thing* (1978). In this scene Jake stays up late to watch 'Rendezvous with Terror: *The Brass Golem*'. 'Despite everything the background bass clarinet could do, and it did indeed get a lot done in quantity, terror as expected failed altogether to turn up at the prearranged spot.' He might have taken a pasting over *Psycho*, but Kingsley really did like terror, particularly antique terror (*The Mask* dates from 1932). I warm to the tone of youthful and unvalorous excitement in his essay 'Dracula, Frankenstein, Sons & Co.': 'Apart from the adventures of the incredibly shrunken man, I recall chiefly *The Fly* (1958) and its successors. Here, the hastiest of mumbo-jumbo was run through with the palpable design of proceeding to the disagreeable activities and physical appearance of a fly with a chap's head and a chap with a fly's head – especially him' (*What Became of Jane Austen?*).

surroundings (if not to their geographical location). Women aren't like that. As my mother would say to me a couple of years later (she was nomadic at the time): 'If you're a woman, then you are your house and your house is you.' I was doubly impressed when Jane, who had no desire to leave, seemed to accept Kingsley's proposal without argument. 'No matter how much you've put into it,' she told me, 'you can't go on living in a place that makes one of you unhappy.' I was twenty-six. I thought: this is maturity. This is civilisation. What happened next, however, amounted to a fulminant *folie à deux* . . . In the interests of 'economy' Jane decided to dispense with the services of professional house-movers: instead, she would do it all herself. This not only prolonged the agony but hugely vivified it. And the domestic atmosphere was soon close to excruciating. The move had begun with a movie; and here was another motion picture: a long one, with a long title, something like: Moving House, And Very Obviously Moving House, While Very Obviously Not Wanting to Move House, As Husband Looks On. After a while I said,

– Dad, what's happening here is insane. You've got to insist on getting the movers in.

– She says we can't afford it.

– You're going from one enormous place to another enormous place. The move would be only a fraction of the sums involved.

– She says we can't afford it.

– Then go into debt.

– We've already gone into debt, apparently.

– Then go deeper.

We fell silent while Jane, with Karloffian gait (*Frankenstein*, 1931), trudged through the hall, sighing under the weight of a loaded tea-chest. Kingsley looked incapacitated: gently incapacitated. The Amis paralysis was upon him. Of course, there had never been any question of my father 'lending a hand', as the saying goes. In any case that would have frustrated Jane's subliminal purpose, which I can only conclude was sadomasochistic in tendency. 'My main job so far,' KA uneasily boasted to Robert Conquest in May, 1976, 'has been drinking up the nearly-empty bottles' ('horrible stuff like cherry vodka, Mavrodaphne, raki etc.'). Later that day, as usual, my father

[217]

and I set off to drive to the Two Brewers. In the courtyard Jane was struggling to wedge an armchair into the martyred minivan, for yet another round trip to London . . . She must have hired some muscle at some point: I never saw her carrying a refrigerator or a double bed. One way or the other the thing got done in the end. Finally the Amises were established in the house in Hampstead (listed, freestanding, eighteenth-century, with walled garden front and back), on a massive foundation of resentment. And it would get worse.

When I was going through *Girl, 20* the other month I was chilled to see that Kingsley's evocation of the house on Hadley Common was persistently necrotic. The phrases I am about to quote serve their general purpose in this funny, sad and unautobiographical novel, but I couldn't avoid seeing them as indices of a dormant disaffection:* the 'paved courtyard adorned with small trees in a sickly or dead condition', the old coats on the old coatstand, the empty bottles, 'the gloom of the barn', the 'avenue littered with fallen wood', the 'overgrown path that proved to be two or three inches deep in rotting leaves', 'the ruins of the greenhouse', the 'vases of decaying flowers'. And what am I to make of the fate of the Furry Barrel, a character very closely based on the comical and voluptuous Rosie Plush? Unlike Nancy in *The Anti-Death League*, Rosie just about survives *Girl, 20*. The novel ends in divorce and dilapidation; and the narrator (an outsider, making his last visit to the house) sees that the dog, too, has been caught up in this final convulsion, crippled by the child of the breaking home: 'One hind leg, with what looked like a rubber bandage on it, stuck out at an angle, and there was an arrangement of straps over her rump.' And what am I to make of *this*?

> I stooped down and stroked the dog's silky head, feeling as if something dismal had happened right in the middle of my own life and concerns, something major, something irretrievable, as

---

* Because that's what novels are (among other things): not almanacs of your waking life but messages from your unconscious history. They come from the back of your mind, not from its forefront. This would eventually be made very clear to me.

if I had taken a fatally wrong decision years ago and only now
seen how much I had lost by it.

Girl, 20 was published in 1971. (My copy is inscribed: 'To good old
graduand Martin. Love from Dad'). *The Green Man* was published in
1969. So *Girl, 20* belongs to 1970.

And this is 'Wasted', which appeared in 1973:

> That cold winter evening
> The fire would not draw,
> And the whole family hung
> Over the dismal grate
> Where rain-soaked logs
> Bubbled, hissed and steamed.
> Then, when the others had gone
> Up to their chilly beds,
> And I was ready to go,
> The wood began to flame
> In clear rose and violet,
> Heating the small hearth.
>
> Why should that memory cling
> Now the children are all grown up,
> And the house – a different house –
> Is warm at any season?

What is, what has been 'wasted'? Not just the surge of warmth from
the fire, clearly enough. 'A different house': there is something
dismissive, something warding-off, in the dashes that gird these three
words. The poem is about the recurrent grief, endemic to the male
divorcee – grief for the lost family. More than that, though, the
sadness here is defeatist. It is saying that it wasn't worth it. The
aggregate of familial pain, of familial disconnection: that is what has
been wasted.

Around now I hear a subversive voice from the other camp,
claiming (with some basis) that it was *Kingsley* who was wasted, in

1973. And I find that a certain themelet in these pages – the Two Brewers, the cherry vodka, the Mavrodaphne, the raki – is doing its best to intrude. We will, perforce, come back to that . . . I want to end this subsection with two images of my father's face. The images are identical, though separated by twenty years. There is a connection between them that I know to be there but cannot quite locate.

First image. This comes in the aftermath of an altercation in the library of the house on Hadley Common. The row, I seem to remember, was tripartite: I was involved in some way, perhaps taking sides (and not necessarily with my father). It ended, anyway, and in the dazed lull that followed Jane reached out impulsively towards Kingsley, who glimpsed her movement late, and flinched as he reflexively raised a protective arm. And then it was Jane's turn to rear back, in vindicated astonishment, as if to say, 'See? See how it is with me and you?' My father's face: childish, softly frowning, entering a plea for mitigation, for leniency, asking for things to be seen in a kinder light.

The second image. This was Swansea, and I had been sent upstairs to be beaten, or at any rate hit, by my father in his tiny study at the end of the long corridor. The long corridor, the tiny, tawny study facing the steeply sloped back garden: that means we were still at 24 The Grove, and hadn't yet moved up the hill to Glanmore Road, making me unbelievably and embarrassingly young to have committed such crimes – six and three-quarters at the outside. More and more recklessly I had been stealing money and cigarettes from my mother's handbag and coat pocket. I knew a reckoning was coming. Earlier that day, almost legless with apprehension and self-disgust, I had secreted a handful of stolen change under a bench in a bus shelter – and gone home, where my mother told me to present myself at my father's study, to be hit . . . I remember the increasing gloom of the corridor. I knocked (we always knocked). He stood with his back to me at the window. He turned – with the significant face. What happened next is darkly shadowed and escapes all memory. My mind knows nothing about it. Afterwards he said: 'What do you want to do now?' I said: 'I want to go to bed.' It was a summer evening. Plenty of fervently hurrying footsteps in the street, and people calling out to one another with a buoyancy and hopefulness unimaginable in the nighttime . . . As for the cancelled memory of the beating: the void is so perfect and entire that I sometimes suspect it never happened. But I would have remembered its not happening. And my mother told me he wept that night, as he always did when he hit us.*

He turned from the study window. His face was in quarter-profile (and shouldn't this have been *my* face?): childish, softly frowning, entering a plea for mitigation, for leniency, asking for things to be seen in a kinder light.

Although, in the novels, with their permanent blitzkrieg against bores and boredom, pointmissers, poseurs, much violence is summoned, hammers, pokers, bayonets, knuckledusters, flaming stakes, swarming anthills, starving crocodiles (Dad. Yes? If three anthills and two crocodiles . . .), firearms, mortars, flamethrowers (this list is by no means complete), together with common assault ('Ronnie had been standing for about half a minute . . . considering whether to run up and hit Mansfield a lot would convey to him something of what he felt about him'), Kingsley was in some sense a profoundly unviolent man. He didn't leave my mother and he didn't leave Jane. They left him. Divorce 'is an incredibly violent thing to happen to you'. Above all he feared escalation.

The Pain Schedule

'We'll have a ball yet,' Bellow kept saying when, still numb from the monotone of Haifa, we were all temporarily gazumped at Mishkenot

---

* A rare occurrence, and it should be added that Kingsley could be a pretty pathetic chastiser of his children. During a party, one night hereabouts, Philip and I kept going downstairs and hiding behind the furniture. It got out of hand. Kingsley eventually took a hairbrush to us, but so limply that we giggled about it for an hour after he had gone downstairs. Hysterical anyway, we disguised these giggles as wails of anguish, and that, too, got funnier and funnier. Meanwhile, downstairs, our father's tears were unfeigned, and later I was sorry that we had deceived him.

Sha'ananim, the official guesthouse, and had to cast about for a hotel. And we did have a ball. There was a dinner, an occasion where I felt a liveliness that went beyond the excitement guaranteed by the location: Jerusalem, the city without smalltalk. That night the dramatis personae, it now seems, was drawn up with ominous care: my wife and I, Saul and Janis, Allan Bloom (the political philosopher), Teddy Kolleck (the city Mayor), and Amschel and Anita Rothschild. Bloom and I had a long, loud, and in the end unrancorous argument about nuclear weapons.* I climbed down, carefully, that night. I saw all the deep attractions of escalation, of arsenal-clearing escalation. For a while, as in a countdown tingler set in the Situation Room, I stood on the brink and saw the abyss. But down I climbed. There are times when manners are more important than the end of the world. In fact I often felt myself among my elders and betters in Israel, and I was furtively honoured to be staying in the city guesthouse – where Bloom and the Bellows seemed to me to be rightfully installed. I was attracted by Bloom's demeanour (one of constant expectation of amusement) and the physical greed with which he went through his Marlboros. And I was alive to the pleasure Saul took in him. Their friendship was a nice sight: two fugitives from *Ulysses* (Bloom, Moses Herzog), happily conspiring . . . Teddy Kolleck tended to disappear between courses and then potently rematerialise, his city so much the calmer or the more solvent after some appearance he had put in or

---

* Bloom considered nuclear weapons to be a heavy-handed but effective means of deterring conventional war. I said that it was indefensible to gamble the future on an arrangement that, somehow or other (and so far and no further), had succeeded in containing the present. Et cetera. Bloom, I now know, had an immensely capacious intellect; but I felt at times that I was arguing with my father, who on this subject was often capable of 'thinking with the blood', in Kipling's phrase (instead of *about* the blood, as you ought soberly to do). With the collapse of the Soviet Union and the erosion of deterrence, the planet has 'become safe for war' (in Don DeLillo's phrase). The bloodbaths and ethnic cleansings – ethnic foulings – in the Balkans would never have been allowed to destabilise an era of continued Mutual Assured Destruction. But the moral case against MAD remains watertight. Therefore: down. 1987 was a time (SDI, space shields) when many voices were still saying *up*.

phone call he had made. The young Rothschilds – old friends of mine despite their youth – were also engaged in that (to me) mysterious arena of power and public relations, of endowments, of pro-bono unveilings. 'I'm the Princess Di of Israel,' said Anita (née Guinness), semi-seriously: 'I *am*.' Her husband Amschel looked on with his usual unassertive benignity, his usual (curiously elastic) physical elegance, his hot brown eyes. What did we talk about? Israel. I didn't want the evening to end.

The next day at Mishkenot Sha'ananim I sent Bellow a note. In a spirit of extreme diffidence. I think I know as well as anyone that writers are *always* nursing and protecting a preoccupation. 'We are usually waiting', as he says, 'for someone to clear out and let us go on with the business of life (to cultivate the little obsessional garden).' No writer has inveighed so feelingly against distraction ('What is going on will not let us alone'); and I suspected, once again, that I was there as a representative of the moronic inferno, which *is* distraction. So my note to Saul, I repeat, was tentatively couched. 'Towards the end of your life,' says Benn Crader in *More Die of Heartbreak*,

you have something like a pain schedule to fill out – a long schedule like a federal document, only it's your pain schedule. Endless categories. First, physical causes – like arthritis, gallstones, menstrual cramps. Next category, injured vanity, betrayal, swindle, injustice. But the hardest items of all have to do with love. The question then is: So why does everybody persist? If love cuts them up so much, and you see the ravages everywhere, why not be sensible and sign off early?

In my note, therefore, I asked after the state of Bellow's pain schedule,★ saying that I had no wish to add to it, but if he should happen to – unless of course he . . .

★ I was of course aware that Bellow's situation had changed since our first meeting in 1983. He was no longer living with his fourth wife, Alexandra . . . But I couldn't claim to be aware of what all this meant for the heart, because it hadn't yet happened to mine. I had watched my father, and read him; I had read Bellow, and many others. This remains the great deficiency

He replied, and we had afternoon tea at the guesthouse (me milk, him lemon) on a balcony or rooftop in the undecided landscape of Jerusalem, tropical, barren, rubbish-laden. It was our first entirely non-professional encounter; and in a way I wish I had had the tools of my sometime trade about me: the pen, the notebook, the tape-recorder to stare at distrustfully, the trembling hands.* Because I don't remember what we talked about. But I can guess. It has often been said of Saul Bellow that he speaks just as he writes. In my view this couldn't be an accurate description of any literary novelist (and think how grotesque it would be to say it of a poet). Still, it is more nearly true of him than of any other writer I have known. His speech shows the same habits of rhythm, the same vigilance and circumspection together with the same willingness to ascend and expand.† Talking to him, that day, was not so very different from curling up with *Mr Sammler's Planet* (the sense of being plugged into a talent), and this suggests no passivity on my part. Here we come close to one of the definitions of literary fiction. Even the best kind of popular novel just comes straight at you; you have no conversation with a popular novel. Whereas you do have a conversation (you have an intense argument) with *Herzog*, with *Henderson*, with *Humboldt*,

---

of literature: its imitation of nature cannot prepare you for the main events. For the main events, only experience will answer. 'If love cuts them up so much . . . why not be sensible and sign off early?' My father had taken that advice. In 1987 he was sixty-five; Bellow was seventy-two, and by no means done.

* John Updike has written about the young men who come to see him, with their questions and their shaking hands. My hands would shake for Updike, in the summer of that same year. As I loaded the tea tray (me milk, him . . . camomile?) in the cafeteria of Massachusetts General Hospital, he noticed this and said smoothly, 'Why don't *I* carry that?' I learned from the experience. When young men come to see me, with their questions and their shaking hands (only the true fans tremble), I place their drinks on the table before them and avert my gaze while they take their first sip or splash.

† A three-draft man myself, I was shocked to learn that Bellow had *dictated* certain passages in *Humboldt's Gift*. (Then again, I know he can be an obsessional reworker.) Most writers have at least this in common with Nabokov: 'I think like a genius, I write like a distinguished author, and I speak like a child' (*Strong Opinions*).

frowning, nodding, withholding, qualifying, objecting, conceding –
and smiling, smiling first with reluctant admiration, then smiling with
unreluctant admiration. That's how it was on the rooftop in
Jerusalem. And that's how it was last night (18/7/99), long-distance,
when I sat in a London kitchen and reread *Seize the Day*.

So there was happiness for me in Israel; and happiness, I keep
finding, contains a strong admixture of paranoia. Now that you're
happy (you suspect), an aeroplane will come and crash on your head.
Later that year Bellow published *More Die of Heartbreak*, I published
Einstein's Monsters, and Allan Bloom published *The Closing of the
American Mind*.★ And among all this productivity and vigour I can
now only see a sneer of eventual calamity. Let us move seven years
on. I am being let off lightest, with my convulsion of middle age.
Whereas Allan Bloom is dying of AIDS. And that red snapper in St
Martin is feeding off the reef, turning itself into a cyanide capsule,
ready for the Bellows. Of the others at that table in Jerusalem, Teddy
Kolleck would by then have lost his mayoralty to Likud; and his life's
work, the city, which in the mid-1980s was a bazaar of febrile
ecumenicism, would become something much more monolithic,
conservative, and orthodox. The last time I saw Amschel Rothschild
was at a party in London in 1996. As we talked, I picked his brains
about firearms for my suicide novel *Night Train*. Three months later
he hanged himself in a Paris hotel room.†

★ The deserved popularity of this freak bestseller almost unhinged its thesis,
because the unregarded morbidity of the American soul turned out to be
something that millions of Americans wanted to read about. Bloom's book
is gripping, funny, and bruisingly erudite; all the same (and I mustn't go into
italics here), it is consistently obtuse on the subject of nuclear weapons.
These weapons irritate Bloom, but only inasmuch as they provide a pretext
for undergraduate self-pity. Strange to say, he didn't think hard enough – he
didn't think philosophically – about the question and the way it affects some
of the propositions he takes for granted. 'Concern for the safety of one's
family', writes Bloom (he is summarising Hobbes and Locke), 'is a powerful
reason for loyalty to the state, which protects them.' A nuclearised world,
where the state puts one's family in the front line, entirely undoes this
apparent verity.
† Suicide is the most sombre of all human outcomes; it really is the saddest
story. My novel was about a suicide that seemed inexplicable, but Amschel's

There is no bringing Amschel back, although he still half-exists, in each of his three children. Others did come back. After twenty-five days in the waiting-room of death Saul Bellow came back. Then he undertook another retrieval. Allan Bloom 'is' Ravelstein. I use inverted commas but I feel that I am soon going to have to discard them – along with much other critical punctilia. Of course, only a semiliterate would say that Harold Skimpole *is* Leigh Hunt or that Rupert Birkin *is* D.H. Lawrence; of course, even the most precisely recreated character is nonetheless *recreated*, transfigured; of course, autobiographical fiction is still fiction – an autonomous construct; and, of course, the *roman-à-clef* is the lowest form of wit. I know Bellow's novel far, far better than I ever knew Bellow's friend. Yet *Ravelstein* comes close to persuading me otherwise. This book is numinous. It constitutes an act of resuscitation, and in its pages Bloom lives.

Climacteric

– I want to put Rob in a novel, said Kingsley.

The time was 1982 (post-Jane); the place was the sitting-room of the pokey, wonky little corner house in Kentish Town. My brother

---

suicide was far more dumbfounding, because it was real and because it was near. Some probable precipitants did emerge (death of mother; pressure of work). But perhaps the most striking disclosure, a mere detail at first glance, was to be found in the statement of the chambermaid who, that afternoon, delivered some towels to his room. She described his manner towards her as impatient and abrupt. And the idea of Amschel behaving overweeningly seemed so unrecognisable, so impossible . . . Generally suicide comes about at the moment when the pain schedule suddenly contains no air and no prospect of it. But the literature tells us that it can also be triggered by ungovernable impulse, by a kind of mental spasm. I back away, as you must do, believing that Amschel's *felo de se* was involuntary. He is part of my fundamental trinity of significant suicides, along with Susannah Tomalin (daughter of Claire and Nicolas) and Lamorna Seale, the mother of my daughter Delilah. Whatever else it did, the other suicide recently mentioned in these pages, that of Frederick West, was entirely intelligible and caused not a flicker in the moral cosmos.

Philip was also present . . . We had recently had a visit from Philip's namesake: Larkin. I was getting out of my car on the appointed evening when I saw Philip L. and his girlfriend, the virile Monica, as they moved questingly up Leighton Road. They had been to the cricket, at Lord's,* and were now slightly lost; they looked apologetic and provincial, Larkin reminding me of one of his own self-deprecations (an imaginary headline, to accompany an unfortunate photograph: Faith-Healer, Or Heartless Fraud?). I approached them slowly and obliquely, not wishing to cause alarm, and got them safely indoors. Where my brother, to my surprise, crossed the room and embraced his godfather. Larkin's response surprised me too (because I knew his poems better than I knew their author); it exactly corroborated a remark that Kingsley would make in December 1985, in Hull, at Larkin's funeral:

it was impossible to meet him without being aware in the first few seconds of his impeccable attentive courtesy: grave but at the same time sunlit, always ready to respond to a gleam of humour or warmth.

And of course he and Hilly always took delight in each other . . . This was the last time I saw Larkin. A bad time was coming for our household poets. And what a luxury it is, to have these poets in your past. John Betjeman† went in 1984. We had seen a fair bit of Betjeman in the Seventies: he was (ominously, for the marriage) one of the very few friends whom Jane and Kingsley equally liked.

* Monica berated me for underestimating the skills of legspinner Abdul Qadir, of Pakistan. It was a browse through my younger son's *Wisden Cricketers' Almanack* (touchingly to be found on his bedside table) that gave me the date for this meeting.
† Cecil Day Lewis was Poet Laureate from 1968 to 1972 (he succeeded the antique figure of John Masefield, who filled the post for thirty-seven years). Betjeman was Poet Laureate from 1972 to 1984. Larkin, the obvious successor, let it be known that he would turn the job down. I wrote an obituary of Larkin, and almost a decade later I would write about him at much greater length – to protect him from his biographer, Andrew Motion, who the other week (5/99) was appointed Poet Laureate.

In a late letter KA passes on a posthumous rumour about 'Betch' reducing a secretary to tears, adding something like: And he'll be remembered as the sweetie, while the real teddybear (KA) will be remembered as just another old swine. I never saw anything but the party-animal side of Betjeman (once a summer lunch that went on till dark) and the sweetie side of Betjeman (whenever he came to the house on Hadley Common, even late on, he would always insist on climbing however many stairs it took to visit you if you were sick).

I said,

– Rob?

– Yeah. I thought I'd put him in a book. You know, just a minor character.

– What sort of thing?

– A drinker who's trying to produce films.

– Rob never tried to produce films. He was an assistant director.

– There you are then. Would he mind?

– I shouldn't think so. I won't tell him about it.

– What shall I call him?

There was a silence. Then my brother said,

– Call him *Rob*.

Quite a while later, in 1990, Kingsley published *The Folks That Live on the Hill*. Among the minor characters is a heavy-drinking would-be film producer called *Rob*. But 'Rob' *isn't* Rob. The truth is that you can't put real people into a novel, because a novel, if it is alive, will inexorably distort them, will tug them all out of shape, to fulfil its own designs. Accordingly, *The Folks That Live on the Hill* is very broadly about kindness, and the main point about 'Rob' is that he is indifferent to kindness, or takes kindness as no more than his due – an entirely unRoblike trait. In this regard Rob makes me think of Aziz's plangent but puzzling lines (they are spoken 'gravely') in *A Passage to India*: 'Mr Fielding, no one can ever realise how much kindness we Indians need, we do not even realise it ourselves. But we know when it has been given.' And being mildly and casually generous to Rob is its own reward, or I probably wouldn't do it . . . In his essay of 1973, 'Real and Made-up

People',★ KA wrote: 'By what is either a paradox or a truism, the closer the likeness of the real . . . person, the less interesting he will be in the novel.' This was something that my father and I had always agreed about: until 1978. Calling the minor character 'Rob', though, was no more than Kingsley's continuation of an amusing moment with his sons.

In the same essay he wrote the sentence I quoted early on: 'I did once, out of laziness or sagging imagination, try to put real people on paper and produced what is by common consent my worst novel, *I Like It Here*.' In my view KA's worst, or least-good, novel is the alternate-world fantasy *Russian Hide-and-Seek* (1980),† which is flanked by the problematic *Jake's Thing* (1978) and, after the longest gap in his career, the superproblematic *Stanley and the Women* (1984). This period was climacteric – and how brutally the *COD* defines that word: '*a.* constituting a crisis, critical; (Med.) occurring at period of

★ Reprinted in *The Amis Collection* (1990). The autobiographical writer, he goes on, is peculiar to this century: '. . . D.H. Lawrence started writing about himself, people he knew and what there was of what had actually happened to him, and his knowing or unknowing heirs are all around us today. They have raised the ghosts of long-dead Philistines who thought the poet a liar and history the only truth, and Katherine Mansfield is called "the most autobiographical of writers" in unadorned commendation . . .' Lawrence regularly faced legal pressure not just for obscenity but also for libel. If he were writing today, he would also have to moderate such sentiments as the following, from *Lady Chatterley's Lover*, when Connie questions the value of her loyalty to Clifford: 'What was she serving, after all? A cold spirit of vanity, that had no warm human contacts, and that was as corrupt as any low-born Jew, in craving for prostitution to the bitch-goddess, Success.' I quoted this passage to Saul Bellow, who calmly agreed that it belonged on the debit side of the ledger. I remain less tolerant. The anti-Semitism of the comically despicable 'citizen' in *Ulysses* is more subtle than this. Lawrence's slur is a double commonplace: a cliché of the head and a cliché of the heart. † I said to him, 'What's the point of the title?' He said, 'It's a play on Russian roulette.' I said, 'People won't get that. *I* didn't get it.' And he said, 'Ah, but don't forget that you're incredibly thick.' Set in the twenty-first century, the novel describes an England almost medievalised by fifty years of Russian rule. At a dinner on publication day Kingsley presented a copy to Margaret Thatcher. 'What's it about?' she asked. He told her. 'Get another crystal ball,' said the Iron Lady.

[229]

life (45-60) at which vital force begins to decline.' Kingsley's fiction would recover, and triumphantly. But from my vantage it seemed that he was somehow adrift in art and life. *Russian Hide-and-Seek* was a depressed book. He didn't have the energy to travel so far from his own concerns. *Jake* and *Stanley*, on the other hand, were asphyxiatingly close to the pain schedule. In Kingsley I sensed lost equilibrium. His life, obviously and demonstrably, had (half) survived a *tormenta*, a raging sea. But what had happened to the work? Only other writers, perhaps, will believe me when I say that this question felt just as serious.

The day I finished *Jake's Thing* I went over to the house in Hampstead. When Jane left the room I said,

– All that sex-therapy stuff. Did you really *do* any of that?

I knew something about my father's sex life. One source was Jane, who even in 1975 was telling me more about my father's growing remissness in that area than I really wanted to know. Another source was *Jake's Thing*.

– Yes!

– Christ! That genital-focusing stuff and going to bed with a ring round your cock?

– Yes! Some of it.

– Christ!

– Well, in a case like this you have to show willing . . .

– Yeah, but the *novel* didn't show willing, did it?

And he gave me that look again. Incapacitated: gently incapacitated. Jane came back into the room. We changed the subject.

In happier times the two writers used to end the working day by reading out to each other, over evening drinks, the results of their labours. I don't think they did that with *Jake's Thing*. And they certainly didn't do it with *Stanley and the Women*.

He was a man who couldn't be alone in a house after dark. I had no idea what action to take but I expected the call and at once knew my brother's meaning when he said,

– Mart. It's happened.

Letter from College

Exeter College, Oxford

[July? 1971]

Dearest Dad and Jane,

Sorry I haven't written sooner – this is my first letter this
term – but it's so nice here in the summer that it's difficult not to
spend the whole time lying drunkenly in punts or in the Fellows'
garden pretending to read. Also I'm spending a lot of time
looking for somewhere to live next year. I could use your advice:
we want somewhere quite far out and with 3 bedrooms. The
prices are around £12 and, bearing in mind that it costs
£8–£9 living in college, how much should I allow for food
and how much for rent.* I'm sharing with two other boys
(I can't look far enough ahead about Gully),† so that's £4 each
on rent, or thereabouts. The thing is that unless you're incredibly
lucky you have to take it for the holidays since it's virtually‡

---

* No question-mark in the original. It seems that these letters, now, were
being addressed to Jane only – hence the domestic/amatory emphasis.
† A couple of crossings-out and insertions here. It at least makes a change to
find Osric enfeebled, not by getting out of bed every day, but by emotion.
Gully, or Alexandra Wells, is the dedicatee of *The Rachel Papers*, though she
was not its heroine, whom we have yet to get to. I had been introduced to
Gully much earlier, in about 1965 ('But you said you hated him! You said
he had a jukebox!': this was Gully's confidante, Anna Haycraft – a.k.a. the
novelist Alice Thomas Ellis). We started going out together when she came
to St Hilda's to read History in 1969, and it lasted in its intermittent way
about as long as the average marriage. Ten years?
‡ 'Virtually': the signature tune of the idler and charlatan.

[231]

impossible to get a place in October. Anyway, tell me what you think.

Things are more or less O.K. with Gully but I keep on wishing I weren't tied down and that I'm wasting the best years of my life etc., since, as far as I'm concerned, the relationship isn't getting any better: it just seems to consist of me trying to maintain the illusion that I'm as keen on her as ever (which I'm not). I know it's all a question of responsibility but I keep thinking that it's my life too. It's at that awful stage where I think I'd be equally pissed off without her, so I'm frightened as well as squeamish about ending it.

I had an incredible talk with Wordsworth★ the other day. He said Shakespeare was probably queer, anyway disgusted with heterosexuality, and we started talking about queers generally. He said he was used to the idea since his father and brother are queer: another minute went by and he said casually that his mother had been queer too and had lived with another woman all through the war.† He said he wasn't sure where his heterosexual genes came from and I saw what he meant. I'm doing Shakespeare all this term which is good fun, and Wordsworth is talking about all the prizes I should go in for. I don't know about that but he agrees that I should stay up a month or so at the end of term since this is the last chance I'll get to do some big reading before finals – a good idea don't you think? Also this term I'm attending a series of seminars given by Prof. Northrop Frye – very high-powered, one man from each college.

I've fixed it all for Sall & I'll take her punting and so on. Write to me about Gully & the house business & I'll see you soon (I'll let you know if it's for a weekend).

    Lots of Love,
    Martin.

★ My tutor's biological connection with the poet, still of interest to an Osric becoming slowly more literary, was real but nepotic. His then wife Ann sent me, three years later, the following comment on my first novel. 'Have read your very [*something*] book.' The difficult word was three letters long and took me about a week to decipher. It was: het.
† My tutor advises me now that 'bisexual' would have been more accurate.

Could you send the £50 to the Bursar by the end of the week if poss. & the following for me. Dry cleaning £1 – 5, coffee etc., £1. Dinner credits £2, and filing pads £1 = £5 – 5 – 0.

Love to everyone & Miss Plush.

Feasts of Friends

There was a discreet but persistent knocking on my bedroom door. I awoke.

– May I come in?

My younger son stood at the foot of the bed. This was during the lugubrious Christmas of 1994 when the three of us still used to camp out in the flat at weekends: there is the carton of chocolate yoghurt with a used teabag in it. The point was that the boys (then aged eight and ten) would usually wake me, of a Sunday morning, by jumping up and down on my head. Jacob now whispered,

– Daddy, I'm sorry to disturb you.

– Are you? Why?

– I'm sorry to disturb you. But it's the Jackal on the phone.

The Jackal was my agent, Andrew Wylie. My sons had seen things in the papers and asked me some questions about them. Who, they wanted to know, was this man they were calling the Jackal? The Jackal, I explained, was called the Jackal because of his claws and his jaws and the tail-slit in the back of his pinstripe suit. They didn't really believe it, but Jacob, here, was erring on the side of caution.

I can't remember the details of this particular call. But it must have been an important one and I'm sure I attended to it closely and uneasily at the time. Negotiations for my novel *The Information* would continue into the New Year. I have in front of me Julian Barnes's friendship-ending letter, which arrived the day after the deal went through and is dated 12 January 1995. It is a remarkable document. It merits a reply . . .

And I can't remember the details of all those months of crucifixion in the press. 'Why always you?' I was asked. I'm tired of saying that I don't understand it. I am tired of saying that I am tired of saying that I don't understand it. When it was happening I kept murmuring to myself, Lord, I am ignorant and a stranger to my fellow man. It was chastening, it was even stimulating, to be taken aback by an entity you thought you understood: England. This wasn't a story about me, because there was no story. 'Where is the *story* here?' foreign journalists would ask me, as they tried to grasp it: you could see their foreheads straining to grasp it. But this wasn't a story about me. It was a story about England.

On 16 January 1995, Kinch soared free of London's Heathrow Airport and flew to Boston's Logan. As I climbed from the cab I was imagining the kind of looks that Saul Bellow and I would soon exchange. He was thirty-seven years my senior, and his ordeal had been immeasurably more serious. Still, to paraphrase Philip Larkin, in the *Letters*: his was the harder course, but mine had to be lived by me. I outsuffered Saul only in one paltry particular: so far, he was not being widely attacked for being sick. Nobody was saying that his submission to intensive care was 'cosmetic'. He was, as always, being attacked about other things. But not about that.

As we cautiously embraced I said,

– You feel a little lighter.

– But *you* feel a little lighter too . . .

It was a fish, a red snapper ('clammy' to the palate, and served with mayonnaise like 'zinc ointment') – it was a reef-feeding 'pescavore' that had almost done for him. Prying at the living coral, this fish had armed itself with a toxin exorbitantly hostile to human life . . .

As I write, I keep apprehending Bellow's ordeal through the radiance of the novel *Ravelstein*, in which events are given point, order and meaning – and, in this case, intimations of universal grandeur. I should remind myself of the ordinary misery of the thing, the meshugga ill luck of it. And I too stood there in the hall, clothed in the appalling quiddity of my case: modern, local, lurid. In *Seize the Day* (1959) Bellow wrote that 'a man's griefs with his teeth' accounted for about 2 per cent of the whole. Whereas I would revise this percentage in accordance with Clive James's dictum, emphatically and empathetically urged on me when I was about twenty-seven: 'Nine out of ten bad things happen at the dentist's.' Saul's bad thing had happened in a paradisal setting. Not as beautiful, true, as the New Guinea rain forest and its orchid waterfall, where the nostrils of the traveller are greeted by the fragrance of fallen warriors turning on the spit. But the Caribbean (with its seascape, its sudden sunsets) was a good place to be taught a lesson about the weakness of our 'life tenure': the lack of cosmic support for it. When he was back in Boston, medical technology imposed itself. Machines did his living for him, and he went under for three and a half weeks. Thus consciousness was abandoned. All that was left was the subliminal mind. 'Sub: under as regards position + L *limen-inis* threshold.' That's where he went, for twenty-five days: under the threshold.

We all talked a storm that night: we had good stories to tell – chillers, tinglers. In those days the Bellows were living in a semi-ambassadorial residence provided by Boston University; their guest-room was in the next house along, and it must have been about five a.m., my time, when I strolled into it and took out my pen . . . On the table by the window, I have seen fit to record, lay a copy of *Too Much Too Soon*, 'the spellbinding new novel by the bestselling author of *Everything and More*'. The room also contained a pair of globes. Two worlds. Everything and *more*? Certain people are not easily satisfied. I was satisfied. Notebook: 'Sometimes the same light in the eyes, sometimes a different light.' It seemed to me that he was mentally intact and entire;* Janis made it clear, though, that he was alternately desolated and infuriated by his physical shortfalls. (*Ravelstein*, early draft of the penultimate page: '[The neurologist] put me through some simple tests, all of which I failed . . . The degree of

---

* With one fascinating lacuna. He described the 'visions' he had experienced during deep unconsciousness ('I was in a vault of a bank in Paris . . .') as if they were real experiences, and not with the tentative air of a man reassembling a dream. He was very definite. The visions are fully dealt with in the early version of *Ravelstein* but most are expunged in the final draft. Bellow must have felt that they didn't measure up structurally, or that their tendency was to deuniversalise.

recovery possible could not be estimated; I would soon be eighty years of age.') Notebook: 'I swear he has gone from being bigger than me to being smaller than me. Confident (?) that he will renew.' And he did renew.

And I was satisfied. Princess Diana used to claim that her favourite poem was 'Ye Wearie Wayfarer' by Adam Lindsay Gordon, four lines of harmonial Victorian rubbish that go as follows:

> Life is mostly froth and bubble,
> Two things stand like stone.
> Kindness in another's trouble,
> Courage in your own.

For fun, Kingsley had recently rewritten 'Ye Wearie Wayfarer', imbuing it with something of the spirit of the times:

> Life is mainly grief and labour.
> Two things get you through.
> Chortling when it hits your neighbour,
> Whingeing when it's you.

Friendship, as I see it, lies at the midpoint between these two stanzas. It is a mysterious power: you show your friend your weakness, and somehow you are both the stronger . . .

The next morning I demanded to be taken, for my breakfast, to a place called something like We Are Pancakes. Largely because I like the look of reproach she gives me when I do it, I often tease Janis Bellow about modern Americana – unaccountably, really, for she is Canadian.*

---

* You can faintly hear it in her *ow* sounds, which sometimes resemble *oh* sounds. Linguisticians call this phenomenon 'Canadian raising' (the tongue lifts on the vowel). Once, while Kingsley was in the room, I watched a tennis match broadcast from Montreal, and the line-judges kept shouting 'Oat!' Kingsley said, 'Do Canadians say "the Moanties"?' The next time I saw my Canadian brother-in-law (as he was then), Chaim Tannenbaum, I said, 'Do Canadians say "the Moanties"?' He was uncharacteristically defensive about it. 'Canadians do *not* say "the Moanties",' said Chaim.

We did in fact end up in a cafeteria called, not We Are Pancakes or Pancakes Are Us, but something like Home of the Pancake or Mike's Pancake World. Saul, I thought, was significantly improved: overnight. When I said goodbye to him I was mildly scandalised to ascertain that he had gone back to being bigger than me. (I take no credit for this, though maybe *I* got smaller.) 'He just *decided* to get better,' Janis would tell me, months later, when the recovery, the remarkable recovery, was achieved. And I believe her. He did it with his head.

I flew to Hollywood – to visit an *actor* who had come back from the grave: Mr John Travolta.

He Hugged It to Him

Readers of Kingsley's *Letters* will follow the emotional arc that the book describes. We begin, after an interesting stutter,★ with a massive and unbroken tranche of prose addressed to Philip Larkin – several tens of thousands of words, even after abridgment. It was love, unquestionably love, on my father's part. He wanted to be with Larkin *all the time*; that this was impossible continued to irk and puzzle him. Larkin, I think, felt the same way, or rather he felt the Larkinesque equivalent. But he had less talent for love . . . Then life started to happen to Kingsley, beginning with war, then marriage, children, teaching, travel, divorce, remarriage, divorce. And success happened too (it had the odd effect of calming him: success cooled him down). Meanwhile, life was happening to Larkin, but he had *no* talent for that, remaining, to the end, single, childless and site-tenacious. He did this quietly and heroically, as I now see it. He hugged melancholy to him, in the poems – *for* the poems, it might even have been. It wasn't that he cultivated misery. It was more the feeling: unhappiness is ordinary

★ In which KA humourlessly chivvies a recusant member of the Communist Party. In Oxford in 1940/41, Kingsley was Comrade Amis. (And Comrade Murdoch was Iris.)

and everyday and in abundant supply; let's see if I can make something out of mine, which is otherwise unalleviable.

My sense of Larkin comes from my childhood. I had several good times with him as an adult or near-adult. He had Osric over to dinner at All Souls, where he was in residence while working on the *Oxford Book of Twentieth-Century English Verse*.★ In his room before dinner he gave me, or maybe just showed me (was it a present for his niece? I already had it, anyway), a copy of the Rolling Stones' live LP, *Get Yer Ya-Yas Out*. We agreed that it had clear strengths – particularly 'Stray Cat Blues'. Then in to dinner with the Warden, John Sparrow, and others. Attired in an improvised tuxedo (black velvet suit with some black rag around the neck), I felt myself simultaneously sneered at and fancied by Sparrow and by additional pewter-haired relicts in this all-male sanctuary. Who else was there? Bowra? Rowse, the 'biographer' of Shakespeare? And the conversation?

> Tonight we dine without the Master
> (Nocturnal vapours do not please);
> The port goes round so much the faster,
> Topics are raised with no less ease –
> Which advowson looks the fairest,
> What the wood from Snape will fetch,
> Names for *pudendum mulieris*,
> Why is Judas like Jack Ketch?†

Larkin and I, in any event, contentedly formed a lower-middle-class

★ 'I read *all* Alan Bold today,' he told me. 'How many did you pick?' 'None,' he said. The book would appear two years later, in 1973. I was by then at the *TLS*, and I remember Peter Porter, flushed and brisk with roused feeling and anxiety (because he didn't enjoy the business of dispraise), stalking into the office with his front-page review. The anthology inspired broad debate, even controversy. Everyone seemed to be talking about it. That's how it was, in 1973.

† From Part III (dated 21 December 1971) of the great poem 'Livings'. Part II is perhaps the most extraordinary, with its modernist sprung-rhythm ending (the narrator is the keeper of a lighthouse): 'Lit shelved liners/Grope like mad worlds westward.'

enclave, among all the silver and the servants and the connoisseurial punctilio. We felt solidarity, against this.* And we ate and drank to remarkable effect. Two or three months later, when the Finals results were published, Larkin wrote to me saying how relieved he was: he feared that his hospitality might have damaged my brain. 'Every century has its cushy profession,' he said that night in All Souls. 'It used to be the church. Now it's academe.' We sat at a high-church High Table, with its salvers and chalices, its monstrances and chrismatories: academe at its most epicurean and pseudo-aristocratic. All three sections of the poem 'Livings' conclude with a nightscape. This is the ending of Part II, quoted above:

> The bells discuss the hour's gradations,
> Dusty shelves hold prayers and proofs:
> Above, Chaldean constellations
> Sparkle over crowded roofs.†

Larkin could get a mild kick out of the pompous glamour of All Souls, and so could I.‡ My education was winding up. Life was about

---

* Osric's suzerainty was coming to an end. Twenty-one, and in my last year, I was living in one of the bedsits of a college annex on Iffley Road. My usual evening meal was the basis of the daily diet I served up, nearly two decades later, to Keith Talent in *London Fields*: a vacuum-packed Chicken Korma, say, followed by a Bramley Apple Pie. I was working so hard for my Finals – at least fifteen hours a day – that it would have been an embarrassment if I hadn't got a first. Also, late at night, influenced by (a) one glass of whisky, and (b) my father, I was trying out my first paragraphs of fiction (scenes, descriptions) and feeling an ominous but also energising intimation of the long haul. Despite all this I was frequently as blue as a Larkin line-ending, prematurely aged by Old English, emphatically without a girlfriend (again), my face pale and breakfastless-looking as I went round the corner, in the rain, with my one-and-nine or however much it was, to buy an *Escort* or a *Parade*.
† The Chaldeans ruled Babylonia from 625 to 538 BC. They were celebrated astronomers. Babylon, of course, was famous not only for its Hanging Gardens but also for its impregnable fortifications and its luxury.
‡ And so could the hot Balliol radical, Christopher Hitchens, who was a frequent dinner guest of the Warden's.

to start happening to me. Academe, in humbler form, was something
I felt I might have to fall back on. But what excited me, that night,
was the company of the poet – his presence, his example, his
dedication to the use of words.★

'Philip, you should *spend more*,' I told him, a decade or so later –
dogmatically and fatuously and above all childishly. Because my sense
of him begins in childhood . . . There was always this ritual, in
Swansea, every time he came to stay: Tipping the Boys. I described
the procedure in an obituary I wrote in 1985:

> At first it was sixpence for Philip and threepence for Martin;
> years later it was tenpence against sixpence; later still it was a
> shilling against ninepence: always index-linked and carefully
> graded.

This account contains a grotesque exaggeration: it was *fourpence* for
Philip and threepence for Martin. The heavy, blackened coins were
counted out by Larkin on the kitchen table, in two squat stacks. My
brother and I exchanged uncertain glances (this was the closest we
had come to a religious experience); urged on by our mother, we
darted forward and made the snatch – out from under Larkin's
mournful and priestly gaze. I now see my father hanging back, with
a half-suppressed smile. A smile of what? Of affectionate sadism as
he forced his friend to surrender 7d.? Partly, perhaps. When I

★ I was moving, hereabouts, from foppery to overearnestness. Six or seven
years later, at a regular gathering that would have typically included Clive
James, Russell Davies, Julian Barnes, Terence Kilmartin, Mark Boxer, James
Fenton, the Hitch and (for a while) my father, I put to the table the
following question: Who would you side with, if the choice were limited
to Leavis or Bloomsbury? Everyone else said Bloomsbury. I said Leavis. The
loved and lamented Mark Boxer ('cartoonist and dandy': his own favoured
description) gave a quiet whinny of incredulity. I had never been a Leavisite
and I had written several attacks on his doctrines and followers. But I think
I would cast the same vote, even today. What could be more antipathetic
than Woolf's dismissal of *Ulysses* on the grounds of Joyce's *class*? No, give
me F.R. and Q.D., give me Frank and Queenie, despite all the
humourlessness, the hysteria, and the Soviet gloom.

search the periphery of this memory, though, I come across an earlier scene, with Mum telling us that we would get our tips but we had to remember that this was a serious business for our miserly visitor. 'He's not like Bruce,' she said, with dissimulated levity.* So it was a setup! And my brother and I, in our avarice and awe, were part of the charade. Was Larkin in on it – was Larkin the straight man? Well, whichever way you look at his life he was certainly the strait man, careful, mean, tight, close. *Niggardly* has many fine synonyms (including the welcome Americanism *cheap*, with its simplifying imputation of inadequate income), but *near* is the adjective for Philip Larkin. Near: holding everything to him.

– You should spend more, Philip.

He didn't answer.

– You've just bought the car and that's good. Now you –

– I wish they wouldn't keep sending me these *bills*.

– For the car.

– They keep sending me these *bills*.

– You can afford them. Now you should –

– I wish they wouldn't keep on sending me all these *bills*.

He understood the inhibition perfectly, of course. And it was altogether characteristic of him (of him, of his time, of his place) that having identified the difficulty he did nothing to relieve it. Again, he just hugged it to him. These are the first and last stanzas of the sixteen-line poem 'Money' (1973):

---

* Bruce Montgomery, *my* godfather, and a legend of generosity. He was a minor composer who had some early success with his film scores (*Doctor in the House*, a *Carry On* or two). Bruce tipped the boys with silver, not with brass; he once caused us to rub our eyes, on the afternoon of an unforgettable Guy Fawkes' Night, by giving us *ten bob* for fireworks. It was said of Bruce that when he moved about in public he always held a cocked pound note in his hand. When he needed something, he tended to need it soon and badly. His fate was of the cake-in-the-rain variety often reserved for precocious and flamboyant talents. My last, indirect memory of him is Kingsley's elegiac sigh on being called to the telephone: Bruce was having one of his sessions with the whisky bottle and the address book.

Quarterly, is it, money reproaches me:
'Why do you let me lie here wastefully?
I am all you never had of goods and sex.
You could get them still by writing a few cheques' . . .

I listen to money singing. It's like looking down
From long french windows at a provincial town,
The slums, the canal, the churches ornate and mad
In the evening sun. It is intensely sad.*

'Do you feel you could have had a much happier life?' an interviewer once asked him. And he answered, 'Not without being someone else.' You should spend more, Philip. He didn't, naturally. Someone else would have had to get the goods and the sex. But Larkin did get the poems.

One morning I looked on, through the stair banisters, as Larkin readied himself to walk out into the Swansea rain. Tall beyond utility, bespectacled, prematurely and almost ideally bald, with the beginnings of heaviness in his movements, he sighingly marshalled his mack, his scarf, his hat. Everything about him expressed stoicism (he didn't have a choice) and the opposite of ease . . . Famously, Larkin hated or professed to hate children† and of course never fathered

---

* 'Money' was a favourite of mine; and when I published a novel with the same title, in 1984, I sent Larkin a copy. Unlike my father, he succeeded in finishing it. But in his reply he made it inoffensively clear that he disliked the postmodernist liberties I took with the reader, and that he found the prose too dense and worked-at. Parts of the book amused him. I haven't kept Larkin's letters, I'm afraid (nor any from my father, to Zachary Leader's silent disgust), but I do remember the sentence: 'My big shriek came on page 275 line 3.' And I found *that* funny. Because Larkin seized on a moment where extravagant (and expensive) sexual temptation is greeted by the prediction of extravagant (and deflationary) disappointment. I couldn't take much pride in Larkin's big shriek. The joke was Ian McEwan's; it interrupted a salacious anecdote I was passing on about a Far Eastern brothel. In the British paperback the moment comes on page 292 line 33; in the American paperback, page 271 line 3.
† 'Children are very horrible, aren't they? Selfish, noisy, cruel little brutes.' As a child himself, he has said, he thought he hated everybody: 'but when

any.★ I used to wonder, when I began to read him, if it was my brother and me who put him off. When I was a child Larkin was mythologised for me, at home, as a mock-epic miser and misanthrope. But I trust my sense of him then. Whenever our eyes met and held for a moment he looked on me gently, and I felt, as well as pleasure and reassurance, a peculiarly childish disappointment. Because he was supposed to be a red squirrel, an exotic, and here he was being kind and grey.

So life started happening to Philip, the novelist, and to Kingsley, the poet, as they then saw themselves in 1942. The correspondence remained intense into the middle of the next decade. After *Lucky Jim* it starts to thin and cool. I don't imagine that Larkin coveted his friend's wife and three children;† but in his remote and martyred imaginings it seemed that Kingsley had disappeared, past all recall, into a carwash of goods and sex – and 'all I never had'. From Kingsley's end of it, I sense, there is an impatient awareness of this fantasy and a certain defiance in relishing such vulgar triumphs as

---

I grew up I realised it was just children I didn't like.' I take this to be self-stylisation. Both intellectually and emotionally null, the anti-child position is only good for a joke or two. Kingsley used to occupy it a bit, as we shall learn. But he never aspired to the genuine artistic venom of Larkin's 'children, with their shallow, violent eyes'.

★ The concluding stanza of 'This Be the Verse' – 'Man hands on misery to man./It deepens like a coastal shelf./Get out as quickly as you can,/And don't have any kids yourself' – should be considered alongside the concluding stanza of what I take to be the companion poem (they are technically near-identical), 'The Trees': 'Yet still the unresting castles thresh/In fullgrown thickness every May./Last year is dead, they seem to say,/Begin afresh, afresh, afresh.'

† 'Self's the Man' addresses the nipper option with brilliant brutality: 'He married a woman to stop her getting away/Now she's there all day,/And the money he gets for wasting his life on work/She takes as her perk/To pay for the kiddies' clobber and the drier/And the electric fire . . .' I love the perfect boredom clinched by that last rhyme. And I love the clear injustice of it: as if the eponymous Self benefits not at all from the drier, and the electric fire. Marriage, the poet foresees, would certainly make him mad; he will head for the alternative, unopposed selfhood, where madness looks to be no more than a strong probability.

come his way; and also a vaguer agenda, having to do with Larkin's emotional parsimony, his earlier retreat from full fraternal love. As you follow the thinning, cooling trail of the letters you begin to feel that life has scored a dreary victory here, coarsely skewing an intricate alignment.

Then, eventually, *life* thins and cools. The children grow up, the wives leave (or reconfigure); the world is not so much with us . . . And Larkin is still there, up in Hull, and the neglected intimacy is still there, awaiting reconnection. When in KA's *Letters* you see 'Dear Philip' (and when, in Larkin's, you see 'Dear Kingsley'), then you ready yourself for a different order of disclosure: something much closer in. It is of course delightful, as the intimacy is taken up again, to see the reappearance of familiar endearments, long-disused (Larkin: 'Well, dalling, I cried at the end, 'cos that's just how I feel about you'), delightful, too, to see the rejuvenation of the juvenile in their thrashed jokes and obscene misspellings and yelping capitalisations. But what stays with you is the sense that the two of them, in age, are at last transparent to each other. They are finally equal, equal before God and a godless death, and also physically and – for the first time – sexually equal.* It is now very terrible to watch Larkin falling from this plateau and accelerating

---

* In all likelihood this question deserves more attention than the longish footnote I am going to give it. Whereas Nabokov thought the greatest human division was between those who slept well (complacent dopes, as he saw them) and the great twisting insomniacs (like himself), Graham McClintock, an ensemble character in *Take a Girl Like You* (1960), thinks that the greatest human division is that between 'the attractive and the unattractive'. 'You can have no conception,' unattractive Graham tells attractive Jenny Bunn, 'of the difference between the lives of those who look like you and those who look like me . . . unattractive men don't want unattractive girls, you see. They want attractive girls. They merely *get* unattractive girls.' The beautiful Miss Bunn doesn't end up with Graham. She ends up with Patrick Standish (clearly attractive, and impartially described by another male character as 'beautiful'). Now look at Larkin's unpublished poem 'Letter to a Friend about Girls' (1959): 'After comparing lives with you for years/I see how I've been losing: all the while/I've met a different gauge of girl from yours./Grant that, and all the rest makes sense as well'. The titular 'friend' belongs to a world 'where to want/Is straightway to be wanted', where 'beauty is accepted slang for yes'. In contrast to the

[245]

towards extinction. When he dies, in 1985, the narrative of Kingsley's *Letters* takes on a stunned and deafened feel. It seems like more than the loss of a friend and a poet, he writes to Robert Conquest. What? 'A presence?' The remaining decade of my father's life, as seen here, could almost be considered detachable, like an addendum. As for Larkin's *Letters*, the volume ends with a dictated letter signed in his absence (he is going in for 'the big one'), which itself ends:

> I must mention Sally's★ letter and photograph which arrived this morning. Of course they deserve a separate acknowledgement, and *may* one day get one. I am so glad to see strong resemblances in her to Hilly, who is the most beautiful woman I have ever seen without being in the least pretty (I am sure you know what I mean, and I hope she will too).†
>
> Well, the tape draws to an end; think of me packing up my pyjamas and shaving things for today's ordeal, and hope all goes well. I really feel this year has been more than I deserve; I suppose it's all come at once, instead of being spread out as with most people.
>
> You will excuse the absence of the usual valediction,
>> Yours ever,
>> Philip

---

girls whom the poet comes across: 'They have their world, not much compared with yours,/But where they work, and age, and put off men/By being unattractive, or too shy,/Or having morals – anyhow, none give in . . .' The poem makes rather a show of failing to draw the obvious conclusion: that the 'I' is unattractive too. Scientists of attraction tell us that what we look for, in the other, are the features of babyhood: curves of eye and brow and mouth. Which at least means that we have all been beautiful. And will all be ugly, in the end. Writing to Larkin on 14 January 1980, Kingsley tersely introduces himself to the final commonalty. 'I am getting ugly now', he writes, 'because I am getting old.'

★ My sister.

† My mother had her own rules, or grades, of attraction. Members of both sexes were ranked as one of the following: a dud, a possible, a smasher. I once asked her where Larkin stood on this scale. She surprised me by saying, 'Oh, a definite possible' – but then the fact that she quite fancied him was on record in an earlier Amis-to-Larkin letter. She knew his qualities.

Fuck Off – I

It was said that I turned away. It was said that I took a friendship lightly – that I took friendship lightly.

I have before me Julian Barnes's letter of 12 January 1995. Technically this piece of paper is my property, but the text is Julian's copyright. I won't quote from it, except to say that its last phrase is a well-known colloquialism. That phrase consists of two words. The words consist of seven letters. Three of them are *f*s.

The hit-him-again-Dai treatment I was getting in the press ('Martin Amis in Greed Storm')* over *The Information*, still un-published, still unfinished, seemed to me *ipso facto* evidence that the negotiation had already taken the wrong turning. So finally I went all in with my American agent, Wylie, and this meant breaking with my English agent of twenty-three years, Pat Kavanagh. The second half of that process I found decisively dismal (in spite of rich and recent experience of more intimate separations), making me feel that such griefs do their work by straightforward accumulation, that a limit could be reached, and that I had suddenly reached mine. Still, years earlier my father, too, had broken with Pat's agency, and no friendships had been lost. That professional rupture had gone unremarked, though, and mine was far more painfully public, magnifying everything, distorting everything . . .

Now Julian, of course, was and is married to Pat Kavanagh, and I knew him to be an uxorious man. But as I recognised his handwriting, over breakfast on the morning of the thirteenth, I found myself expecting him to say that he knew the difference between

---

* To turn a fuss into a storm the press must procure the censure of at least one peer. Two is better, but one will do. So you work the switchboard until you find a writer who happens to be in a lousy mood. This time they got A.S. Byatt, justly famous for her novels, her short stories, and her inability to get off the telephone. While conceding that I might need money (there was the divorce, and the costs involved in having my 'teeth fixed'), she said she didn't see why she should 'subsidise' my greed. Later, in her note of apology, she said she'd had a toothache when the journalist rang.

church and state, and that the two would go on being separate in his mind. Then I read the letter.

My first response was guilt that I had reduced him to writing something so blunderingly ugly. And so self-defeating, too. Christ, I thought: he never liked me anyway! The letter made me question the substance, let alone the value, of the friendship it cancelled. That may sound implausibly neat, I realise. And the feeling didn't last. As the reader will be exhaustively aware, I had more proximate worries – and Julian listed the ones he knew about, and in no sympathetic spirit, either. January 13 was in fact a good day, an epochal day. That letter was in my pocket while I sat talking equably with my ex-wife for the first time in twenty months. Then in the evening I spent an hour with it and wrote my reply.

The last time I lost a friend was in childhood. Since then I have suffered temporary rifts but no excommunications. In this case, as is the way of such things, I was losing two friends, not one. The letter I wrote was conciliatory. And I did try to revive the friendship, about a year later, after signs of a thaw. His rebuff was civil. Its phrasing tended to confirm my feeling that all this went back a lot further than 1995.

What am I doing? Setting the record straight?* As Christopher Hitchens learned when he signed the house managers' affidavit (contradicting the sworn testimony of presidential aide Sidney Blumenthal), the sacrifice of a friendship is a terrible affront to the Sauls and Jonathans of the media (each to each an Achilles, a Patroclus). The slant they'll always give it is that the sacrifice was, at once, utterly calculating and utterly blithe. And never regretted. Whereas in the real world, the world of experience, a vanished friendship leaves you with many doubts and questions; it is an amorphous absence that haunts your present, your future and, most unwelcomely, your past. I should think this is how it is for Julian, too.

That letter I wrote to Julian is his property but my copyright:

---

* The most that will happen here, I suppose, is that one or two journalists will take the friendship stuff out of the shithead factfile devoted to me and put it into the shithead factfile devoted to Julian.

54A Leamington Road Villas,
London W11 1HT

Dear Jules

I was going to write to you and say something like:

Twelve years ago you rang me up and said, 'Mart, tell me to
fuck off and everything if you want – but have you left
Antonia?' As it happened, I went back to Antonia, that time,
twelve years ago. But I liked the way you framed the question.
It was characteristic.

I was then going to say something like:

Jules, tell me to fuck off and everything if you want – but try
and stay my friend, and try and help me be a friend to Pat.

Now I have your answer before I asked the question. I will call
you in a while – quite a long while. I'll miss you.
Martin

For the first time in these pages I sense the twist of rancour in me,
and my hands, as I write, feel loath and cold. But I had to assert it, to
my readers, and also to my friends. It was said that I turned away –
and I don't do that. I won't be the one to turn away.

Letter from College

Exeter College, Oxford
Monday, [*sic*. Summer 1971]

Dearest Jane,*

Here are my Battels. I've arranged to stay up about six weeks (until 1st August) and I'll probably come back a couple of weeks early (in September) if we've got somewhere to live by then. I'm applying for a vacation grant which will be handy since I'll have to eat out and so on. I want to come down for some of the weekends, but this is going to be my last chance to do any really thorough reading, so it's going to be like a 14 week term. I hope my tutor will still take the trouble to bully me a bit.

I still haven't been able to bring myself to tell Gully that I don't think our living together will work and it's getting to be pretty worrying since we're supposed to be looking for suitable places to live. I think she knows I'm not happy about [it] but I suppose she's just hoping for the best. It's such an awful responsibility. A friend of mine here is getting married on Friday (I'm being best man) – I haven't said anything to him but the whole thing makes me increasingly convinced that I'm not going to get married until I'm about 70. It's all too harrowing.

* So Dad has dropped out, rather hurtfully in retrospect, now that I know how many letters he wrote to everyone else. The only other time we corresponded at all regularly was during the fiscal year 1979–80, when I was abroad. That was his climacteric, and I'm sorry I wasn't around. But Philip was. Philip also came to see me in Paris where, in seven months, I wrote the novel of mine that annoyed Kingsley most, *Other People*.

I hope things are O.K. at home – Rob and Olivia said you were all very jolly when they came up for the day. I want to come down the week-end after next, but I'll let you know for sure before then. Give my love to everyone inc. K. (I saw two *stunning* Blenheims the other day – R[osie] should definitely have one for her 2nd husband).

  Lots of Love,
   Mart XX

P.S. Could I also have a cheque for £8 – £3-10 for the tip for my scout (extra because I'm staying up, Dry Cleaning 30/-, [writing?] Pads 10/-, Coffee 10/-, and Dinner Credits £2-
   See you soon.

Thinking With the Blood

– So you won in the end, said my mother, in mid-January, 1995.

   – Have you really been following all this, Mum?

   – Not at first. Until they started attacking you. Then I thought: *où* . . . Anyway you won in the end, dear.

   – Did I? I suppose I did.

I flew to Boston and then I flew to Los Angeles and checked into the Beverly Wilshire Hotel. This is the hotel showcased in *Pretty Woman*. *Pretty Woman*, if you remember, tells the story of an LA hooker (Julia Roberts) redeemed by a handsome businessman (Richard Gere). There is a scene, set in one of the very best rooms of the Beverly Wilshire, that features strawberries, champagne and (if I remember rightly) oral sex. Under the auspices of a vigorously postmodern PR move, each newly arrived guest now finds in his room a bowl of strawberries and a (half) bottle of champagne. Which might prompt the literalminded to ring room service and ask after the whereabouts of Julia Roberts or, at least, an LA hooker . . . Luridly Kinch prepared for his *à deux* dinners with Travolta. On the first night John's wife, Kelly Preston, appeared with their two-year-old son: little Jett ('Jett's eyelashes', I would write, 'are an inch long'). Jett Travolta, the life of Jett Travolta: this is a tremendously good idea for a novel . . . The *New Yorker*'s Caroline Graham came to see me poolside at the Wilshire. She was slightly dismayed, I think, by the condition of my face. 'But you won,' she said. Did I? What did I beat? A few days later Caroline improvised a black bowtie for me in the carpark beneath the venue for the Golden Globes, where I would be rooting for my boy John (Best Actor, *Pulp Fiction*). We entered the building, preceded by Sharon Stone, a circus horse of blonde stardom, fiercely cheered by the cordoned crowd. Inside I was immediately and humblingly face to face with Sophia Loren (a 'proud' beauty whose habitual expression suggests that she is always an instant away from imperial indignation). Over by the door was the slouching, sidling figure of Quentin Tarantino. He won (Best Screenplay). Travolta lost. Who beat him? Tom Hanks? Jessica Lange won (Best Actress, *Blue Sky*). In her speech she thanked absolutely everyone. 'Lastly but not leastly.' Open widely. What nextly? . . . John Travolta is one of the sanest men I have ever met. He wastes no time pretending not to be a movie star. Even the Scientology stuff (depicted, in the clippings, as a cross between yoga and satanism) turns out to be almost shockingly hardnosed: life as a duty-roster. I have never felt uglier than when I dined with Travolta (or poorer: me with my VW Golf, him with his three aeroplanes). He gave no sign that he noticed my difficulty: the absence, the loss, in the middle of my face. And on the set of *Get Shorty*, on the last day, after pizza in his trailer (like a deluxe mobile home), he embraced me as I left – the man whose androgynous beauty was praised by Truffaut . . . I went to New York and wrote the piece in a hotel room. 'You won,' an American journalist would soon be saying to me, 'but it wasn't a clear victory, was it?' And I said, 'Over what?' . . .

One day ten months later, when I hailed a cab outside St Pancras's Hospital, where my father lay, the driver said,

– Notting Hill? I thought you lived in Camden Town.

– Not yet.

– I was reading somewhere you lived in Camden Town.

– I'm moving next month.

Into my father's street. Half a mile from his house – but my father's street.

– Ah! So they're one step ahead of you now. They're *dictating* to you now.

When I returned from New York (after more dentistry: much more dentistry) my new publishers told me that they were going to rush my novel out to exploit 'all the publicity'. But hang on, I thought: all the publicity was *bad* publicity. Shouldn't we, rather, be waiting for it to wear off?★

★ All publicity isn't good publicity. As a New York publicist put it: 'What: the guy's an asshole so I'll go and buy his novel?'

[253]

They *were* dictating to me. And I lost, because I felt for my novel. It was a disinterested use of words but it didn't *look* like that, arriving noisily and as it were triumphantly, and creating a cognitive dissonance about itself. Because the book was about losing, not winning, about failure, my failure.

This only happened here, of course. I was being dictated to. I was being directed in a film about England.

The Hitch: New England, 1989

Ravelstein threw his head back at this. Shutting his eyes he flung himself bodily back into laughter. In my own way I did the same thing. As I've said before it was our sense of what was funny that brought us together, but that would have been a thin, anemic way to put it. A joyful noise – *immenso giubilo*, an outsize joint agreement picked us up together, and it would get you nowhere to try to formulate it.

I said in the car, the hired Chevrolet Celebrity,
 – Now no sinister balls, okay?
 – . . . No sinister balls.
 – Promise?
 – Promise.

My passenger was Christopher Hitchens and I was taking him to Vermont to meet Saul Bellow. We would have dinner and stay the night and drive back to Cape Cod the following morning. Cape Cod was where I spent eight or nine summers with my first wife, and with the boys, on Horseleech Pond, south of Wellfleet . . . The trope *sinister balls* went back to our days at the *New Statesman*. In 1978 the incumbent editor, Anthony Howard, bowed to historical forces and honourably stepped down. I and the Hitch were part of the complicated, two-tier, six-member committee that would decide on his successor. During an interview Neal Ascherson, one of the three candidates on the final shortlist,★ came up with the following: 'Anyone who resists the closed shop is going to get the biggest bloody nose of all time.' I said afterwards that this was sinister balls, and Christopher, whether or not he agreed (he was, of course, much more pro-union than I was), certainly seemed to be taken by the phrase. So 'no sinister balls' meant no vehement assertions of a left-wing tendency. In 1989 temporary fluctuations – going under the name of Political Correctness – had rigged up Saul Bellow as a figure of the right; he was under frequent attack, and I felt that he deserved a peaceful evening in his own house. As it happens I now believe that Bellow and Hitchens are not dissimilar in their political intuitions – especially in their sense of how America is managed or carved up. When I read Christopher's book on Clinton, *No One Left to Lie To* (1999), I was physiologically reminded of an hour I spent with Saul, in 1988. I was on my way down to New Orleans to cover the Republican Convention (where Bush unleashed Dan Quayle), and I requested a political tutorial to prepare me for it. Bellow's illusionless vision of Beltway jobbery and pelf caused the hairs on the back of my head to tingle . . . As the Chevrolet Celebrity moved boldly down Route 6, I was pretty confident that the evening would go well. There would be no sinister balls.

A drive of five or six hours, but the buddy-movie, radio-on feel of the journey was part of the treat. Stops were made for the huge uneaten meals and many powerful drinks desiderated by the Hitch. At this time my friend was still attached by one boot to the steer of his mid-life crisis, which began in earnest at the end of 1987. As Commander Eric Hitchens was going about the business of dying, Christopher's younger brother Peter revealed some family news:

★ The other two were James Fenton and Bruce Page of the *Sunday Times*. Hitch and I pushed our luck in an attempt to secure the job for our friend (impracticably, because James was still in his twenties). The great V.S. Pritchett, who was on the committee, voted for Ascherson. That would have been the logical and achievable outcome. With the committee split, the job went to Bruce Page, and the decline of the *NS* was thereafter sharply accelerated. All this was national news at the time, which tells its own story.

My brother's account was simple, but very surprising. Our mother had died tragically and young in 1973,* but her mother still lived, enjoying a very spry tenth decade. When my brother had married, he had taken his wife to be presented to her. The old lady later complimented him on his choice, adding rather alarmingly, 'She's Jewish, isn't she?' Peter, who had not said as much, agreed rather guardedly that this was so. 'Well,' said the woman we had known all our lives as 'Dodo', 'I've got something to tell you. So are you.'†

This information provoked a complicated sort of pleasure, and was certainly a stimulus. But it had all come hard upon: realignment of mother, death of father (the two imagos now transfigured), end of first marriage, separation from children; and here he was, turning forty as a member of a different race. I will always regret that I was a lesser friend to Christopher in his climacteric than he was to me in mine, when it came. True, he already knew the ground: he had experienced the main events, including divorce, while I was still a few years behind . . . In filling out the pain schedule 'the hardest items of all have to do with love'. Christopher and I, in leaving home, did what we did 'for love'. But how does it look, the love ledger, by the time you're done? Because you are also the enemy of love and – for your children – its despoiler. 'I hate love,' said my son Louis at the age of five or six (he was complaining about the love interest in a book we were reading). He didn't mean that, but he could now say, 'I no longer trust it.' When Dryden retold the story of Antony and Cleopatra he called his tragedy *All for Love* (or 'The World Well

* As I see it this event marks the beginning of our friendship. I knew Christopher only slightly when I read about his mother's death – in a Sunday tabloid. I wrote to him and he wrote to me, and the friendship began. (It was a suicide, by the way: another suicide.)
† See 'On Not Knowing the Half of It: Homage to Telegraphist Jacobs' in *Prepared for the Worst* (1988). Christopher's mother had kept her Jewishness a secret from her husband, children and (perhaps wisely) from the Oxford she grew up in during the early-middle decades of the century. It was an admirable – an indispensable – decision of Dodo's to tell the truth to her grandsons.

Lost'). Those stupendous sweethearts sacrificed empires, but they were certain that love, the primary value, was being exalted even in their defeats and their suicides. I envy them the flourish. We who absent ourselves from the daily company of our children must reckon it differently. Love comes out of it with gains but also with losses. And whenever death is losing, the force of death makes gains. Divorce: the incredibly violent thing. What parent, involved in it, has not wished for the death of the once-loved one? This is universal. And this is why your heart feels gangrenous inside your chest. This is why (as I put it to myself) you want men in white to come and take you away and wash your blood.

The cream Celebrity moved softly on, through the high-morale farmlands and pastures of New Hampshire and into the unsculpted landscapes of Vermont. When the roads got darker and twistier and we paused again, in a high tunnel of orange foliage, to buy the several bottles of wine nominated by the Hitch (and seconded by me: the Bellows are generous hosts, and Saul knew John Berryman and Delmore Schwartz, but they could have no conception of what they faced here), plus plenty of honey and maple syrup to take back to Cape Cod. Signalling left, the Celebrity turned off the main road and down into the valley. The Bellows were waiting in their garden.

I want to say here that when I returned from Jerusalem in 1987 my faith in my father's artistic health – and that means everything I saw as vital to the state of his spirit – was once again fervent. A year earlier he had published the book he will be remembered for: *The Old Devils*.★ It is his longest novel, and his most unflagging. In my view

★ Along with *Lucky Jim* of course, and, I would hope, preeminently *The Green Man*, *The Alteration*, *Girl, 20*, *Ending Up*, the stories 'Dear Illusion', 'All the Blood Within Me' and 'A Twitch on the Thread', the *Collected Poems*, *The King's English* and perhaps the *Letters*. *The Old Devils* won the Booker Prize, or should I say the 'prestigious' Booker Prize, because that adjective has got itself firmly attached to the Booker Prize, particularly in America; I would bet that there are many Americans who think the thing is called the Prestigious Booker Prize, which is as it should be. Here is the Fowlers'

it stands comparison with any English novel of the century (except of course *Ulysses*, which is Shakespearean). It fears no man – no, nor woman either. And what mattered to me most at the time was that it announced a *surrender of intransigence*. I had hoped for this, as ardently as you hope for the cessation of an infant's crying-fit, of a child's marathon sulk, of a lover's disaffection. *The Old Devils* marked the end of his willed solitude. He backed off, he climbed down. And we all have to do this, at some point; we all have to come out of the room we have sent ourselves to. My father emerged with a novel about forgiveness. He hadn't forgiven Jane, and never would, but he had forgiven women, he had forgiven love; he had returned to the supreme value (and would go on returning to it, in five more novels). 'I hate love,' said my son. I hate love: not a credo you ought to want to go on propounding. At the time my relief was purely instinctive, a voice saying, Your dad is okay again. Now I see that Kingsley's snarl of disappointment had finally run out of breath. And I know why . . . Anyway, there was of course no father-vacancy to be filled, just as Saul Bellow, with three of his own, had no opening for a son.*

At about 11.15 a silence slowly elongated itself over the dinner table. Christopher, utterly sober but with his eyes lowered, was crushing in his hands an empty packet of Benson & Hedges. The Bellows, too, had their gazes downcast. I sat with my head in my palms, staring at the aftermath of the dinner – that evening's road smash, with its buckled headlights, its yawing hinges, its still-oscillating hubcap. My right foot was injured because I had kicked the shins of the Hitch so much with it.†

---

article in the *COD*: **prestigious** (-j*us*) *a.* having or showing prestige; hence [-]LY *adv.*, [-]NESS *n.* [orig. = deceptive, f. L. *praestigiosus* (*praestigiae* juggler's tricks; see -OUS)]. But the award is administered by an *ad hoc* and not a standing committee. So what it signally lacks is *prestige*, in every sense except the etymological: 'F, = illusion, glamour.'

* The situation changed after 1995 (and again after 1999), as we shall see. And I would eventually say the words to Saul, in 1997, across the table of a Boston diner.

† Against the Hitch physical and intellectual opposition are equally futile. When in 1978 he left the *New Statesman* (we would all soon leave it) for the

It would be simplification to say that Christopher had spent the last ninety minutes talking up a blue streak of sinister balls. But let us not run in fear of simplification. Simplification is sometimes exactly what you want . . . The theme of discord was, of course, Israel. Christopher was already on record with a piece called 'Holy Land Heretic' (*Raritan*, Spring 1987), where he had adduced 'the generalised idealisations of Israel commonly offered by Saul Bellow, Elie Wiesel, and others'. Much of Christopher's discourse, at the dinner table in Vermont, can be found in this 8,000-word essay, which he wrote, so to speak, as a gentile. And the rest of his discourse can be found in 'On Not Knowing the Half of It: Homage to Telegraphist Jacobs' (*Grand Street*, Summer 1988), which he wrote as a Jew. Needless to say, it was a point of fundamental, of elementary intellectual honour that Christopher's changed ethnicity should have no effect whatever on questions of political science and political morality. Grandmother Dodo's disclosure had not rendered Israel any less messianic or expansionist or quasi-democratic. Christopher would do no thinking with his blood, neither at the desk nor at the

---

bourgeois broadsheet, the *Daily Express*, I went *mano a mano* with him among the sawdust and fagsmoke and bumcrack of an infernal Irish pub in a basement off Piccadilly Circus. I was in the unwonted position of attacking Christopher from the left: for defection, for betrayal, for taking the rich man's shilling. Sadly watched by James Fenton (and the altercation had something wretched and near-tearful in it), our wills, my will and the will of the Hitch, became concentrated in the glass we were both holding with our right hands. It was a wine glass, and it contained a single whisky. We were squeezing it, while looking implacably into each other's eyes, squeezing it till it began to creak . . . I desisted. I climbed down. Because I suddenly knew that he would not desist, not in a million years, and when we went off to Casualty together (James squaring the cabdriver and sadly accompanying us), the Hitch would have no regrets, no regrets about that gashed palm, that missing finger, lost in the sawdust: none. Later that year James and I, and Christopher, would journey by train together to cover the Conservative Party Conference in Blackpool. There was a difference but not a lessening in our affections. The *Express* had installed the Hitch at the Grand, with its view of the Irish Sea. James and I were in a fiver-a-night bed-and-breakfast up some distant backstreet. Now *that's* being left-wing: you lie awake on your narrow cot, listening to the only other piece of furniture in the room – the hulking wardrobe, as the beetles eat it.

dinner table. Emotions, atavisms, would be set aside, while reason – the nabob of all the faculties – went about its work.

Saul was on record too, at book length in *To Jerusalem and Back*, in his journalism, his essays. And Jewishness is close to the hub of the wheel of his fiction, which is another way of saying that it pervades his unconscious mind. (Whereas Christopher's soul, I am suggesting, is essentially gentile. He doesn't have a Jewish unconscious – though his beautiful premonitory dream, stirringly described in the piece of 1988, suggests that there are traces of it in him.) It would be pointless to deny that on the question of Israel Bellow to some extent thinks with the blood: the unconscious always thinks with the blood. If the writer is made up of three different beings – littérateur, innocent, everyman – then the innocent is very strong in Saul Bellow, despite great learning, experience, and nous. This is how he does it as a writer: he runs everything past his innocence, his nethermind, his first soul. He runs everything past his soul. The blood thinks, and Israel, therefore, is bound to him by consanguinity – 'Jewish consanguinity, an archaism of which the Jews, until the present century stopped them, were in the course of divesting themselves'. Israel is consanguineous with Exodus★ and Diaspora, with Pogrom, Ghetto and Holocaust. I once heard him say that the Jews would have been 'finished' without Israel, 'after the beating they'd taken'. The next

---

★ Once, in a Boston restaurant, I brought up the subject of capital punishment. Carla Faye Tucker had just received the lethal injection, down in Texas. (Governor Bush had prayed for 'guidance' in the matter; his prayers had been answered by a lowered thumb.) After a short while I noticed that my lament for the Abolition movement was being greeted without noticeable sympathy. I was saying,

– What is it with Americans and the death penalty? Instead of talking about Rickey Ray Rector, they were all talking about Gennifer Flowers. Instead of talking about Karla Faye Tucker, they're all talking about Monica Lewinsky.

Saul remained silent. I said,

– Don't tell me *you're* not against it either.

– Well. Look at . . . Eichmann. What are you supposed to *do* with a son of a bitch like that?

– Christ, you're really Old Testament, aren't you!

And he shrugged, and gave a sideways nod.

chapter would be Assimilation; and that would be the end of it. That would be the end of the connection to all the significant dead.

Naturally Bellow was capable of a rational – indeed a Benthamite – discussion of Israel, pros and cons. But it wasn't that kind of evening. No, it wasn't that kind of evening. Very soon Janis and I were reduced to the occasional phoneme of remonstration. And Saul, packed down over the table, shoulders forward, legs tensed beneath his chair, became more laconic in his contributions, steadily submitting to a cataract of pure reason, matter-of-fact chapter and verse, with its interjected historical precedents, its high-decibel statistics, its fortissimo fine distinctions – Christopher's cerebral stampede.

Then it was over, and we faced the silence. My right foot throbbed from the warm work it had done beneath the table on the shins of the Hitch, availing me nothing . . . As I shall explain, I too think about Israel with the blood. But my blood wasn't thinking about Israel, not then. A consensus was forming in the room, silently: that the evening could not be salvaged. A change of subject and a cleansing cup of coffee? No. Nothing for it, now, but to finish up and seek our bedding. But for the time being we sat there, rigid, as the silence raged on.

Christopher was still softly compacting his little gold box of Benson & Hedges. He seemed to be giving this job his full attention. Before him in the silence lay the stilled battlefield: the state of Israel, thoroughly outmanoeuvred, comprehensively overthrown . . . In his *clefish* novel of London literary life, *Brilliant Creatures* (1983), Clive James said of the Hitchens-based character that the phrase 'no whit abashed' might have been invented for him. But Christopher did now seem to be entertaining the conception of self-reproof. During the argument the opinions of Professor Edward Said had been weighed, and this is what Christopher, in closing, wished to emphasise. The silence still felt like a gnat in my ear.

– Well, he said. I'm sorry if I went on a bit. But Edward is a friend of mine. And if I hadn't defended him . . . I would have felt bad.

– How d'you feel *now*? said Saul.

* * *

[261]

Rachel

Suppose I were to talk to him about the roots of memory in feeling – about the themes that collect and hold the memory; if I were to tell him what retention of the past really means. Things like: 'If sleep is forgetting, forgetting is also sleep, and sleep is to consciousness what death is to life. So that the Jews ask even God to remember, *"Yiskor Elohim"*.'

God doesn't forget, but your prayer requests him particularly to remember your dead. But how was I to make an impression on a kid like that?*

1987 was not my first time in Israel. I had been there the year before, as a guest of the Friends of Israel Educational Trust, with four other writers: Marina Warner, Hermione Lee, Melvyn Bragg and Julian Barnes. We had audiences with rabbis and academics, we had a cafeteria lunch with a couple of politicians in the Knesset, we went to Harodian, Masada, the Dead Sea, Bethlehem, Jericho, we stayed at a kibbutz on the Golan Heights.† We had a glass of tea with the postcard Bedouin in his tent, and took a ride on his camel. And we had a great time. But we were not introduced to any Palestinians or to any of the Holy Land Heretics – people like Israel Shahak, Witold Jedlicki and Emmanuel Faradjun – with whom Christopher

---

* From Bellow's *The Bellarosa Connection* (1989) – published a couple of months before the visit to Vermont. Christopher, who had read it, was not like the kid in the book: a 'low-grade cheap-shot' nihilist. Christopher's complications were far more human. When my crisis came I was reduced to a kind of inaudibility. With the Hitch it went the other way. During his stay in Cape Cod he spent the days writing a long, learned and supereloquent defence of another great (future) friend of mine, whose life, that year, was also suddenly changed, transformed utterly: Salman Rushdie.

† About half an hour into an informal lecture on the history of the kibbutz movement, I raised a hand and said: 'There's something I want to know about the kibbutz movement, and I know this is a question of deep concern also to my colleague Julian Barnes. Do you have a ping-pong table here?' I felt (rightly) that this was sayable, in 1986. Would it feel sayable in 1999?

Hitchens, around now, was stimulatingly engaged. V.S. Naipaul, in his travel books, puts nation states on the psychiatrist's couch and then takes a reading of their mental health. All writers, all travellers, do something of the kind. After a couple of days your body gives you a verdict on the place you're in; and I felt invigorated – rejuvenated. The Palestinians, true, remained invisible; but no one I spoke to was anything less than earnest about their situation and its affront to justice and democracy.

A year later this society already seemed to me to be turning. The health check I gave it left me feeling underrelaxed.* My wife was at my side, and I kept noticing certain unreflecting male emphases – the anxiety about female hygiene, for example. To see the guy in the beanie doing his stuff at the Wailing Wall now put me in mind of Nabokov's remark about chimpanzees dressed up for circus tricks and how this demeaned their animal nature. What was being demeaned here? Something like human autonomy. And who were these scholars and cantors who kept sweeping unseeingly past you on their wild-goose chases, their fool's errands? (They would be accosted, now and then, by proselytising home-church Americans: 'Friend! There's another way!') And once, in the Arab Quarter, I had a mild altercation with one of the gatekeepers of the Holy Mosque, and I saw in his eyes the assertion that he could do *anything* to me, to my wife, to my children, to my mother, and that this would only validate his rectitude. Humankind, or I myself, cannot bear very much religion. Politically, too, it seemed a little harder to speak your mind. Naipaul, perhaps, would have drawn attention to certain symptoms of longterm (and largely justified) persecution mania. This is the garrison state, and this is the attrition of beleaguerment.

I have hopes for Israel and will never be entirely reasonable about her. I think about Israel with the blood.

In 1967, while Saul Bellow was nosing corpses in the Sinai (the 'sour-sweet, decayed-cardboard smell becomes a taste in the

---

* Kingsley was sympathetic to Israel but he would not have liked it there. At one dinner party I was forcibly reminded of a line from *Lucky Jim*: I held in my hand the smallest drink I had ever been seriously offered.

mouth'),★ I was lying in the arms of a Sephardic Jewess in Golders
Green. When the invasion began, on 5 June, she went off, hectically,
to give blood for Israel. And at that moment I knew that this was love:
first love . . . My only friend, Rob, resignedly said that she was the
most beautiful girl he had ever seen: her mouth was wide, her nose
unignorably warlike, her hair an ebony shoeshine. She lived with her
mother (who worked for Lord Sieff of Marks and Spencer) and her
grandmother, who was ancient, tiny, humorous, and orthodox: in her
pantry even the instant coffee was kosher. My girlfriend was a year
older than me, and she was a virgin. When, eventually, it happened,
we looked for the blood and found none. We were inseparable for
half a year. And then, of course, we separated.

The affair has a coda. Six years later she read *The Rachel Papers* and
rang me up. We arranged to have dinner in 'our' bistro, off Baker
Street, and I went along there, I must confess, expecting a three-hour
denunciation, a slap in the face, and a libel suit. There has been much
talk, in these pages, about real and made-up people. When you begin
a novel at the age of twenty-one (or so I found), all you've got is your
own consciousness; autobiography is forced on you because there
isn't anything else. Rachel, in the book, is sympathetic but also sad
and baffled; and I enormously exaggerated the coldness with which
she is finally spurned. I arrived at the bistro and looked for my first
love. But she wasn't there. In her place sat a woman of twenty-five,
and fully formed† . . . It was one of those meals where the waiters
keep asking you if there's something wrong with the food. Because
the body is full, tight, sated, and nothing can be added to it; the body
is already too rich. I was powerfully delighted, gorgeously relieved,
greatly moved – and astonished, all the same, when she finally said,
'Do you want to come back to my room? For coffee.' And then she
added, uncharacteristically (I thought. But what did I know?), 'As

★ He was there as a reporter. The Six Day War (the Arabs call it the June
War) ended, I see, on Saul's fifty-second birthday.
† In the novel, I realise, I de-exoticised her. Rachel seems to be Jewish but
turns out not to be. I don't know what idiotic scruple possessed me. I did
change her name. *That* I did transform, in the crucible, in the grappledrome,
of my imagination.

well as the obvious' . . . I spent the first of several nights in the residential wing of her training college, down the Metropolitan Line. She was studying medicine and would soon be leaving the country: for ever. Where did she end up? Australia? Canada? Israel, whose army her blood had fuelled? In the morning I took the train straight into Blackfriars and the *TLS*. Climbing aboard I would say to myself that the 'obvious' was ineffable, and remember my amazement (even my alarm) at the elevation of my blood.

So I will never be entirely reasonable about Israel. I will always think about her with the blood. Not *my* blood. The blood of my first love.

Death of a Feeling

The Forest Ranger tends to be cheerful in the morning and will normally give you a couple of numbers over the toast and cereal – 'K-K-K-Katie', for instance, and, if there are children to be entertained, the one about O'Hogan's goat. Unsurprisingly, perhaps, there were no songs, no nursery rhymes, to be heard as Christopher, pausing to extinguish a cigarette in the fireplace, reoccupied his spot at the table. Breakfast was polite. He and I didn't linger, and soon we were steering off into the mist and the Eastern Woodlands – 'the beeches, the yellow birches, and maples, the basswoods, the locusts, the rocks, the drainage ditches, the birds, and the wildlife, right down to the red newts on the roads . . . The poplar leaves, when you narrow your eyes, are like a shower of small change.' That was the trouble, or part of it: Vermont was meant to be the green world, a distraction from distraction. Vermont was *the good place*.★

On the way back to the Cape I exacted – the phrase is James Fenton's – an SBIR: a small but interesting revenge. I didn't see my

★ 'Vermont: The Good Place' (1990), collected in *It All Adds Up*. My father, typing out his home address in early letters to Larkin, would usually write not 'Berkhamsted' but 'The Bad Town'. For him, and for different sorts of reasons, home was the bad place.

[265]

stunt as a retributive act, not at the time (for our return journey was marked by the usual fraternal ease); I thought I was merely surrendering to some juvenile impulse. Now I clearly apprehend that I did, in fact, want satisfaction . . . Somewhere in rural Massachusetts we took the necessary break – for the many powerful drinks and the huge uneaten meal without which the Hitch could not long subsist. It was when we crossed the bridge and joined Route 6, gaining the peninsula of the Cape, that Christopher began to press the case, not for a repartitioned Jerusalem, but for an immediate rest-stop. The cream Celebrity bowled on. After another twenty minutes or so, by which point Christopher's whimpers had become a whine for mercy (he reminded me of my sons and their terminal cry: 'Dad, quick! I'm *desperate!*'), I veered on to a slip-road and, at sixty miles per hour, ground my sore right foot into the brake pedal. The bladder of the Hitch, so intimately pleached and triced in the seatbelt, jackknifed forward and then, even more horribly, twanged back into its bucket. I find it difficult to duplicate the double-groan he gave, approximately Uh-*da*! – as alarm quickly modulated into the most earnest suspense. And he remained resolutely unamused by the incident. When he came back from the drenched spinney and I in my turn slipped into it (the shrub, the scrub, the butt-ends, the air always tangy with the gasps of human relief), the Hitch attempted a finessing getaway in the Celebrity, abandoning me to a walk of, I guessed, several miles. As it turned out he couldn't make the car start.★

★ That he didn't know how to drive was a testimony to my friend's poet-like (and pasha-like) qualities. Poets can't, don't, shouldn't drive. (British poets can't or don't drive. American poets drive, but shouldn't.) I wrote a piece about this, in the mid-1990s. Soon afterwards, at an event in Raleigh-Durham, North Carolina, as I signed books in the public square, a local poet stepped forward and, in droll repudiation, tossed on to the table a slim vol and a driver's licence. This poet was lean, weathered, sandily handsome. He also wore a plaster support on his right arm. 'What have you been up to?' I said. 'Out driving your car?' Christopher Hitchens has since learnt how to drive. He looks endearingly bizarre behind the wheel – as if he were wearing a ballgown or a King Kong suit. The delight in his eyes is proof enough that he shouldn't be sitting there. Larkin, after many travails, learnt how to drive, and learnt to rue his profligacy (see the later *Letters*). Fenton, the essential, the crystallised poet, made attempts to learn how to drive that bordered on the Sisyphean: 'everlastingly laborious' (*COD*).

THINKING WITH THE BLOOD

That evening, in the house on Horseleech Pond, Christopher and I had our longest and loudest laughing-fit, ever, followed by our longest and loudest fight. The laughing-fit I will return to. The fight was predictable, and had to come: 'So you were defending your friend! Your friend Edward! Well Edward *wasn't there*! The friend who was there was *me*! What about *that* friend! And what about MY friend! *AND* you were doing that horrible thing with your lips!' I then broadened my fire, arraigning Christopher as the *cause* of the recent upheavals in his life.* But there are times when manners are more important than the state of Israel – just as there was a time, in Israel, when manners were more important than the end of the world . . . Life, just here, is behaving like a short story, and everything is connected. Everything is connected: all for love, the world well lost, the deaths of feelings. Christopher was coming to the end of a world, with great shiftings, massive rearrangements. All the imagos, all the picture cards – the face cards – were being shuffled, king and queen and jack.

On the phone the next day, still shocked, indignant and guilty, I was saying,

– And tell Janis I'm sorry.

– Please don't worry about it.

– You deserved a night off, I thought.

Saul was emphatic:

– Martin, you're *not* to be hard on yourself about it.

– Thank you. But when you bring –

– Listen, I'm used to it. I get that kind of thing all the time.

– That's what the *Hitch* said!

We couldn't avoid laughing at that; and accordingly the case began to close. Some summers later I was in the same kitchen in Vermont when Christopher sent the Bellows an apology, or at least a thankyou note, enciphered in a piece he published in the *London Review of Books*. The communication was leniently – no, warmly –

---

* An ignorant solecism that Christopher not only forgave (I would expect forgiveness) but, much more generously, contrived to forget, leaving it unevoked, for ever unactivated. It doesn't haunt him: it haunts me.

received. And so was my wife, a different wife, who came with me on that later visit; and I was reaccepted in my new reality . . . It is a simple desire, to try to triangulate your friends; and I am ready, on this one, to go in again. What gives the thing justice is that it was Hitchens who introduced me to Bellow – as a reader. 'Look at *Humboldt's Gift*,' he told me, with a serious inclination of the head, on the staircase at the *New Statesman*, in (I think) 1977. I looked instead at *The Victim*, and after very few pages I felt a recognition threading itself through me, whose form of words (more solemn than exhilarated) went approximately as follows: 'Here is a writer I will have to read all of.' Everything else followed from this, and it remains the basis of the connection. I see Bellow perhaps twice a year, and we call, and we write. But that accounts for only a fraction of the time I spend in his company. He is on the shelves, on the desk, he is all over the house, and always in the mood to talk. That's what writing is, not communication but a means of communion. And here are the other writers who swirl around you, like friends, patient, intimate, sleeplessly accessible, over centuries. This is the definition of literature.

Oh yes: that laughing-jag. It was the kind of paroxysm that turns you inside out and leaves you with a new set of bodily fluids. *Immenso giubilo.* The joke – the improvisation – had nothing to do with Israel, or Vermont, but we are still in this short story, and everything measures up. In one of his most stunning utterances Nietzsche said that a joke is an epigram on the death of a feeling.* Our improvisation was violently scatological, and would not survive transcription. But feelings *were* being mourned: feelings about the first half of life. Youth can perhaps be defined as the illusion of your own durability. The final evaporation of this illusion parches the skin beneath the eyes and makes your hair crackle to the brush. It was over. There would be hell to pay. Dying suns of a certain size perform the alchemist's nightmare: they turn gold into lead. And there we were, in 1989,

* A passing note. When Princess Diana died it took four or five days for the jokes to marinate. When John Kennedy Jr. died the jokes were instantaneous, electronic, light-speed. The feeling, in other words, had no chance to exist; it was born dead. One wonders, too, about subsequent road kill on the information highway.

heading towards base metal. Transmutation had come to him, and would soon come to me.

'It has all followed hard upon,' I said to him, that lugubrious Christmas, when suddenly it was my turn. 'Breakup, separation from children, health-crisis.' Lucy Partington, Bruno Fonseca, Saul Bellow in the ITU. And a five-year novel, *The Information*, begun in peace and finishing, now, in spasm war . . . Christopher sat there, offering his presence. Say as much as you like or as little as you like. He could contemplate me, I felt, from a vantage of senior humanity. Acknowledging this, I said, 'All I need now is the death of a parent.'

But here, for a little while longer, is the house on Horseleech Pond. Here are the trees where Christopher and I, at the age of thirty-six, stood posing for photographs with our sons in our arms: Louis, Alexander. The women taking the photographs were Antonia and Eleni. And there would be other births: Jacob, Sophia. All this is going to go. All this is going to disappear. This will fail. I will fail. I said to myself, Look at it: look at what you've done. There is the rented car, a different rented car, in which you will drive alone to Logan. There is your wife, crying in the drive. Beyond her are your boys on the patch of grass, with that zoo of theirs – the frogs, the turtles.

Letter from the Old Forge

The Old Forge
Shilton,
Oxon.
[Autumn, 1971]

Dearest Wog,*

    Thanks for the cheque + note. There have been such
interminable dramas here: it all seems to be getting out of hand. As a
result of the happily varied events of last weekend, Z, whom you
know, is now at the local looney bin in Oxford. What happened was
Friday: he beat up a girl whom he's been unrealistically in love with
for 6 mths, whom he'd asked for the w.end & found in bed with
another guest.† Saturday: prolonged looney behaviour (stealing my
car for the afternoon, spending all his money) followed by a suicide
bid (some sleeping pills), us trying to make him sick and keep him
awake, and then an 80 m.p.h. mercy dash to the Radcliffe with me at

---

* This is the last letter in the Osric archive, and for the first time I have not
censored or bowdlerised Jane's nickname. I took against it after seeing
William Boyd's early TV play *Good and Bad at Games*. It is set in a public
school and its main character is called Woggie. Woggie was born in the East.
You used to feel that English people were going to get called Wog or
Woggie if they had ever been north of the Trent or south of the Tweed.
But Wog, I am reminded, was called Wog because of her hair: golliwog. I
favour the nickname now because this is a goodbye of a kind and I want to
thank her for her help. Osric had moved into a distant cottage – with a
husband and wife (X and Y) and a further man (Z). It did not turn out well.
† Rob.

the wheel. He turned out to be O.K. and Sunday: he returned while
only Gully and Y were here – a scuffle ensued (with Y) and after this
becoming scene, she called the police saying she wasn't 'going to
have him in the house'. I came back and sorted things out,
temporarily. He went to the bin (where he's since had a *fit*) and Y has
gone to the London Clinic . . . The last weeks have been
characterised by pretty well permanent hysteria and high volume
rows between Y and X . . . Things like: 'You don't love me! If you
loved me, you'd look *after* me!' (Meaning, I suspect, you'd spend
more time licking the kitchen floor). It's novel-fodder,★ but that's
about all. I've never seen people so intent on advertising their own
vulgar and selfish emotionalism: and making themselves so horribly
and flabbily *vulnerable*. Y's new edicts, transmitted to us from the
hospital, feature: *no* friends at the house, *no* pop records etc, because
she simply just 'can't take it'. It also means my rent, because of the
ejection of Z, has gone up to £6. My money's come through & I can
handle the difference & and I hope Gully can soon come and live
here which would be better in every imaginable way.† But, on the
other hand, and I shall certainly use this as a threat, this isn't a good
Finals Year atmosphere, combined with all the tiring and expensive
driving in and out; so I'll say if things don't calm down I'm getting
the hell out – Y's not a student, and it's not X's Finals Year, so what's
it to her? *She's* the landlady, as she screamed many times at Z, so *she* is
in a position to throw him out. She's therefore in a position to be left
paying all the rent herself if she gets too unbearable.‡

★ *Dead Babies* (1975). I recently visited (10/99) the set of the film they have
made of it. The actors and actresses were all astonishing but the Little Keith
was *astonishing*. They fired the first Keith, the producer told me. He was a
good actor, and widely liked, but they wanted a crueller Keith. They found
a crueller Keith. And all the other actors and actresses said with due regret
that, in fact, they felt more comfortable with a crueller Keith.
† There are many psychological transparencies in this letter. Anyway, soon
after Gully moved in (and she was very sweet about this), I went up to our
bedroom and said, 'I've just taken a death pill and I'm going to have horrific
hallucinations for the next seven hours.' It was MDA and I was right.
‡ Gully and Osric made their escape in the small hours of the night, loading
the Mini and driving off in second gear.

[271]

As you see, I could use some advice and support. Jonathan [Wordsworth] says he'd love to be taken out on the 11th & I'm looking forward to seeing your sane faces. Could you drop a line saying what you've got in mind for Jonathan and to say what you think of all this? I'm perfectly O.K., but I'm getting increasingly angry about the whole set-up here as regards my work and so on. See you both soon & give all my love to Col (say Insurance is O.K.). Lots of love to you and Dad.

Love Mart X X X.

Part Two

THE MAIN EVENTS

1: Delilah Seale

It was the late spring of 1995 and I had just returned from a three-week book tour of North America. On such tours, Ian McEwan once said, you feel like 'the employee of a former self', because the book is now out there to be championed and squired, while you have moved on. Well, my book, *The Information* (and all its impedimenta), was still with me, was too much with me, soon and late. But I won't tender any further complaints about the book tour. Some writers find the role of the double more degrading/deracinating/boring/tiring and so on than others find it; some writers are not easily divisible, and must cloister themselves behind moats and barbed wire.★ Once an outrageous novelty, the book tour is now accepted as a fact of life and a matter of professional routine. You arrive in each city and present yourself to its media; after that, in the evening, a mediated individual, you appear at the bookshop and perform. And now something salutary happens, as you are confronted by your most priceless asset: your readers. How badly you need them – because they know who you really are; they are the confidants of your unconscious mind. It does the author good to Meet the Reader. Sometimes, in the signing queue, I see a pair of eyes quietly telling me that communion has occurred, and I feel a proportional transfusion.

I had come in on the overnight, that spring morning. My plane,

★ J.D. Salinger is the obvious example. Only one journalist ever went in there and she took years to come out. Gore Vidal told me in 1975 that he'd heard it was 'very cold' where Salinger lives: an extraordinarily delicate suggestion that the great man seeks warmth in alcohol. Still, you can only love a writer who has a character say 'Jeat jet?' when asking another if he has dined. These literary spectres are not always as impalpable as they seem. Salman Rushdie has been to the baseball with Don DeLillo. And Ian McEwan, for a time, used to have *lunch* with Thomas Pynchon.

in addition, had peeled off for a rest-stop in the Arctic and arrived four or five hours late. The *après*-book-tour condition, I think, would be indistinguishable from extreme jet-lag, with or without the extreme jet-lag that usually accompanies it. All split and scoured, the author (that not particularly fragile being) must now shed his executive self and repossess his former shape. It was a Sunday. I and my ghost were alone in the studio apartment. We had coffee – or I made it and my ghost drank it. He had a bath, sluicing off all that jumbo, and I felt a little better. We passed round a cigarette as I went through my mail. One letter caused me to sit down suddenly when I was halfway through its first sentence. This, I might have murmured to my ghost, is probably for you . . .

That night, carrying the letter in my chest pocket, I escorted Isabel to the Coronet in Notting Hill Gate, where we saw *An Awfully Big Adventure* – the screen adaptation of Beryl Bainbridge's novel. And I'm very sorry, Beryl, but I slept through most of it (a sleep both deep and fitful) and then walked out. We regrouped for dinner at that pizza/pasta place just down the street. Its menu featured a dish translatable as 'from grandmother's handbag'; on an earlier visit Isabel asked Kinch if he fancied a plate of hairgrips and DentuFix. I took the letter from my jacket and passed it across the table.

Isabel finished reading it and said,

– . . . *Good*.

– There isn't any reason, is there, why this shouldn't be a great thing.

– None.

I rang my mother in the morning and sent her mind back almost twenty years. She said immediately,

– I've still got the photograph.

– Do you think you could dig it out, Mum?

– It's here on the dressing-table, she said.

And now it's on the shelf in the study, within arm's reach of my desk.

*　*　*

I felt it was important to tell the story in the simplest possible terms. My interlocutors, after all, were aged eleven and ten: number-one son, Louis, and number-two son, Jacob. For the occasion I had taken the boys to a Chinese restaurant called the Spice Market, prized by them at the time for its serve-yourself and all-you-can-eat facilities plus its powerfully sizzling Mongolian Grill. What I was about to reveal to them was a family matter, a private matter, but I knew it couldn't remain private. There was a feeling among my intimates that I should wait, that 'the boys weren't ready' for the news. But it seemed to me that I didn't have a choice. To give the emphasis: my free will was being compromised. The Fourth Estate wasn't going to care whether or not the boys were ready.* Over and above this, though, I thought that the boys *were* ready, had always been ready. I trusted the morality of my sons.

– There was once a little girl, I said.

I said, I'm going to tell a story. There was once a little girl called Delilah. She had a brother and a mother and a father. When she was two years old her mother died. Her mother killed herself. She hanged herself. Delilah grew up with her brother, raised by her father, who remarried. Then when she was eighteen it was revealed that her father wasn't her real father. And so suddenly it seemed that she had no parents at all.

Louis and Jacob spoke in one voice. They had a habit, that night, of speaking in one voice.

– Poor her, they said.

– Well, boys, the real father . . . is me.

– Good, they said.

And we talked on.

Good, good – it seemed good.

The meeting was set for seven o'clock in the bar of a Knightsbridge hotel called the Rembrandt. A potent name and a challenging spirit, for students of the human face; and very soon two human faces would be opposed, as in a mirror, each addressing the

---

* And soon enough I would be sitting in my flat patiently and sincerely saying 'Fuck *off*' every twenty seconds while a woman in a brown mackintosh went on ringing the doorbell.

other with unprecedented curiosity. I arrived twenty minutes early, accompanied by an indispensable Isabel. My hands were shaking. They always shake, my hands, but that evening they felt quite disconnected from me. A cup and saucer would sound like a pair of castanets in my grip; an iced drink would become a maraca. We sat on a sofa among lamps and low tables, doilies, antimacassars. I watched the door. She knew what *I* looked like. And I knew that she was nineteen and would arrive on the very stroke of the hour.

This time the day before, in the same bar of the same hotel, I had had a long conversation with Delilah's father, or co-father, Patrick Seale (a figure of well-established versatility: literary agent, art-dealer, foreign correspondent and Middle East specialist). He was the author of several books; he was also the author of the letter in my jacket pocket. On this occasion his manner, like his letter, was impeccably straightforward. Patrick told me that his original plan had been to tell Delilah everything when she turned twenty-one. Family politics had intervened (there was the stepmother, and two further children), and now Delilah knew. She had known for some months. And how had she reacted? Patrick described a process that began in grief and had since moved on towards something more resilient. In his super-evolved fashion he had given Delilah a box of my books (a kind of kit) plus a video cassette of an hour-long interview. I would be coming at her partly as a mediated being, mediated by myself – and others: Delilah would presumably be aware that I had abandoned my sons to go and live with an heiress in New York, the better to squander my advances on a Liberace smile . . . But this was a secondary or tertiary matter. At the moment of revelation she must have been wholly indifferent to my identity (and never mind its carapace). When I tried to imagine it I saw her aswim in a panic of lost connection. The connection – with her father, her brother – seemed lost, but it wasn't. And here was another connection waiting to be made. I thought, too, of the courage she would need on this summer evening as she mounted the steps and opened the door.

She entered.

– It's *you*, said Isabel.

Then hugs and kisses for the girl with my face.

UNDESIRABLE ALIEN

p (left and right): These are the two photos kept by my desk: Delilah Seale, Lucy Partington.

ve: Marian and Lucy at Fountains Abbey, a month before Lucy disappeared in December 1973.

This Bee Gee dates from 1974. The photograph was taken by the dedicatee of my second no

Christopher Hitchens and I are flanking James Fenton: Sacré Coeur, Paris, the winter of 198
The photograph was taken by my companion of many years, Angela Gorgas.

and my father are flanking Elizabeth Jane Howard. Hampstead, late 1970s: towards the end. (*Dmitri Kasterine/Camera Press*)

My parents in the early 1990s.

Anticlockwise from top: Antonia Phillips; Jacob Amis; Louis Amis. We think that these photographs, by Jo Ryan, were taken in late 1990, making Louis just six and Jacob four and a half.

Above: Standing by my father in 1991. (*Frank Martin/Guardian*)

Right: Larkin. (*Fay Godwin/Network*)

ow: With Saul and Janis Bellow, Vermont, 98. For structural reasons the baby I am wielding cannot be named.

Left: Isabel Fonseca on the day a
we returned from the Condado
Casino in Puerto Rico: January 1
(*Marion Ettlinger*)

Right: Bruno Fonseca, 1958-199
Clockwise from top left: 1988 (*L
Vignelli*), 1968, and 1994, on the
day before he died. The drawing
by his mother, Elizabeth Fonseca

Below: With unnamed baby, Long
Island, 1998. Photograph by Par
Morgan.

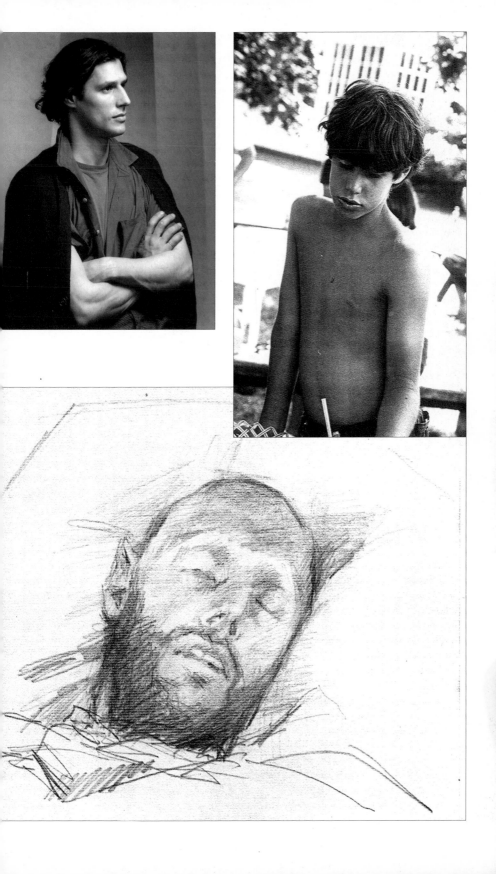

Kingsley with Sarah Snow.

On the telephone the next day Patrick and I had a conversation of surrealistic urbanity. It felt likely that these sentences had never been heard before. I congratulated him on his daughter. And he congratulated me on mine.

'Poor her,' said the boys, in one voice, when they heard her story. 'Good,' they said, when I told them who the father was. 'I'm very pleased and proud that you've taken it this way.' And very relieved, I might have added – but I don't think I felt any relief, because I don't think I felt any doubt. And again the eerie unison, with the frowning duo saying, 'Why would we not?' Yes, exactly. Why would you not. And when a day or two afterwards Delilah came to dinner for the first time, the boys leapt to the sound of the buzzer and ran upstairs to open the door and let her in.

Six weeks later I went to pick up Louis from one of his guitar lessons (hey: what *happened* to those guitar lessons?) and we looked into a newsagent's for a comic or a football magazine. The *Daily Express* had Delilah and me on its front page. I don't often use the adverb *wryly* but that is how he said it:

– More bad publicity, Daddy?

– I don't know. Maybe not.

Without acknowledgment I quoted his grandfather at him: on the correspondences between cruelty and sentimentality.

– They've only got two ways to go, I said. And I think they'll be playing this one as a heartwarmer.

– Jesus. Still.

– I know.

Delilah was in a safe place, or at least a distant one, and would be away for three months. But then the *Express* sent their journalist after her – to Quito, Ecuador. Delilah cooperated (it was our policy, formulated by Patrick, to cooperate), and the subsequent article wore an indulgent smile. All the coverage was like that: it beamed fondly on us. No doubt it was Delilah's youth – her manifest innocence and vulnerability – that softened the mood. I was very glad that they hadn't tried to hurt her. But I sat through it all in the way that one tolerates (counting one's immediate blessings) the tearful interlude of a notoriously violent drunk. Our story did the rounds of the dailies and was picked up for more thoughtful treatment at the weekend. Then came another revelation.

In his essay on *The Old Curiosity Shop* G.K. Chesterton talks about the kind of criticism or commentary that makes a writer 'jump out of his boots'. Such an occurrence is vanishingly rare. Nine out of ten writers, I imagine, get through life without once experiencing it. But it does happen, and it happened to me. In the Sunday *Observer* the novelist Maureen Freely staged a straightforward retrospective of my fiction and noted the punctual arrival – just in time for my third novel, *Success* (1978) – of a stream of lost or wandering daughters and putative or fugitive fathers, and that these figures recurred, with variations, in every subsequent book. There was nothing I could do about this diagnosis. It chimed with something Patrick had said during our first talk on the telephone: 'I expect it's been in the back of your mind.' Yes, exactly: in the back of my mind. Your writing comes from the back of your mind, where thoughts are unformulated and anxiety is silent. That's where it comes from: silent anxiety. I felt there was something almost embarrassing about the neatness and obviousness of the Freely interpretation. But it also sharply consoled me, because it meant that I had been with Delilah in spirit far more than I knew.

The interpretation is incomplete. There is at least one other eidolon, one other wraith idealised and feared for. A yard from my right shoulder stands the transparent picture-frame containing the two photographs, back to back (how did they get in there together?), of Delilah Seale (two years old, in the print dress and sandals) and Lucy Partington, bespectacled, school-uniformed, sitting in a curtained booth . . . There is a third presence, a third absence: Delilah's mother, Lamorna, who hanged herself in 1978.

I find I have written a great deal about and around suicide. Suicide, the most sombre of all subjects – the saddest story. It awakens terror and pity in me, yet it compels me, it compels my writing hand. Perhaps because what I do all day and what they do, the suicides, in an instant, are so close to being antithetical. Chesterton (again) said that suicide was a heavier undertaking than murder. The murderer kills just one person. The suicide kills everybody. And what *other* submerged memory had me going downstairs, yesterday, to look out a certain novel that after thirteen pages confronted me with

> I saw now . . . how conventional were my former ideas on pre-suicidal preoccupations; a man who has decided upon self-destruction is far removed from mundane affairs, and to sit down and write his will would be, at that moment, an act just as absurd as winding up one's watch, since, together with the man, the whole world is destroyed; the last letter is instantly reduced to dust and, with it, all the postmen; and like smoke, vanishes the estate bequeathed to a nonexistent progeny.★

'All the postmen': that is genius. I feel a strong and constant resistance to the harshness of Chesterton's great formulation. Nabokov, moral but not moralistic, is more painfully persuasive. He shows, too, in this short novel, that the writer is the opposite of the suicide, constantly applauding life and, furthermore, creating it, assigning breath and pulse to 'a nonexistent progeny'. Suicide is omnicide. But it's not in me to pass any judgment on it. It escapes morality. Throughout history suicide has been arduously detaching itself from human censure: the curses and penalties, the rock-heaped graves in unsanctified ground, the defiled cadavers. Why drive a stake through their hearts when, as Joyce knew, their hearts have been broken already?

In the novel *Night Train* I had my woman narrator make the following observation: 'It used to be said, not so long ago, that every suicide gave Satan special pleasure. I don't think that's true – unless it isn't true either that the Devil is a gentleman.' But the Devil is *not* a gentleman. The gentle *do* come to grief. And when Satan, in *Paradise Lost*, sets out from Pandemonium (abode of all demons), this was his mission: 'To waste His whole creation',

★ *The Eye* by Vladimir Nabokov (1930, 1965). I hadn't looked at it in fifteen years.

to confound the race
Of mankind in one root, and earth with hell
To mingle and involve . . .

Suicides, too, are worldkillers; they are, in that critical moment, everyman and everywoman. But no blame attaches. If what she was suffering had been endurable, then she would have endured.

Delilah was a two-year-old standing on the stairs. Her older brother Orlando, who led the way, could see the hanging body. And it was Patrick who had to go in and 'take her down'. That void world up there is, of course, the central fact behind Delilah's origin and evolution, and not the little mystery of the lost-found father, which is good, good, only good. No mother, but more than one father, now – and much else. It does go on. When the revelation came Delilah forfeited technical consanguinity with her half-brother and half-sister. But there were two more, a half-brother and another half-brother, waiting, like a team, just as they wait for the sound of the buzzer and then run upstairs to let her in.

– What do you think, Mum? I said, as she snatched the photograph from my hand.

– . . . *Definitely*.

– What should I do?

– Nothing. Don't do anything, dear.

I had always wanted a girl and suddenly there she was, in the Rembrandt, like a mirror. For seventeen years I had been worrying about her, in the back of my mind. Time, thus affronted (I thought), would give us work to do; but it hasn't been like that. Love flowed (and was soon declared). And now she and I can say the words in unison: why would it not?

2: One Little More Hug

Onset

So before I lost a father, I did find a child . . .

It began with the news of a fall. I wasn't alarmed when I heard about it, for the simple reason that Kingsley fell over all the time. Falling over (as I used to say to him) was all he ever did. There were the slow and majestic subsidences, such as the one I had tried to stage-manage in the middle of the Edgware Road (see following). And there were other types of trips, tumbles and purlers, usually performed in his rooms at home and monitored by my mother and stepfather in the garden flat below. To hear my mother tell it, some of these collapses sounded like a chest-of-drawers jettisoned from an aeroplane. 'Absolutely deafening. But you're not supposed to mention it. It happens so often that we don't even go up. Unless he's wedged. Then he bangs on the floor and I send Ali.' So there was nothing alarming about the news of the fall: nothing alarming *per se*.★

★ From *The Biographer's Moustache*, published earlier in the year (Gordon is the biographer, Jimmie the subject):

> Gordon likewise rose. 'I will. I'll also send you my c.v.'
> 'Send me your what?'
> 'My c.v. My curriculum vitae.' He pronounced the first word like curriculum and the second like vee-tye.
> 'Your *what*?'
> Gordon said it again . . .
> 'Oh, presumably you mean a curriculum vitae,' said Jimmie, pronouncing the first word like curriculum and the second like vie-tee.

The author's sympathy is here with Gordon; but Kingsley, you may be sure,

Still, when I heard about it I was visited not by a premonition but by something anterior to that: a coloration, a change in the light. My father had fallen over, on a stone stairway, in South Wales, Swansea, where he still betook himself for a few weeks every August, rather grimly, and visibly conscious of his own fortitude. He was solidly attached to the friends who put him up there (the Thomases, the Rushes), and he liked all the talking and the drinking,★ but by now he was no longer a creature of annual habits; his habits had become daily, hourly, and he feared all disruption. When he went to Wales, we were to understand, he was bowing to family pressure to give Hilly a break which, in his view, she did not need. There was one thing he admitted he really enjoyed: the minibus tours. The minibus tours began in the mid-1980s. In the *Memoirs* there is a photograph of KA and the gang outside the Plough Inn in a Carmarthenshire village. And on the next page, at some other valley hamlet, we see him cooperatively kneeling on the ground with his head and hands in the stocks; thoroughly inauthentically, the words YE OLDE VILLAGE IDIOT are painted on to the upper arm of the contraption, and Kingsley's face is obligingly (and brilliantly) abject and benighted. He was slightly bashful, with me, about the minibus tours: motorised pubcrawls, in effect, but with places to be visited and undulating Wales to be driven through. It wasn't the pubcrawl aspect that made

———

would have pronounced *per se* like per-see and not like per-say. He was energetically old-school on this question. If you pronounced *sine qua non* sinny-qua-non he would yodel it back to you in music-hall Italian. It had to be sigh-nee-kway-non. My favourite was his treatment of *pace*. No pah-kay for him, and certainly not pah-chay (more of the music-hall Italian). He said pay-see, as if describing a car or a fast bowler.

★ *The Old Devils*, which is set in South Wales, tells of a *lunch* 'firmly washed down with aquavit and Special Brew and tamped in place with Irish Cream. By a step of doubtful legitimacy the men thinned their glasses of the heavy liqueur with Scotch'. Special Brew is a beer specially popular with hooligans and heroin-addicts. Kingsley wrote a whole piece about it, if not two – about how the Danes had brewed it as a tribute to Winston Churchill and how incredibly strong it was. Rob argues, with deference, with fear, that Special Brew has restorative powers and virtues rivalled by no other drink – indeed, by no other substance.

him uneasy. It was the other stuff, which made him feel like Daddy B. (a great and voluble expert on Wales, as he knew). When he talked about how much he liked the minibus tours his manner suggested that I wasn't wrong to be sceptical about them. But I wasn't sceptical about them. I was enjoying the animation in him . . . I still don't know if the fall took place on one of the minibus tours. I do know it happened after lunch. 'He bumped his head,' my mother told me. He hit his head.

I said that Kingsley annually betook himself to Swansea but the reflexive verb is misleading as well as archaic (or *arch.*).* He never in his life travelled alone without dread. Even in his twenties he needed escort. To have a child, an infant, with him (I am thinking of a particularly triumphant letter in the *Letters*, recounting a brief but successful train ride with my one-year-old brother) – this could shame him into courage. I also remember the times he was helped into my room at night after attacks of depersonalisation; I also remember the family visit to the scenic roof of the Empire State Building, in 1959, when he said that it was only the presence of his children that stopped him from screaming . . . Sally it was, these days, who took him west past Offa's Dyke and then, after a cup of tea in the station cafeteria, reboarded the train to Paddington. Three weeks later she would go up and bring him back again. But this year his return journey was unscheduled and had the air of an emergency. I know more about it now than I did then, how he slipped backwards on the steps, how his head met concrete – how he began to feel as bad as he had ever felt. I was relieved and grateful to learn that there was a friend on hand to drive my father back to London. The friend was Kingsley's biographer.†

It was late August and the family was reconverging. I heard the

---

* My father proposed that *illit.* should be a standard dictionary abbreviation. *Vulg.* was something else entirely. Even his *COD*, on occasion, cried out for *illit.* How he loved that dictionary – as I too love it. My current edition has just snapped in half and will have to be replaced. When it was near by and he was praising it ('This, this is the one'), he would sometimes pat and even stroke the squat black book, as if it were one of his cats.

† Eric Jacobs. The biography was out. See Appendix. But don't see it now.

news on the day that Kingsley was expected back in town, where he would be admitted to the Chelsea and Westminster Hospital in the Fulham Road. My mother, exhaustively familiar with her ex-husband's scrapes and scares, was non-alarmist and formulaic: Kingsley had had 'another fall', was 'shaken up', would be 'under observation'. With what now seems like farcical indecorum I had arranged to play snooker that night. I called my friend and put him on hold, and began trying the hospital. Around seven I got through.

– Dad.

And I cannot for the life of me remember the two words he said in reply – except that there was something wrong with them. If you want to remember the neologisms of a child you have to write them down immediately: they are alphabet soup, and defy memory just as they defy meaning. My father sounded as if he was making a somnolent attempt at a quite ordinary greeting, 'It's you', perhaps, or 'There you are'. What *did* he say? 'That's you'? 'You're there'?

– I'll come over.

And he went on, entirely recognisably,

– No. I'd rather save you up for tomorrow, if you know what I mean.

– You're sure.

– I'm sure.

So I went out and played snooker among all the other etiolated slouchers and anaemic sidlers at the Portobello Health and Fitness Club, under the Westway. I visualised the biographer, earlier that day, speeding eastwards down the M4 in an anonymous but highly evolved machine. This was a job I might have been expected to do myself. The gratitude I felt was qualified by guilt, partly inapposite, as it turned out, because the biographer had gone to Wales not to fetch Kingsley but to visit him: he was already there. To put it another way, I was pleased that I hadn't had to drive to Wales. In my other health and fitness club, Paddington Sports, there is a great man called Ray Gibbs who, when once glancingly challenged about his fitness, climbed from his chair and *ran* to Wales. Ray is sixty. As my body played snooker that night, as my body tensed and crouched and executed, and did all this not very well, significantly worse than usual, my body kept thinking: I could have done that. I could have *driven* to Wales. What was it my father said? 'There you are.' Or: 'It's you.' It sounded like the answer to that question about love in *The Anti-Death League*. 1994 and 1995 had not gone out of their way to persuade me that I was immune to disaster; and no one is spared the main events. Stealing over me now, working its way through my body, I felt a presentiment, not about love, but about its opposite. Was it now? Was it him?

During the summer I had several times imagined the first meeting of Kingsley and Delilah. She was still in South America, going up and down it, with others, in a trucksized people-carrier. That would give them something to talk about: minibus tours. I knew that introducing Delilah to my mother would be a breeze, and a warm and gentle one; but my father wasn't quite so reliable.★ I did feel sure that he would like her laugh, her laughter, its breathiness and drive. And this would be an important thing. He would want to hear more of that laughter. He would exert himself to excite it.

In the aftermath of one of his earlier falls or motor mishaps (they were often accompanied by the suspicion of an infarction, a thrombus: a minor stroke), my father had gone temporarily insane. He wrote about it, with all the freshness and detail of returned perspicuity, in a great little thing called 'A Peep Round the Twist' (which concludes the prose matter in the *Memoirs*). Illusions, delusions,† willed hallucinations, imagined psychokinetic powers. He was in hospital – in hospital already, so to speak, with his broken leg; and he seemed more or less all right in the head when we visited him. But there was a difference. He told me about the voices:

★ Minutes before meeting Kingsley for the first time, Carol Blue (the second Mrs Christopher Hitchens) sought my guidance. 'Don't say anything left-wing,' I said. 'Okay,' she said eagerly. 'Don't say much of anything,' I said. 'Okay,' she said. 'In fact, don't say anything at all,' I said. 'Okay,' she said. After shaking his hand Carol found herself embarked on a long speech in praise of the high literacy-rate in Cuba. It was a *coup de théâtre* of counter-suggestibility. Perhaps Kingsley sensed this. Anyway he liked Carol fine, describing her, afterwards, as a good kid.

† Cementing the distinction in *The King's English*, he quotes Fowler: 'That the sun moves round the earth was once a delusion, and is still an illusion.'

– A little girl called me an old fascist.

– But she didn't really.

– . . . No.

– It's like *Pinfold*.★ How does it go? 'Of course you know he's homosexual. Jews always are.'

Kingsley frowned vigilantly. We talked on. Another visitor appeared, evidently an ex-student of Kingsley's, who had read about the accident in the newspapers. There was something unreassuring about this new arrival (was he drunk?), and it didn't seem strange – only strangely candid – when Kingsley asked him, mildly enough, if he wouldn't mind going away. And he did. My father and I talked on. He seemed all right in the head, but there was a difference. I finally identified it, and it frightened me.

Now I think of *Stanley*, which he was working on at the time, and the thrilling disquisition on madness by the old psychiatrist, Nash, which concludes: 'The rewards for being sane may not be very many but knowing what's funny is one of them. And that's an end of the matter.'

Down the Fulham Road

Specialising as they do in arrivals and departures, hospitals invite comparison with airports. But the Chelsea and Westminster seemed to be taking it too far. The ground floor was a mall of outlets, concessions – of opportunistic commerce. You looked around for Duty Free . . . Saturday morning. Saturday morning comes after Friday night and this hospital did what hospitals do, so somewhere, presumably, there were waiting-rooms and dressing-stations for the axe-in-the-head fraternity – not to mention the proliferating wards for the elderly; but you saw absolutely none of this, no Coach, no Steerage. Kingsley was up in the private wing, Club World, waiting at the other end of the elevator.

★ Evelyn Waugh's *The Ordeal of Gilbert Pinfold* (1957).

If my father had been playing the adverb game (to borrow another line from *Stanley*), then the adverb in question would have been 'normally'. He received and returned my kiss normally, he sipped his juice or soda normally, he steered his way through the *Daily Telegraph* normally. He said little, but said it with clarity. And he said he wanted to go home . . . Philip was there: we exchanged a look that went back to childhood, to infancy – a wary flinch that said, half-comically, '*Now* what?' Sally was there too. She was on the phone, summoning a prawn cocktail from room service. So that's where we were: in one of the better rooms of the airport hotel. Only the bathroom, with its metal handholds, its rubber mats with their squidlike suction-cups, disclosed the luggage of incapacity. One by one (life must go on) the Amis children descended in turn to the sulphurous pit of the Smoking Room and sat beside a trembling spectre in a dressing-gown buckled up with gratitude over his crafty burn . . .

A doctor came, enormously tall and further elongated by his pinstriped suit, and as suave as a Mayfair estate-agent. Doctors. Who are these doctors?★ This particular doctor said that Sir Kingsley had been 'shaken up' and 'needed rest'. My father fidgeted more concertedly than hitherto until the doctor left the room. Then the afternoon, like a five-hour flight delay, sprawled out in front of us.

Dadsitting was what we called it. It was what *he* called it too. Being with Dad, keeping him company, had over the years become an activity or experience of increasingly frank torpor. He read his paper. You read yours. Usually he would offer the odd complaint about illiteracies, barbarisms, punning headlines with their single entendres. Not today. Old age, for him, was like privacy, thickening and deepening around him.

– Here, Dad. Help me with this.

★ I too have my phobias. '[Doctors]: intimates of bacilli and trichinae, of trauma and mortification, with their disgusting vocabulary and their disgusting furniture . . . They are life's gatekeepers. And why would anyone want to be that?' From the first page of *Time's Arrow* (1991), which, admittedly, describes an extreme case: it is narrated by the soul of one of Mengele's lesser assistants at Auschwitz-Birkenau.

I handed him my copy of the *Independent*, folded in four to isolate the Prize Crossword. Kingsley was of course very well-equipped for crosswords but lost interest over the years, saying he felt 'buggered about' by the setters.* Another objection was that crosswords were 'too much like work'. He said the same about chess. Once, in Princeton (making me nine), he contrived to lose a game in four moves. It wasn't the classic Fool's Mate, which demands the informed cooperation of your opponent. Fool's Mate lasts *two* moves. In the more protracted version Black has only to ignore an unignorable – and shamefully corny – pincer threat to his King's Bishop's pawn. (1. P-K4 . . . 2. Q-KB3 . . . 3. B-B4). 'Mate,' I said with astonishment, thinking, for a moment, that he would be sure to grant me a rematch. But there he was, ruefully climbing to his feet (and going back to his study). No, he *really* doesn't like chess, I thought. It was the last time we played . . . Up on the Empire State (that day was famous also for its unprecedented costliness: ‡100) I stared out and down at Manhattan with a sense of boundless privilege and achievement. That this glittering immensity inspired only terror in my father seemed to me painfully discrepant. I was sorry for him, and also generally bewildered, because I thought all adults lived beyond the reach of fear.

Lying in his hospital bed he accepted delivery of the *Independent* and its Prize Crossword (the prize was an Oxford reference-book: surely a worthy grail). I watched him: the compression of the lips, slightly vexed and put-upon; the emphatic exhalation through the nose; the preparatory wag of the head, as it settled down to reluctant concentration. And I understood the gravamen: more words, more dealings with words. And pointless dealings, because some crossword wonk† would get there before you (somebody who *did nothing else*) and you would never win that Companion to English

---

* Alun Weaver in *The Old Devils*: 'While he ate [his breakfast] he worked animatedly at the *Times* crossword. "You *fiend*," he said, writing in a solution. "Oh, you . . . you *swine*."'

† Mr Slang, a.k.a. Jonathon Green, in his great *Dictionary* (Cassell), fails to intuit the derivation of *wonk*. Surely (my father and I agreed) it's backslang, like *yob*, only wittier. 'Know backwards': a crossword clue in itself.

Literature or that Dictionary of Quotations. And he already had them. And he was already *in* them . . . All the same, Kingsley would usually help me out, on Sunday lunchtimes, filling in the last half-dozen clues of the Saturday puzzle I brought along – while the boys watched *Tom and Jerry* or the tape of *Aliens* – with irritation and imposing ease.

He returned the *Independent* to me (he would have no more of it), saying,

– Eight across is *stop*.

I *think* it was *stop*. It was a four-letter answer involving two abbreviations and a tactical synonym. The clue might have been: 'Prevent roadwork (4)' (road=*st.*, work=*op.*, prevent=*stop*).

– Thanks, Dad.

Very soon I would be looking back on this moment with veneration, like an apostate remembering the unction and ardour of faith.

He stayed a week and, although it was my mother he really wanted and needed, the children, too, worked to a rough rota, and I was a good deal back and forth.

Larkin, long dead it now seemed, began his monumental hospital poem, 'The Building' (1972), as follows:

> Higher than the handsomest hotel
> The lucent comb shows up for miles, but see,
> All round it close-ribbed streets rise and fall
> Like a great sigh out of the last century.

Fulham Road didn't feel like a great sigh out of the last century. It felt like a great sigh out of the next century – no, not a sigh, a ditty, a jingle. The area was undergoing plutocratic Italianisation (Milan being the model, not Florence or Rome), deriving its character from Chelsea Football Club – from Roberto Di Matteo, from Gianfranco Zola, from Gianluca Vialli. On the street everybody is impeccably groomed, beautifully shod, wasp-waisted, leather-jacketed. They all look as though they earn thirty thousand pounds a week and eat pasta three times a day. Their hearts, in repose, beat once an hour.

We used to live here, just a couple of blocks east, 128 Fulham Road: me, brother, sister, mother. This was in the early 1960s, after the dissolution of the marriage, after the fatherless interlude in Soller, Majorca. I enrolled at a grammar in Battersea, over the river (where my mother worked, later, at Battersea Zoo; she had been a kennel-maid in her youth, and groomed many horses). Philip had gone back to his Cambridge-axis boarding-school. During the vacations, with various friends, in various combinations, we cruised all day* and played Scrabble all night.† In 1963 my mother had a form of breakdown. Hilly went away to recover and, unaccountably, for several days, maybe a week, maybe more, the children ran wild. One afternoon George Gale rang the doorbell. He went from room to room in solemn consternation. Every cupboard he opened had a fourteen-year-old girl in it. Kingsley and Jane came to stay. Jane took the house in hand, transforming it from low- to middle-Bohemian (until then the front door had been seldom locked). A friend of Jane's stopped by for a drink, Alexander Mackendrick, the director (*Whisky Galore*, *The Ladykillers*, *Sweet Smell of Success*), and a few weeks later I was taking my mother – first-class, BOAC – on a highly paid as well as complimentary two-month holiday in the West Indies. I got fifty quid a week and she, as my Chaperone, got twenty (the rent on our four-floor house in South Kensington was forty-eight a month).‡ I talentlessly played one of the children in Mackendrick's version of the Richard

* The method: you wrote out visiting-cards, with your name and number, and distributed them, by the tens of thousands, to every girl you could find on the London Underground; then you hurried home to wait, often in vain, for your one or two calls.
† I hallucinated Scrabble boards; Scrabble boards stayed with me like the sun's imprint or logo; I would stare into the lavatory bowl, at three in the morning, and see a Scrabble board, its diagonals of pink, its corners of red.
‡ I gave Philip fifty. He told me what he was going to do with it. He was going to hail a taxi (we only used taxis in emergencies) and say, 'Carnaby Street.'

Hughes novel *A High Wind in Jamaica*.* Sally came out and was a busy extra. I played chess with my co-star, the consistently avuncular Anthony Quinn, and the divinely pretty daughter – Lisa Coburn – of my other co-star, genial James, was in love with me and followed me everywhere, even down into the deep end of the pool of the hotel on Runaway Bay. I loved her too but I wanted moments of reprieve. She was seven. The film's central character was an extraordinary girl called Deborah Baxter, who played my younger sister. I had eyes (but no lips, no hands) for her *older* sister: *Beverly* Baxter. My smallest sister (there were three, the middle one, Roberta Tovey, going on to star in *Dr Who and the Daleks*) was called Karen Flack, who was even younger than Lisa Coburn. Hilly and I told each other again and again that Karen was destined to be a star. Once or twice I babysat for her when our mothers went out on the town with the feature actors and the stuntmen. Karen was asleep by the time they left. 'Go in the big bed with Karen,' said my mother. 'Then when you're older you can say that you've slept with Karen Flack.' This was unlike my mother, more like my father; but we both knew it was funny. In Jamaica I laughed a lot with my mother and ceased to play host to anxieties about her breakdown. (That night in London I had been restrained from entering the

---

* 1929. I didn't know it then but this is a thrillingly good book: an historical novel (the setting is Victorian) about children running wild. As a visit to this theme it is more continuously sinuous and inward (and enjoyable) than the Golding. Hughes came to the set at Pinewood. Otiosely tall, Gravesian in cast and colouring and background (they both went to Charterhouse, a public school of louche reputation), accompanied by his wife and perhaps a grown child (Hughes was in his sixties), he was pleased, impressed, tickled (they might have been making *Thunderball* in the next lot along). His dress was like my costume: oatmeal trousers, oatmeal jacket, straw hat . . . I keep meaning to read more of him but something prevents me. In that year of 1963, I learn from my *Companion*, he was one novel into a silence-breaking multivolume sequence unwisely entitled 'The Human Predicament' . . . These potted lives are often sinister in their adumbrations. *The Fox in the Attic* had appeared in 1961. Volume 2, *The Wooden Shepherdess*, published in 1973 (and so joining *The Rachel Papers* on that year's fiction lists), was ill-received (meeting 'with little critical enthusiasm'). And then, in 1976, he died.

room where she lay.) When she trod on a spiked sea-anemone in the rocks, towards the end of the trip, I expected her to be courageous, and she was: as indifferent to self-pity as to self-dramatisation. My acting duties were light compared to those of the other children, because I died just over halfway through; blood-thirstily watching a cockfight in the square below, I fell from a window of the bordello run by Lila Kedrova . . . We flew back to England (second-class: my mother cashed in the tickets) and the summer was spent going back and forth to Pinewood until the film was done.* Wearing a brand-new blazer I returned to the grammar in Battersea, on the first day of the academic year – and was instantly expelled (for chronic truancy). This was stunning and also laughable. Sir Walter St John's was a violent school, with violent pupils and violent staff. It seemed to me that you could do *anything* there and expect just an hour's detention. I enrolled at a chaotic crammer in Notting Hill, and went back to cruising all day and playing Scrabble all night. 'Do they sleep with these girls?' my aunt Miggy, visiting, asked my mother. 'No,' said Hilly. Well, Philip did, and I didn't. Then after an aeon of petting and pleading I suddenly lost my virginity to a girl I met in a Wimpy Bar earlier the same day. I was fifteen. My amatory career was launched. My cinematic career immediately disappeared. And my academic career, as mentioned earlier, started to fall into a pattern: one O-level every other year. I didn't have much time for reading but when I did read I read comics and, after I'd done that, I reread them. Quietly, patiently, unobtrusively reeking, I lay there on the bed as my mother yelled my A-level English result up the stairs: 'You *failed*.' I arose, and spent the rest of the day transferring a sock from

---

* It was years before I steeled myself to see it – and then only on the small screen, where my adolescent panic would, I thought, look more contained. And that wasn't all. During the filming my voice had finally broken: I had been dubbed (this was standard practice) by an old lady. The other anxiety concerned my physique. I was pleased when I heard, the other day, that someone had written a whole novel called *Does My Bum Look Big in This?* I might have asked the same question of *A High Wind in Jamaica*. The answer would have been yes. Now picture it in CinemaScope.

one end of the room to the other. This had to end. My brother and I moved in with Kingsley and Jane, and my mother remarried and went to Ann Arbor, Michigan, and Sally went too.

On my visits to the Chelsea and Westminster Hospital I didn't bother to go along to the old house. Because I pass it all the time. It is now a choice, a bijou residence. I find it hard to believe that so much guileless disorder played itself out behind that pearly, Belgravian façade. Tellies and trannies, cats and lodgers, fires and floods – and dope, and speed.* It seems now that my faculties were entirely inert. I knew there were higher inklings out there, and they had to do with the soul. *Soul* was a quality much discussed, or rather referred to as understood, by my brother and me, and was the first attribute you looked for in everyone and everything (and especially girls). In addition, I did claim to myself that I wanted to be a writer.† So what did I do all the time? Did I dream and doodle, did I read, did I pray? No. I was groping my way back across the bedroom, looking for the other sock.

My mother's breakdown, in 1963, culminated in an accidental overdose: sleeping-pills. She lay in a curtained room. I looked in and could see the bedside light and its pink lampshade. Someone, an adult, barred my entry. Her recovery was swift and total. When she talked to me about it afterwards she said she had been depressed because she was still in love with my father.

I cannot overemphasise how thoroughly this was not the case, in 1995. All was reversed. By this stage my mother still contemplated death as an escape from her feelings about Kingsley – but an escape in the opposite direction. 'I've been *dying* for a heart attack for years,'

---

* But no drink. We considered alcohol barbaric – surprisingly, perhaps. Was this rebellion? One morning in Swansea Philip risked the anger of my underslept mother as he sat down at the table in his school uniform. 'Ah,' he said. 'Breakfast in the wine shop.' We were both about twenty when we began to see the point.

† Such a claim, at such an age, may be near-universal, as articulate self-communion dawns. The writers are supposedly the ones who 'move on' from this, but you could say that the writers are the ones who never leave – that part of them just doesn't grow up.

she told me. Still, there were days, there were weeks, when she really meant it. Always difficult, and more recently impossible, Kingsley was now proceeding towards the unbelievable. 'Courage . . . means not scaring others.' My father did a fair job of not frightening his children: the Empire State Effect. But he didn't think to spare my mother. Because she was everything to him now: the full imago. It had always struck me, concerned me, that for as long as I can remember Dad called her what we called her. He called her Mum.

On 6 September, just over a week after his fall, Hilly and Sally went in to get him and bring him home.

Seagulls

First I wanted to know what was happening on his side of the desk. All else would follow from this.

I was with my mother in her sitting-room downstairs. It opened on to the asymmetrical little garden, in past summers the scene of al fresco lunches and hosed-down grandchildren. Kingsley was upstairs, with friends.

– He sits in the red chair.

This was said ominously. The tomato-red leather armchair lived in Kingsley's study. Its significance lay in the fact that it wasn't the chair on the business side of the desk. The red chair was where he sat when he wasn't writing.

– Reading?

– Yes, or trying to . . .

The diagnosis, as it came down to me (or got diffused in my direction), was still a string of contented clichés. Kingsley had (a) been up against it and gone through it, this bad patch, and was still out of sorts and one degree under, out of kilter and a bit green around the gills, but if he (b) looked after himself and took it easy and had some peace and quiet and drew the line and kept within bounds, then, he would (c) yes, he would soon be his old self again. His old self.

Upstairs, the sound of voices – the laughter of the biographer.

– Dad's drinking, is he?

– Of course he is. He was *desperate* to get back to the Garrick. *Desperate*.

It was the first thing he did. He went to the Garrick for an all-day lunch.

– Was he drunk?

– Oh, paralytic . . . I like the sound of a typewriter. It seems to me like a natural background noise.

And she missed it. As you would, after nearly half a century (with one interregnum, 1963-81; but my mother's other husbands were writers too). All those novels, poems, essays, letters. Kingsley was a brisk two-finger typist; some of the more often-used keys bore a deep lateral cleft from his nails. My mother was unsettled by the silence of the typewriter; it was like vanished traffic or birdsong.

Hilly had been saving this up. She said,

– He keeps typing the word *seagulls*.

– Seagulls?

– Seagulls.

This seemed much stranger to me then than it does now. Now I live on my father's street, and seagulls, in the temperate months, are part of my daily life. Attracted by the nearby canals, they fill the sky above Regent's Park Road. Plump, cumbersome and pompous, they flock to the shitlashed terrace outside my study. All day they honk and shriek, practising on their ten-pee harmonicas, their warped kazoos. A mother seagull has a nest in the chimney. She knocks on the glass of the terrace door with her questing yellow beak. She once strode into the room: the size of an ostrich.

– He types *i*'s and *o*'s.

– What?

– He gets up at five in the morning and types *i*'s and *o*'s.

A week later. I hadn't seen Kingsley for three days and suddenly he was shorter than me. What happened to those four inches? Gravity ate them. It would be another week before I took this in.

He looked as though he had gone halfway through a car-compactor: the vertical compression had taken place, but they had yet to attempt the horizontal. I went and lay on his bed while he crouched opposite in a low armchair. The expression he wore seemed unfamiliar, and at first I took it for anger. I said experimentally, knowing that this was just the kind of thing my father liked,

– If we were all Icelandic, you would be called Kingsley Williamson. I would be called Martin Kingsleyson and Louis would be called Louis Martinson. Sally would be called Sally Kingsleysdottir and Jessica would be called Jessica Philipsdottir.

– Mm, he said, unamused.

Now I hoped he *was* angry with me. I hoped it . . . And Delilah, what would she be called? Delilah Patricksdottir or Delilah Martinsdottir? The former, surely. She calls *him* Daddy, and that's as it should be. I did the nature but he did the nurture. He did the hours . . . I had just returned from a two-night trip to Iceland (and I hoped that that was what Kingsley was angry about). There I saw a rainbow entire, bandily bestriding a fjord in austere isolation. Round-topped mountains loomed on the horizon, like planets. Now I was back in the small world, the sickroom, with my father using whisky to swallow his pills, and with that look on his face. What was that look? Not anger. More defiance: a defiant self-neglect.

As we changed guard my brother and I had a few words in the hall. Philip said,

– He's poisoning himself.

– Those pills are all jumbled up in the shoebox.

– I see him sitting there really *sweating* . . .

Downstairs. I sensed, now, that my mother too had changed, had contracted. It was no longer a question of rolling your eyes and blowing the fringe off your brow. This was going to be warm human work from here on in. I said, uselessly (do we *ever* need to be told this, beyond the age of about thirty?),

– You look tired.

– He screams for his Nurofen at five in the morning. I mean screams . . .

The doorbell rang.

– He waits all day for people to visit. And when they come he switches the TV on. Then he asks, 'What's for dinner? What's for dinner?' But he's *had* dinner.

But he *hasn't* had dinner. He eats nothing at all.

Upstairs. There was a good showing that night: me, Philip, Moira and Percy Lubbock, Dick Hough. And the ever-dependable biographer. Saying little, his eyes lowered, Kingsley was established in his chair, with the Macallan and the Evian water on the side table. But he seemed to me to be miming his congeniality, as if saying to himself – This is what I like. Drink, talk, friends, family. This is what I'm supposed to like. Then why . . . ? Suddenly he lifted his head and professed an opinion. His novel *The Biographer's Moustache* had recently appeared. And the reviews, on the whole, were eagerly unfavourable. I found the notices and interviews more onerous than anything that had been written about me that year, and I hoped that my father (on this subject at least) was past caring. Never one to go on for long about such things, he spoke up now about a detail, saying, out of the blue,

– Someone complained that I put a 'real' restaurant into it. But once it's in the novel, even if it's a real place, it isn't real any more. Not quite.

I thought I understood him and I thought I agreed with him. Perhaps this is all that needs to be said on the subject. The real/made-up question is for biographers and memoir-writers and other literalists. Anyway, I would hear no more critical theory from my father. Amusement would return, but that was his last attempt at anything abstract. Over the following weeks I would look back on it as a summit, along with the crossword clue.

Next door in his study there were sheets of paper covered with *i*'s and *o*'s and *seagulls*.

Fuck Off – 2

Here are some glimpses of the morning routine of an old devil, Charlie, in *The Old Devils*:

When Charlie Norris noticed that the smallest man in the submarine railwaycarriage had a face made out of carpeting he decided it was time to be off.

He wakes, and tormentedly dozes. It is just after 5 a.m. Several hours later:

He rolled over and fixed his eye on the stout timber that framed the quilted bed-head, counted a hundred, then, with a convulsive overarm bowling movement, got a hand to it, gripped it, counted another hundred and hauled with all his strength, thus pulling himself half upright.

Later, wholly upright, Charlie looks out of the bedroom window,

. . . looking but not seeing. With a conviction undimmed by having survived countless previous run-offs he felt that everything he had was lost and everyone he knew was gone.

With infinite difficulty he dresses and goes downstairs:

After ten minutes Charlie had made it all the way from the breakfast-room table to the refrigerator in the kitchen . . . The sight of a coffee-bag out in the open near an unused mug was not quite enough to make up his mind for him, but finding the electric kettle half full turned the scale . . . When a speck of saliva caught at the back of his throat he managed to lay the mug down before the father and mother of a coughing-fit sent him spinning about the room and landing up face to face with Mr Bridgeman [the gardener], round the back now, eighteen inches away on the other side of the window-pane.★

★ Kingsley's own approach to breakfast actually bears closer resemblances to that of Peter, the fattest of the old devils. Here he is with his grapefruit: 'Some [segments] clung tenaciously to their compartments after being to all appearance cut free, others came only half-way out, still joined on by a band of pith. He dealt with such cases by lifting the whole works into the air by the segment and waggling the main body of the fruit in circles until the bond parted and it crashed back on to or near its plate.'

Charlie has a 'weakish' whisky and water at 10.45 or so and climbs into a minicab. He is off to the official unveiling of a statue of the unofficial national poet, Brydan (a figure based on Dylan Thomas). At the ceremony Charlie is accosted by an American who introduces himself as Llywelyn Caswallon Pugh:

'I am an official of the Cymric Companionship of the USA,' said Pugh.

At this point something terrible happened to Charlie's brain. Pugh went on speaking in just the same way as before, with no change of pace or inflection, but Charlie could no longer distinguish any words, only noises. His eyes swam a little. He stepped backwards and trod heavily on someone's foot. Then he picked out a noise he recognized and nearly fell over the other way with relief. It had not been fair to expect an old soak whose Welsh vocabulary started and stopped with *yr* and *bach* and *myn* to recognize the rubbish when it came at him unheralded in an American accent. 'M'm,' he said with feeling. 'M'm.'

Pugh's wide stare widened further in a way that made Charlie wonder what he had assented to, but that was soon over and more English came . . .

A capful of rain blew refreshingly into Charlie's face and a seagull passed close enough overhead to make him flinch.

That seagull . . . Charlie is now rescued by Alun, the flyest and most priapic of the old devils. As their car moves off Alun sticks his head out of the window and tells Pugh to fuck off. The two men settle back in their seats:

'They do say fuck off in America, don't they?' asked Alun anxiously.

'I'm sure they understand it.'

. . . Alun laughed quietly for a short time, shaking his head in indulgent self-reproach . . . He lowered his voice and went on, 'Hey – timing really was important for that. I got badly caught in Kilburn once telling a Bulgarian short-story writer . . . to fuck off for two or three minutes while the chap driving the open car I was sitting in turned round in the cul-de-sac I hadn't noticed we were at the end of. Amazing how quickly the bloom fades on fuck off, you know. Say it a couple of times running and you've got out of it nearly all you're going to get.'

'And there's not a lot you can go on to later,' said Charlie.

'Well exactly.'

Sunday, 17 September. I have just learned how Kingsley spent Saturday night. He was, as my mother said, 'very active'. Whereas I can feel the essential family flaw – passivity – seeping over the rest of us. Mum is a ghost. Shouldn't I be the strong one? Kingsley needs to go to hospital. But he doesn't *want* to go to hospital. I don't want to frighten him. I don't want him to frighten me.

Who is in charge? Where is the doctor? His bowel specialist will not make housecalls – he is too grand, too gastroenteritic.* We are reduced to looking in the Yellow Pages – for the jobbers and cowboys. Mum got a quote for a home visit: sixty quid . . . We are an articulate family but we are heading towards speechlessness. We are doing what Kingsley is doing. We are becoming speechless.

But last night he was very active. He wanted, he said, to have a party. Then he told everybody – Mum, Ali, Connie† – to fuck off. Everybody went downstairs. He followed everybody into the basement

---

* This was the physician Kingsley seemed closest to. He used to ring him up practically every time he used the bathroom. In his sixties my father became a martyr to IBS, or Irritable Bowel Syndrome. The condition was aggravated in him by mild but undeniable paranoia. Sometimes I had to drive him around because he feared having a mishap in a taxi. His condition and his paranoia were at their worst when he was summoned to Buckingham Palace to receive his knighthood from the Queen. KA had his doctor lay down a firewall of Omidium, and there was some doubt, afterwards, whether he would ever again go to the toilet. When the crisis was over I told him that he would have been remembered as the prick who died for a Sir. He laughed at this, to my surprise, because he was as sensitive about IBS as he was about HRH.

† Connie Basil, the co-proprietress, while it lasted, of Lucky Jim's fish-and-chip shop in Ann Arbor.

flat★ and told everybody to fuck off. Then he went upstairs. Everybody followed, with caution. Then he told everybody to fuck off.

I heard this on Sunday. Sunday was the day I almost always brought Louis and Jacob here, for lunch; this had been going on for ten years. He was an observant, if wholly immobile, grandparent. He enjoyed them and admired them and was proud of them. Louis's birth caused him grave happiness. He bestirred himself, accompanying my mother to the hospital. We met and had drinks at my flat. It was November; I trained a bar fire on his knees. The baby was six weeks premature (but beautiful), and the mother happy . . . Afterwards the three of us had a reverent lunch in a Chinese restaurant. I was, I suppose, still in clinical shock, but I felt far more warmed than stunned. Jacob, in his turn (and only four weeks early), had his name posted on the Garrick noticeboard and phoned in just in time to join Louis on the dedication page of *The Old Devils* (where, in the first of many editions, it is followed by a harassed-looking full stop). The boys were main events. But the only thing he ever actually did with them or about them, apart from hug them hello and goodbye, was reach out with his hand (this was when they were very small) to cover a sharp edge of low furniture as they crawled or toddled by.

On this Sunday the boys are elsewhere, absent. As they will be next Sunday, too. He never saw them again.

My father and I often had occasion to agree that 'fuck off' was very funny. One naturally admired its brutality and brevity – but it was also terribly *good*.†

★ Where he also openly peed into a mop-bucket. I would have spared my father this detail, but it is already in print (see Appendix).
† It is in fact Stephen and not Rosemary West who does so very well here with 'fuck off' ('Childhood', *Inside 25 Cromwell Street*): 'I didn't have many friends for the simple reason Mum told them to fuck off when they came to the door.' I will promiscuously mention in this note that my father once told Christopher Hitchens and me to fuck off after we took him to Leicester Square to see *Beverly Hills Cop*. No: he liked it and we didn't. And I think we must have curled our lips at him. Most uncharacteristically he walked away on his own and had to be coaxed into the next pub or cab.

But the best fuck off of all time had Dad at the receiving end of it. Or at least he stagemanaged it so. One afternoon, in Hampstead (it must have been before 1980, when Jane was still around, because he had a lightness about his person which left him when she did), he came in through the front door after posting a letter, laughing quietly and richly to himself. I said,

– What was so funny?

– I saw a bloody fool of a dog just now . . .

It was a genuine summer's day, concerted and cloudless. On his walk to the letterbox my father had passed a fullgrown Alsatian apparently asleep on the boiling breast of a parked car. He looked interestedly at the dog and the dog roused itself and stared back, as if to say: I'm lying on this car – all right? On his walk back from the letterbox he looked at the dog again, and the dog stared back, adding: It may be hot but I'm still lying on this car. Before opening the garden door he turned for a final glance.

– What did it do? I urged him, because he was laughing quietly and richly to himself.

It lifted its head from its paws and straightened its neck and went . . . Kingsley did one of two things. Either he made the bark sound exactly like fuck off. Or he made fuck off sound exactly like the bark.

When he made you laugh he sometimes made you laugh – not continuously, but punctually – for the rest of your life. This was his superhumour: the great engine of his comedy. And now the engine was winding down.

He got up in the middle of the night and showered and dressed – and packed. He packed a suitcase. I hear this from my mother. On that night he told Hilly that he had to take a train – Kingsley, alone, in the middle of the night, taking a train? He was expected at a very important meeting. Advised against it by my mother at the doorstep, he went out into the street and approached a driverless parked car and demanded to be taken to the Garrick. He called to my mother,

– Why won't he take me to the Garrick?

* * *

A brief visit. He looks comatose in his chair and I'm surprised when he speaks.

– What time is it?

– Two.

– Two in the afternoon? What day are we?

On my way out I look at the sheet of paper recurled into Kingsley's typewriter. I see no *seagulls*. He is still on page 106 of his new novel. It has been page 106 ever since the fall. Something seems to have been added. The page ends with the words: '"On the contrary," countered Holmes.'★

Another brief visit. The night before Kingsley had again been active. But now he slumbers in his chair. With that expression on his face: the face of a boy who might have done wrong, according to some, but is definitely not yet ready to admit it – and who is anyway tired now, tired by the struggle (the fight for truth), and is turning away from the world in sleep.

Mum reminds me of a nurse. More than this, she reminds me of a nursery: my own . . . Of course we keep discussing the idea of nurses, of hired professionals. But my mother says that they wouldn't be able to stand Kingsley (arguable) and that he wouldn't be able to stand them (certain: it has to be Mum). Hospital is different. Hospital plays on some instinct of obedience in him. And hospital is where he needs to go, at least for a while. He ought to be 'under the doctor', as the English say. When you're under the weather, that's where you ought to be: under the doctor.

Kingsley stirs, or jolts.

– Do you want a cardy? says my mother, stroking and patting his shoulder.

I am still some distance from any apprehension that my father is

★ I have since read these 106 pages. The unfinished work is called *Black and White*, and it is about the development of an attraction between a white homosexual man and a black heterosexual girl. Rather slow, and perhaps rather weakly focused, the half-novel nonetheless sets about its tasks with acuity. The Sherlock Holmes stuff is a digression, but it makes perfect sense.

dying. But I am closing in on the belief that I will never again see amusement in his eyes. Seeming to confirm this, my mother says,

– All you can do is be kind to him now.

She is in it for the duration. There is no love any more, only the memory of love, but it's simpler than that. Her conscience would permit nothing less. Kingsley was right:

> In '46 when I was twenty-four
> I met someone harmless, someone defenceless,
> But till then whole, unadapted within;
> Awkward, gentle, healthy, straight-backed,
> Who spoke to say something, laughed when amused;
> If things went wrong, feared she might be at fault . . .

But wait a minute. In '63 he broke her heart, and she left him.

> . . . Whose eye I could have met for ever then,
> Oh yes, and who was also beautiful.
> Well, that was as much as women were meant to be,
> I thought, and set about looking further.
> How can we tell, with nothing to compare?

And now she is there for the duration, even if he lives on – persists, lasts – until the end of the century. 1963 was thirty-two years ago. How did she get into this?

Night of the Peach

I was sitting in my sock* in Bayswater, starting *Money*, when the call came through.

* Family and friends usually referred to my two-room apartment in Kensington Gardens Square as 'the sock', and the term gained wider currency after *Money*. Its etymology begins with Tina Brown, who, in a

– Mart.

– Phil.

– It's happened.

– What? I said. But I knew.

– She's left him.

– . . . Jesus Christ.

Philip felt no surprise either. That was just the way the whole thing was *tending* . . .

We made arrangements. It wasn't a question of two sons planning to console a father who had lost his wife. It was much more elementary. One or other of us had to be there all the time. Not round the clock but every evening, every night, every morning. He still had his housekeeper there, loyal Mrs Uniacke, and her presence would help him get through the day; but only family or thoroughly trusted friends were any good to him for the hours of darkness. It was now late afternoon. It was November. When I went over Philip was already there.

My memory of that night has Kingsley perched on the brink of the low armchair (this was his characteristic back-favouring posture: in Philip's imitation of it, he is attached to his seat by about a millimetre of outer coccyx), blinking more rapidly than usual, and fiercely worrying his thumb cuticles with the nails of his forefingers. And saying almost nothing. He would answer questions about the logistical end of it (Jane's failure to return from the health farm; the note delivered by her solicitor's office) but nothing was ventured about his feelings, about love, about broken hearts, broken vows. His needs, at that moment, seemed basic, almost animal: shelter, warmth, the heat of known beasts. My brother and I repeated what was most immediately necessary for him to hear:

———

piece in the *Tatler* (I think), wrote that some young man's flat was 'like a sock'. Christopher Hitchens then promoted the simile to a common noun (he was also responsible for 'rug-rethink': haircut). At this time – 1980 – the Hitch had just spent a year in the sock, while I travelled. My cleaning-lady, Ana, who continued to come every week, told me: 'I only see him *once*. In the middle of the afternoon. This terrible groan come from the bedroom. And, Miss Tramis, I *RUN*.'

– Dad, you won't spend a night alone. One of us will always be here.

– Thank you both for that.

It was solemnly said. But I can see now that he was heartsick: romantically mortified, and (in a sense) incurably so. Later, in his revisionist mode, when he had unpersoned Jane, had unloved her, he looked back on his suffering with ridicule and disbelief. Yet the suffering was there. That very night he was writing to her and about her in his head – a pleading letter, and also a poem. He had lost something that he had made enormous efforts to keep, and undergone detailed indignities to that end.* Perhaps most importantly, two marriages, not one, had been cancelled, wiped out. As he put it to Larkin in a letter of 24 June 1981, describing a meeting with an old friend: 'She said how miserable I had made Hilly, thus (unnecessarily) reminding me that Jane's departure has stopped me pretending to myself that my treatment of H was at least sort of worth while somehow a bit.' 'It's only half a life without a woman,' he said to me, later; the woman, the wife, the other half,† was gone – and no successor would be sought. My father never again kissed a woman with passion. This from a man who used to

* I mean all the psychological and sexual therapy described in *Jake's Thing*. What really impresses me now is how much *boredom* he put up with. '[The shrink] had also . . . stated a major theme of the Workshop's activities, namely that every single one of them without any exception whatsoever lasted for very much longer than you would ever have thought possible'; 'There followed [from another patient] a passage in praise of women so intense, categorical and of course long that a confession of hyperactive homosexuality seemed almost boringly inevitable'; 'To limit the danger of cardiac arrest from indignation and incredulity Jake had made an agreement with himself not to look at his watch . . .' Elsewhere KA wrote of 'the burning sincerity of all boredom'. What sustained him here? The burning sincerity of not wanting to be left.

† Kingsley's malicious glee is admirably controlled in his article on 'Sexist language' in the much later (indeed posthumous) book, *The King's English*. The language does it all for him: English, 'which regularly includes some less than respectful affix meaning *man* in its words for *female*. The word *female* itself, from *femella*, diminutive of Latin *femina*, assimilates its second syllable to *male*, thus implying that a female is a mere appendage or subsection of a

2: ONE LITTLE MORE HUG

live for adultery.★ Over the years I have worked my way towards a psychological explanation, and like all such it is zero-rudimentary. But it explains and therefore forgives a good deal. My most obliterating experience of Kingsley (soon to occur) has since been softened in its light.

The letter to Jane got written. And replied to. There was a fruitless exchange of conditions and ultimatums. I can't help feeling that there was something doctrinaire in Jane's insistence that Kingsley should, in effect, join Alcoholics Anonymous. What didn't get written was the love poem. What got written, now, was the hate novel: *Stanley and the Women*. There was something humanly open-ended about *Jake* (1978). Rather formulaically, in my view (there is simply too much of this in my father's corpus), the outgoing woman gets all the best moral lines.†
And I know several female readers who admire and partly assent to the novel's magnificent final period. Our libidoless and now wifeless hero has just been asked by the doctor if he would like to try a course of what *Girl, 20* calls 'horn pills' (or ur-Viagra):

> Jake did a quick run-through of women in his mind, not the
> ones he had known and dealt with in the past few months or
> years so much as all of them: their concern with the surface of
> things, with objects and appearances, with their surroundings
> and how they looked and sounded in them, with seeming to be
> better and to be right while getting everything wrong, their

---

male . . . The almost archaic term *lady* is free from any linguistically built-in put-down or sneer, though perhaps none was felt to be necessary in a word originally signifying nothing more than *loaf-kneader* (*hlafdige*) beside a *lord* who at any rate was guard or warden of that loaf (*hlafweard*).'
★ I think he was more or less faithful in his second marriage. He did tell me about an inconclusive but pretty graphic incident in the sitting-room at Lemmons. 'Where was Jane?' I asked. 'In bed.' 'In bed? Christ. I thought you were going to say, "In *Greece*."'
† It appears that I was already complaining about this, or rebelling against it, when I wrote *The Rachel Papers*. On the last page the narrator notes that the (rejected) heroine leaves the house 'without telling me a thing or two about myself, without asking if I knew what my trouble was, without providing any sort of comeuppance at all'.

automatic assumption of the role of injured party in any clash of wills, their certainty that a view is the more credible and useful for the fact that they hold it, their use of misunderstanding and misrepresentation as weapons of debate, their selective sensitivity to tones of voice, their unawareness of the difference in themselves between sincerity and insincerity, their interest in importance (together with noticeable inability to discriminate in that sphere), their fondness for general conversation and directionless discussion, their preemption of the major share of feeling, their exaggerated estimate of their own plausibility, their never listening and lots of other things like that, all according to him.

So it was quite easy. 'No thanks,' he said.

Stan (1984), on the other hand, is all closed up and walled off. It made my head drop, during this time, when my father, elaborately and not entirely unmordantly, started to liken women to the USSR (department of propaganda): when *they* do it they say *this*; when *you* do it they say *that*; and so on. Around now, too, he started referring to the opposite sex as 'females'. 'Dad, don't *say* that word!' I used to tell him; and he partly moderated this habit when I was present, in the spirit of someone doing absolutely anything for a quiet life . . . *Stanley* is in fact a mean little novel in every sense, sour, spare, and viciously well-organised. But there is an ignobility in the performance. Here the author implements – and literalises – Jake's poetical promise: i.e., men only. There is certainly no sexual disgust in it (Kingsley was never that kind of woman-hater). The grounds are purely intellectual.

I always thought it was suicide: artistic suicide. He didn't kill the world. He just killed half of it.★

★ 'A snarl of disappointment', maybe, but also a snarl of something else. Here is the violence of the defeated: delegated violence, surrogate violence. '"According to some bloke on the telly the other night," he said, "twenty-five per cent of violent crimes in England and Wales is husbands assaulting wives. Amazing figure that, don't you think? You'd expect it to be more like eighty per cent. Just goes to show what an easy-going lot English husbands are . . ."' The speaker, a gruff 'medical johnny' named Cliff,

Over the next few weeks Philip and I conferred regularly on the Kingsley question. Either he had to go somewhere (club, set of rooms, hotel?) or someone had to come to him. Whoever came to him would have to be . . . How to define it? It would have to be someone who understood, and so forgave, his fragility. And it would have to be someone he liked very much indeed. I was thirty-one, Philip thirty-two: a bit early, we felt, to commit our lives to Dadsitting – but we couldn't rule it out. It seemed to me that the Kingsley question was oddly shaped. The answer, too, therefore, would have to be oddly shaped.

In the interstices of worrying about my father I worried about my mother. Her third marriage was a complete success, but she and her husband, and little Jaime, were confined to a tiny cottage in the Midlands and couldn't afford to move to London . . . Surely it would be no great feat to attempt an answer here. Philip had already reached the same conclusion. When canvassed, the principals appeared keen. An introductory dinner was scheduled. Everyone else, by the way, considered the idea both bizarre and impracticable. 'Like an Iris Murdoch novel,' they kept saying. Yes, and it would have been even more like an Iris Murdoch novel if Kingsley had been called Otto and Hilly had been called George. It was an unconventional proposal, true; but they were an unconventional crowd. Philip and I thought it might work for a good six months, maybe even a year.

We all gathered at the house in Flask Walk and the inaugural dinner began.

In later life Kingsley would deny it ever happened, deny it hotly, stoutly, despite the presence of four adult witnesses. I think my father did manage on some level to expunge the incident from his memory. It was, after all, completely unbelievable.

---

delivers these lines in a savage pub called the Admiral Byron (''Tis women's whole existence'). Another character, a high-ranking police officer, observes that the Arab nations 'do seem to have got the woman problem sorted out nice and neat. Whether you like it or not'.

Our dinner was going beautifully. My brother and I were already exchanging complacent smiles. Everyone present was coming across as a model of flexibility and discretion. When the dessert course began, Jaime, eight years old and unimprovable throughout, reached for the fruitbowl. It contained oranges, apples, grapes – and a single peach. As Jaime's fingers met its surface, Kingsley, like a man hailing a cab across the length of Oxford Circus during a downpour on Christmas Eve, shouted:

– *HEY!!!*

. . . It was an extraordinary manifestation, hideously harsh, hideously sudden. The sound Kingsley had uttered would have been just about appropriate if Jaime had reached, not for a peach, but for the pin of a hand grenade. There was no silence: everyone reeled back, groaning, swearing. Even Jaime whispered 'Jesus Christ' as he shrivelled up in his chair. I can't remember – I can't even imagine – how we survived the rest of the evening.

But the *ménage* lasted for fifteen years.

'Philip had a biscuit.' Jaime had a peach.

If you're a grown man who is frightened of the dark – what happens when someone leaves you? When they leave you alone in the dark like that, what happens to you? It is rudimentary, it is zero-rudimentary. Part of you becomes a child that wants its mother.

I think it's right that it should have been Jaime who gave my father his last episode of pleasure on this earth. Jaime was then twenty-three. By that time it would be strictly true to say that Kingsley had forgotten about the night of the peach. It would be strictly true to say that.

So I should tell my mother: I know you hated it when he played on your feelings ('The sentimentality', you said, 'makes you want to reach'), but you did bring him back to life and love. That's the best way of looking at it, Mum. He got *Stanley* out of the way and then he wrote *The Old Devils* and *Difficulties with Girls* and *The Folks that Live on the Hill* and the *Memoirs* and 'A Twitch on the Thread' and *The Russian Girl* and *You Can't Do Both* and *The Biographer's*

Moustache and *The King's English* and a few more poems.

He could never have written them without you, because you reminded him of love. Mum: you were the peach.

That's the best way of looking at it.

Completely Relahible

Wednesday, 20 September. The biographer has taken Kingsley into University College Hospital in Gower Street. Oh happy day. I experience deep and furtive gratitude. All afternoon I go around muttering, Muchas gracias, señor. O, muchissimo gracias . . .

I learn details later. I know I couldn't have done it.

In the ambulance the attendant revealed that he had read some of Kingsley's novels but more of mine. Luckily Dad didn't take this in.

When he reached Casualty they put him in a wheeled bed. The biographer tried to prevent him from (deliberately) sliding out of it and Kingsley yelled: 'Doctor! Nurse! Stop this man!'

A porter and two nurses had to manhandle him into his room.

Before he fell asleep he beseeched the biographer, saying, 'Don't leave, oh, please don't leave.'

I definitely couldn't have done it. But maybe, if I had, *he* wouldn't have done it: beseeched. How effective, now, is the Empire State Effect?

At six-thirty I rose up from Goodge Street tube. My brother and I had a cup of coffee and entered the hospital, entered the lift. Briefly we clutched each other, seized each other's arms with clawed hands, as the lift climbed: ordeal readiness.

Alone in his private room Kingsley is in bed lying on his side, turned away from the door. *Top of the Pops*, of all things (he always used to mock us for watching it), is playing on the small TV: 'uncouth minstrelsy', and couples 'performing at rather than with each other, making rope-climbing or gunshot-dodging motions with an air of

[313]

dedication, as if all this were only by way of prelude to some vaster ordeal they must ultimately share'.★

'I'm in hell.'

This comes out of nowhere. Philip and I have an expression – eyes abruptly focused and widened – that denotes growing alarm. We have need of it now as our father, with worrying agility, climbs out of bed and sets about removing his pyjamas, which are light green. When did I last see him naked? Cambridge?

Sitting on the side of the bed (an affectingly bear-shaped figure, softly hulking in the dusk), he says,

– I'm not going to attack you.

I am more surprised by the fluency than the content. Fluency is now soon lost, but his agitation, and his sudden wariness, are eloquent enough. Philip asks,

– What's actually worrying you, Dad?

– The people here.

– But they're all right. They're there to help you.

– No they're not. Not *really*.

– Do you think we're deceiving you too?

– No. I trust you two. It's more that I think there are things you're not seeing.

– You wrote about this, Dad, I said. Don't you remember? The last thing in your *Memoirs*. Called 'A Peep Round the Twist'. You broke your leg and went to hospital. You went slightly nuts for a little while. You thought they were all out to get you. Like now. It's the same.

This undoubtedly interested him, and he attended to it. I thought I saw amusement in his eyes, but it wasn't amusement, not quite. It was the undesigning pleasure his face showed when he was being flattered. Modesty contending with something hoity-toity in the elevation of the head.

★ *Girl, 20*. Earlier in this chapter the narrator has gone to a wrestling-match and watched a contestant called the Thing from Borneo. 'In-nuh the red-duh cornah, at eighteen-nuh stoh-oon-nuh five-vuh pounds . . . the Thing-nguh . . . from-muh Borneo-oo-uh!'

He put his pyjamas back on again. Then he took his pyjamas back off again. Eventually in near-darkness he got into bed and turned away from us and from the world.

We went to the nearby pub with the wonderful name: the Jeremy Bentham. That old utilitarian (1748-1832) was a philosopher whom Kingsley, probably, would have considered worthy of having a pub named after him. Unlike some. My father wouldn't like to see his sons drinking in the Bertrand Russell or the A.J. Ayer. I knew A.J. Ayer, and thought about him now, during one of the silences: his death, his memorial service, Roy Jenkins's puzzling eulogy (he talked about Ayer's 'obituary impact'). A.J. Ayer was the stepfather of my second great love: the dedicatee of my first novel. *He* used to play chess with me, on a pocket set usually passed from lap to lap. And he almost always won. Your only hope was to make it into the end game with your knights intact. Then you could get him so frazzled by proliferating possibilities that he would disgustedly resign or even throw the whole set in the air . . . Allan Bloom: 'It is the hardest task of all to face the lack of cosmic support for what we care about. Socrates, therefore, defines the task of philosophy as "learning how to die".' I was not yet thinking about death, only of ravages and qualified recovery. But is there a philosophy of it? Is there a philosophy of death?

The next day Philip goes in to see him and Kingsley's opening words are: fuck off.

And the day after that I go alone, peering, first, through the square, head-high window set into the door. I imagine that this precaution is now general among his visitors. Almost anything at all could be happening in there . . .

That sunny Saturday I looked through the spy window and jerked back with delight, with profusely gratified hope. Groomed and shaved, my father sat hooked forward in the armchair with a pen in his hand. His face was set in fascinated concentration. Maybe he's *writing*, I thought. I'm going to walk in and he'll tell me that he has come out of this with a great novel, a sequence of sonnets, an epic poem.

    – Ah. Now come and look at this.

    I stand over his shoulder. The sheet of A4 consists of variously slanted columns of arabic numerals, something like:

017 212 2010	0175687278
017 222 [weakly crossed out] 2100	0175867278
017 221 2100 [weakly crossed out]	0175687872
017-221 6102	017 586 7872
	[weakly crossed out]

The figures on the left are attempts at my phone number, the figures on the right attempts at his own. One of the wrong numbers has this spelt out next to it: COMPLETELY RELAHIBLE. I didn't know then that my mother, hating to do it, had had the house number changed. Kingsley was ringing home all day. And Kingsley was ringing home all night.

    – Let's go through that again, he says.

    – Wait. Here. You don't need the 017, Dad. We're all on the same prefix. All on the same exchange. Here.

    I write out: MART: 221 6110. HIL: 586 7872.

    – That's completely reliable, Dad.

    – Let's go through it again.

    And we go through it again, with him writing it out. Thirty times. Forty times. Only your children and your parents (it transpires) demand of you these marathons of repetition. He pauses, apparently satisfied for now, and casually asks, 'Why am I here?' I tell him. He can't remember any of it. Then he sits up and says with enthusiasm,

    – Let's go through it again.

    Meaning the numbers.

    – We've got it!

    When the time came for me to go he didn't plead with me. He only said, as I hugged him,

– Little hug.
I straightened up. He said,
– One little more hug.
And I hugged him again.

Women's Breasts

Alzheimer's, my mother tells me, is the most likely diagnosis. 'He could go on like this for years.' What do you do at such a prospect, if you're English? You don't weep and wring your hands. You shrug, and laugh 'dryly'. You do what Cliff does at the end of *Stanley and the Women*:

> [He] did the brief lift of the chin South London people use to mean Told you so or Here we go again or Wouldn't you bleeding know. People elsewhere too. Perhaps all over the world.

– Well you certainly broke new ground with *Stan*, I told him, one day in 1984.
He was vigilant. He knew I had my reasons (trend-crazed and bleeding-heart, according to him) for questioning the argument of the book. Literature affirmeth nothing, we're told. But *Stan* affirmed something. Still, I wasn't about to go through all that with him.
– How do you mean?
– There's a woman in it with big breasts who isn't sympathetic.
– Who?
– The ex-wife. Nowell. That's a first for you, isn't it?
– Balls.
He thought about it quickly. He could name a couple of sympathetic women with small breasts, but he struggled to find any unsympathetic women with big breasts.
– There's too much in general about women's breasts in your

[317]

stuff, I said. What's the line in *That Uncertain Feeling?*★ And remember Ann Jones?

– Ann Jones?

Ann Jones won Wimbledon in 1969. She was, as the English say, a big girl; there was some talk about Billie Jean King, her opponent in the final, exploiting this fact by 'crowding' Ann on her volleys.

– She had a wonderful body and a goofy face. And you used to put your thumb over it on the TV so you could look at her breasts.

– What of it?

– You once told me that the sexiest part of a naked woman was her face. And I remember another conversation. Jane was there. I said, 'Are you a total tit-man? Don't you like any other bits? Don't you like legs?' And you said, 'Well I like to know they're both there.'

– What of it?

– Nothing, really. But you might think about reducing Nowell's breasts in the second edition. And by the way. There's a huge piece in the *London Review* by Marilyn Butler saying that *Stanley* is pro-women after all. That's balls, isn't it.

– Oh, absolutely.

Kingsley's legs are both there. And so are his animal parts. In these he has begun to take a new interest – symptomatic behaviour, for one in his condition. He seizes himself (but only for a moment), like a child with many siblings who comes across an unattended toy. Philip had a biscuit. Jaime had a peach.

Here a terrible symmetry beckons. I am thinking of Kingsley's father and his propaganda about insanity and self-abuse. The wards. The thinning of the blood.

How does it go in *Dead Souls*? 'Old age, inevitable and inescapable, is terrible and menacing, for it never gives anything back, it returns nothing!' No, that's right. It mocks you, but it never gives anything back.

★ 'Why did I like women's breasts so much? I was clear on why I liked them, thanks, but why did I like them so much?'

Aren't Old Boulders All?

Sunday, 24 September. When I entered he turned over in bed and looked at me.

– Oh, *Christ*, he said feelingly.

The biographer was standing in front of the window and wearing a helpless smile. Kingsley said,

– What time is it?

– Six, I said.

– In the morning?

– Six in the evening.

– Six in the evening? But that one – the biographer – was telling me it was six in the *evening*.

– It *is* six in the evening.

Kingsley was having no more of this. He spun round, not huffily so much as decisively and finally. He spun round, swivelling away from the world.

Six, six, six. What he actually said to Philip on Friday, I learn, was not fuck off. What he said was: 'Kill me, you fucking fool!' His room stands at the median height of the westward skyline. A vast sun is aimed at the window. 'I'm in hell,' Kingsley had said. And at six in the evening you do feel that the room is about to burst into flames.

I Want It Now. Ronnie and Simona are eloping (this is the American South) to a place called Old Boulder State Park. Ronnie falls asleep. The jolting of the car wakes him:

> 'Aren't old boulders all?' Ronnie fumbled for a cigarette. 'I mean old boulders all? Jesus, I mean all boulders old? What made them name a bloody park after this one, I wonder?'

Aren't old boulders all. Perhaps this is Kingsley's state: like waking from a tragic nap at a strange time of day. Ronnie is soon saying all boulders old. But what if you get stuck on old boulders all?

Here is a notebook entry for Wednesday, 27 September:

K's agitation. Some internal psychodrama that he will never say anything about to you or anyone else. He hasn't got the words. Though he might do it on the page, if he gets back.

This is strenuous moonshine. He wasn't coming back. Words and memories were leaving him: like banks of lights and switches, sighing as they closed down.

– I feel a bit . . . You know.

– What, Dad?

– You know.

– Anxious? Uneasy?

– Not really. Just a bit . . . *You* know.

I know? In his choice of words my father is not a delegator, particularly in accounts of his own state of mind. But here he is, smiling trustingly and, it seems, calmly, and lost for words. I now see that this was an alternate-world Kingsley, an anti-Kingsley, confined from now on to a regime of tautologies and commonplaces. What his brain was doing was the *opposite of writing*★ . . . His hands today are all over the place, waving, interclasping, and again waving. Should I regale him with his description of the critic and writer John Berger?†

'All this with my hands. It's nothing sinister.'

I am impressed by the rare and immediate success with the adjective ('Or is that a complement, Dad?' I once asked him. 'Yes but it's *first-and-foremost* an adjective,' he said, momentarily enraged by a competing pedantry).

– It's just so I know where they are, he says.

– Gives them somewhere to be.

– Ex*actly*.

Then I went through with something I had planned to say. I said,

– Do you remember the book you wrote called *Ending Up*? They

★ Joyce does this, of set purpose, in the Cabman's Shelter in *Ulysses*.
† Kingsley once saw Berger, who stood for many of the things he hated, gesturing with violent extravagance – in a restaurant. My father said he thought a fight was about to break out but all Berger was doing was confirming his reservation. His hands, Kingsley said, looked like two warplanes in mid dogfight.

did it on TV, with John Mills and Michael Horden and Wendy Hiller and Googie Withers. Remember? Anyway, one of the characters in the book you wrote, a nice old boy called George Zeyer, suffers from nominal aphasia. He can't remember common nouns, he can't remember the names of common objects. In the book you wrote this gives him the chance to be very entertainingly *boring* in three different ways. In the first phase he's incredibly boring because he just stumbles along improvising as he goes. Like: 'This chap's got a thing, you drive around in it. It's got a, you know, it turns round.'* In the second phase he's incredibly boring because he tries to get over the difficulty with rehearsed formulas and paraphrases. Like: 'They hit him with a screwing-up job and the iron thingummy for the fire.'† In the third phase he's incredibly boring because he's cured! He's completely back to normal and he can't stop displaying his mastery of the common noun. Like: 'Table, sheet, chair, glass, bottle, spoon.'‡ All this, Dad, in the book *you wrote*.

He is contemplating me with delighted admiration.

* The old folks are sharing their impressions of an emergent African dictator. George says, 'Well, anyway, to start with he must have a, a thing, you know, you go about in it, it's got, er, they turn round. A very expensive one, you can be sure . . . Probably gold, gold on the outside. Like that other chap. A bar – no. And probably a gold, er, going to sleep on it . . . And eating off a gold – eating off it, you know. Not to speak of a private, um, uses it whenever he wants to go somewhere special . . . Engine. No. With a fellow to fly it for him. A plate. No, but you know what I mean.'
† 'I was reading where a chap wrote this morning . . . about those four young swine who broke into the place to rob it, but there was hardly any money in where they keep the money . . . so they hit him with a tightening-up affair and the iron business for the fire and so on, and took the money in what he was wearing and how you tell the time and even his smoking stuff. What can you do about people like that?' ('I suppose you rush them to hospital,' replies Adela, his saintly but ever-vague interlocutor.)
‡ '"I've yet to come across an object I can't name . . . Door, knob, hinge, lintel, jamb, panel, window, frame, catch, pane, sash, cord, glass, dressing-table . . . drawer, handle, mirror, clothes-brush, hair-brush, comb, dressing-gown, cord, pocket, table, lamp, bulb, switch, flex, plug, socket . . ." By saying slowly and continuously and more and more loudly that it was very interesting and quite remarkable and most extraordinary, Dr Mainwaring brought about silence at last.'

– Do you remember?

– *No*, he said.

After a pause I probed on for a while. His amnesia was turning out to be strangely selective. He remembered the first lunch he had with Isabel and me ('very clearly'), but not the second, which was much more recent . . . As I took my leave I unthinkingly quoted from an old Peter Sellers record (a family catchphrase), and he repeated it. Perhaps he was experiencing the simple pleasure of recognition; but I saw in his face something I hadn't seen for a month: the willingness, the readiness, the capacity to laugh. Why take that from him? Why take *that* from him, and the words?

Back at the flat I looked through *Ending Up*. Frequently I wiped my eyes, from laughter, and from the opposite of laughter. Here is George Zeyer again, fully recovered (this is just before his riff of unstoppable *chosisme*):

> 'I was just saying to Bernard here that a sense of humour is
> more precious than pearls or rubies or any number of motor-
> cars or luxury yachts or private aeroplanes or castles . . . I mean
> to say, supposing you do eat off silver plate with a pearl-handled
> knife and fork and drink your wine out of cut glass . . .' After
> listing further concrete signs of affluence, George went on to
> question their real worth to anybody without a sense of
> humour.

Now (but not then) I think of *Stan* and the psychiatrist's great speech:

> 'When [mad people] laugh at things the rest of us don't think
> are funny, like the death of a parent, they're not being
> penetrating . . . They're laughing because they're mad, too mad
> to be able to tell what's funny any more. The rewards of being
> sane may not be very many but knowing what's funny is one of
> them. And that's an end of the matter.'

Kingsley isn't laughing at unfunny things. Thank God. He isn't laughing at all. Because he's no longer sane? Or because he's in a world where there's nothing funny to laugh at? That would be *another* end of the matter.

The Subject of Last Words

Tuesday, 3 October. 'Martin,' says my mother on the telephone.

The use of the full forename prepares me, and already, without addition, informs me of everything I need to know.

One Sunday, while the boys were eating their red chicken ('the best meal of the week') and watching a cartoon or a billion-dollar blood-bath, and Hilly was in and out of the kitchen . . . It must have been 1992. I was reviewing the Larkin *Letters* and the Larkin Life, and I said,

– And I suppose *your Letters* are going to be even worse. From the PC point of view. There'll be even more fuss.

– But I won't be around for that.

– I'll be around for that.

– Yes *you'll* be around for that.

Another Sunday, maybe the next Sunday, we talked about Larkin's last words. I quoted:

– 'I am going to the inevitable.'

– Not bad, said Kingsley.

Not bad: stressed as a standard spondee, like *outdoors*. It was hard to tell whether he was being sceptical about the whole business of Last Words or about Larkin's contribution to it. But I sensed some approval in him – approval of these last words, their particular nature, death being inevitable because he, Larkin, could never avoid it in his thoughts. No, nor Kingsley either.

– Have you got any ready? Have you done any work on it?

I asked this question cautiously but his response was tolerant, interested.

– Yes I have. Now you mention it.

– I don't suppose you're going to tell me what they are.

[323]

– No.

Read *en masse*, in anthology form, Last Words are a sorry lot, making you wonder what all the fuss was about: I mean the fuss about death, the fuss about life. Last Words, on the whole, consist of inadvertencies, non sequiturs, bet-covering pieties and pompous self-dramatisations. Henry James belongs in the last section: his high-style 'So here it is at last, the distinguished thing' is weighty and evocative, but it reeks of the lamp. Blake is both plangent and ecstatic (asked by his wife whose songs he was singing: 'My beloved, they are not mine, no, they are not mine'), Jane Austen terse (asked what she needed: 'Nothing but death'), Byron resilient ('I want to sleep now. Shall I sue for mercy? Come come, no weakness. Let me be a man to the last'). Marx is, as usual, pertinent: 'Go on, get out! Last words are for fools who haven't said enough' . . . D.H. Lawrence, like many another failing whisperer, believed or at least announced that he was suddenly on the mend: 'I feel better now,' he said.

– Your boy Hopkins had a good one.

My father, who hated Hopkins, looked up from his newspaper.

– Uh, 'I am so happy, so happy!'

And Kingsley gave a slowly nodding sneer.

– There's another thing about Last Words, I said. The question of whether you can get them out.

– Yes. There is that.

Earlier in the day Lawrence had hallucinated that he was leaving his body. He said to Maria Huxley: 'Look at *him* in the bed there!' Earlier still he said to Frieda: 'Don't cry.' Now those *are* good last words. I recommend them for general use – provided you can get them out.

The fiercest in his refusal of all consolation was Kafka. Demanding that his papers should be destroyed in their entirety, he said, 'There will be no proof that I ever was a writer.' Because if you are a writer your books – all your books – are your last words.

– Martin.

– Yes, Mum.

Words are leaving Kingsley, they are fleeing him. But he too will have his last words.

– Your father is going to die *very soon*.

And that feeling again: one of impending levitation.

Close That Naughty Eye Now

Saturday, 7 October.

Under this date my notebook yields the following:

I beat Zach 6-1, 6-0 in 55 minutes, so nothing wrong with my constitution. I mean my concentration.

Which was the day I played five sets – just to stop thinking?

That night I said to my mother, in a voice that struck my inner ear as distinctly childlike (baffled, wondering), 'What's he dying of, Mum?'

– *Drink*, she said.

We were sitting, over drinks, of course, in the Jeremy Bentham . . . Jeremy Bentham, like Kingsley Amis, was a man who addicted himself to the endorsement of unattractive opinions. He championed usury, and was opposed to the French Revolution and the 'Declaration of Human Rights' ('nonsense on stilts'). In his ethical system – which promoted 'the greatest happiness of the greatest number' – pains and pleasures were quantified according to four considerations: intensity, duration, certainty and propinquity. As we sat in the Jeremy Bentham that night, all four considerations obtained.

A day or two earlier my mother had said that there needed to be 'a terrible meeting' – about nurses and sunset homes – but *duration*, now, is giving way to *certainty*. And as well as *drink* there is also *cerebrovascular accident* to be taken into account. When I visited, that day, he sat sleeping (I felt a cur's relief) in his Thinker pose, but with the mouth bitterly set. A beautiful middle-aged woman of Persian

[325]

cast was hoovering his room. She buffeted about beneath his chair as if its occupant were not only non-human but also inorganic: a refrigerator or an old X-ray machine. This was the private wing. We were still enjoying the benefits of business class.

For some days the silent work in the back of my mind has been prompting me to give in to something: my Englishness, our Englishness. I notice it most acutely in my many conversations with Isabel. Her instinct is to explore, and if necessary exhaust, all medical-remedial possibilities before thinking further. I see myself, or I don't see myself, wheeling Kingsley on to a plane to go and see that top man in Zürich or Toronto. I see myself, or I don't see myself, administering to Kingsley an innovative diet consisting of barium and basmati rice. Isabel comes from a place where the first thing you do about death is throw your life-savings at it. She wants, at the least, a second opinion, and I don't even want a *first* opinion, and had to will myself to keep the phone near my ear while Kingsley's case-doctor, named Croker (and no, this is not an irony that Kingsley would have 'relished'), brayingly and yet with full professional sympathy spoke about the brain damage, the loss of motor control, and the incontinence now being visited on 'your poor father'. I engage in my discussions with Isabel from behind a net curtain of Englishness, Old Englishness. How palpable, how commonplace it is. In England, when you see death coming, you just ask if you've joined the right queue.

– He always said, my mother reemphasised in the Jeremy Bentham, 'If I ever have a *turn*, and get into a *state*, then I don't want to be *messed with*. D'you understand?'

Kingsley had gone on to say: 'Get the cheapest coffin there is and bury me without a word.'

We went back to the hospital. The patient was restive; he was pitching himself about in inarticulate protest. My mother dabbed his face with 4711. You could feel his anxiety submit to a trusted ritual as she said,

– You can go to sleep now, darling. You've done everything you needed to do.

His lazy left eye stayed open for a moment longer.

– Close that naughty eye now. You've done everything. You've done all your work.

The next day Kingsley's room is again an arc-lit crucible. My stepfather Alastair is patiently helping Kingsley in his efforts with the tube of a slosh-capped bottle; and in the same spirit he is also, in effect, asking him where he wants to die.

– How do you feel about coming home? . . . A bad idea? . . . A good idea?

One of Alastair's antecedents, William Boyd, fourth Earl of Kilmarnock – now *he* had some good last words, unremarkable in themselves but exalted by circumstance. He was holding a handkerchief which he proposed to relinquish after his final prayers. He said, 'In two minutes I will give the signal.' A prominent Jacobite, William Boyd was beheaded on Tower Hill in 1746.

– How about coming home? . . . A good idea?

Dad is having trouble with his grip, trouble achieving it, trouble releasing it. His face is still his face, but his hand is unrecognisable: the hand of a Marfan.

– You could come home . . . Bad idea? . . . Good idea?

– Not particularly, he at last decided.

June | Haggle Unction

I had been reading to him earlier in the day. I suggested Chesterton – *The Napoleon of Notting Hill* or *The Man who was Thursday*. I suggested Anthony Powell. I suggested George Macdonald Fraser (the Flashman books),★ and Kingsley gave a sudden nod.

As *Flash for Freedom* opens, our hero is contemplating a new career: politics. At a houseparty in Wiltshire his father-in-law

★ The Flashman books purport to be the memoirs of Harry Flashman, the notorious bully in *Tom Brown's Schooldays*. A great cad and coward, he goes on to win fame, in uniform, as a bester of Her Majesty's enemies.

introduces him to a clique of Tory bigwigs, among them a certain novelist: 'that cocky little sheeny D'Israeli'. I read on:

> 'Bad work for your lot in the Lords, hey?' says I, and he lowered his lids at me in that smart-affected way he had. 'You know,' says I, 'the Jewish Bill getting thrown out. Bellows to mend in Whitechapel, what? Bad luck all round,' I went on, 'what with Shylock running second at Epsom, too. I had twenty quid on him myself.'
>
> I heard Locke mutter 'Good God', but friend Codlingsby★ just put back his head and looked at me thoughtfully. 'Indeed,' says he. 'How remarkable. And you aspire to politics, Mr Flashman?'
>
> 'That's my ticket,' says I.

I looked up in (forgetful) expectation. My father was glaring at me with intense and futile concentration; and, of course, no humour . . . There are perhaps half a dozen descriptions, in his corpus, of grown men trying to read: drunkenly trying to read. Generally their first response is to blame the book. This is Shorty in *Ending Up*:

> Shorty was doing his best to read a paperback book that told, it seemed to him, of some men on a wartime mission to blow something up. His state of mind, normal for him at this time of day, lent the narrative an air of deep mystery. New characters kept making unceremonious appearances, or, more exactly, he would find that he had been in a sense following their activities for several pages without having noticed their arrival, or, more exactly still, they would turn out, on consultation of the first couple of chapters, to have been about the place from the start. The prose style was tortuous, elliptic, allusive, full of strange poeticisms . . . Every so often he would come across some detail that nearly convinced him he had read the whole thing before, perhaps more than once.

★ Disraeli's novel *Coningsby* was published in 1844.

Kingsley had read *Flash for Freedom* before: more than once. And now it was sounding like *Finnegans Wake*.

So I continued. Why not? We bring Kingsley comfort, by being here, but only one visitor has brought him any pleasure: Jaime. He enjoyed, he exulted in Jaime – because the dew is yet on him, the glamour is yet on him. Jaime brought his youth, in all its Conradian force (youth, that 'mighty power'). I haven't got any youth to offer my father. This year has closed my youth. I'm sorry, Dad: I haven't got any . . . Sometimes I imagine that the dead are allowed to watch their children. This would be one of their privileges. But there must come a point where the dead really wouldn't want to look. William Amis, even Rosa Amis: they wouldn't be watching now.

Skipping a page here and there, I pressed on. Having drunkenly murdered a fellow guest at the Tory houseparty, Flashman is packed off to sea by his father-in-law. I had just reached the point where Flashman realises that the *Balliol College* is not a merchant ship but a slaver. Greatly alarmed (though utterly unscandalised), he reviews the attendant dangers. 'But what was the use,' I read,

> of thinking that way in my present plight? In the end, as usual, one thought came uppermost in my mind – survive, Flashy, and let the rest wait. But I resolved to keep my spite warm in the meantime.

Abruptly Kingsley sat up in his bed and pronounced a string of words of sentence length. I couldn't understand them.

– What? I said.

He tried again. Now *he* was *Finnegans Wake*. His drift was more or less clear, but that was incomprehensible too. In straight contravention of the book's comic premise, Kingsley was giving me to understand that he very much disapproved of Flashman: of his selfishness, of his spite.

– I'm sorry, Dad, I don't follow.

My father made his inconvenienced face and tried again. It was at least very like him to imply that I was simply too deaf, or too thick (or too drunk), to take his meaning.

– Sorry, I said.
– Christ!

I'll show you what his sentence or sentences sounded like. In *Take a Girl Like You* Patrick Standish lurches into a London flat to be introduced to two women. He approaches one of them – Joan:

> On the way he came to the edge of a rug, which he surmounted as one might step over a sleeping Great Dane . . .
>   'Hallo, I parry stashed a nowhere hermes peck humour speech own,' he heard himself say. 'June I haggle unction when donned ring gone oh swear.'

'June I haggle unction': a *good* way to spend the early summer. Given some time and thought and help, I can decipher that: Hello, I'm Patrick Standish and now we're here I expect you must be Joan. Julian and I had lunch and went on drinking elsewhere.

But I couldn't decipher a syllable of his case against Flashman.

The themes, then, were duly convening. Although he wasn't now drunk, he had in the past very often been drunk, so now he thought like a drunk and talked like a drunk. And his wordhoard (how viscerally he hated those compounds, with their reminder of cursing his way through Old English at Oxford – compounds, the one mannerism he balked at in Larkin) was being roughly scoured.

He had gone to sleep. Sleep: death's brother.

'I *used* to be important,' he'd said to Jaime, apparently quite cheerfully. I used to be important. 'But I'm not any more.'

On Drink

'Now and then I become conscious of having the reputation of being one of the great drinkers, if not one of the great drunks, of our time,' writes Kingsley in his *Memoirs*.

Drink. Yes, as he would say: there *was* that.

— I got home last night rather the worse for wear, he told me (one day in, I think, 1985). And I didn't have any cash for the cab. I said, 'Will you take a cheque?' and he said, 'Well I suppose I'll have to, won't I?' He did a bit of complaining. Quite reasonably. I felt his eyes on me as I tried to write out a cheque on his bonnet. Halfway through my third go he said: 'You're obviously an educated man. Why d'you want to go and get yourself into *this* states.'*

— Good question.

— Very good question.

Very good question. Kingsley wrote three books about alcohol, *On Drink*, *How's Your Glass?* and *Every Day Drinking* (the hyphen is tellingly dropped). And alcohol infuses and even saturates his fiction.†
Alcohol meant many things to Kingsley. These things included oblivion, in perhaps two senses, but there were innocent gradations along the way. Part of his enthusiasm was hobbyistic, particularly in the expansive days at Lemmons: the heated wine glass, the chilled cream poured over the back of a spoon, the mint leaves and the cucumber juice, the strips of orange peel, the rims of salt, the squeezers and strainers. It was the only time I ever saw him busy in a kitchen. And there was something boyish, owlish, about the way he cosseted his little barrel of malt, feeding it, nurturing it. Kingsley

---

* *States* is singular. The *s* is there for phonetic effect. The cabby was overarticulating the terminal *t*, having perhaps willed himself, over the years, to stop saying *stay*-plus-glottal-stop. We first noticed this tendency in a Seventies TV ad. It was an ad for drink, too. A genial fellow says to camera, against a festive and hugely populous background: 'My wife and I like to have a few friends over in the evening. It gives you a chance to get the ports outs.' It was Kingsley who instantly hit upon this simple but unobvious means of transcription. After getting an okay I used it for *my* Stanley – Stanley Veale in *Success*.

† I always thought that Alan Sillitoe's first novel, *Saturday Night and Sunday Morning*, should have been called 'Saturday Night and *Monday* Morning'. It is about self-gratification versus work, whereas the Saturday night/Sunday morning axis does in fact set the rhythm for a great deal of my father's stuff: self-gratification versus self-examination and self-reproach and (often) self-hatred.

could claim, then, that he was researching his regular drink column, but of course it was more the other way around. He wrote about booze to salvage something from all the hours he devoted to it.

As well as sincere and humble esteem for the rituals, the flavours and above all the immediate effects of alcohol, there was also, in my father, compulsion – a trait that reappeared, on and off, in all three of his children. He couldn't afford to drink anything like as much as he wanted until the appearance of *Lucky Jim* in 1954. After that he drank less than he could afford, but more than he wanted – or more than he wanted to want. 'I want a lot of it, I need a lot of it,' Peter Porter once said to me, before going on to qualify his attachment to alcohol. Kingsley wanted a lot of it and needed a lot of it. Alcohol was ominously connected to greed, to satiety. 'Imprisoned in every fat man', wrote Cyril Connolly, 'a thin one is wildly signalling to be let out.' Kingsley, in *One Fat Englishman*, is much truer and funnier: 'Outside every fat man there was an even fatter man trying to close in.'

Biagi's on a Thursday night in the spring of 1994. Warily I watched him enter, with weighty tread, and scan the restaurant like a man in search of the face of his enemy. I stood up. We kissed. I eased him into his seat and said,

– Big lunch?

– Mm. The trouble is . . . The trouble is, when you get to my age, lunch is dinner.★

– You mean lunch is your shot. And everything else . . .

– Yeah.

He ordered a Campari and soda: his usual route to a second wind . . . In restaurants my father always wore an air of vigilance, as if in expectation of being patronised, stiffed, neglected, or regaled by pretension (pretension, not transparent vulgarity, which he normally

★ Cf. *The Old Devils*: 'It's quite a problem for retired people, I do see. All of a sudden the evening starts starting after breakfast. All those hours with nothing to stay sober for. Or nothing to naturally stay sober during . . .'

enjoyed).★ Even in Biagi's, his occasional haunt for three decades, Kingsley was on permanent alert. One sure infuriant was the unbidden approach of a waiter (he felt they always timed it to ruin his anecdotes). Waiters bearing peppermills drew his special scorn.

– Would you like some pepper, sir?

– . . . Well I don't know yet, do I? Because I haven't tasted it.

When my turn came I accepted a thick coat of pepper on my unbroached starter. Kingsley stared hard at me. I said,

– If you like it you like it. It's not the same as salt. That's why they don't go around with a salt cellar.

He seemed to find this genuinely enlightening. But then he closed his eyes and his head dropped sideways: a nearby infant was crying.

– Formerly, he said, she'd have to take it off and deal with it. Formerly, they'd be lucky to be taken out at all.

– Well then. A clear improvement.

– A change, anyway, he said, now raising his chin.

I had never understood his anti-baby shtick, or Larkin's, or anybody else's. At least I wasn't responsible for the sentiment, because it antedated both me and my brother. 'It is the *single-minded intensity*,' he wrote to Larkin, 'even more than the *brutish self-interest*, of babies' crying that angers me most; it is as if they feared that by omitting to yell for a second or two, they might be deprived of *a drop* of milk.' That was Easter Monday, 1948 – when my father was twenty-five. To this sort of thing one simply answers: Hark at the pot calling the kettle black. Or: So the raven chides blackness. Because Kingsley was a baby too. And (my mother would argue) sometimes behaves like one now, seventy years on.

The baby continued to cry and Kingsley continued to be melodramatically longsuffering about it. I didn't want to provoke him

---

★ The food, too, had to be honestly tailored to the clientele. From a review of a book about British eating-habits: '"A Hong Kong meal . . . is a statement to which customers are secondary." I know that sort of meal, and the statement is Fuck You, and you haven't got to go to Hong Kong for it. Soho is far enough.'

(I wanted to provoke him later), but I never wanted to roll over for him either. I said,

– That sort of stuff is funny in the books★ but it's a complete non-starter otherwise. What's that mad poem of yours? 'Women and queers and babies/Cry when things go wrong.'

– 'Women and queers and children . . .'

– And when do you come in? When do the good chaps come in? 'But other kinds of men . . .'

– 'The usual sort of men/Who hold the world together/Manage to face their front/In any sort of weather.'†

– Like you. Quiet heroes like you.

And I imitated him – Kingsley with crenellated lips, looking quietly heroic. He liked being imitated by his sons so much that he would nearly always ask for encores ('Do that again. Do that one last time'). He didn't ask for an encore – and anyway the waiter reappeared to showcase the wine bottle, sending my father into another saturnalia of ogreish sighs and scowls. That night I had been wondering where to position him on his personal scale of inebriation. Seven-point-five? Eight? For I intended to revive a political argument with him, begun the week before, and I was trying to gauge his tolerance. Kingsley had never been a Jekyll-Hyde kind of drinker,

★ For instance, I do like this from *One Fat Englishman*, the most persistently anti-child novel (we were fourteen, thirteen and nine when it was published): 'Joe had something of the child in him, a grave demerit, but he was . . . [we now hear about his better points].' And there is something invigoratingly unsympathetic about 'mess' in this good bit from *I Want It Now*. The hero, Ronnie, surrounded by rich people, is wondering about the forename of an American called Student Mansfield: 'As a nickname it could hardly have been appropriate at any stage of Mansfield's career, unless on the *lucus a non lucendo* principle that had got bony Upshot called Tubby. But this was British, and Mansfield was not. The same applied to another possibility, whereby you had made a roughly reproducible mess of saying your name as a child and "somehow it had stuck" – hence many a rich/upper-class Oggie and Ayya and Brumber and Ploof and Jawp of Ronnie's acquaintance.'

† This poem, his last, was never published. The third and final stanza, ridiculously to my ear, goes: 'With rueful grins and curses/They push the world along;/But women and queers and children/Cry when things go wrong.'

but alcohol could create, in his discourse, certain dead ends and forbidden zones – undebatable lands.

I wondered how he would take to being put in his place about Nelson Mandela.

Symposium is a word that has strayed, or lurched, a fair distance from its classical derivation. When F.R. Leavis died in 1978 I assembled a valuation of his career, by various hands, in the *New Statesman*, and called the thing 'F.R. Leavis: A Symposium'. Consisting as it did of sober and discrete contributions put together over several months, the heading could hardly have been a greater affront to etymology. Because *symposium* means, or meant, 'a drinking party', 'a convivial discussion': from *syn-* 'together' + *potes* 'drinker'.

And that is what Kingsley liked, above all things. Well, he probably liked adultery even better, in his manly noon;★ but the symposium was a far more durable and unambivalent pleasure – a love whose month was ever May. The prospect of *that* was what made him rub his hands together so fast that you thought they might take fire. Argument, anecdote (not gossip), imitations, set-pieces, quotes, recitations . . . Recitations. When the two of us were up late at night I would sometimes think, 'My God. He knows *all English poetry*.' Ten lines here, twenty lines there, of Shakespeare, Milton, Marvell, Rochester, Pope, Gray, Keats, Wordsworth, Byron, Tennyson, Christina Rossetti, Housman, Owen, Kipling, Auden, Graves, and of course Larkin. Drunkenness is in some sense the opposite of the composition of poetry (drunkenness is nonsense verse), but at the other end of the business there is a clear connection.

I used to think that Kingsley's review of Larkin's *High Windows* (1974) was slightly hearty or perfunctory or bathetic. It began: 'When everyone else has gone to bed, how many poets compete successfully with a new recording of the Tchaikovsky B flat minor as

---

★ My father once took my mother to dinner at the house of his married mistress. Another husband was present, accompanied by his wife; and that night Kingsley made a date with *her*.

accompaniment to the final Scotch?' He goes on to list some but not all of the poets mentioned above (inserting Betjeman, the Macaulay of 'Horatius', and the early R.S. Thomas). 'The quality they share', he goes on, 'is immediacy, density, strength in a sense analogous to that in which the Scotch is strong.' I objected to this as an indecorum, partly because *High Windows* was so clearly Larkin's greatest book and partly because it was so clearly his last. But I now accept it, just as Larkin would have accepted it, probably, if the drink in question had been gin. One day a decade later, in the early months of the *ménage*, Kingsley told me,

– I had a strange experience with Byron the other night. There was an hour to kill before a dinner party in Chelsea and I went into a pub and started reading *Don Juan*. After half an hour I couldn't believe how absolutely marvellous it was. I knew I liked *Don Juan* but this was oh, something of a completely different *order*. By the time I had to go I was looking round the pub wanting to say, 'Has anyone here got any *idea* how wonderful *Don Juan* is?'

– So you really, I said uncertainly, you really revised your opinion.

– No, he said. I was drunk. They were the first drinks of the day and what was happening was that I was getting drunk.

– And *Don Juan* being pretty useful anyway.

– Well yes.

Getting drunk: there was no doubt that that was always the quest. Being drunk had its points, but getting drunk was the good bit. Kingsley has written often and poignantly about that moment when getting drunk suddenly turns into being drunk; and he is, of course, the laureate of the hangover. Still, there was never anything namby-pamby about his admission that getting drunk, or, failing that, being drunk, was what he had in mind. Take these cheerful sentences from *I Like It Here* (where the word 'property' is laudably precise):

> [Bowen] had added to Barbara [his wife] that beer was cheaper while sharing with gin and Burgundy the property of making him drunk. This last factor had received insufficient acclaim. He thought to himself now that if he ever went into the brewing

business his posters would have written across the top 'Bowen's Beer', and then underneath that in the middle a picture of [his mother-in-law] drinking a lot of it and falling about, and then across the bottom in bold or salient lettering the words *'Makes You Drunk'*.

Why then? Why did he want to go and get himself into *that* state? A writer's life is all anxiety and ambition – and ambition, here, is not readily distinguishable from anxiety; it is a part of your desire to do right by what talent you have. So some of us will be wanting a break from that, if we can manageably get it. In the Preface to his *Memoirs* Kingsley observes: 'I have already written an account of myself in twenty or more volumes, most of them called novels'. These novels are 'firmly unautobiographical, but at the same time every word of them inevitably says something about the kind of person I am. "In vino veritas – I don't know," Anthony Powell once said to me, "but in scribendo veritas – a certainty."' And that's another connection. In vino and in scribendo alike, the conscious mind steps back and the unconscious mind steps forward. They both need a change of scene. There's just the usual trouble: age, and the only end of age.

Kingsley's fish cakes have arrived. Every Thursday, he goes with the fish cakes. When he found something he liked (or could get down without bother) he tended to stick with it. In Indian restaurants it was rogan josh. Always the rogan. 'You can't go far wrong with rogan josh,' he would say, ritually. I now say:

– You can't go far wrong with fish cakes.

– Exac –

But now Kingsley *is* going far wrong with fish cakes. He reaches into his mouth and removes a section of his lower dental plate. This device will spend the rest of the evening in open view beside his wine glass, a faithful reminder of what will soon be happening to me. When my novel is done I must fly to America and submit to the hands of Mike Szabatura. I am flying to America next week anyway: to see Bruno Fonseca before he dies . . . The waiter appears and I can sense him eyeing the prosthesis. For a moment I fear that he will mistake it for a fallen strip of prosciutto and briskly sweep it from the table. But Kingsley's furious writhings are in themselves enough to daunt him, and he backs away. I begin measuredly:

– Last week I asked you whether you were excited by the events in South Africa and you looked at me as if I was nuts. You said Mandela was a terrorist who had murdered women and children and never denied it.

– Yeah, that's right.

– Well you're . . . *wrong*. You'd have trouble finding an Afrikaner extremist who agreed with you. Your views would get you chucked out of a bar called the Kaffir-Flogger. The only people who feel the way you do are a few hundred-year-olds called Viernicht.

Then I hit him with chapter and verse.

When I was young my father gave me a tip about lunchtime drinking and the shadow it cast over dinnertime drinking. Take everything you had at lunch (he said), double it, and imagine you swallowed it in one at 5.55 pm. I was reminded of that rule when, an hour later, Kingsley finished his *grappa* and climbed wonderingly to his feet. He had taken my Mandela defence in fairly good part, merely rolling around in his seat and saying 'You don't understand. *You don't understand.* YOU DON'T UNDERSTAND' until, finally and unprecedentedly, he clamped his hands over his ears and stared at his plate. I fell silent. He paused and said,

– Let's change the subject.

– Okay. Just one thing. Get some new dirt on Mandela while I'm in America. Because your old dirt is *hopeless*. Let's change the subject. Let's go back to women and queers and children.

– Agreed. Just one thing. You're a leaf in the wind of trend.

Sealed with the fiery liqueurs, the dinner ended amicably, as it always did. But Kingsley's face, now rising from the table, registered real alarm. What I was seeing was an exponential alcoholic kick-in of trouncing efficacy. I reached out towards him.

On a traffic island in the middle of the Edgware Road (that

eternally disreputable thoroughfare, with its northwestward trek from mammonic Marble Arch, past the pubs and offies and slot-arcades beneath the Westway, past Little Venice, until it subsides into Maida Vale, where we lived in a house with Philip and Jane, thirty years ago), Kingsley fell over. And this was no brisk trip or tumble. It was a work of colossal administration. First came a kind of slow-leak effect, giving me the immediate worry that Kingsley, when fully deflated, would spread out into the street on both sides of the island, where there were cars, trucks, sneezing buses. Next, as I grabbed and tugged, he felt like a great ship settling on its side: would it right itself, or go under? Then came an impression of overall dissolution and the loss of basic physical coherence. I groped around him, looking for places to shore him up, but every bit of him was falling, dropping, seeking the lowest level, like a mudslide.

I got him home in the end. He found some balance, some elevation; I wedged my shoulder in his armpit, and slowly hauled. The incident never stopped being about 3 per cent comic. Even with his face at knee height, and his eyes stark with apprehension, like a man disappearing into a swamp, he never lost that glimmer of astonished amusement at what was happening to him – at the weight he carried, at the greed of gravity, at the wheel of years. Dad, you're too old for this shit, I might have said to him. But why bother? Do you think he didn't know? You're too old for this, Dad – this kind of lark, this kind of caper. You're too old for this.

The Corner

Thursday, 12 October. Kingsley has been moved to St Pancras's, behind King's Cross: the Phoenix Ward. I am at his bedside, pressing on with *Flash for Freedom* (we are now nearing the Dahomey Coast). I don't honestly know how much Dad is getting out of this. His head is thrown back (the eyes open moistly for a while and then close again). But I'm glad that he isn't turned over on his side, away from me.

[339]

The biographer later wrote (rather implausibly – I must check this) that my mother expected me to be appalled by the Phoenix Ward, so much so that I would insist on Kingsley being moved. Anyway, this is not the case. I am not appalled by the Phoenix Ward.

This ward is a hospice ward. This ward is what prison inmates call death row: the Corner.

Eric Shorter, a good egg from the Garrick, pays a visit. The biographer, a clubmate of Shorter's, has already been in. After a word or two with me the visitor leans over the bed and says, very affectionately, rather formally,

'How are *you* then, Kingsley?'

My father has hardly said a word to me for days. So he impresses me a great deal, and makes me laugh, when he turns his face up to Eric Shorter, and says with full clarity,

'Absolutely fucking awful, mate!'

After a pause Eric talks speculatively of further visits by himself, of subsequent visits by others . . .

'I don't want to see *anyone* . . . *Anyone*,' my father says, and turns emphatically on his side.

As Eric prepares to go he looks round about himself, shakes his head, and shudders. This shudder utterly rejects what he contemplates.

I don't want to see anyone. This can't be literally true. He certainly wants to see his most faithful visitor: Sally.

Eric walks off, through it all.

This is death on what some Londoners call the National Elf. From now on there is no messing about with all that stuff in Club World, the room service, the cleaning-lady with her indifferent vacuum chute. This is the Corner and this is public transport: one-class.

The men are upright in their beds with the censorious stares of schoolmasters, of indignant motorists in ancient cars, the women are more clustered, huddled, grouped round small tables or lined up in front of the TV in the day room. On the floor there is a cancer-sufferer so shrunken and wasted that he crawls up his mattress towards his pillow, the size of a two-year-old.

But this is all right and I would like to die here. Pritchett has a bit about hospitals making the body 'feel important' because you are bringing your 'talent of pain' to the total. I very much like talent of pain.

What surrounds me now, though, and fills me with awe, is talent of love. Or supererogatory love. That's what the nurses here, who are of all colours, suffer from: supererogatory love. It overflows in them and so they have to come here and do all this.★

There seems to be a film, a fine rain of dust or vapour, but everything and everyone is clean. Kingsley is very clean, and starting, unaccountably, to be handsome again.

Now he jolts me by sitting up in bed and saying something incomprehensible. He repeats it, but it still makes no sense.

He seems to be saying, '– Borges.'

Bore-hess, as in Jorge Luis Borges. I think he is trying to swear at me. Philip has been sworn at, and I have had my share of *Christs* as I encroach on his vision. He may have been trying to swear at Eric Shorter, conceivably, or at Bernard, the ward wag. Buggers. Bastard. Maybe 'Bernard'. Bore-hess . . . What Kingsley was very definitely not trying to say (as a suggestion for further reading) was 'Borges' – another of my gods – whom he was instinctively suspicious of and had no time for and never got started on.

But that's all right too. Mum was just being accurate: 'You've done all your work.' You've done everything you needed to do. You've done all your work.

His perturbation lasted less than half a minute. Then he turned on to his side, away from me.

All Flash

'Dad's coming back. Dad's coming back from hospital,' said Philip. 'All flash.'

★ I checked. My mother expected me to be 'appalled' that Kingsley's illness had reached hospice-point. 'I was actually more apalled by the U.C.H. private bit,' she writes (16/11/99). '[T]he nursing staff knocked U.C.H. out of the picture for care, respect & gentleness. So really I should change apalled to sad, & loss of Father & the realisation of it actually happening.'

This had nothing to do with Flashman, who had in any case been abandoned a day or two earlier. It was Philip and I, in fact, who were coming back from hospital, where Kingsley lay. My brother was telling me about a dream. I said,

'Coming back all flash?'

'He only went to hospital to detox and slim down. But now he's coming back – all flash.'

All flash. When we were about sixteen and seventeen Philip and I, at that chaotic crammer in Notting Hill, shared an eighty-year-old maths master called Flash Crunch. We called him Flash Crunch. The 'Crunch' part is easily explained: he used to crunch his false teeth together. Under the name of Mr Greenchurch the old boy features in *The Rachel Papers*: there is something about him letting the coltish dentures slurp halfway down his chin before drinking them back into place. The 'Flash' bit is harder to justify. Anybody might have reached for the sobriquet 'Crunch'. But how could this wizened, quivering relic – who once scythed his head open on the door jamb of his Morris 1000 *without noticing* – come by the epithet 'Flash'? Because on two occasions he had subjected my brother and me to unlofty censure on a point of punctuality. It just seemed odd, coming from him. And that was all it took. So, thereafter: 'I got extra homework.' 'Who from?' 'Flash Crunch.' Or: 'I'm late for a lesson.' 'Who with?' 'Flash Crunch.'

'His hair was flash,' said Philip, continuing to describe his dream about Kingsley's return. 'He had a car. And he was back with Jane. All flash.'

On Regent's Park Road we climbed from the cab and rang the front doorbell. Alastair let us in. My mother was standing on the stairs.

'He's coming back, Mum,' we called out to her.

She peered cautiously over the banisters.

'He looks great. He's wearing that gold-coloured overcoat.'

My mother peered on. She wasn't convinced one way or the other.

'And he's driving his own car.'

'All flash.'

*　　*　　*

Such moments of comic reprieve are the least of it. I am now faced, in my notebook, with some embarrassing achievements on the tennis court.

I beat Zach 6-2, 6-2. I beat the tireless David 6-2, 2-6, 6-4. I beat George 6-3, 6-3. I beat Ray – him who runs to Wales – 6-3, 6-1. I even beat *Chris*, technically. The score was 4-6, 4-3. At this point he broke *two* new rackets and walked off the court.

That last result is the most remarkable, because Chris, a onetime judo champion, is no dinker and poker: he plays proper tennis, and usually beats me at a stroll. But that day he was up against a Martin Amis whose father was dying – an altogether different proposition. The first racket he broke in anger. As for the second, he calmly removed it from its pouch and placed it on the ground; he stood on the grip and, with both hands, bent the head almost double. 'No more tennis this year,' he murmured, shouldering his way off a court scattered with shop-fresh garbage. The two rackets looked like coathangers.

The summer I left home I could hardly lift a tennis ball. Lift a racket? I could hardly lift a hand to my brow. On the court I felt more or less okay only when playing mixed doubles with people in their seventies.

But now, with my old man pegging out at St Pancras's? Watch me leap as high as the umpire's chair for those slam-dunk overheads. Watch me twirl beyond the tramlines for that topspin backhand pass. Watch me run that dropshot down – look at that *get* . . .

Why do I climb out of bed with a spring in my step? Why do I wake up and feel the ignition of the idea that some palpable good is being prosecuted, being carried forward? Why is my body excited? Why am I all flash?

'What's the *matter* with me?' it says in my notebook. 'Do I just want my bit of his money?' 'Do I *not love* him?' 'Does he not love *me*?'

'Oh, Bernard's got a head on his shoulders.'
'Oh, Bernard wasn't born yesterday. You can be sure of that.'
'Bernard uses his noodle all right.'

[343]

'Bernard knows which side his bread is buttered on.'

At St Pancras's my mother is not slow to join in the banter with, or about, Bernard, the ward wag. Bernard gives the impression that he has been in the Phoenix Ward all his life. Lolling, slurring, gurgling, slackly smiling, and almost wholly speechless, Bernard looms and Bernard hovers. It is hard to see how he has gained his reputation as a byword for pertinence and wit. But Bernard's reputation, it seems, is perfectly secure.

'I bet Bernard does all right. Don't you, dear?' says my mother.

'Oh, Bernard gets his fair share,' one of the nurses joins in.

'I bet there are no flies on Bernard.'

'Bernard? Oh, he can look out for himself, don't you worry.'

'Oh no. I wouldn't worry about Bernard.'

And Bernard gives a leer, and hovers there: all flash.

Meanwhile the leading comic novelist of his generation lies on his side in mute obscurity. The biographer evidently got a hesitant 'Hello, old chap' out of him the other day, but the most I elicit is a tolerant grunt as I embrace him on arriving and parting. Kingsley has 'the old man's friend': pneumonia. He is on morphine and antibiotics. When pneumonia recurs, which it will, the morphine will remain but the antibiotics will go. This is the English way . . . When I visit alone I no longer read to my father. I read to myself, while keeping an eye on him and hoping, and not hoping, that he will wake. The book most often to be found on my lap is Gore Vidal's memoir, *Palimpsest*, which I will be reviewing at length for the *Sunday Times*. My mind seems clear but my emotions keep striking me as woefully disordered. For instance, in *Palimpsest* there is a sub-theme or running joke about the Curse of Gore: all his enemies and traducers receive prompt and often conclusive punishment. Fate is on Vidal's side, and I don't want to tempt it. What more, what extra, could the Curse now do to my father? It could return to his dying body all the things he is fortunately without: reason, judgment, awareness. I don't want that.

'Oh, Bernard knows what's what.'

'Bernard knows a thing or two.'

'Bernard knows the score all right.'

'Bernard knows how many beans make five.'

Suddenly and agonisingly my father rises up from the gravity-well of his bed, and says,

'Oh *come* on.'

At first, ludicrously, I assume he is referring to Bernard – to Bernard's drastic and undeserved elevation. But the words are said so sweetly, so pleadingly. Perhaps he is saying 'oh *come* on' to us, to my mother and me: this fiendish charade has continued so far beyond all conscience that we cannot possibly persist in it now. Perhaps he is saying it to life: no more detailing, please, no more skew-whiff nostril-hairs in the madhouse and poorhouse of old age. Perhaps he is saying it to death.

He subsides and my mother tucks him in.

These were his last words and we know their drift. Either resume or finish. Enough. Be done.

I tell myself what I have always told myself. It is what all writers have always told themselves, consciously or otherwise. The things you feel are universal.

The father is dying, as did his (and as did his). The inevitable is coming and there is a readiness in you to rise and meet it. 'A sense of impending levitation.' *Levitation* is right. *Levitation* is no less than the truth.

Those superdrugs inside the body that wait for shock and pain. They can make you lift a bus off a baby. They are there to get you through, to carry you along to the other side.

Hospitals make the body feel important. The dying father makes the body feel important. It does what the father does not: it lives. There was no reason, until now, why that should have struck you: that your body lives.

It is 1995 and he has been there since 1949. The intercessionary figure is now being effaced, and there is nobody there between you and extinction. Death is nearer, reminding you that there is much to be done. There are children to be raised and books to be written. You have got work to do.

Now it is 1999, four years on to the day, and his books are all over my room, on the desk, on the table, on the floor, on the shelves. I keep having to go and look for the one I want and I keep thinking: What a lot of books you wrote, Dad, and what a lot of work you did. *These* are your last words. *New Maps of Hell* is under *The Anti-Death League*. *The King's English* is on top of the *Collected Poems*. *What Became of Jane Austen?* is leaning on *The Alteration*. *The Old Devils* is hiding behind *Ending Up*. All this is you and is the best of you, and it is still here and I still have it.

Bernard Speaks

Tuesday, 17 October. I hear a thud and suddenly there is commotion in the Phoenix Ward: Bernard has taken a fall. Bernard has taken a toss and the upsurging nurses gather round his bent, dressing-gowned figure.

'Whoops. A little accident. There you are, my love.'

'Bernard's all right.'

'Bernard's as sound as a bell.'

'Bernard? He's as fit as a fiddle . . .'

This week I am in the newspapers for a familiar reason. Yes, the newspapers still exist, but they seem to be reporting on an alternative universe which bears only fleeting resemblances to my own. This week I am in the newspapers because of the absence of *The Information* from the shortlist for the Booker Prize. So far as I am aware no one has remarked on the similar absence of Kingsley's latest novel, *The Biographer's Moustache*, whose appearance, if you recall, tested the patience of reviewers and interviewers alike. Kingsley, dying, is not in the newspapers. All we have had is a jovial diary paragraph about his mishap and subsequent admission to hospital. Not much, when you consider that the Fourth Estate is still agog about my dental work. For example, no reporter, hoping for the inside story, has wormed his way into the Phoenix Ward (as one journalist wormed her way into the office of Mike Szabatura). Unless that reporter be Bernard – who, I see, is successfully shuffling around

again, and often draws close, as if to listen. There is nothing to hear
. . . The newspapers, particularly the tabloids, are much concerned
with the trial of Rosemary West. When the *Sun* does run a piece on
Kingsley it describes him as the author of *Lucky Jim* and the uncle of
Lucy Partington.

Kingsley looks smoothly beautiful. His hair is longer than he
would normally wear it, and seems to me more suave and silvery. Loss
of weight is finding the face within the face, the old face, which is the
young face. On the day Kingsley took up his job in Swansea, one of
his students turned to her friends and said, 'Get a load of this, girls.
This is talent with a capital T.' Not bad – for his tombstone, along
with the lines from his poem, 'A Dream of Fair Women':

> The door still swinging to, and girls revive,
> Aeronauts in the utmost altitudes
>   Of boredom fainting, dive
> Into the bright oxygen of my nod . . .
> 'Me first, Kingsley; I'm cleverest' each declares,
> But no gourmet races downstairs to dine,
>   Nor will I race upstairs.

But I don't know what nature is playing at here, reconfiguring his
beauty for me. Nature should be making him ugly, so that I will be
readier to let him go.

The patient stirs and opens his mouth. I am obliged to say that
Kingsley's teeth were his only unpleasing feature. Hence the many
early photographs of him with that fully amused but reliably undis-
closing smile. His mouth is empty now. It looks like the socket of an
upturned angle lamp expecting to have its bulb replaced.

'*He* had a fall.'

This, startlingly, is Bernard.

'That's right,' I tell him.

'Pissed?'

'Well, yes.'

Bernard now takes it upon himself to give me far more thematic
consistency than I feel the need of. I really would have preferred to

[347]

change the subject. If this were a novel, don't you think I'd want to give the things a rest?

But no. Dislodged, perhaps, by the effort or novelty of speech, Bernard's *teeth*, his *false teeth* – the upper set – have started to slide out of his mouth. Whoops, here they come. For a moment he looks all youthful and nerdy, like a beaver who trainspots, then instantly goes back to looking very old – disastrously old. Is Bernard the *son* of Flash Crunch? A nurse steps forward and fondly and spryly removes the coltish denture, placing it – *there* we are! – in a white plastic tub bearing the label (in black capitals) DENTURES. Bernard grins on.

A year ago this would have freaked me out. But now? Now?

I have guardedly handed in my review of Gore Vidal's memoir. Eighteen hundred words, dispatched with great fluency and ease. I think my endorphins wrote it. The piece is solidly and sincerely favourable, but I did draw attention to certain anomalies in the author's character: the simultaneous desire to be in the thick of it and above the fray. I am beginning to wish I hadn't said that Vidal (like Lear) has always but slenderly known himself. It has an impressive record – the Curse of Gore. It is not that I'm superstitious. We know, pretty much, what is going to happen to Kingsley. The thing we don't know is what is going to happen to us. My review will be published on Sunday.

Unawakened (2)

The time was January, 1974, the place Lemmons, the house that looked out over Hadley Common and Hadley Wood.

I remember that at breakfast Kingsley had looked truly stricken, as if experiencing the father and mother of a hangover – but it was just his daily penance, his union dues to authorial anxiety. He paid them every day. Every day he believed that he would go into his study and there'd be nothing. There'd be nothing left . . . Eventually he did his wounded-elephant trumpet — a noise that always signalled furious submission — and pushed himself up from the table.

His study was directly beneath the bedroom I still claimed as mine on weekends and other visits. So I could hear him that morning when, after an hour at his desk, he started laughing: the sound of a man succumbing, after a certain amount of resistance, to unshirkable amusement. He was writing *Ending Up*, I was writing *Dead Babies* (and Jane, down the passage from me, was writing *Something in Disguise*). Both Amis novels were black comedies set in country houses. In his book they all died. In my book they all died except one.

He came up to ask me something and found me looking out of the window. Seventy-five yards from the house, on the common across the road, there was a small circular pond, and a team of plainclothes policemen stood around it. When I think about this I can feel my memory trying to elaborate. It keeps trying to add someone in uniform. It keeps trying to add a frogman in flippers and mask. I don't know: three men, four men, standing around the pond. I said,

— I want to go out and ask them if they're going to drag it for Lucy.

This was the only time my father and I ever talked about Lucy Partington. Some hired fantasist of the press has since written that she was a great favourite of Kingsley's, but he barely knew her (and is very hard, in the *Letters*, on her sister, Marian, then aged one). He said,

— What was she like?

What did I say? . . . I recently dreamt about Lucy, in the summer of 1999. In the dream she was about eighteen, and she was showing me how to play an antique and complicated musical instrument. Lucy was animated, amused, encouraging. And I felt what an *addition* she was. I felt I had discovered a great *addition*. When I woke up, and focused, I duly felt the other thing: subtraction, subtraction.

What did I say to my father? Something like: Sweet. Intense. Religious, I think. Highbrow, but innocent too. She hadn't got round to boyfriends.

— Unawakened, as they used to say.

— Unawakened.

I don't know if they ever dragged that pond. Twenty years later,

[349]

when we learned what had happened to her, I remember Kingsley tending to stay out of the various conversations I had with my mother. But I knew exactly what Lucy's fate awakened in him: hatred of God.

When I run the Phoenix Ward past my soul I know it is good and I always want to say to the nurses, 'Bless you. Bless you.' But this is a place of death. And sometimes the sights and sounds combine calamitously with what I am learning about the things that might have been done to Lucy and to all the other girls. I have to struggle against a kind of end-time vision where human flesh has been utterly pauperised and all its significance stripped of it.*

* At her trial Rosemary West had nothing to tell us about Lucy's death – probably because she was innocent of it (see Brian Masters's *'She Must Have Known'*). Anyway, she had nothing to tell us. Another writer, Geoffrey Wansell, in his disgraceful book, *An Evil Love: The Life of Frederick West*, permits himself to concoct a decathlon of torments for my cousin ('The possibility must be that . . . there must be a suspicion that . . . there must at least be every possibility that . . . may have . . . may have . . . almost certainly . . . It seems only too probable that . . . It seems only too possible that . . . It seems only too possible that . . . The only possible conclusion is that . . .'). But the fact is that we don't know – and almost certainly never will. A section of packing-tape was found with Lucy's body (along with a length of rope, several strands of hair, and two hairgrips), circumstantially suggesting that she was at some point gagged. Another victim, fifteen-year-old Shirley Hubbard, was found with her face almost entirely engulfed in packing-tape. Plastic tubes, of the kind West used for siphoning petrol, had been inserted through the mask and into her nostrils. Did he walk around Shirley Hubbard, holding the tape by its quoit? I find myself thinking of Kingsley's words about the significance of the female face . . . It was over quickly with Lucy. I feel I can say I do now believe this. Stephen West, a perceptive young man, observed that his father, when faced with determined opposition, invariably cowered. And Lucy, Lucy's presence, was very *powerful*. Fear, that night, travelled in more than one direction, and West was intensely susceptible to fear. This is the essence of it. The quality of that fear would *not* excite him. He would want to get the thing over quickly.

Night Visit

Friday.

We were coming back from dinner with friends and we drove past the hospital at midnight . . . I was first struck by the collective profundity of medicated sleep. It is more than sleep because there is also anaesthetisation. All the pain, in here, is drugged and trapped. Unfelt, unregistered, pain is still working the room, death is still working the room. The air is heavy with trapped pain. But no one cries or moans; all are prone and silent, in lines and clusters and rectangles. You can sense their demotion, and the fact that only animal work lies ahead of them now, because of the barnyard feel, the feel of a starlit barnyard, the old sheep and hens on one side, the old dogs and donkeys on the other. The old dears on one side, the old devils on the other.

Isabel rearranged his bedclothes and smoothed his hair with her hand.

In Homer the gods really do enjoy it when sacrifices are made to them. The adoration gives them physical pleasure but they also relish the smoke, the smells. How the heart of the god of pain must have hummed to see all the sacrifices, all the propitiations, made to him here tonight, with bolus and enema and hypodermic.

Sweat of Death

Saturday.

When I go in around lunchtime Sally is there. She has been there all morning. She sits with him for hours and hours – smoothing him, lulling him. After a while I offer to drive her home, but just for a break, because Sally will be back.

Her flat is spotless, as always. It is also (again as always) amazingly small. I often say that when you call Sally you can hang up after only one ring: it is not possible for the phone to be out of arm's reach. Despite the want of space a whole corner of the flatlet is made over to what the newspapers would call a 'shrine'. A shrine to Kingsley: signed copies of his books, photographs, memorabilia. On the shelf, too, is a volume published by the University of South Carolina Press called *Understanding Kingsley Amis*. I produce from my bag a newly arrived instalment in the same series, *Understanding Martin Amis*. Sally and I agree that we need to read these books with attention and could do with a couple more.

Sall's place *is* tiny. When I get back to my flat in Notting Hill (bedroom, study, sitting-room, kitchen) I feel I am entering an edifice the size of Harrod's. These hours have a hollow ring.

The Phoenix Ward in the middle of the night reminds me of a book I know well: *Big Red Barn* (by the author of *Goodnight, Moon*). There they all are in their stalls, fast asleep, 'While the moon sailed high/In the dark night sky'. 'The little black bats flew away/Out of the barn at the end of the day': and from a distance you can see the bats escaping through an upper window, like smoke. The fleeing bats make me think about all the trapped pain.

In 1948 the University of Tucuman in Argentina commissioned my father to write a book about Graham Greene: as it might be, *Understanding Graham Greene*. The fee offered was ‡1,500: it seemed a stunning sum. On 6 August, nine days before the birth of my brother and three months before I was conceived, Kingsley wrote to Larkin:

> There's some not so good news about them dollars; I asked my father to find out about them and he reports, on the best authority, that the fucking things are only worth about 1s. each, and 1500 of them come to £75-7-6 point something, which is nice, but nothing like so nice as we first thought.

He finished the book and sent it off. And somebody lost it at the other end. It was never published. And he was never paid. There would hardly be room, now, for *Understanding Graham Greene* on KA's title page. Yet the most persistent theme in the massive volume of his

Letters is self-reproach: self-reproach for idleness.

If there is any disquiet left in him now, then self-reproach is its source. He can't believe that the work has all been done. At home, on the desk in his study, half a novel called *Black and White* is waiting. And the other half is still inside him somewhere.

Kingsley's pneumonia has recurred and is not being treated. I sense that his body isn't without some ultimate constitutional strength, but it is awfully confused, his body, struggling to stay, struggling to go. The air sacs in his lungs are filling with matter. He must breathe so much the harder and faster to get the oxygen he needs. How hard it is to die. You have to chase it, panting. Great sweat of death, said the divine poet, meaning battle. We can expand the application. My father is doing what he always did. When he went to his study in the middle of the night and typed his i's and o's, and seagulls, seagulls . . . He is working, working, working, working his passage to the main event.

My father has turned away, on his side. He is showing me how you do it. You turn away, on your side, and do the dying.

Sunday.

During one of the very last Thursday dinners Kingsley told me that in his most defenceless insomnias he tended to worry about Sally and what it would be like for her when he was dead. The diminution of general support, he said – and the diminution of purpose, too . . . An intuition, a 'funny feeling', woke Sally at two o'clock in the morning ('I felt he needed me'). She got dressed and gathered her things and went quickly to the hospital.

The clocks were changed that night (spring forward, fall back) and we found ourselves in the new time, where dusk would come early. By arrangement I met up with Philip outside the hospital gates. It was noon. Under my arm was the Sunday paper containing my review of Gore Vidal . . . I suggested that we linger for a smoke; we sat and talked for ten minutes, and it was quite easy for us, because although there was dread there was no regret. And that *isn't* universal. When you read writers on the death of the father, when you read

Kingsley on the death of the father, what you are mostly told about is regret. My brother and I felt regret in that we wanted him to live for ever. But we had had our say with him and had our time with him. And while we smoked our cigarettes, sitting on the ledge of a circular flowerbed, in patchy sunlight, under rapid clouds, our father died.

Absolutely right, absolutely right that it was Sally who was with him. She had been with him for ten hours . . . When we pressed in there the white screens were being drawn, and Sally stood, as if electrified, as if italicised – as if so many urgent tasks awaited her that she couldn't for the life of her think where to begin. Philip flinched away from seeing the body and I said but you must, you must; and as we moved forward I felt his fingers clutching my arm, the way we had clutched each other a thousand times, in childhood, when there was a reckoning to be faced. Next came a moment of outlandish horror. In Kingsley's bed a sheeted figure thrashed (they're killing him!) – but this was someone different, someone else, a new arrival being battened down into his blankets. Our father lay further in, on the other side of the screens, which I now parted. Instant chemistry of death, already changing him from alkaline to acid. And the death colours, greens and indigos, like dyes of caste, so much more garish than the colours of life. As if to ward something off, his right hand was raised (contorted, mottled), with the plastic nametag on its wrist.

I walked the ward. There were things to be done (Sall to be comforted, Mum to be called, nurses to be thanked, forms to be signed), and then I walked the ward. The trolleys and Zimmer-frames and wheelchairs; This Hamper for Linen, This Hamper for Soiled; the 'day room' with its jigsaws, boardgames, prewar paperbacks, and a film in black and white on the raised TV. Bernard was always there, just off to the side. I contemplated him – how? I contemplated him defeatedly. Defeatedly. Bernard was as blasé and insouciant as ever, resting on his laurels. It would take more than the death of a writer, we may be sure, to discountenance Bernard. You would have to get up much earlier in the morning to put one over on Bernard . . . The new arrival, Kingsley's replacement, had stopped struggling. He repeatedly summoned me towards him with an authoritative frown.

I remember that frown. When I ran out into the street and caused a portly car to swerve or break, then I would see that frown, through the windscreen, on a frozen face. Such authority, now, is lapsed or dwindling in the brows of the old headmasters. This is school (this redbrick pile), this is Swansea, this is childhood: everything is half a century out of date. The clock with its sloping shoulders, the Monopoly board, the black-and-white TV. Here are my brother and sister; my mother will be coming; my father is absent but near by, in his study, probably, getting down to some work.

Sally, I'm sorry, but no urgent tasks await you. He has finished his work and you have finished yours. There is nothing left to be done.

3: The Magics

November 1996

– Now there is a man, said my opponent (Zachary Leader), who is going to have a baby.

He had gone to the clubhouse bathroom in the break between sets. When he returned to the court he expected to see me smoking a cigarette on the bench.

I was doing pressups on the baseline.

I was a man who was going to have a baby.

The week before I had MC'd Kingsley's memorial service at St Martin-in-the-Fields, Trafalgar Square, before a large audience rich in novelists, among them Ian McEwan, Salman Rushdie, Piers Paul Read, A.N. Wilson, William Boyd, David Lodge, V.S. Naipaul★

★ My relationship with V.S. Naipaul bears a light but pleasing symmetry – enough for a (perhaps rather old-fashioned) short story. Two of his precepts are well-known: unpunctuality is inexpiable and 'never give anyone a second chance'. So when I first met him I simply thought, Well that's that. Because I read a poem at his brother Shiva's memorial service, and I was late. Seriously and basely late. My contribution to the remembrance of the endearing and talented Shiva was the unself-censored Auden: 'Time that is intolerant/Of the brave and innocent,/And indifferent in a week/To a beautiful physique,//Worships language and forgives/Everyone by whom it lives.' But Sir Vidia has appeared to pardon me. When I sent him the invitation to Kingsley's wake an impulse made me add (was this a plea for tacit forgiveness?), 'Don't be late.' In the pews at St Martin-in-the-Fields I reminded him of this, and his eyes swiftly sought the apex of the church at the notion of such a solecism. 'I was not . . . late,' he said. And, perhaps mistakenly, perhaps wishfully, I felt the gratitude of the absolved. Or the gratitude of somebody who had been given a second chance.

and Iris Murdoch.* Hilly was there and Jane was there. Delilah was there, of course, as were Louis and Jacob, as was my niece Jessica, Philip's daughter. And there was a further grandchild present, but one not yet abroad in the outside world. Kingsley never met his eldest grandchild. And of course he would never meet his youngest. He had been dead a year to the day.

The main events are these ordinary miracles and ordinary disasters.

When I told Salman Rushdie about Delilah he said,

– So she's at Oxford now. She's already at Oxford.

– Reading History. Second year.

– Quite an interesting way of doing it. Skip the nappy stage and go straight to gowns and mortar-boards.

– Exactly.

I calmed myself (I was forty-seven) by whimsically elaborating on this way of doing it. The Oxford alternative, the *emeritus* alternative (in which the father's title is merely honorary), accounted for the fact that we were having the baby at St Mary's – so convenient for Paddington Station. As soon as the baby was born I would pack it off to Oxford. I knew the plan contained a flaw. I didn't expect to be all that surprised when the call came through, saying that the baby was unable to read or write, or walk or talk, and was permanently in tears. And so would be sent down or sent back . . . The truth was that I was

* Iris, a great friend of my father's (he bowed to her in brainpower), died of Alzheimer's in 1998. At this stage her condition was being discreetly camouflaged as a case of writers' block. During the reception afterwards, at the Garrick, I said to her that she would live to look back on this, and that the words would come again. They did not. In 1990 or thereabouts I was named writer of the year by the *Sunday Times*, precipitating a public dinner where readers could mingle with literary types at so much a plate, this being the object of the exercise. Iris and John were there, and Iris drew me to her and, with plumped lips, kissed me firmly on the mouth. Now that *was* an honour, and I told her so. The Bayleys were genuinely eccentric, genuinely dreamy, while also being vivid physical presences, tousled, humid, intimate; John would take an olive out of his deep trouser pocket and say, 'Have one. They're frightfully good.'

ready for another child (I was in training for another child), but I made no secret of my longing for a girl. Although I now had Delilah, I had not raised Delilah. And I wanted to raise a girl. I was desperate to see how the other half lived.

At this stage, though, I had to admit that the baby was doing an excellent imitation of a boy. It rode high in its mother's womb, as boys are said to do, and was putting itself about in there with suspiciously masculine violence. You didn't need to 'feel the baby move'. You could watch the baby move: it seemed to be trying to punch its way out. We could have settled the matter with a telephone call – but that was a modern convenience I wanted to do without; that was a modern temptation I wanted to resist. *You shouldn't know.* And the moment of birth confirms this. As labour nears its end, you stop thinking 'girl' or 'boy' and start thinking *baby*. Baby, baby, baby. At the moment of birth, nature seems to obliterate the question of sex; it isn't even a detail. You shouldn't know. If you do, the experience is, moreover, deuniversalised. You isolate yourself from your ancestors and from all past humanity.

Of course I was ready. The main events are these ordinary miracles and ordinary disasters. In the ordinary miracle, two people go into that room and three come out. In the ordinary disaster, well, I was going to say that two people go into that room and only one comes out. But in fact only one person goes into that room and none comes out.

The Day the Clocks Go Back

I called Rob and I told him, 'The King is dead.' And he said, 'Well I think that's *very sad* . . .' And that's what I thought too. I thought it was *very sad* . . . 'It's like losing a part of yourself, isn't it?' said Chris, at the club. Yes, that is exactly what it was like. And you know you're dealing with experience, with main-event experience, when a cliché grips you with all its original power. Other words and acts of condolence stay in my mind: the gentleness of the nurses at the hospital; the long and impassioned message from Dmitri Nabokov;* the letter from Pat Kavanagh; the letter from Gore Vidal. And yet the Curse of Gore didn't really work this time; it was punctual, but somehow missed its mark.

The day my father died I took my two boys and their two lifelong friends (also brothers) for pizza in Shepherd's Bush, and then to Wormwood Scrubs, the vast and desolately moor-like recreation ground in White City, overlooked by its tutelary institutions: hospital, prison (where Rob once served and I once read from *London Fields*). All four of these boys I had seen on the breast, and here they were now, like half a football team . . . The incredulity my children excite in me never diminishes. I contemplate a child of mine, and I can't believe that a creation in which I shared has gone on to gain such contour and quiddity and mass. Watch the way they fill up a car, a room. In the bath – look at all the water they displace.

Later, sitting motionless in the kitchen, I seemed to be positioned at the centre of a great circular vacancy. When a child is born you reel in the apparent emptiness of the street, because the world has shoved up, making way for the new one, and the world has overdone it, and there is all this space to reel in. Death does not act symmetrically here. Death too creates space but isolates you and cuts you off within it. How like Kingsley to die on a Sunday. How uncompromising of him: to die on the Sunday when the clocks go back.

In the plastic light of the bathroom, for a full minute as I stood susceptibly before the mirror: a kind of half-willed hallucination came and daubed the death colours on me, the yellows and greens I had witnessed in the Phoenix Ward. Death is supposed to give nothing back (nothing!), but it probably does do *that* much for the son. In my case death was forthcoming, and literal, showing – screening – my own death in the colours of my father's corpse. Now the clocks had already changed and I had never faced a dusk so gigantic. 'The King is dead,' I told the telephone. 'Well I think that's *very sad* . . .' And,

* Vladimir and Véra Nabokov's only child: mountaineer, racing driver, opera singer, and, of course, the chief translator of his father's work and the guardian of his memory.

[359]

having phoned Rob, I phoned Saul. Whom I am usually most reluctant to disturb. For selfish reasons, I never want to disturb or distract him. I want him to get on with what he is writing so that I can read it when he's finished. But I made the call; I made the call, without scruple, without forethought. I said in a dull voice, 'My father died today.' And he told me what I badly needed to hear.

Dusk did indeed come early, as was to be expected in the new time.

– You've changed since your father died, he said.
  – In what way?
  – More gravitas. Not the kid any more.
  – God, no. The *kid*?

This was much later: 1997. We sat, with Janis, in the booth of a Boston diner. Around us a TV crew was cumbrously packing its things; they had just shot the last scenes of a 'Bookmark' programme called *Saul Bellow's Gift* (I had argued for 'Saul Bellow and the Actual'). The artificiality, the controlled environment, of the last couple of days (the staged conversations, the innocent harassments of background noise and curious passersby) was now receding, and we were approximately ourselves again. I was turning forty-eight. He was turning eighty-two. In the course of our talks I had asked him about death, about 'the more or less pleasant lucidity at this end of the line', and he had surprised me by saying, 'I sometimes think I *am* dead.' That seemed to adumbrate a new and unsuspected struggle: the struggle to believe you're alive.

In the diner I had said, as I had been meaning to say,
– Do you remember I called you on the day my father died? And you were great. You said the only thing that could have possibly been of any use to me. The only thing that would help me through to the other side.★ And I said dully, 'You'll have to be my father now.' It worked, and still works. As long as you're alive I'll never feel entirely fatherless.

★ He said, in parting, 'Well I love you very much.' I am not his son, of course. What I am is his ideal reader. I am not my father's ideal reader, however. *His* ideal reader, funnily enough, is Christopher Hitchens.

It is still working, in 1999. But I mustn't encroach on the territory occupied by Gregory, Adam and Daniel – and by a fourth child, expected at the end of the millennium. I feel it is okay to quote from a letter I wrote Janis, when I heard, because I am only quoting my father:★ 'The greatest difficulty is believing in the baby's resilience. But they *are* resilient, fanatically resilient . . . You do know this, don't you, about Saul? You will have a bit of him, half of him, for ever.'

Envoy

My life, it seems to me, is ridiculously shapeless. I know what makes a good narrative, and lives don't have much of that – pattern and balance, form, completion, commensurateness. It is often the case that a Life, at least to start with, will resemble a success story; but the only shape that *life* dependably exhibits is that of tragedy – minus all the grand stuff about nemesis, fortune's wheel, and the fatal flaw. Tragedy follows the line of the mouth on the tragic mask (and the equivalent is true of comedy). You rise to the crest and then you curve down to a further point along the same latitude. That's the only real shape lives usually have – and, again, forget about coherence of imagery and the Uniting Theme.†

I had a cigarette in my mouth. It pleaded, it yelped to be torched. We were waiting on words that had to be handed down from the

★ See the closing lines of *Difficulties with Girls*. Naomi Rose Bellow was born on 23 December 1999.
† Kingsley has a good poem on this, 'The Huge Artifice', in which all creation is reviewed by a moralising (and specifically Leavisite) littérateur. 'We can be certain, even at this stage,/That seriousness adequate to engage/Our deepest critical concern is not/To be found here,' he says, by way of preamble, before deciding: 'Concepts that have not often been surpassed/For ignorance or downright nastiness – /That the habit of indifference is less/Destructive than the embrace of love, that crimes/Are paid for never or a thousand times,/That the gentle come to grief – all these are forced/Into scenes, dialogue, comment, and endorsed/By the main action, manifesting there/An inhumanity beyond despair.'

people upstairs . . . It was early April, 1996, in New York, and I was coming to the end of a brief book-tour. I now sat in the dressing-room at the TV studios with my lighter cocked. Then the message from above came through: 'The talent can smoke.' And I did smoke. And the talent found it good.

The next day, as I staggered into the hotel foyer, I was greeted by an old friend.

    – *Again*? he said.

    – *Again*, I said.

'Again' had two applications. The first followed up on certain hints given by my appearance: the bloodstained paper tissue pressed to a swollen mouth with bits of gauze sticking out of it. The second application, the second 'again', had to do with the Affair of KA's Biographer (or the affair of KA's 'wishes'),* a storm that was still feebly raging in the newspapers back home.

    – It won't ever be over, I said. There'll always be another *again*.

Todd Berman had just yanked out a molar in my underjaw: open widely. The tooth had announced itself as finished down in Nashville, the Athens of the South; but it had hung on, practically at right angles to the gum, through Miami and Philadelphia. Nor was the extraction a formality: three jabs, two stitches, and a sanguinary interlude in the recovery room.† I was then the subject of a

---

* His posthumous wishes, which I stood accused of contravening. See Appendix.

† The underjaw finally collapsed as late as the summer of my forty-ninth year. I only had to do without it for the ten minutes it took to walk from Todd Berman's to Mike Szabatura's. My lower lip, flaccid with anaesthetic, hung over my chin like the tongue of a dog. 'Hey, you look great!' quipped Mike when I hauled myself into his chair. He meant the cowbone graft under the vanished incisors. Then he screwed and welded the implant into place, and there it was, like iron, like the grate of a fire. Halfway whole, I was ready for the next *again*. Mike Szabatura got off early that day. I rode down in the lift with him. Mike Szabatura was in civvies now: polo shirt, white slacks. How did it go? 'I dare not withstand the cold touch that I dread./Draw from me still/My slow life! Bend deeper on me, threatening head,/Proud by my downfall, remembering, pitying,/Him who is, him who was!' Mike Szabatura will always glow in myth for me. But here he stood, in 1998, just another dentist heading back to Westchester.

'panoramic' X-ray: wearing the lead vest, you sit clamped into a chair while the camera sluggishly but sedulously patrols your face. Claustrophobia, as usual, presented itself with a muted cough of polite introduction. You can't turn away from it because there is nowhere to turn away to. I spent those minutes with my cousin, secure in the knowledge that suffering (*contra* Bernard Shaw) *is* relative. There's a scale of it, going from zero to the googolplex.

That night my father came to me in a dream. He was all business. He came not as shade but as envoy.

I fell asleep and it seemed that he was already there, waiting patiently, although his time was far from limitless. He was about sixty; he looked respectable to the point of mild dowdiness, and more self-sufficient and obviously benign than he ever was in life. And sexless – crucially sexless: free of gender or desire.

In dreams of the dead you always want to say: Clever *you*. You fooled everyone, you outmanoeuvred everyone . . .

Well, Dad, I said, how do you want things to go, now you're back?

And I didn't mean back from the dead. I meant back in the neighbourhood. But then, too, there was a countervailing sense that he would now have no need to involve himself in these surface concerns, stiflingly human, perhaps, which had no power to distress or fascinate him now.

He said nothing (and I felt he didn't want to be touched). With gestures only, with looks, with pauses, he gave me to understand that I had all his trust – in the prosecution of his wishes, and in everything else. Because my wishes were his wishes and the other way around. Then he left, he briskly absented himself, returning not to death but to an intermediate vantage. He was resolute. This dream was all business. He came not as shade but as messenger.

A messenger from my own unconscious, naturally. But that's all right. Because my mind is his mind and the other way around.

So it was incredibly warming to see you, Dad. And why don't you come more often like that? As a messenger, and not just as a shade whom I swamp and harass and bore with obeisances.

[363]

It was incredibly warming to see you, but I didn't really need the reassurance about your wishes. Because my wishes are your wishes, and I am you and you are me.

The Cunning of Babies

When my first son was born I wanted a girl, but I was quick to take his point (traditionalist and Kingsleyish though it was) about starting off with a boy. When my second son was born I wanted a girl, and it took me several minutes to forgive him for not being a daughter. My second son was delivered by caesarian section. I had not been present at the moment when 'boy' and 'girl' get lost in the more general urgency – hence my puzzlement on being told, by a nurse, that the girl was, in fact, a boy. Nevertheless, all my life I wanted a girl. Even when I was a boy I wanted a girl.

At St Mary's I had been wondering, off and on, whether the baby would arrive in time to make the four-o'clock to Oxford; but the joke was definitely over well before parturition. Earlier, for a full minute, the baby's heart had stopped beating; and from then on all thoughts were primitive and choric – just a steady whine for mercy. But my faith in the cunning of babies was strong; I knew that in this process they were neither passive nor disinterested – they did mean to live, to persist in their being. Both the boys had come early, dangerously early, and they had persisted. The new baby had gone to term and would be even better prepared, even more resourceful and resolute and sly . . . In the delivery room there was now an atmosphere of industrious crisis-management. Auxiliaries – a pediatrician, two more midwives – stood ready as the Venteuse, the suction instrument, was decisively applied.

Dr Marwood parted the baby's thighs with a matador's flourish. I took this in; but what riveted me more was the lower lip, which was still trembling, as if in an attempt to resist tears. Well, it *had* been a difficult journey, through all kinds of freak weather. After a while I took the hot soul next door to be washed, weighed, measured and tagged, and to receive the prefatory instalment of administered pain, in the thigh, from the nurse's needle.

Our first visitor the next day was Delilah Seale. On her way up she had stopped at the in-house florist's on the ground floor. She said,

– When she was wrapping the flowers the woman asked me, 'Nephew or niece?'

– What did you tell her?

Delilah's words made me happy, but they also made me realise how many days and nights I had spent on the planet.

– 'No, sister,' I said. 'Sister.'

Two had gone into that room and three had come out. Later I told Isabel that motherhood brought with it another and less tangible privilege: she would now be able to complete or round out her love for her parents, an outcome unavailable to the childless. At the birth of your child, you forgive your parents *everything*, without a second thought, like a velvet revolution. This is part of the cunning of babies. There was time for that, but not much time, because Gonzalo Fonseca died the following year. Death was lenient with him, and came suddenly. After a day of spartan travel from New York, he had his dinner and sought his bed in the house near Pietrasanta, home of sculptors and quarrymen. One went into that room and none came out. So the new baby would be doubly bereft. Grandmothers, yes; but no Abu, no Nonno, for the unbelievable Fernanda. Fernanda is a girl. She is also a Jew. She is also quarter-Kingsley, quarter-Betty, quarter-Hilly, quarter-Gonzalo.

Gonzalo was the one who was sitting with Bruno when he died, just as Sally was the one who was sitting with Kingsley. Everyone agreed that that was how it should have been.

'Life is mainly grief and labour . . .' That's true, Dad. Life is mainly deaths and babies; ordinary miracles and ordinary disasters, the white magic of growth, and then the other magic at the other end of the line, the black magic, just as strange, just as feverish, and just as out-of-nowhere.

Four years on, Sally is still capable of calling me in tears when she is having 'a bad Dad day'. After Kingsley died we were all chastened by the dimensions of the void that replaced him. It goes all right for me, pretty much, because the books are still here and, therefore, so is his presence: sleeplessly available.

I hated it, in the Phoenix Ward, when he turned away from me – when he turned away. I hate it, now, when they turn away. It could be anyone, even an animal: the Alsatian sleeping by the side of the road, that elephant-seal beached on a tropical shore. My daughter, revolving on her axis for the first time in her life, and turning away from me. I hate it when they turn away.

Postscript: Poland, 1995

Three weeks after my father died I journeyed alone to Warsaw, where I was met at the airport by Alexandra, the lady from the publishers, and by Jeff, the man from the British Council. On the way into the city the oily weight of traffic seemed to be making a direct contribution to the smog-enhanced sunset. There was a press conference in a basement bar – and a good fracas involving the official interpreter and Alexandra, who kept reinterpreting him. One journalist commiserated with my bereavement, and I found myself freely discussing my father for the first time outside the family huddle. I said how terrible it must have been: the defection of the words. And that this was surely the inner death-moment for him . . . Then a signing-session without a reading in a bookshop (always painful the world over). Then a dinner. Having read so widely about my teeth, Alexandra had gone and cleansed the menu of all things *al dente* (she sympathetically divulged her own meandering upper gumline). This was thoughtful of her, though it lent no savour to the untoothsome jellied carp (and I could, now, have eaten a steak). I liked the people there, and I liked the way they exercised their English. 'Between you, me and the lamppost.' 'So put in the word for us.' Then a radio show: Radio Zet. The host began with the results of a vox pop establishing that no one in Poland had ever heard of me. So when I was asked the question 'What do you think about Poland?' I said that I hadn't ever heard of her – although, of course, I had heard of Poland, and thought several things about her. I thought that she was one of the planet's greatly wronged nations and that you felt an intimation of this in every question, every glance. The next morning I met up with an old friend, Zbigniew, now a Warsaw businessman valued for his perfect English (conversational and technical), but once a skilled carpenter moonlighting in

London.* Zbigniew had made the bookcases in my Notting Hill flat, a place characterised by him (he had in mind its bar, its dartboard, its pinball machine) as 'a fucking *paradise*'. That morning we drank some coffee and then visited, first, the Warsaw Uprising Monument, the great highstyle socialist frieze commemorating the events of 31 July 1944 (the retreating Nazis reduced Warsaw to 'a name on the map' and left it to the Red Army), and then, secondly, the black marble statue of Nicolaus Copernicus, the man who exploded the anthropocentric universe – the man who said that the illusion was in fact a delusion, and the sun was not our satellite. He powered the Enlightenment. I ate lunch with publishers and translators, and gave my lecture (on *Lolita*) . . . At the hotel that night I relaxed on an Expo metal chair in the club-world brothel of the bar. I had been warned against these women: after renting pass-keys from the concierge they would let themselves into your room and start negotiating while you were already in bed.† Zbig had told me that Warsaw was now 'a money city', and on the way out in the plane I had noticed that Poland was coverboy on the issue of *Business Week* that everyone was reading. So the hotel bar would put forward its version of that: the blondes in pink pants-suits would have been inevitably conjured up, like a market force, by the arrival of the ponderous entrepreneurs in their jackets of suede and leather. Meanwhile the piped music preached free love: 'If You Go to San Francisco' by the Flowerpot Men.

I went to Cracow, and on to Oswiecim.

It was as a ten-year-old that I first came across the images: the railtracks, the smokestacks.

* After he watched Jerzy Skolimowski's film *Moonlighting* (1982), Zbigniew became convinced that Jeremy Irons was Polish – was, in fact, a Pole moonlighting in London. He was scandalised when I showed him a few clips of Irons as Charles Ryder, simpering his way through the TV version of *Brideshead Revisited*.

† The already-in-bed or part-way-there principle reminded me, obliquely, of the impoverished backstreet abortionist in William Burroughs's *The Naked Lunch*. Times are so hard, he says, that he is reduced to hustling pregnant women in the street.

– Mum. Who was Hitler?

– Don't worry about Hitler. You've got blond hair and blue eyes. Hitler would have loved *you*.

I often think that this exchange, and the unworthy relief it gave me, formed the first pang of a novel I would write thirty years later: a novel about the Holocaust narrated by a man with blond hair and blue eyes. My book was partly set there, but I had never been to Auschwitz.

Here is the town: Oswiecim (1 KM). And here is the train station, in its day the size of a Victoria, a Gare du Nord, a Grand Central. There too is the cafeteria, the hotel. And here is my guide, a young woman called Dovota.

From which dream do you escape with the greater hunger for full consciousness, the dream where you are murdered, or the dream where you are the murderer (or his abettor, his familiar, his host)? The first kind of dream will shake you more, perhaps, but the second kind will stay with you longer. Auschwitz is now a museum, an inert monument to memory; inertly it continues to generate mortal shame, for Germany, and unending insult, for Poland.

When we touched on this my guide said,

– Poland had ceased to exist.

Yes of course. And not for the first time. 1939: Arianised, Sovietised; Hitlerised, Stalinised. When the war was over Poland found herself reduced in size (and shifted westward); the capital was razed; the population was reduced by one quarter. What Poland was left with was Auschwitz, and the other islands of the Kat-Zet archipelago . . . My guide was called Dovota; sturdily elegant, soberly soft-voiced. Her makeup had been applied with care, and her skin had a glazed look. But her eyes were not glazed; they were fresh and uninured.

– We now have people coming here, she said, who think that all this has been constructed to deceive them. Not just from Germany. From Holland, from Scandinavia. They believe that nothing happened here and the Holocaust is a myth.

How did she deal with them?

– I concentrate on *proof*. Point by point. They deny it, though. They don't believe it.

[369]

One has to admit that Auschwitz-Birkenau is very difficult to believe. But the unaverted heart can still feel its fierce rhythms. Auschwitz itself is disgustingly intimate (Hoess's house nestles in behind the gallows; his wife and children used to play in the garden there), Birkenau disgustingly vast. It is easier to believe in the cruelty than it is to believe in the contempt, the unbelievable contempt. And what about the bottomless literalmindedness of the project (*all* the Jews in Europe? Even the Jews of Ireland were slated – all the Blooms and Herzogs)? And what about the patina of efficiency and thrift? How efficient is a work camp where the slaves last three months (it was always three months. You were killed immediately, or you organised yourself and survived. Otherwise it was always three months)? How cost-effective were those mounds of toothbrushes, those mad trains full of human hair? During the war there was a meteorology department in the *Ahnenerbe* dedicated to 'proving' that the Aryan race, untainted by evolution, had been preserved in ice from the beginning of time on the lost continent of Atlantis. Ideologically it was all on that level, tubthumping, tabloidal – the world of talking animals, resurrected celebrities, miracle panaceas, alien abductions, two-headed babies. The other end of it, Auschwitz-Birkenau, where ideology becomes action, is like a formal dystopia dramatising the mind of the babbler, the monologuist, the man on the milk-crate with the flickering eyes.

Any serious immersion in this subject will take you through several phases. I found that these were: fully replenished incredulity, despite all previous acquaintance with the facts; thwarted anger, as the body casts about for a way to make itself felt; obscene vituperation, swearing and weeping, cursing and sobbing and thinking of the dead; a sense of *lousiness*, like an infestation; a nausea resembling, though not representing, extreme guilt (this is species-shame, perhaps); and, towards the end, capitulation, defeated assent. At last you have toiled your way from incredulity to belief. Or the mind has. The body, I suspect, takes longer to surrender and dumbly struggles to do so. It does this slow work at night, churning, mashing, heaving. Maybe this is also physical empathy, or an attempt at it. The internal rearrangements used to wake me suddenly, and I would feel as you do after a day spent in a speeding car or on rough water, with the torso committed to motion and also tensing itself against it . . . I had been through this process before and I recognised every stop along the way as I fought for sleep in the hotel bed in Cracow.

I think now of that meeting with my cousin, David Partington. He told me that he couldn't see the word *west* (as in westerly, southwest, the West) without horror (West: the one-man Kat-Zet). He told me that when he carried his sister's coffin he was grateful for the way the strap chafed his hand – grateful for the pain and its insistence on reality. It was for this insistence, too, that Marian went to see and touch her sister's bones . . . David told me about the hours of swearing and weeping, how he rose in the night to swear and weep. And I felt then that atrocity does this; when you are close in, as he is, the task is not to accept but simply to believe. Atrocity defies belief and also *persecutes* it, demanding something that can never be freely given: one's assent. Lucy Partington was my mother's sister's child. She was my cousin, not my sibling, not my daughter. I have never been told to believe something really unbelievable, just the usual articles of faith for a man of fifty (and they seem unlikely enough): that the parents are going, the children are staying, and I am somewhere in between.

Appendix: The Biographer and the Fourth Estate

I was once walking down the Portobello Road, slowly (there was an elderly woman in my path), and in enforced single file (there were roadworks on this market street), when I felt a pair of powerful hands seize me round the base of the neck. Startled, I turned; but in that half-second I had decided that this was a friend, not an assailant. I even had time to think: Redmond! Redmond O'Hanlon. The bearish (and affectionate) Redmond is always doing this kind of thing. I recalled that moment in his first travel book, when he deliberately visited mortal fear on his companion, James Fenton. But that was in Borneo, a more frightening place than Portobello, on a Saturday morning. So I turned, with the words 'Fuck off, Redsi!' forming in the back of my throat. It wasn't Redsi. It was a young, black, grinning stranger, who moved me to one side and stepped past me with his girlfriend, saying, 'No, man. You don't walk on the street like that.' Meaning: so slowly. Just then the obstruction, the elderly woman, turned left, and the couple walked out into the crossroads with a flourish of freedom. The girl, who was white, took her boyfriend's arm and said approvingly, 'Did you see him? He was shit nisself!' I felt . . . I felt intense weariness; I almost sank back against the wall under the weight of it. No, I wasn't *choosing* to walk slowly and, no, you don't seize strangers round the back of the neck and, no, I wasn't shitting myself and, no I . . . The sense of compound injustice, and compound futility, the conviction that the universe was without reason or redress: this reminded me of something.

It was like being in the newspapers.

If these pages have so far been free of a sense of grievance, it is not because I have been trying to keep it out. It is because it isn't there. But we now find ourselves in an appendix, a realm of separable matter, and I am going to put the record straight. What follows should not be taken as an attack on an erring individual so much as an attack on the Fourth Estate. This Fourth Estate is at a peculiar stage in its evolution. It is, on the one hand, ever more contented with the power that corrupts it; and it is, on the other, heading towards an elephantine impotence on all the questions that really matter.

Three days after my father died I got a call from the Biographer, Eric Jacobs. He said he had kept some 'jottings' on Kingsley – notes for a second book he was intending to write about him. As if putting in their claim for an exclamation mark at the end of this sentence, surprise and amusement joined in his voice as he told me that the *Sunday Times* considered these jottings publishable. I said something like,

– Well that probably sounds okay.

– It seemed right that you should see it first.

And I felt no apprehension. I was grateful to Eric. With his energy and congeniality he had lightened the load of Kingsley's death. Or the load of his dying. And that stands. I expected these jottings to be affectionate and anodyne. I parenthetically liked the idea of the hard-up biographer making some money as he added to the general glow of the obituaries. At a certain stage, towards the end, I had thought that even the *obituaries* would be hostile . . .

I went on working. The package arrived and I went on working. At 2.15 I started to take a look at Eric's piece and at 2.45 I remembered I had a tennis match, which I turned up for. But after a couple of games I had to concede, and apologise (my opponent, again, was Zachary Leader, and he understood, quickly) and go back and start to deal with it all.

The jottings consisted of about thirty pages of typescript and included an episodic chronicle of Kingsley's last days written from the viewpoint of an insider. And into our china shop of familial sensitivities Eric had come lurching and bucking and blundering. Every time he bent over to inspect a shattered vase he would clear another shelf with the sweep of his backside. What was he *doing* in here? And what was he doing in here *now*? Agonising violation was inflicted on the immediate family (and on peripheral figures too: my sons, for example), and the central event, the rite of passage, was unbearably demeaned. It was quite something, like a visit to a world without affect, to see my father, at his most helpless, and literally naked, described without a particle of decorum. He had been dead for seventy-two hours.

When I finished the piece I shed tears of pure misery; and in this state I began making all the calls.

– So . . . *rude*, said my mother.

She always got a lot of mileage out of this word. She meant: so abrupt, so rough, so coarse.

– Get your man on it, she said. What's his name? That's right: Sly.

– His name is Wylie, Mum. And he's already on it.

Eric immediately agreed to withdraw the piece (and I have his letter of apology somewhere). He then confessed that he had shown his jottings not only to the *Sunday Times* but also to the *Daily Mail*. So that day, and the next, were spent trying to expunge Eric's delineations from the journalistic bloodstream. I had some leverage at the *Sunday Times*, where I was Chief Book Reviewer or some such designation. And I spoke to Gillon Aitken, Andrew Wylie's partner, who, bafflingly, was representing *Eric*. (Gillon had long been Eric's agent; but the effect, for me, was still baffling.) This wasn't what I wanted to be doing, with my father not yet in his coffin and the funeral only days away.

The family, of course, wanted no further dealings with Eric. This meant, or entailed, firing him from the job, not yet begun, of editing Kingsley's *Letters*. The word was passed to Eric that he would not be welcome at St Mark's on 31 October. Later I wrote Eric a sorrowfully worded letter. I felt sorry for him – and gratitude lingered.

Four and a half months later the jottings were published in three instalments by the *Sunday Times*. The first I heard of it was when a biker appeared on the Saturday evening with a copy of the next day's paper and a note from the section editor: something about the bark being worse than the bite. On the cover of the Book Review was my piece about Hillary Clinton. On the cover of another section was the first of Eric's three pieces about Kingsley.

My father's biographer, in my newspaper, the deal having been brokered by my co-agent, Gillon Aitken. For a moment I was back on the Portobello Road.

What tipped Eric over? My mentioning, in an interview, that somebody else was going to edit the *Letters*: my friend Zachary Leader. Eric typically assumed that it was mere propinquity and cronyism that led me to toss the job to my 'tennis partner', whom he later stigmatised, in a letter to one of KA's correspondents, as being 'curiously named'. Yes, I wanted to say, and Zachary Leader has a curious *title*, too: Professor.

As before, Eric's move involved me in various exertions and contortions. He also obliged me to behave dishonestly, for which I do not forgive him. To maintain any influence at the *Sunday Times* I had to tell the literary editor, Geordie Greig, that I might be persuaded to continue in his employ – whereas my connection with that paper had ended in the couple of seconds it took me to open the relevant envelope at the door, with the biker looking on; Greig behaved throughout with sympathy and a despairing decency, and it was a humiliation to mislead him. More taxingly still, I had to keep talking in a calm voice to Eric on the telephone, urging this or that cut or emendation on him. These conversations were among the strangest I have ever participated in. Example:

– I see you've added an account of the funeral.

– Well, yes.

– Which you describe as a perfunctory affair. You end your description of it with the following: 'Only Sally cried.' If I were you, Eric, I would take that out. Because it isn't true.

– Oh really?

– And there were many people present who can confirm that it isn't true.

– Oh.

– You weren't there, were you, Eric. Who told you only Sally cried?

– Someone who was . . . who was there.

– Whoever it was was mistaken.

– Oh. Then I . . . Then I'll . . .

– Everybody cried.

Now the whole business was going public. You will smile pityingly, O my reader, when I tell you that I expected press opinion to be firmly on the side of the family. If Eric had done what he had done in Italy, say, he would now be in jail. But so would half the journalists in the UK. Newspapers reveal things and print things, so they will always take the side of those that reveal things and print things. Journalist will always fall in with journalist, and Eric was a journalist who was just being a journalist. There were other forces at work, or at play. The existence of several established broadsheets in the capital is often assumed to be a sign of diversity and health. What you end up getting, though, is a relativists' echo chamber – what Kingsley called pernicious neutrality. Every 'public feud' or 'literary dogfight' or 'undignified scrap' must have two sides to it, mustn't it, or how will it run? Over the next couple of weeks I looked on with fascination as the press came out and then shadowboxed its way back into the vacuum.

Because this was zero-rudimentary, a no-brainer. You didn't need a brain for it. All you needed was a reasonable heart. It came down to what Eric did to us and what we did to him. The effect of his actions was to assail us in our grief. We did what all families known to me would have done and severed all connections with him. The 'painful revenge' we allegedly took – firing him from the *Letters* – was just another severed connection. I blush for Eric, now, when I see him talking about Kingsley's 'wishes'. 'I thought executors were supposed to follow the wishes of the person they represent,' he told the *Sunday Times*, 'but this is the exact opposite of what Kingsley wanted.' (Eric being the exact opposite of somebody called Zachary, I suppose.) If he hereby convinces you that my father – or indeed any conceivable being – would posthumously endorse the man who hurt his family, while they grieved for him, then the day is his.

It says it *in the Bible*. It says it on the column in the churchyard behind St Pancras's, where my father lay: Blessed are they that mourn, for they shall be comforted. What Eric did was not only wrong but wrong in itself. And what was wrong in October was still wrong in March. It is very much to Eric's credit that he, at least, came to realise this.★

On the second Saturday after Kingsley died I found myself alone in the flat, unable to work or even to read. The only thing I seemed to be any good at was staring at my shoe. I didn't feel ill so much as deafeningly medicated; we were all like this, we were all on the antibiotics of grief. The weekend had been boyless: the camp beds were stowed, the flat stood unlittered by yoghurt cartons and crisp packets and monstrous toys; no spent teabag lay slumped against the toothpaste tube. I decided that I wanted to see my sons, and sued for an hour or two with them. And it felt like a mistake, with the rain, the cars, the visit to the miserable mall in the worst kind of Sunday light . . . Our mission was to buy Louis a pair of trainers. The young salesman opened a lot of boxes and did a lot of staring at their contents. Eventually he held up two shoes and said,

– Them's the same size innit.

I contemplated them dully. Showing a failure of tolerance, perhaps, I felt that shoe-sizing lay at his end of the operation, not mine. I said,

– No. Clearly not.

One shoe was handily larger than the other. It was also a slightly different colour. The assistant went on staring and said,

– Them's a pair.

The outing must have been partly successful, because my notebook reads: 'But Louis sweetly grateful, and more sympathetic. And

★ In October, 1996, Eric Jacobs and Christopher Hitchens had this exchange. EJ: 'I suppose you think I've been a bit of a shit.' CH: 'Yes I do. What could possibly have come over you? And how did you imagine you'd get away with it?' EJ: 'All right. I know I've been a bit of a shit.' And, as we shall see, Eric went further in his expression of remorse.

lots of pats from Jacob.' Comforting pats being Jacob's speciality . . .

As for the shoe-seller: I now think that this kid was in the wrong job. He had no kind of future in the footwear business. He should have been writing for a quality newspaper, where it is quite customary to stare at a jackboot and a glass slipper and mumble, Them's a pair . . .

Everybody cried.

'Only Sally cried.' No, everybody cried. Sally cried the hardest ('I wish I had a Valium,' she said, and Rob instantly produced one, like a slot machine), but everybody cried. It was a contagion. Throughout Jacob held my hand or comfortingly patted my shaking shoulders. The boys had seen me crying before, but not out in the open; and they hadn't seen Sally crying and Isabel crying and Hilly crying and Philip crying. And their own mother, too, was crying. So the boys cried. Afterwards, in the street: Louis, normally so gracefully self-sufficient, looked as baffled and crumpled in his uniform as he sometimes did when he was four or five. Poor him. He had thought of this ceremony as just an hour out of school. He hadn't reckoned on a main event.

The senior Amises (all smoking, all coughing) rode the Daimler to Golders Green, and then returned in it, all smoking, all coughing. At the wake the first person I talked to was the first person I ever kissed on the lips: my cousin Marian Partington, who had been attending the trial of Rosemary West.

– When you pronounce the name *Jacobs*, said Jacob repeatedly at this time, could you please stress the *s*. I keep thinking you're talking about *me*.

Yes of course, Jake. We can't have that. But how do things rest with your near-namesake? What in the end are we to make of him?

The night that the final instalment of the jottings was put to bed at the *Sunday Times* I rang Eric and violently denounced him: 'And go to sleep wondering what Kingsley would think of you now.' I wonder what *I* think of him now. I find him far less unsympathetic in the memory than I find his agent and adviser, Gillon Aitken. Eric's behaviour was foolish and chaotic and, perhaps, disorganised by grief. And I charitably assume that he needed the money. But what did Aitken think he was doing?★ If he had advised his client differently, Eric would have gone on to edit the *Letters*. He would have done the job controversially, no doubt; but he would have done it with a clear conscience.

And Eric does have a conscience. This we know.

At Kingsley's memorial service, held a year after his death, Karl Miller talked about the fiction and Blake Morrison talked about the poems; Mavis Nicholson talked about Kingsley as a teacher; Richard Hough and Eric Shorter evoked Kingsley as a social being; and Christopher Hitchens touched on all these aspects. I talked about Kingsley's last days and about his attitude towards God; and I said that now we would begin to see him differently, and not just as the old devil; we would begin to see the whole man. The service ended with a tape of one of KA's imitations: Franklin Roosevelt vying with a brass band on a short-wave radio in the darkest days of World War II. There was laughter, there was applause, there was jazz; we came out into Trafalgar Square and made our way to the Garrick, where we talked and drank in Kingsley's cenotaph. It was, for most of us, a happy day.

Only Eric cried, I am tempted to type. Only Eric cried. But the words have a journalistic feel, and are therefore unlikely to be true.

Marigold Johnson also cried, while her husband, Paul, stalked off with his nose in the air, claiming that Kingsley had been 'body-snatched by the Left'.

I cannot rid myself of some vestigial gratitude to Eric. But you can only forgive what you can claim to understand, and he remains a

★ Everybody assumed that part of what he was doing was sending a smoke signal to Andrew Wylie. Aitken's second approach to the *Sunday Times* entrained the dissolution of their partnership. I gave a low whistle when Aitken later described his part in the negotiations for *The Information* as 'unedifying'. How edifying were his negotiations with the *Sunday Times*?

mystery to me. Even if he stepped into a novel of mine I wouldn't know what to do with him. Eric often struck me as a character out of fiction. So the question is: whose?

Looking through the 'jottings' again, I was reminded of the great modernist convention of the Unreliable Narrator – the 'I' whose version of events is not to be taken at face value. If the trick is to work, the unreliable narrator must in fact be very reliable indeed: reliably partial, reliably unaware of his own egotism. It occurred to me that Eric might have been a distant cousin of Kinbote, the devouring 'editor' in Nabokov's *Pale Fire*, who thinks, wrongly, that the poem he sets out to annotate is an admiring version of his own life story.* Listen to Eric on KA's last novel, *The Biographer's Moustache*:

> I said: 'Kingsley, this sounds rather like me – a Scotsman writing about a writer.' Oh yes, said he quickly, but 'he's not *like* you' . . . I wondered – did he choose the name Cedric, with which he's rather pleased, because it contains the name Eric? . . . I am beginning to wonder whether the novel, which seems so much closer to the story of his own life, has been brought on by the fact of my writing his biography.

The Cedric/Eric stuff (the character's name was subsequently changed to Gordon), and that 'said he quickly', might have come from Kinbote – admittedly on a very quiet day. And, incidentally, Gordon does not resemble Eric, and the novel is, unlike many others, wholly unautobiographical . . . I keep thinking about that sentence – 'Only Sally cried' – with which, in their unamended form, the extracts tollingly concluded. Eric's surrogate at the funeral (by any standards a remarkably lachrymose occasion) was presumably sentient. Maybe Eric just needed to imagine it this way, with himself tragically barred from adding his tears to Sally's. He loved Kingsley,

* Here's a florid example of Kinbote's talent for missing the point: '[T]here was at least one evil practical joker; I knew it ever since the time I came home . . . and found in my coat pocket a brutal anonymous note saying: "You have hal- - - - -s real bad, chum," meaning evidently "hallucinations" . . .'

as best he could, just as Kinbote loved his poet, John Shade.

L'affaire Jacobs, of course, showed us the *crème de la crème* of the culture pundits at their very, very best, impossibly stretched towards the absolute zenith of their game. They failed miserably, but at least they were trying to be serious. Even Eric was trying to be serious . . . As for the others, all those toiling smallholders of the Fourth Estate: to their world-famous attributes of intrusiveness, negligence, vulgarity, and dipsomania we may add what Kingsley called their 'non-committal superiority of manner', their habit of 'pervasive unspecific irony', and their 'cruising hostility'.* After a short search we found an archetype for Eric Jacobs. But it is the work of a moment to find the archetype for an average journo on an average day. We find him in the primary source, Shakespeare, where everybody is to be found, sooner or later. He is Thersites: a one-speech phenomenon in the *Iliad*, but a fully developed argument in *Troilus and Cressida*. 'Thou crusty batch of nature', as the (here) despicable Achilles calls him. '[T]hou core of envy.' Thersites – 'A slave whose gall coins slanders like a mint.' He is the 'deformed and scurrilous Greek', compelled by his own baseness to see deformity everywhere.†

✢   ✢   ✢

* 1999 saw another centenary: that of Jorge Luis Borges. Ian McEwan and I paid tribute to him at the London Library. The event, which passed off in a spirit of warm celebration, was written up with almost Leninine corrosiveness in a quality broadsheet. This example is supertrivial but illustrative. The writer said that I was wearing an 'unfashionable' suit. Well, a 'fashionable' suit, you may be sure, wouldn't have been any good either.
† The only trouble is that Thersites, being Shakespearean, remains irresistible. My favourite bit is not very typical of him, showing us, rather, another key facet of his character. During a battle:

> *Enter Hector.*
> *Hector*: What art thou, Greek? Art thou for Hector's match?
>   Art thou of blood and honour?
> *Thersites*: No, no, I am a rascal, a scurvy railing knave, a very filthy rogue.
> *Hector*: I do believe thee; live. [*Exit.*]
> *Thersites*: God-a-mercy, that thou wilt believe me; but a plague break thy neck – for frighting me.

Enough. Nabokov, I fear, would have found this particular biographer too slow-moving for his purposes. And the schemers and shafters of Balzac, say, would have immediately frogmarched him from their pages – on the grounds of sheer naïvety. Anyway, Eric is too British. I now think that V.S. Pritchett would have read him in an instant. And there's another writer who, had he heard the whole story, might have made a pretty good fist of him: Kingsley Amis.

Addendum: Letter to my Aunt

November 8, 1999

Dear Miggy,

This is a letter I will never send, in a book you will never read. Still, I couldn't conclude without addressing some words to you, however briefly and tentatively.

In the spring Isabel and I took Fernanda and the boys to Spain – to see your sister. I know you visited the house in Ronda, twenty-five years ago, because I was there too; but I don't know if you ever saw their casita in the campo, just outside town, which is where she and Ali live now (Jaime, based in Seville, is always coming and going). It's pretty basic down there. In the cold months, Mum says, it takes her at least an hour to get dressed for bed – layer upon layer. Her new knee is a great success and she says she is pain-free for the first time in many years. But it's not just the knee. She's a country girl, and she now has what we all wanted for her: a life after Kingsley. She has chickens and dogs. (She no longer has the two goats who could jump up on each other's backs and stay put.) It reminded me of your courtyard when I was ten – anarchically alive, with a cluck-cluck here and a whoof-whoof there, and crisscrossed by the busiest children you ever saw. Fernanda wrenched her clothes off and disappeared into the coop to 'collect' the eggs. She was quick to annex this word – quick to collect 'collect'.

I knew from Marian that you had had doubts about my attempting to memorialise your other daughter, Lucy. Then we exchanged letters and you elaborated in your own hand – your hand, so strong and upright, but still reminiscent of my mother's

[383]

(minus the famous phoneticisms). And your doubts remained. I had already begun the book but I found I couldn't proceed with it. When I sat down to write I felt the physical absence of your blessing. Then it came to me with an unfamiliar kind of certainty. I knew there was only one person who could secure it: your blessing.

We drove up for lunch, remember? It wasn't the first time I had revisited the Mill as an adult. The village, the lane, the circular drive with its millstone, your lawn, your ponds, your Michaelmas daisies. I recalled covering this garden in a series of desperately ardent sprints, moving from clue to clue (those were your rhymes, I think) in a hunt for Easter eggs, nearly forty years ago. The village seems sanitised now. No longer do the cattle come steaming down the lane ('The cays are coming!'). And your garden is no longer the finite but boundless universe that I made of it as a boy. 'How small it's all!' Yet the place still transports me, and I am back in an unfallen world. I could feel the fascinated excitement it awakened in my daughter: then not quite two. Today is her third birthday. The party has just ended and the house is still full of balloons.

That afternoon you and I were supposedly going to talk about Lucy, and the propriety of my writing about her. But we both knew that we were never going to do that. To do that, we would have to be alone together for, I would say, about six months. Besides, it would have been pointless to try to change your mind. A change of mind wasn't what was needed; something more than that was needed. I couldn't bring it about. Only my daughter could bring it about.

Soon after that visit you wrote to me. You said that one day you woke up to find that your doubts had been replaced by a feeling of peace. And you gave me your blessing. You also added your impression of Fernanda . . . I pulled your letter out of the box on the front gate and read it as I walked to Camden Town. On my return I handed the envelope to Isabel and said, not at all triumphantly but with sober respect, 'The power of Fernanda.' I never doubted it, but it is still extraordinary: the power of these girls.

I didn't predict that she would remind you of Lucy, although you said that she had. All I knew for certain was that she would leave you with something, she would impart something. She was not sent here just to come and go. As with Lucy, Fernanda always leaves you with something. You cannot be in her company without something being imparted. Lucy had that, entire: she had the magics. And when the time came to go Fernanda refused to leave the courtyard and reached out to you as her deliverer.

Enclosed are some more pictures of Fernanda, and a couple of her older sister, Delilah (whom I wrote to you about – discoursing on the unconscious, and silent anxiety), and a couple of her *younger* sister: tiny Clio.

And Louis and Jacob are there too.

With love as always from your nephew,

X

X Martin X

X

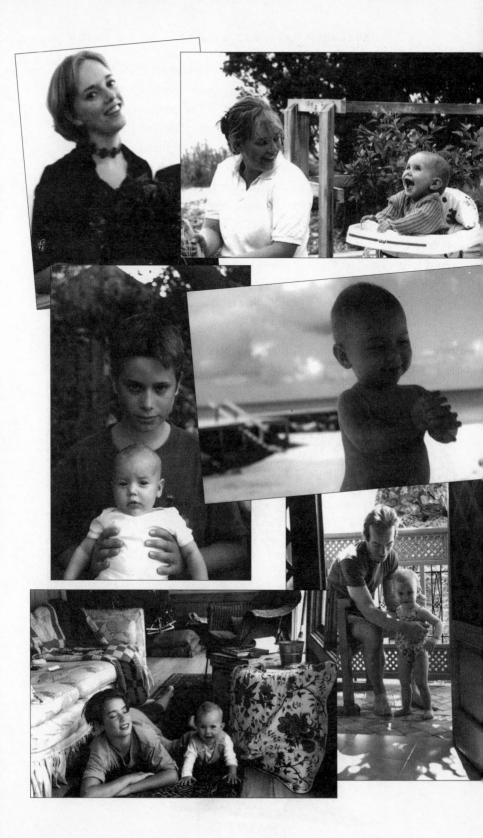

Index